D1384722

An Introduction to the
Philosophy of Mind

To the memory of my mother,
Dorothy Vera Maslin
(1921–89)

An Introduction to the Philosophy of Mind

K. T. Maslin

Polity

First published in 2001 by Polity Press in association with Blackwell Publishers Ltd

Editorial office:
Polity Press
65 Bridge Street
Cambridge CB2 1UR, UK

Marketing and production:
Blackwell Publishers Ltd
108 Cowley Road
Oxford OX4 1JF, UK

Published in the USA by
Blackwell Publishers Inc.
350 Main Street
Malden, MA 02148, USA

A catalogue record for this book is available from the British Library.

Library of Congress Cataloging-in-Publication Data

Maslin, Keith.
    An introduction to the philosophy of mind / Keith Maslin.
        p.   cm.
    Includes index.
    ISBN 0-7456-1687-9 (alk. paper)—ISBN 0-7456-1688-7 (pbk. : alk. paper)
    1. Philosophy of mind.   I. Title.
BD418.3 .M37   2001
128′.2—dc21   00-053755

Typeset in 10½ on 12 pt Times New Roman
by Best-set Typesetter Ltd., Hong Kong
Printed in Great Britain by MPG Books Ltd, Bodmin, Cornwall

This book is printed on acid-free paper.

CONTENTS

102532

DETAILED CHAPTER CONTENTS

ACKNOWLEDGEMENTS

I would like to express my gratitude to numerous people without whom this book could never have been written.

I am grateful to Rebecca Harkin, formerly at Polity, now at Blackwell, who commissioned the book. Her patience, advice and constant support kept me going when I might otherwise have given up. I would also like to thank John Thompson, Louise Knight and Gill Motley at Polity, Cambridge for their helpful suggestions and, in particular, three anonymous referees whose positive comments and useful criticisms enabled me to make substantial improvements to the text. Pam Thomas, the editorial manager at Polity, also gave much useful advice and support; and I must thank Kathryn Murphy, the production controller, for all the hard work that she has put into producing the book. A very special note of thanks must go to the copy-editor, Sarah Dancy, who read the entire book with immense care, and who not only enabled me to avoid numerous errors, but made excellent suggestions for making the book more accessible and user-friendly.

In 1996, not long after I had begun writing a first draft, I was fortunate to be the recipient of a Fellowship, awarded by the Farmington Institute of Christian Studies, for one term at Harris Manchester College, University of Oxford. This time, when I was free from teaching and administrative duties at Esher Sixth Form College, was invaluable. I must give thanks, firstly to the Rt Hon. Bobby Wills, who created the Institute, and, secondly, to Martin Rogers, OBE, the Director, for his continual encouragement and advice. Thanks also to Ron Glithero, who read and discussed much of the first draft, and to Suzanne Tetsell and Elizabeth Machin who gave much needed secretarial and administrative support during my time at Harris Manchester. The Reverend Dr Ralph Waller, Principal of the College, made we feel very welcome, but especial thanks must go to Roger Trigg, Professor of Philosophy at Warwick University, who was a Visiting Fellow at the time I was in Oxford. Roger very generously offered to read everything I wrote, and to discuss it afterwards in the sanctity of the Wykeham tea-rooms. I look back on those conversations with great pleasure.

My taking up the Fellowship would not, however, have been possible without the support of Dr Patrick Miller, then Principal of Esher College, and I am grateful also to the then Deputy Principal, Geoff Mason, for his willingness to make the necessary arrangements for my absence. I was also pleased that Dr Miller was able to attend the presentation of the work I had completed towards the end of my Fellowship at Oxford. Dr Nick McAdoo very generously stepped into my shoes for one term whilst I was away from Esher and helped keep the philosophy department on track.

I must not forget to mention the members of the South-West London Gastronomico-Philosophical Society who heard, and usefully commented upon, various chapters, as well as a large number of my students at Esher on whom I tried out much of the material in the book, and who gave me valuable feedback in addition to strong encouragement to see the project through. Basil Hunt, formerly Head of Classical Civilization at Esher College, also made useful suggestions for improving the writing style, as well as providing stimulating discussions of some of the main ideas in the book.

I must also thank my wife Zielfa, our daughter Philippa, and my father, for their tolerance and support whilst the project was underway.

My debts to the work of philosophers from Descartes to Wittgenstein, as well as to many contemporary writers on the philosophy of mind, too numerous to mention, will be obvious from the text. I do not claim to have made original contributions to the philosophy of mind, but the book is no mere neutral survey of the subject and in general the reader should be left in no doubt of my own views on various topics throughout the text. I have not wanted to create the impression that no questions remain and that all difficulties have been solved, when they quite clearly have not. I hope that readers will take forward for themselves the many issues that remain for discussion. Above all, because this is an introductory text, aimed primarily at A-level students and first-year undergraduates, I have tried to write clearly and accessibly, assuming as little previous knowledge of the area as is reasonable to suppose.

Lastly, I owe a special debt of gratitude to my mother, Dorothy Vera Maslin, who, from my earliest years, taught me to love reading and the life of the mind, and who was a mainstay over the years, especially in difficult and discouraging times. She always encouraged me to write, and would have been delighted to see the publication of the book, had she lived. This book is dedicated to her memory.

The author and publisher would like to thank the following for permission to quote copyrighted material: Faber and Faber Ltd and Harcourt Inc. for an extract from T. S. Eliot's poem 'Morning at the Window' from *Collected Poems 1909–1962*; Penguin, UK for permission to reproduce a diagram and to quote from *The Mechanical Mind* by Tim Crane (Penguin Books, 1995).

Every effort has been made to trace copyright holders, but if any have been inadvertently overlooked, the publishers will be pleased to make the necessary arrangements at the first opportunity.

HOW TO USE THIS BOOK

This book contains a number of features which are designed to help you quickly find your way around it, and to help you achieve a sound and thorough understanding of what you need to know.

Firstly, a quick overview of what you can expect to find in each chapter is provided by the list of objectives at the start of the chapter. These objectives specify the main things you must know if you are to gain a good understanding of the issues with which the chapter deals. It is hoped they will provide you with a valuable check-list.

Secondly, exercises designed to help you think about various topics for yourself are integrated into the text throughout the book. You could attempt these exercises on your own, but frequently you will get more benefit by discussing the issue with someone else, as the exercises suggest. In any case, my strong recommendation is that you resist reading my responses to the questions raised until you have first formulated your own reactions. In that way you will be helping to strengthen your own powers of analysis and criticism, as well as avoiding being over-influenced by, or too dependent upon, what I have to say.

One way to avoid inadvertently reading what I have written would be to use a masking card and uncover the text gradually. Similarly, a teacher who wanted to generate small group discussions could use the exercises as a stimulus before asking the students to read my discussions of the various topics, or before proceeding to a formal presentation of the issues.

Thirdly, a selection of questions typical of those asked by examiners at A-level and degree level are to be found at chapter ends, together with details of further reading for those keen to take the topics forward for themselves. Clearly, teachers could set these essays for students. Alternatively, students might try planning or writing these essays for themselves.

In the fourth place, whilst I have tried to write as non-technically as possible, and to introduce and explain terms that may be unfamiliar to you as I go along, there is still the danger that I might have taken too much for granted. Accordingly, a glossary of philosophical terms whose meanings may not be clear is provided at the end of the book.

Lastly, a short select bibliography is included at the end of the book for those who wish to pursue the subject further than covered by the reading lists at the end of each chapter.

I

THE MIND/BODY PROBLEM

Objectives

As a result of reading this chapter you should:

- have a preliminary understanding of the nature of the mind/body problem and how it arises;
- have an understanding of some of the major theories of mind and body available;
- understand the differences between intentional and non-intentional states;
- understand what is meant by the qualia associated with some types of mental state;
- understand the structure of the propositional attitudes and why they have been thought to pose a problem for materialist theories of the mind;
- appreciate the distinction between intrinsic and derivative intentionality;
- understand what is meant by first- and third-person perspectives and why mental states have been thought to be radically private to the person;
- understand why doubt can be cast on the claim that a person always has a privileged access to, and infallible knowledge of, his intentional states;
- understand why the existence of first- and third-person perspectives have been thought to pose a problem for achieving a unitary account of the mind;
- understand what is meant by the holistic character of intentional states and why self-consciousness is necessary for rationality to be possible;
- understand possible criteria for demarcating the mental from the physical.

1.1   Introduction

As I begin writing this first chapter I can hear the hum of the computer in front of me. My cat, perched on a large folded duvet, is purring, and when I swivel round I can see her cleaning herself. There is a slight ache and stiffness in my right shoulder, and I feel slightly full, not long having eaten lunch. I pause from writing momentarily to visualize my wife, who is visiting her home country, the Philippines; and I remember the time when I lived there and we went to the mountains for a holiday. I also think about picking her up from the airport in a week's time and vaguely wonder whether she will need a meal and what I should cook.

Why have I supplied you with this tiny fragment of my life-history? The reason is to remind you of the very obvious fact that as a human being I am a conscious, experiencing subject, and the possessor of a variety of mental states – hearing, seeing, feeling an ache or pain, seeing in the mind's eye, remembering, thinking and wondering – to mention a few instances of states of mind selected from a very long possible list. I am the centre of a universe of experiences – and you are too. Animals, birds, fish, insects and possibly even molluscs also have mental lives, however underdeveloped and rudimentary some of these minds might be.

But what, ultimately, is it to have a mind? At one level this question is easy to answer. As the brief excursion into my mental history which began this chapter helps to illustrate, in talking about the mind – your own and other people's – you are describing the sorts of state or event that go to make up a mind – the thoughts, beliefs, emotions, sensations, intentions, desires, perceptions, purposes and so forth that help to comprise it. Moreover, in your own case, it seems impossible to get closer to your own states of mind than you already are, since these states literally comprise the stuff of your experience, your mental life, without which you, as a person, would not exist.

As far as it goes, this characterization of what I shall generally call 'mental phenomena' is satisfactory. But, in the end, it fails to satisfy, because it seems to give us very little idea, if any, of the nature of mental states. By contrast, consider physical phenomena. There are well-developed theories about the nature and behaviour of physical bodies, processes and events, as exemplified in sciences such as chemistry, physics and biology. Obviously there is plenty we do not yet know about the ultimate nature of physical reality, but it seems reasonable to say that we have a better grasp of what is going on when physical occurrences take place than when mental events happen. For example, scientific investigation is uncovering more and more about the processes that take place in our bodies and brains, and although our understanding is far from complete, we do at least have a good idea of what further kinds of detail we need to discover and how to set about this task.

By contrast, gaining an understanding of the nature of mental states does not seem to bear comparison with what is entailed in reaching a better understanding of physical states. Thus, while we all know what it is like to ponder over an intellectual problem, such as solving an algebraic equation, or, at the other extreme, to feel a pain, our experience seems to provide no clue regarding the intrinsic nature of what takes place within us when we think, or when a part of our body hurts. Admittedly, active engagement in teasing out the solution to a problem in mathematics, on the one hand, and the passive experience of a painful sensation, on the other, are extremely different sorts of mental phenomena, so disparate, in fact, that one almost hesitates to mention them in the same breath. But nevertheless, very unlike in character though they are, both thinking and feeling a pain belong on the mental, as opposed to the physical, side of the fence. That said, however, we are still left with the question of what precisely is going on in us when either of these two sorts of mental event occur. In what kind of medium, one wants to ask, do the thinking and the experience of the pain take place?

It is this kind of puzzle that leads to, and helps to constitute, the mind/body problem. Three questions, I suggest, insistently press themselves upon us. Firstly, what is the nature of the mind, of mental states and events generally? What, to put it more grandly, is their mode of being? This is what philosophers call the ontological question about the status of the mind. The word 'ontology' is derived from the Greek word *ontia* which means 'things that exist'. In asking what the ontology of mental states is, philosophers want to know what mental states consist in, what actually constitutes them. Are they ultimately physical in nature, like the processes involved in, say, photosynthesis, or are they totally immaterial in character, sharing nothing in common with the physical world, like souls or spirits as these are traditionally conceived? Alternatively, should the dilemma, either physical or non-physical, which seems to force itself upon us here, be rejected in favour of other accounts of the nature of the mind?

Secondly, experiences, it seems, must exist as someone's, or some being's, experiences. The idea that there could be loose and separate experiences floating around, as it were, unattached to some subject or other does not appear to make sense, although this issue is controversial.[1] If we are prepared to grant, at least for the time being, that experiences must have owners, we are led naturally to wonder what the nature is of the possessors of mental states – those persons, as well as animals, whose sets of experiences comprise various sorts of mental phenomena. Should these subjects be conceived of as existing over and above the experiences themselves, or as somehow constituted out of them, as a jigsaw puzzle is nothing over and above the pieces that go to make it up? On the other hand, if subjects of experiences are different in kind from the experiences themselves, and are not reducible to them, are such subjects non-physical or physical in character? Various answers to these questions are returned by the five different theories of the mind/body relation that comprise chapters 2–6.

Thirdly, implicit in the issues raised by the last two questions is the puzzle of how mental states and subjects relate to the physical world. Can mental phenomena exist independently of physical phenomena, or do they depend upon them for their existence? If physical states do indeed give rise to mental states, how can this occur, since the mental and physical seem so different from each other? This problem was brought home to me with special force a few years ago. I was teaching a philosophy of mind course to adult students at Rewley House in Oxford, and I said that I would like, if possible, to be able to show a real human brain to the class. I had, of course, seen brains in photographs and in science museums, but I was intrigued to know what it would be like to have one to inspect at close quarters. The University authorities surpassed my expectations: not only did they deliver a brain, but it had been preserved in such a way that you could actually handle it and pass it around. It certainly gave the class members and myself a weird sensation to think that what we were so casually handling had once been in a living person's skull. At the same time, a feeling of intense wonder was provoked by the reflection: how on earth could this piece of pallid whitish-grey matter, even if it were fully functioning and connected up to the rest of a living human being, be responsible for the amazing technicolour dreamcoat of consciousness? How could this thing be the embodiment of a person's hopes and dreams, fears, beliefs, intentions, memories and thoughts? There did not merely seem to be a gap between, on the one hand, brains and the processes that go on in them and, on the other, consciousness, but an uncrossable gulf which, by its very nature, could not be bridged or eliminated. The great seventeenth-century philosopher Leibniz (1646–1716) encapsulated this puzzlement when he asked us to imagine a machine, the structure of which produces thinking, feeling and perceiving, enlarged to the size of a mill so that we could visit its inside. What would we find there? asked Leibniz. Answer: 'Nothing but parts which push and move each other, and never anything which could explain perception.'[2] The machine Leibniz had in mind was, of course, the brain. What modern scientists find when they investigate its workings are electro-chemical physical events, the equivalents of Leibniz's 'parts which push and move each other'. But if neurology cannot be invoked to explain perception and consciousness, what can?

The answer, according to the dualist (whose arguments form the first major theory of the mind/body relation, which I will expand on and evaluate in chapter 2), is that the machinery of the brain can never in principle explain the existence of mental states. Instead, each of us has to be thought of as a non-physical entity, a soul, whose immaterial states comprise our mental lives. The soul is capable of existing in its own right in complete independence of anything else. During life it is somehow attached to the body, affecting, and being affected by, it, but at death it will separate. Although dualism can be traced back at least as far as the ancient Greeks, René Descartes (1596–1650) gave a distinctive new shape to the doctrine, and original, powerful arguments in its favour. Consequently, the theory is often referred to and discussed under the title 'Cartesian dualism' (Cartesian is the adjective formed from the proper name Descartes).

The strict materialist dismisses the notion of the soul as nonsense, insisting robustly that the mind is nothing but the functioning brain. Mental states do not exist over and above physical processes: they *are* physical processes, and nothing but physical processes. In explaining how the brain works we are, in effect, explaining what consciousness is, because consciousness is identical with brain processes. There is no problem of how the mind is related to the physical world; it is merely one aspect or subset of material events. This account of the mind, a second theory of the mind/body problem, which is known as the mind/brain identity theory, forms the topic of chapter 3.

However, both dualism and the mind/brain identity theory are equally and oppositely wrong, according to a third theory, logical or analytical behaviourism. The mind is not a ghostly immaterial thing, but nor is it the gross material brain. The most fruitful way to construe the mind is to think of it as a pattern of actual and possible behaviour exhibited by both human beings and animals. The workings of a person's mind do not lie hidden behind their behaviour, but find their embodiment within it. This theory, which held sway from the 1930s for twenty-five years or more, will be examined in chapter 4.

Chapter 5 brings us to a fourth theory, functionalism, which evolved, largely independently, from analytical behaviourism, on the one hand, and computational theories of the mind, on the other. Functionalism has been the most recent and fashionable major attempt to account for the mind, although there are now signs that its popularity is waning. According to the functionalist, the mind is strictly neither mental nor physical, but should be conceived more abstractly as a function or program, run on the hardware of the brain, which transforms sensory inputs into behavioural outputs.

Finding none of the theories above satisfactory, my own preferred option, a fifth theory of the mind/body relation – non-reductive monism – forms the subject of chapter 6. I side with the materialists in their rejection of the mind as a non-physical soul, but in opposition to them I find the mind/brain identity theory, analytical behaviourism and functionalism fundamentally and crucially deficient in their stubborn refusal to acknowledge, and to seek to explain, the existence of consciousness as a feature of reality that is not exhausted by physical theory. Despite some of the very considerable problems that non-reductive materialism brings in its wake, it has at least the virtue of taking consciousness seriously.

Apart from the five major theories of the mind, to which I confine myself for reasons of space and because this is an introductory book, there are some important issues outstanding which require an extended and separate treatment in their own right. The first of these, which forms the subject of chapter 7, concerns the issue of how the mind can affect the body when it appears so different in nature from it. How can something as seemingly non-physical as an embarrassing thought make me blush, for example? In an attempt to answer this and related problems, I concentrate largely on a discussion of Donald Davidson's complex theory of anomalous monism.

In chapter 8, I turn from metaphysical questions about the nature of the mind to epistemological issues concerning its knowability. Do we have special knowledge of the existence and nature of our own mental states which we lack in the case of others? Can we, in fact, ever know of the existence of mental states other than our own, or are we doomed to eternal scepticism about such matters?

Finally, in chapters 9 and 10, which are devoted to the issue of personal identity, I undertake an extended discussion of what constitutes the identity of a person over time. What makes a person now, at the present time, one and the same as someone at a past time, despite the considerable changes he or she will have undergone during the intervening period? What, crucially, *cannot* be changed, if the identity of the person is to be preserved? Is it the soul, the body or a specific part of the body, the brain? Alternatively, is none of these answers correct? Is it, rather, the continuity of memory and character, however achieved, that is crucial to someone being one and the same person now as he or she was then? Trying to get clear about this issue, as well as of being of great interest and fascination in its own right, is essential to gaining a better understanding of the nature of the experiencing subject or self.

1.2   Approaching the mind/body problem

In section 1.1, I sketched five major theories which are contenders for the solution to the mind/body problem. Which one, if any, is correct and by what measures or criteria are we to assess the adequacies and inadequacies of the competing theories? A possible way to begin setting about this task is to try to discover what features of the mind and its relation to the body a successful theory must be able to explain and accommodate. The emphasis in this first stage, it must be stressed, is largely on description, rather than on evaluation. Detailed assessment of each of the competing theories of mind and body will take place in subsequent chapters, once the key features of mental states have been characterized in more detail.

1.3   Characteristics of mental states

The sorts of questions that need to be pursued in this and the next few sections are as follows:

1   What are the distinctive features of mental states?
2   Are mental phenomena all alike or are there crucial differences between them?
3   Is it possible to spell out the essential features of various types of mental state?

To get started, we need to collect a good range of samples of different sorts of mental state, so before reading any further, look at Exercise 1.1.

Brainstorm a list of 15 or so items which you would classify as mental phenomena or states. Try to think of a wide variety of examples – it will greatly help if you do this exercise with two or three other people.

Exercise 1.1

How did you do? A preliminary trawl might have yielded the following:

> Pains, itches, dreaming, thinking, hallucinating, seeing, hearing, jealousy, hoping, depression, joy, believing, wanting, remembering, consciousness, indignation, understanding, acting, intending, conceiving, fear, wishing, regretting, imagining, tickles, throbs, tasting, aches, smelling, seeing in the mind's eye, touching, happiness, misery, envy, anger, seeing after-images, trying, anticipating, grief, enjoyment, tingles, knowing, reasoning.

Let us now try a slightly harder task, as set in Exercise 1.2.

Exercise 1.2   Look through the examples of mental states given above and see if you can find ways of classifying them into different groupings. For example, some name sensations, such as pains and itches, whilst others name emotions and yet others are more intellectual, such as thinking and understanding. Again, do this exercise with two or three other people and then compare your results with mine.

I have classified the mental states under six headings:

Sensations – pains, aches, tickles, itches, throbs, tingles
Cognitions – believing, knowing, understanding, conceiving, thinking, reasoning
Emotions – fear, jealousy, envy, anger, grief, indignation, enjoyment
Perceptions – seeing, hearing, tasting, smelling, touching
Quasi-perceptual states – dreaming, imagining, seeing in the mind's eye, hallucinating, seeing after-images
Conative states – acting, trying, wanting, intending, wishing

An inspection of this list reveals some important differences between the items on it, outlined in the remainder of this section.

1.3.1   Bodily location

Sensations have a more or less definite bodily location, whereas all the other states do not. It makes sense to say that you have a pain in your side or an ache in your shoulders, but no sense to say that your belief is just above your right ear, your jealousy in your little finger or your intention to visit Paris in your toe. However, even in the case of sensations, it has to be remembered that their bodily location cannot be understood in the same way in which we talk about the location of physical objects. If a person says that they have a pain in their little finger and we then open it up to look inside, we won't find a thing, not even a mysterious sort of thing called a pain. Pains have a location only in the sense that they are wherever the person who feels the pain truthfully reports it as being.

The difference between talk about the location of sensations and the location of physical objects can be illustrated by looking at Exercise 1.3, which you should attempt before reading any further.

If my coins are in my purse, and my purse is in my pocket, does it follow that my coins are in my pocket?

Exercise 1.3

In one sense, my coins are not in my pocket, i.e. not loose in my pocket, since they are contained in the purse. But clearly, if the purse is in the space bounded by the sides and bottom of the pocket, and the coins are in the space bounded by the material comprising the purse, then the coins are in the pocket. The location of the coins is a literal location in space and one could reach into the pocket and take them out. The same is true, naturally, of bodily organs and parts of the body. The heart and nerves, for example, clearly do have literal locations within the body and could be removed from it.

Now consider Exercise 1.4.

If my pain is in my foot, and my foot is in my shoe, does it follow that my pain is in my shoe? This is a much more complicated case than that in Exercise 1.3.

Exercise 1.4

Firstly, my pain is not in my foot in the way in which my coins are in my purse. I can take the coins out of my purse, but I can't reach into my foot and remove my pain. My pain is not an object like a coin. The pain is in my foot in the sense that my foot hurts. If I say that I am in pain and someone then asks me where it hurts, I will spontaneously point to my foot. But this is not like giving the literal location in space of an object such as a coin. Pains are said to have a phenomenal location – a location as pointed out by the experiencing subject. People who have had limbs amputated often report feeling pains and other sensations in non-existent limbs – this is called phantom-limb pain. Thus, an amputee will point to a region of empty space, the space where the limb would have been before it was amputated, and report that that is where the pain is. Although this sounds strange, it makes sense once you remember that specifying the location of a pain is not like saying where an object such as a coin is. The fact that pains lack spatial locations, unlike material objects, supplies a further reason for not concluding that a pain exists in your shoe when your foot which is hurting is in your shoe. Lastly, if you were to insist that your pain is in your shoe, we would have to remind you that this amounts to saying that your shoe is in pain! This is manifestly absurd, since shoes, unlike people and animals, are not sentient, conscious, experiencing subjects.

1.3.2   Sensations and awareness

The case outlined in Exercise 1.4 can be used to illustrate another crucial difference between sensations and physical objects. The coins in your pocket exist whether or not you are aware of them. However, it would be self-contradictory to say that you had a pain in your foot, but that you couldn't feel anything unpleasant going on in that part of your body. Pains and other sensations exist only when you are aware of them. Consciousness or awareness of them is integral to their very existence. It is not an optional or bolt-on extra.[3]

1.3.3   Non-sensational states and awareness

Prime examples of non-sensational states are provided by cognitive states, which are to do with understanding and thinking, and conative states (deriving from the Latin *conatus*, which means effort or endeavour), which directly or indirectly concern acting, willing, trying, wanting and intending.

By contrast with sensations, it is possible to have beliefs, knowledge and understanding, as well as desires and intentions of which you are not conscious at a given instant. Thus, I am intending to visit the Czech Republic in the summer, but until I needed an example to illustrate the point I am making here, I did not have the intention at the forefront of my mind. Similarly with beliefs and knowledge. There are literally hundreds of things I believe and know, but I am not aware of what they are at the moment. If such beliefs and knowledge are to be attributed truly to me, at least it must be possible that I should be able to bring them to mind if, and when, the occasion demands. This is what is meant by saying that beliefs and knowledge are dispositional, rather than, as in the case of sensations, occurrent.

A sensation such as a pain or tickle exists if, and only if, you are occurrently aware of it, i.e. continuously aware of it. By contrast, a person may be said to have a belief or an intention if, and only if, there are circumstances when he *could* call it to mind, when he would be prone or disposed to bring it to awareness, not that he actually *is* calling it to mind. To put this another way, pains and other sensations exist only when you are actually aware of them. In the case of beliefs and intentions and many other non-sensational states, the requirement is weaker. For beliefs and intentions to be truly attributed to a person, it is sufficient that they are potentially objects of awareness. Should there not be any possible circumstances in which a belief or intention could be called to mind and avowed, then it is highly unlikely that the belief or intention in question exists.[4]

Emotions and moods are harder to deal with. If you are feeling angry at a given time, then it follows that you must be conscious of your anger and aware of your feelings. On the other hand, it seems possible to be angry with someone without constantly being aware that you are. You might stay cross with someone for days, your anger existing even during periods of sleep. This is because emotions, like beliefs and intentions, are dispositional in character.

1.3.4 Qualia and mental states

In the case of sensations, there is something that it is like to experience them. Think of the itchy feel of a rough woollen blanket, the stinging sensation produced by a nettle, the soothing coolness of a lotion for sunburn, the tingling sensation of pins and needles or the throb of a decayed tooth. Philosophers talk of the phenomenology of sensations, that is, the way things seem to the experiencing subject, each type of sensation having a distinctive qualitative feel. This second way of characterizing sensations has led philosophers to invent a special technical expression and to describe sensations as possessing 'qualia' or 'raw feels'.

By contrast with sensations, there seems to be no distinctive phenomenology associated with beliefs and other cognitive states such as understanding and thinking. A belief that the Royal Festival Hall is on the South Bank of the Thames has no particular qualitative look or feel associated with it. Of course, when I affirm this belief, associated memories from frequent visits to it may stray into my mind, but these are purely incidental to the belief and play no part in constituting it. Even if no memories or associations are evoked when the Festival Hall is mentioned, I may nevertheless still be said to believe it is on the South Bank.

Unlike beliefs, and more like sensations, emotions are usually accompanied by feelings, i.e. they have a distinctive phenomenology all of their own. Thus we speak of suffering pangs of jealousy, of going cold with anger, of being agitated by gnawing worry, of a sickening feeling in the pit of one's stomach and so forth. There are also other mental phenomena which resemble the emotions in possessing a phenomenology. For example, we suffer the pangs of regret or remorse, or share the thrill of anticipation, indulge ourselves in the nostalgia of bitter and sweet remembrances and feel the desolation of hopes that have come to nothing.

Some conative states also appear to have a phenomenology associated with them, as when we talk of the fire of desire, the effort involved in trying to accomplish a difficult and dangerous task or when we fervently wish for something to come true. Others, such as intentions, are closer to beliefs and, to adopt an expression originally used by Ludwig Wittgenstein (1889–1951) about actions, seem to have 'no volume of experience', i.e. there is no qualitative content that helps to characterize intentions.

1.3.5   About 'aboutness'

Looking through the various types of mental state outlined above, a vitally important distinction which emerges is between mental states that seem to be 'about', or directed upon, other states of affairs, and those that are not. Sensations are not about, or directed upon, other states of affairs, real or imaginary, that are external to themselves. In other words, sensations do not represent other possible states of affairs. We would be puzzled if we were asked what our pains or tickles were *about*, as opposed to what was causing them.[5] Sensations, we would be inclined to say, just *are*. They are not about anything, just as the table and chair at which I am working do not represent or picture other possible states of affairs.

Contrast this with a belief. You cannot just believe, full stop. There must be some content to your belief, something it concerns, whether or not anything actually corresponds to that content out there in the world. You may believe that the moon is made of green cheese, for example. It isn't, of course, but, nevertheless, 'that the moon is made of green cheese', a non-existent state of affairs, is what your belief concerns, how the belief represents to you what the moon is like. Desires and intentions similarly possess 'aboutness'. You cannot just want or intend without specifying what it is you want to get or aim to do. What makes a belief true is whether the world actually is as the belief represents it as being. What fulfils an intention is whether the state of affairs in the world as specified by the intention is brought about intentionally by the person whose intention it is. The philosopher John Searle has spoken in this connection of the 'direction of fit' of states that exhibit aboutness. In the case of beliefs, the direction of fit is from world to mind; what the world is like dictates whether the belief is true or not. With regard to intentions, the direction of fit is from mind to world: the intention is supposed to bring the world into conformity with its requirements.

Emotions, like beliefs and intentions, must also be directed upon a content. If, for example, you are angry, there must be someone with whom you are angry, or something about which you are angry. But emotions are more complex than beliefs because they presuppose beliefs and are not reducible to them. A belief is a component of an emotion, not the emotion itself. To illustrate this point, suppose that you are angry with someone for betraying a confidence. It follows, then, that you must believe the person in question betrayed your confidence. In the absence of this belief, or should you discover the belief to be false, you will not be angry. Philosophers have wanted to distinguish between the *object* of the emotion – what the emotion is concerned with or directed upon – and the *reason* why the emotion is felt, the belief supplying this reason. The philosopher Elizabeth Anscombe (1921–2001) gives the example of a child who was frightened of a piece of red satin left on a stair. Why should he be terrified of a piece of cloth? Answer: he believed he had been told that it was a bit of Satan. Once the child is disabused of this belief then his fear, if it is rational, will evaporate.

Philosophers often speak, using a special technical term, not of the 'aboutness' of mental states such as beliefs, desires, emotions and intentions, but of their 'intentionality'. Hence, such states are known as intentional states by contrast with pains and other sensations that are non-intentional in character. The content of such states, what they are about, is called the intentional content. A fuller explanation of intentionality and how the term came to be coined by medieval philosophers will be provided in the next section.

Actions also exhibit intentionality. Although there are things that we do for no particular reason out of habit or boredom, such as fiddling with a paperclip or our hair whilst we are talking, actions standardly are undertaken for the fulfilment of purposes, and in this sense are directed upon an end, just like intentions. But are actions physical or mental? There certainly are purely mental actions in the sense that they involve no bodily movements. Doing mental arithmetic, drawing conclusions from premises and detecting presuppositions of arguments are all activities that may take place inwardly without any physical movement. Other activities, such as raising your arm, necessarily involve bodily movements. Such activities are not, however, identical with the movements themselves. If I raise my arm, it follows that my arm rises, but it does not follow that if my arm rises I raised it. My arm might have risen for reasons unconnected with my personal agency – someone else might have lifted it, or I might have suffered a spasm. It seems then that actions are both physical and mental in nature, unlike bodily movements which lack any mental aspect.

Perceptions and quasi-perceptions also exhibit aboutness. By a quasi-perceptual state, I mean a state in which it seems to the person that they really are seeing or hearing something, whereas in fact they are only dreaming, or imagining or hallucinating. Their dreams, imaginations and hallucinations have a mental content, but, as with the case of false beliefs, this content does not represent a really existing state of affairs in the world. By contrast, with regard to genuine perceptual states such as seeing or hearing, for example, what is seen or heard must really exist. This is a consequence of the conditions that perceptual states must satisfy in order to qualify as perceptual states. If I may truly be said to see something, then not only must that thing exist to be seen but it must play an appropriate role in bringing about my perception of it. If this condition is not satisfied, then we would have to describe me as only *seeming* to see the thing in question – I am perhaps imagining it or dreaming it.

It would be tempting to identify the intentional content of the experience of seeing an object with the object itself, but this would be a mistake. This is essentially because a distinction can be drawn between the way in which an object appears to us – the manner, one might say, in which it presents itself to us – and the way it actually is. Some examples can help to make this clear. The sun looks about the size of a five pence piece, but we know it is much larger than the earth. Grass in the far distance looks blue, but close up we see that it is green. Then there are ambiguous pictures that can be seen in different ways. The picture shown in figure 1.1 can be seen first as a duck and then as a rabbit, or perhaps to some people just some lines on paper. Although there is a sense in which both you and I see one and the same picture, the intentional content of our respective perceptions, the manner in which the picture presents itself to us, is different for each of us. You see it as a duck, I as a rabbit. In other words, we perceive different aspects, the picture itself naturally remaining unchanged throughout. The duck/rabbit example helps to explain what is meant by describing visual perception as aspectual in character, and makes clear why the intentional content of perception cannot simply be identified with the external object perceived.

The duck/rabbit example illustrates the situation in which we have one and the same picture which presents two different aspects. But

Figure 1.1

it is not difficult to think of the converse possibility in which two different things present the same aspect. Rosie and Alice are identical twins whom I cannot tell apart. To amuse themselves, the twins play a game in which Rosie tells me she is Alice, and Alice tells me she is Rosie. It thus frequently seems to me that I am speaking to Rose when in fact I am talking to Alice, and vice versa. The intentional content of my perception will be the same in both cases, although in reality I will have been seeing and speaking to two different people.

The aspectuality of perceptual states is not confined solely to cases of 'seeing as', or, to put the point more generally, to cases of 'experiencing as'. There is also 'seeing that', to restrict the discussion to just one of the senses. Thus, after long acquaintance, I finally come to be able to tell Rosie apart from Alice, and can no longer be fooled, since I can now *see that* it is Rosie and not Alice standing before me.

There is always a temptation to think of the intentional content of a perception as if it were a mental object that gets between us and the object seen, as if the way an object appears or looks were like a membrane which could be peeled off the object and contemplated · independently of it. If this move is made, the perceptual content is then said to represent the object that is being perceived. The problem with this way of thinking of perceptual content is that the content becomes a surrogate, a substitution for the object itself, and this surrogate then gets between us and the object. We are then left with the puzzle of explaining how, if we are only aware of the surrogate that represents the object, we can ever know there really is an object out there giving rise to the representation or surrogate in the first place. The antidote is to realize that the way an object seems or appears does not consist in some mysterious entity called an 'appearance' which cuts us off from contact with the object itself. The intentional content of a perception just is the object itself, looking or appearing in a certain way to us. For this reason, philosophers have recommended that the intentional content of perceptions should not be thought of as representing the world to us but, rather, as presenting it in a certain manner. Talk of representing encourages the mistaken belief that in perception we are really only aware of entities called representations which come between us and the object being perceived, rather than the object itself.

1.4 Intentionality

As promised in section 1.3.5, I should now like to say a little more about the concept of 'aboutness', or intentionality, which was a feature of the bulk of the various types of mental state examined.

The adjective 'intentional' and the abstract noun 'intentionality' which derives from it were coinages of medieval or scholastic philosophers. The expression is derived from the Latin *intendere* which means 'to aim at' in the sense of stretching a bow in order to fire an arrow at a target (*intendere ad arcum*). The terms 'intentional' and 'intentionally', which are commonly used to describe actions, derive from the same origin and retain the sense of a goal or target at which the action is aimed. But 'intentionality' is a special technical philosophical term which it is important not to confuse with the everyday 'intentionally'. Having fallen somewhat into neglect after the Middle Ages, the concept of intentionality was revived by Franz Brentano (1838–1917), who wrote:

> Every mental phenomenon is characterised by what the scholastics of the Middle Ages called the Intentional (and also mental) inexistence of an object, and what we would call, although in not entirely unambiguous terms, the reference to a content, a direction upon an object (by which we are not to understand a reality in this case) or immanent objectivity. Every mental phenomenon includes something as object within itself, although they do not all do so in the same way. In presentation, something is presented, in judgement something is affirmed or denied, in love loved, in hate hated, in desire desired and so on. This intentional inexistence is characteristic exclusively of mental phenomena.[6]

Table 1.1   Intentional states (propositional attitudes)

Attitude	Propositional content
Main clause specifying type of intentional state in question by means of a psychological verb which describes the attitude taken towards a content	Embedded that-clause or infinitive of a verb specifying the propositional (representational) content of the intentional state – what the intentional state is about
I believe	that someone in the great somewhere cares for me
Lois Lane imagines	that she is kissing Superman
He wants	to visit the Falklands
They intend	to go abroad for their holidays
He doubts	that there is a God

This passage needs some brief commentary. The faintly obscure term 'intentional inexistence' is Brentano's expression for what is now called the representative content of an intentional state, the state of affairs, real or imaginary, that the state represents. However, as Brentano goes on to point out, anticipating Searle (see section 1.3.5), not all contents are presented in the same way. A belief, for example, asserts that the world is as the belief describes it as being. Desires or intentions, on the other hand, specify what the world should become like if it is to match the content of the desire or intention in question. Ever since the philosopher Bertrand Russell (1872–1970) invented the term, it is now common to call the mode of presentation of an intentional content an 'attitude', a mental stance, as it were, taken towards a given content by a subject and characterized by a psychological verb. The content itself is usually specified by a that-clause, which introduces a proposition or statement, or, alternatively, by a phrase beginning with the infinitive of a verb. Hence, intentional states are also known as the propositional attitudes. Table 1.1 helps to make this clearer.

Brentano was guilty of exaggeration, however, when he claimed that *every* mental phenomenon is characterized by reference to a content, a direction upon an object, since, as I remarked in section 1.3.5, sensations, unlike beliefs and intentions, do not represent states of affairs external to themselves. Moreover, Brentano's other claim, namely that intentionality applies exclusively to mental phenomena, may be challenged because language also appears to be intentional. This book, for instance, is about the nature of the mind. Terry Pratchett's fictions are about a mythical non-existent Disc World, which moves through space carried on the back of a giant elephant. Similarly, computer programs and printouts, films, photographs, maps, diagrams, paintings, models, sculptures and brass-rubbings also represent states of affairs, real or imaginary, other than themselves.

Before reading any further, look at Exercise 1.5.

Exercise 1.5 Can you think of an objection to the claim that things other than mental states, such as words, exhibit intentionality? Working on your own or with someone else, write down your objection.

The objection you might come up with is that language, considered purely in itself, does not possess original or intrinsic intentionality. Intrinsic intentionality is a feature only of human (and animal) minds. The marks and noises that go towards comprising language have a merely derivative or 'as if' intentionality which is bestowed on them by language-users who have minds. Words have meanings and can be about things only in relation to persons for whom they have a meaning and who can interpret them as being about various states of affairs. Imagine that all conscious life in the universe suddenly and permanently ceased, but that all books and documents remained intact. In themselves, intrinsically, none of these items would possess meaning or represent possible states of affairs outside themselves. The ink marks comprising the sentences written in the books would still exist, but with the disappearance of anyone to read and understand those sentences, all meaning would have evaporated. All that would basically exist would be bits of paper with black markings on them. Analogously, the documents printed out by a computer mean nothing to the computer itself, since computers, lacking mental states, do not possess intrinsic intentionality. This is the position taken by the American thinker John Searle. However, as we shall see later, there are philosophers who would vigorously contest these claims. They would view the claim that computers cannot possess genuine intentionality as no more than a prejudice which merely rules out the possibility that genuine intentionality can be found elsewhere other than in human and animal minds.

Trying to explain how intentionality is possible has become a major philosophical industry since about the 1970s. In particular, the aim of many philosophers writing on this subject has been to demonstrate how intentionality can be naturalized. Although there is no definition of naturalism agreed upon by all philosophers, broadly speaking the idea is that in naturalizing intentionality we do not have to appeal to ghostly non-physical states which are supernatural in nature, that is, outside or above the ordinary physical world, in order to explain how mental states can be intentional in character. Using concepts and theories drawn from the sciences, the hope is that intentionality will be shown to be just another feature of the natural world, like digestion or the secretion of bile. However, whilst we shall touch upon some issues concerning intentionality in our examination of theories of the mind/body relation, a full-blown examination of it is beyond the scope of this book.

1.5   First- and third-person perspectives and the alleged privacy of the mental

When I describe another person's physical features, or indeed my own, I do this on the basis of sense-experience, namely through seeing, touching, smelling and so forth. Likewise, when someone else describes what I am like physically, they arrive at their characterization in fundamentally the same way. Neither of us has any special or, in principle, privileged way, of discovering the physical facts about other people and ourselves which the other lacks. The same applies if I wish to discover the internal workings of my own, or another's body. If I wanted to find out what was going on in my brain, for example, I would have no recourse but to employ, or, more likely, get someone else to employ on my behalf, essentially the same techniques I would have to use to find out what was going on in your brain. The most direct method, of course, would be to open your skull and directly observe the living brain. I could even ask for this to be done in my own case – patients under local anaesthetic have seen their own brains during operations reflected in a suitably placed mirror or on a video screen. Less radically, events in my own and others' brains could be probed by the use of scanners or, alternatively, by electroencephalographs which detect and measure the different rhythms of the electrical activity of the brain. We can summarize this position by saying that knowledge of the workings of our bodies, and physical nature generally, whoever we are, is made from a third-person perspective, there being no other perspective available to us in these cases.

The cases of brains and minds seem very different. Look at Exercise 1.6 and think about why this might be so.

Is what is true of brains equally true of minds? How do I find out what is taking place in my mind as opposed to what is occurring in yours? Are there any obstacles to discovering what you are thinking and feeling compared with my being able to say what I myself am thinking and feeling? Think about this for a few minutes and if possible discuss it with someone else.

In relation to my own case, most usually and typically, I do not have to go through any process of observing myself on television or in a mirror to be able to say, accurately and truly, what I am thinking or feeling. In fact, I don't have to go through any procedure of finding these things out at all. It seems I am just aware or conscious of my thoughts and sensations. But in relation to another person, say you, the only way I can find out what your thoughts and feelings are is on the basis of your conduct, what you say and do, since I seem to lack any other more direct way of gaining access to your thoughts and feelings. Moreover, if you choose to keep your thoughts to yourself, perhaps I can never find out what they are. Going further, how can I be sure that your behaviour is not a façade which conceals a bleak mental emptiness? You are, perhaps, a non-minded zombie, or a non-conscious marionette controlled from Mars (to borrow an example from the philosopher Christopher Peacocke).

This line of thought strongly encourages the belief that mental states are radically unlike physical states. Mental states are private to the individual, whereas physical states, by contrast, are public. Furthermore, this privacy is not like the privacy of the contents of my diary, or the code in which Samuel Pepys concealed his concupiscent thoughts. Pepys's code was subsequently broken without difficulty, and with similar ease someone could easily steal my diary and read its boring contents. The privacy of the mind has been characterized as a logical privacy, a privacy that is logically inviolable, so that no one, in principle, can ever get a direct glimpse of the contents of someone else's mind.

Thus, while there is a symmetry regarding my access and yours to physical states, in that neither of us has a privileged access to those states that are denied the other, this is not the case with regard to mental states. I have an access to my own states of mind which is denied to you, just as you have an access to your own mental states which is denied to me. In other words, there is an asymmetry regarding the access each person enjoys to his or her own mental states, by contrast with the access he or she has to the states of mind of others.

This is pictured by Ludwig Wittgenstein in his metaphor of the beetle-in-the-box. I am to be envisaged as having a box into which only I, in principle, can peer – and everyone else has a similar box. We all look in our own box and report that it contains a beetle, but we cannot display what is in our box to others. It is possible that the thing each box contains is very different from the others, but we will never find out since we cannot compare the beetles directly. If only I could somehow look in your box, I might make the alarming discovery that what you call a beetle, I refer to as a spider. The contents of each person's experience, the phenomenology or qualia comprising his or her mental states, might differ drastically from person to person for all we can tell. We have, by the very nature of the case, no way of finding out. At the very limit, the box might even be empty, and there are no qualia, but merely a mental desert. Furthermore, since the meanings of the words we use are determined by the objects to which they are applied, an even more alarming consequence follows, namely that each of us could be speaking a private language, the meanings of whose terms could never in principle be fathomed by others. Whether there could be such a language, a logically private language as it has been called, and whether the contents of experience can be radically private in the way described, has been fiercely contested by Wittgenstein and those philosophers influenced by him. I will return to a further examination of these questions in chapter 8.

1.6   Translucency, incorrigibility and final authority

Historically, the doctrine of privacy and privileged access has been associated with Descartes, as well as with those influenced by him in this respect, such as Locke and Hume. A natural extension of the doctrine is the translucency thesis, the claim that a person cannot be ignorant of the existence of his own states of mind, or in error about the kinds of mental state they are. A person's knowledge of their own mental states, by contrast with their knowledge of other matters, is not only complete, but incorrigible or infallible, i.e. beyond the possibility of mistake or correction. As John Heil perspicuously puts it, the claim precisely is that 'I know all and only the contents of my mind infallibly and completely. Where p is a proposition ascribing a current thought to myself, it is necessarily true both that, if I believe that p, then p is true, and that if p is true, I believe that p.'[7] Hume, a Cartesian in this respect, sums up this attitude: 'Since all actions of the mind are known to us by consciousness, they must necessarily appear in every particular what they are, and be what they appear.'[8] Taking the translucency thesis even further, it has often been thought that the contents of a person's mind are, in some way, self-intimating. They positively clamour to be noticed, and metaphors to characterize this self-advertisement have included thinking of mental items as like jewels glowing in a case, or as resembling phosphorescent seawater.

There are, however, several challenges that can be made to the claim that a person knows his own mental states infallibly. Consider firstly the case of pain and other sensations. If I am in pain, does it follow that I *know that* I am in pain? Here we must be careful. It is true that to feel pain is just to be aware of a painful sensation. The notion of an unfelt pain, a pain of which one had no awareness or consciousness, is surely a contradiction in terms. In this limited sense, ignorance of one's own sensations is not possible, because, as we noted in section 1.3.3, awareness is integral to their existence.

However, to be in pain is one thing, but to be aware *that* one is in pain is something entirely different. The awareness that one is in pain involves a judgement, whereas simply being in pain does not. To judge that you are in pain means that you are ascribing a pain to yourself, and that in turn would appear to involve not only possession of the concept of pain, but in addition the concept of yourself as a subject of experience. Making judgements using these concepts is essentially a linguistic activity and therefore impossible for non-language users such as dogs and cats. Animals can be in pain, but it does not follow that they know that they are in pain, i.e. that they can judge that they are in pain. Making a judgement that one is in pain involves taking a further step beyond the bare fact of experiencing pain. For those who are unable to take that step, propositional knowledge of their own mental states – the kind of knowledge which figures in the ascription of mental states to oneself – is not possible.[9]

1.7   Evaluating the privileged access and translucency doctrines

Exercise 1.7

How convincing do you find the claim that a person has a privileged access to his or her own mental states, and to what extent do you agree that a person's knowledge of his or her own mental states is infallible?

It would seem that in the case of at least some of my mental states, I can ascribe them to myself without having to make any observations or having to engage in any process of drawing conclusions from more basic states of affairs. Pains and other sensations afford some of the clearest examples. I can report that I am in pain without observation and inference. Other people, by contrast, can know that I am in pain, if they can ever really know at all, only on the basis of what I say and do. I would also appear to be the final authority on what my sensations feel like, or whether I am genuinely experiencing them. Providing that I know what the word 'pain' means, it seems I cannot be mistaken in claiming, sincerely, that the drilling the dentist is carrying out is hurting me. In a case like this, I am surely the final authority, and it is difficult to see how third persons could be in a position successfully to deny or correct my sincere claim that I am in pain. The same usually applies to my knowledge of my non-sensational states of mind, such as beliefs, desires and intentions. I can normally avow, without fear of contradiction or correction, what I believe or intend to do.

However, where intentional states are concerned, it is sometimes much less certain that I know better than others what I am thinking and feeling. Whilst I may be the final authority on whether the shoe pinches or not, I am manifestly not the final authority on whether I understand, say, some complex mathematical theorem. Were I to claim that I know, on the basis of a scrutiny of my inner mental landscape, that I really do understand the theorem, I would be laughed, quite rightly, to scorn. What will show whether I do understand it or not will be revealed by things such as whether I can explain the theorem in my own way to someone else, whether I could draw corollaries from it or point out other theorems that it contradicts. Again, sometimes I am not the best person to make an assessment of my own emotional state. It is a stock-in-trade of romantic fiction, e.g. Mills and Boon, that the very last people to realize they are in love with each other are the hero and heroine. An incapacity to know one's own mind is well illustrated in Proust's À la recherche du temps perdu. Bloch, a visitor at the narrator's grandparents, hears the grandmother, whom he has never met before, complain of feeling slightly unwell. Bloch bursts into tears as a result, drawing from the grandmother later the comment that he must be mad to exhibit such paroxysms of grief over such a trivial matter. The point is that although Bloch imagines himself to be sincere in the emotion he feels, or has convinced himself he is sincere, the depth of his feeling and his reaction are disproportionate to its object. The narrator's parents later conclude that although Bloch was sincere in the sense that he was not pretending to feel an emotion when in fact he felt nothing, nevertheless,

> [O]ur early impulsive emotions have but little influence over our later actions and the conduct of our lives; and that regard for moral obligations, loyalty to our friends, obedience to the rule of life, have a surer foundation in habits solidly formed and blindly followed than in these momentary transports, ardent but sterile.[10]

Other varieties of self-deception also provide rich instances of how we may deliberately fail to understand ourselves. In Joseph Conrad's *Lord Jim*, the eponymous hero manages to convince himself that the reason he did not go to the rescue of two men swept overboard was that he was taken unawares by the storm, rather than that he was paralysed by fear and cowardice. Later, he avoids having to confront his jealousy of the boy who did effect the rescue, by labelling the latter's account of his deeds 'a pitiful display of vanity'. And he even manages to persuade himself that by *not* going to the rescue he had 'enlarged his knowledge more than those who had done the work' and achieved something greater than the rescuers, although at the same time, in his heart, he knows perfectly well it is not so.[11]

John Heil, in *The Nature of True Minds*, mentions yet other intriguing possibilities.[12] I might hold the second-order belief, the belief that I believe some proposition, p. But this second-order belief could be mistaken in at least three ways. Firstly, I might not believe p at all: in other words, I believe falsely that I hold the belief that p. Secondly, whilst I have adopted some propositional attitude towards p, I could be mistaken about what this attitude is. Perhaps I don't really believe that p, but fear that p, or want that p, or suspect that p, instead. In the face of these comparatively few examples, it seems implausible to maintain that I possess a privileged, incorrigible knowledge of all the different kinds of mental state I might conceivably be in. Whilst my sincere avowal is sufficient to guarantee the truth of the report of what I am experiencing in the case of a dental drilling, it can sometimes be our behaviour, and the context in which it occurs, that serves as the criterion, the measure, against which the ascription of an intentional mental state to me, even by myself, is assessable for its correctness.

1.8 First- and third-person perspectives and the search for a unitary account of the mind

We are now in a better position to distinguish first-person and third-person perspectives from each other. In the case of knowledge of what happens in and to my body, as well as bodies and material objects in general, my knowledge is, essentially, from an external, third-person perspective. In such a case, this is the only perspective available to me or, indeed, to anyone else. My knowledge of your states of mind is also made from a third-person perspective because it is externally grounded in the public behaviour that you exhibit, just as your knowledge of my mental states must also be from a third-person viewpoint. But at least in some cases, I appear to know what is going on in my mind directly, just as you know what is taking place in yours, from an internal, private, first-person perspective, which requires no observation of, or reference to, any external behaviour.

It is important not to confuse first- and third-person perspectives with first- and third-person ascriptions of mental states. Normally, it will be true that the mental states I ascribe to myself are made from a first-person perspective, as when I have a pain or an itch. Equally, when I ascribe mental states to you, these will necessarily be from a third-person perspective, since I have no way of gaining knowledge of your mental states other than through your actions and behaviour generally. However, there will be those occasions when I am temporarily constrained to take a third-person perspective on my own mental states, owning that third persons know my mind better than I do, and basing my ascription of my mental state on that external basis, rather than on an unreliable (in this instance) first-person perspective.

The fact that mental states may be ascribed in two fundamentally different kinds of way, from a first-person perspective on the basis of inner awareness and from a third-person perspective grounded in the observation of behaviour, has been thought by some philosophers to raise problems. The point has been well made by Colin McGinn: if the meaning of a mental term is governed by the manner in which it is applied, then this seems to render a unitary account of the meanings of such terms impossible.[13] When I ascribe a pain to myself, I do it on the basis of inner awareness, from a first-person perspective. Yet when you ascribe the same pain to me, you do it from a third-person perspective on the basis of my groaning and wincing. Since the meaning of the term cannot be severed from the conditions under which it is applied, and since these conditions are utterly different when made from first- and third-person perspectives respectively, the meaning gets pulled in two opposing directions.

One of these directions is represented by Cartesianism, and leads to the view that states of mind are intrinsically inner, private and non-physical in nature, accessible only to the person whose states of mind they are. The other opposing direction is represented by analytical behaviourism which attempts to reduce mental states to patterns of actual and possible external public behaviour. But how can a given mental state possess such entirely disparate natures? We seem to be forced to choose between one option and the other, since the formation of a unitary concept of the mental appears to be ruled out. Yet cleaving entirely to just one of these perspectives leads to a distorted view of the nature of the mind.

A possible strategy, McGinn suggests, would be to take each type of mental state on its own terms and then try to determine which perspective yields the better account of the state in question. Some mental states, like understanding a theory, will have their applicability governed largely from a behaviourist perspective. Others, like sensations, will be more amenable to a Cartesian stance. An extension of this approach, in line with McGinn's recommendations, would be to treat one perspective as primary in relation to the other, and then try to find a plausible way of connecting the primary use of the concept with its secondary aspect.

Thus, for example, Wittgensteinians have argued that although it is true that we do not ascribe pains to ourselves on the basis of observing our behaviour, our self-ascriptions are only possible because there are behavioural signs available to third persons against which our first-person ascriptions can be assessed for their correctness or incorrectness. In this case, the third-person perspective has been assumed to be of primary importance in reaching a proper understanding of the mental phenomenon in question.

It has to be said, however, that this account is much less plausible in the case of sensations, because, as we have already noted, it seems that these are self-ascribed on the basis of an inner, private awareness, and not in connection with observations of, or reference to, behaviour. That is why Galen Strawson, in his book *Mental Reality*, argues: 'The word "pain" is just a word for a certain kind of unpleasant sensation, considered *independently* of any of its behavioural or other publicly observable causes and effects' (my emphasis).[14] Similarly, James Hopkins has remarked that 'private objects possess determinate natures waiting to be recognised',[15] a claim that has been convincingly fleshed-out by Howard Robinson in his book, *Perception*.[16] Robinson wants to maintain that pains and other sensations should be conceived of as private objects. He writes: 'A subject does not have and does not need public criteria for how it seems to them in such an experience',[17] and, giving a neat twist to Wittgenstein's dictum that 'whatever is going to seem right, will be right, which only means we cannot speak here about what is right', Robinson claims that, in the case in question, '[n]ecessarily, whatever I judge to be right, is right'.[18] Consequently, according to Robinson, pains and other sensations can be re-identified by their possessors in the privacy of their own minds, and hence can be talked about in total independence of public behavioural criteria. Robinson offers a convincing argument in support of this position. He asks us to imagine a case in which someone suffers a pain in their right hand and a pain in their left hand at the same instant. Now it seems entirely believable that purely from the way each of these pains feels, the person can say whether or not they are both instances of the same type of pain. But if the identification of one pain as being like another pain at a given instant – synchronic identification – is plausible, then so must situations in which two pains felt at different times are judged to be qualitatively the same. In that case, Robinson maintains, identification over time of pains as being of the same recurring sort – diachronic identification over time – must be possible.

However, with regard to any particular kind of mental state, it has to be said perhaps that there can be no guarantee in advance that an acceptable way of easing the tension between first- and third-person perspectives will be forthcoming, and this, McGinn thinks, 'may in fact place a permanent obstacle in the way of arriving at a theoretically satisfying conception of the mind'.[19] The same problem, fortunately, does not arise in the case of material objects and events, since knowledge of these is arrived at from purely a third-person perspective. I must, however, for reasons of space, now leave the reader to pursue the issues raised in this section further for him- or herself.

1.9 The holistic character of intentional states and their relation to consciousness

Suppose that you have an ache in the shoulders. The fact that you are experiencing this sensation has no implications whatever regarding whether you are, or are not, also experiencing a tingling sensation in your feet. Suppose, however, that it happens that you are having a tingling sensation in your feet as well as an ache in your shoulders. The occurrence of these two experiences in turn has no implications as to whether you are having a toothache. You might be or you might not. We could describe this situation by saying that sensations are atomistic: the occurrence of an individual sensation has no implications for the existence, or non-existence, of any other sensation, so in this sense sensations can exist loosely and separately apart from each other.

But now think of a non-sensational, intentional state, such as the intention to cancel a cheque. By contrast with sensations, this state of mind does have implications for the existence of other intentional states. For instance, the intention will imply all sorts of beliefs on my part – the existence of a currency system and of banks, of the institution of promising, that there is a good reason why the cheque ought to be cancelled on this occasion, and so forth. By contrast with what is true for non-intentional sensations, it would make no sense to suppose that my intention to cancel a cheque could exist in isolation from a vast network of other intentional states. An intentional state may be compared to a piece of a jigsaw puzzle. The piece owes its identity *as* a piece to the other pieces to which it relates. If all the other pieces of the jigsaw were destroyed, the individual piece would have lost its identity, for it could no longer play the role of constituting part of the puzzle. The piece would have become merely a strange-shaped piece of coloured card. Similarly, the notion of an isolated intentional state all on its own is incoherent, because any individual state, by its very nature, must presuppose the existence of many other related states. Intentional states are like the pieces of jigsaw in other important respects. It is of the nature of the pieces that they may be fitted together to form a coherent whole, but equally it is possible that a mistake might be made in attempting to put a piece in a gap it will not fit. Attempting to force the piece in would merely buckle or distort the rest of the jigsaw. The capacity for intentional states to fit together to form a harmonious whole, or to be inconsistent with each other, as well as to presuppose and entail the existence of other intentional states, is what philosophers refer to as their holistic character.

Consciousness plays a vitally important role in the formation of a coherent set of propositional attitudes. In relation to these attitudes, consciousness strictly means self-consciousness, the ability to recognize that one has certain beliefs, together with other propositional attitudes such as desires. The crucial point is that unless people could become aware of their own beliefs, i.e. can know that they have them and can reflect upon them, they would be unable to spot logical links as well as inconsistencies between them. But without being able to see that subscription to certain beliefs logically commits one to subscribing to certain other beliefs, logical inference would not be possible. Neither would it be possible for someone to detect inconsistency between different beliefs, and this would preclude that person from rationally adjusting his or her beliefs by retaining some, but jettisoning others, in order to bring them into harmony with each other. In addition, beliefs are rationally appraised not merely by comparison with other beliefs, but by looking to see if the evidence available makes it reasonable to hold them. What all this is pointing to is that unless a person could call their beliefs to mind and self-consciously examine them, the capacity for rational thought would not be possible.

This is an interesting and surprising result which helps to demonstrate the evolutionary advantage that self-consciousness brings. Self-consciousness makes rationality possible, and it is only through the exercise of rationality that human beings have been able to understand and explain why things are the way they are. With this knowledge has come the means of manipulating and controlling our surroundings in a way that goes far beyond anything non-human animals can do, thus increasing the likelihood of our survival in the face of hostile changes to the environment. For example, were a large asteroid about to strike the earth and threaten extinction, non-human animals could do nothing about it. By contrast, not only are we aware of the threat and why it exists, but our scientific understanding of this matter is close to providing us with the capability to diminish or avert the danger.

Even more importantly, it is the distinctively human capacity to construct languages and symbolic systems that has made the formation of the propositional attitudes and the exercise of rationality possible. This, in turn, constitutes the necessary condition for the origination and evolution of the social and political arrangements which mark off the human from the animal world, as Aristotle saw so long ago:

> The reason why man is a being meant for political association in a higher degree than bees or other gregarious animals can ever associate, is evident. Nature, according to our theory, makes nothing in vain; and man alone is furnished with the faculty of language. The mere making of sounds serves to indicate pleasure and pain, and is thus a faculty that belongs to animals in general: their nature enables them to attain the point at which they have perceptions of pain and pleasure and can signify those perceptions to one another. But language serves to declare what is advantageous and what is the reverse, and it therefore serves to declare what is just and what is unjust.[20]

1.10   Is there a mark of the mental?

In the light of the extended discussion comprising this chapter, do you think it is possible to state those conditions that will demarcate the mental from the non-mental? Are some elements of this criterion more basic than others? Try briefly to say what is distinctive about the mental as opposed to the non-mental and then read my discussion below.

Exercise 1.

Firstly, physical things, and perhaps abstract entities such as numbers, can exist whether anyone is aware of them or not. By contrast, sensations such as pains and itches exist if, and only if, a person or being is currently conscious of them. To illustrate the point, a physical object like a tree can exist whether or not anyone sees or touches it, but a pain of which no one is aware is surely a contradiction in terms. The importance of consciousness for the mental cannot be overestimated. Even non-sensational intentional states such as beliefs and desires, which can exist temporarily in the absence of consciousness, must ultimately be accessible to consciousness if they are genuinely to be attributable to a person.

Consciousness is also vitally important for ensuring coherence among the propositional attitudes which comprise non-sensational intentional states, because unless a person can becomes aware of the propositional attitudes to which they subscribe, they will not be able to detect and eliminate any inconsistencies between them. Unless this kind of adjustment can be made, rationality would not be possible. In short, the conclusion to which these observations point is that consciousness, and its higher manifestation self-consciousness, are, in their different ways, absolutely integral to the existence of the fully fledged human mind.

Secondly, it is difficult to understand how intentional states could turn out to be purely physical in nature. How can physical states, such as neurophysiological events in the brain, be directed upon a content which in some cases corresponds to nothing in the world outside the mind? Moreover, intentional states are essentially holistic, but there appears to be no counterpart of this feature in purely physical states of affairs.

Thirdly, physical phenomena are accessible only from a third-person perspective, whereas mental states can be accessed, and ascribed, from both first-person – 'inner' – and third-person – 'outer' – viewpoints. Taking this further, people's access to, and knowledge of, their own states of mind would seem to be privileged in the sense that they can say without observation or inference what they are thinking or feeling, and are very often the final authority on their mental states. By contrast, one person is able to ascribe mental states to another solely on the basis of inferences made on the basis of observation of that person's outward, public behaviour. These features of states of mind, their radical privacy, and their ascribability from both first- and third-person perspectives, make it hard to see how the mental can ever be reduced to, or eliminated in favour of, the physical.

Lastly, although I have said nothing about it here, it may have occurred to you that a further important difference between the mental and the physical is that the former would seem to be non-spatial in character, whereas it is of the very essence of physical phenomena that they occur in regions of space – take, for example, magnetic and gravitational fields – and in many cases are the literal occupants of those regions, as is the case with physical objects such as trees, planets and sub-atomic particles. However, any discussion as to whether mental states literally cannot be given a spatial location and, on that basis alone, are not identifiable with any physical states of affairs, will be postponed until chapter 3, section 3.8.1.

1   What is meant by the term 'qualia'?
2   What is intentionality? What is the difference between intrinsic intentionality and derived or 'as if' intentionality? Can this distinction be maintained?
3   Are mental states private?
4   What do you understand by first- and third-person perspectives?
5   'Describe *three* characteristics of mental states which are held to distinguish them from physical states. Assess the view that the characteristics of mental states make it impossible for those states to be within the physical world' (Associated Examining Board A-level question, 1997).
6   Why is self-consciousness alleged to be necessary for rationality to be possible?
7   Is it possible to produce a water-tight definition of the mental which can be used to distinguish it from the physical?

Questions to think about

Suggestions for further reading

- An excellent introduction and reference book is provided by S. Guttenplan (ed.), *A Companion to the Philosophy of Mind* (Oxford: Blackwell, 1994). The opening chapter 'An Essay on the Mind', by Samuel Guttenplan, is highly recommended for its lucidity and interest.
- George Graham's *Philosophy of Mind: An Introduction* (Oxford: Blackwell, 1993), also provides a stimulating and amusing introduction to the mind/body problem and related issues.
- John Heil's *Philosophy of Mind: A Contemporary Introduction* (London: Routledge, 1998), provides a clear overview of this area of philosophy.
- A tougher book, but very worthwhile, is Peter Carruthers's *Introducing Persons* (London: Croom Helm, 1986). A useful feature of the book is its formal presentation of a variety of arguments which the reader is encouraged to assess for himself.

- John Searle's 1984 Reith Lectures, *Minds, Brains and Science* (Harmondsworth: Penguin, 1989) provide a stimulating, accessible and provocative introduction to the main issues involved in the mind/body problem.
- Colin McGinn's *The Character of Mind* (Oxford: OUP, 1982) raises and discusses in depth and with sophistication many of the important questions in the philosophy of mind, but the discussions are amazingly compressed and this is therefore not a book for the absolute beginner.

2

DUALISM

Objectives

As a result of reading this chapter you should:

- be able to describe the main features of dualism as it occurs in the philosophies of Plato and Descartes;
- be able to expound and criticize arguments for dualism constructed by Plato and Descartes;
- understand how Descartes tries to account for the interaction between mind and body and be able to evaluate his attempt;
- be able to explain the main objections to dualism, including, most importantly, the homunculus fallacy and the problem posed by how souls are supposed to be told apart from one another and counted.

2.1   Substance dualism

The basic claim of the dualist is that a human being is a composite of two disparate entities: a non-physical soul or mind and a physical body. The person – the possessor of consciousness and experiences in general – is identical with the soul, not the body. Throughout life, the body and soul are somehow linked together so that each can affect the other, but at death this link is severed. The body then suffers dissolution, but the soul continues to exist independently of the body in its own right. Because it provides for the continued existence of post-mortem persons in a non-physical disembodied form, dualism has seemed an attractive doctrine to many people, especially those who follow a religion of some sort. Physical death is not the end of us: as pure consciousnesses, we continue to exist in a world beyond this present one. There is then no reason ultimately to fear death because it does not amount to annihilation, but merely marks a transition from one state of being to another.

Conceived of as a genuine entity, which can exist in its own right independently of anything else, the soul is traditionally said to be a logical substance, hence the term 'substance dualism'. The term 'substance', when first encountered in a philosophical context, is apt to mislead, and to understand what philosophers mean by it, you must first clear your mind of such usages as are illustrated in an utterance like 'What kind of substance is that in your test-tube?' In this sense, substances are thought of as some kind of stuff or material, such as plastic, glue or water. The philosophical meaning of the term is not at all like this, as an example helps to make clear. Consider the following lines from T. S. Eliot's poem, 'Morning at the Window':

> The brown waves of fog toss up to me
> Twisted faces from the bottom of the street,
> And tear from a passer-by with muddy skirts
> An aimless smile that hovers in the air
> And vanishes along the level of the roofs.[1]

Now, although we can easily conceive of the passer-by as either wearing or not wearing an aimless smile on her face, we cannot conceive of the smile as existing separately from the passer-by. Why is this? Clearly, because a smile is nothing but the disposition – the arrangement if you like – of the parts of the passer-by's face. Logically, a smile cannot exist without a smiler, and the identity of the smile – the particular smile, it is among many possible smiles – is tied logically to the identity of the person who is doing the smiling. The passer-by, by contrast, has the status of a logical substance, of genuine thinghood, because she does not depend logically for her existence on anything else in the manner of the smile. The word 'smile' is, of course, a noun, and many of us were taught at school that nouns acquire their meanings by naming persons, places or things, so there might be a temptation to think, mistakenly, of a smile as a substance.

The ancient Greek philosopher Aristotle (384–322 BC) defined a substance as 'that which is neither said of a subject nor in a subject, e.g. an individual man or horse'.[2] This definition captures the idea that substances can exist in their own right by contrast with what is said *of* them, or is *in* them. The distinction between being 'in' and 'said of' may be explained as follows. Smiles qualify as 'particulars', that is, as individual items. For instance, there can be John's smile, Mary's smile and so forth, and are 'in' subjects. Smiles owe their identities and existence to the substances they are in: they are logically dependent particulars. Unlike a smile, the colour of a face – red, say – does not qualify as a particular. Instead, it is a universal or property, i.e. a completely general feature which can be true of many individual things or substances: the red-faced local butcher, for instance, or my rubicund uncle Arthur. Properties contrast with substances. Properties are possessed by substances and cannot exist loose and separate on their own. You could not find an instance of red floating around independently on its own: rather, someone, or something, must possess the property of being red.

The distinction between substances and properties enables us to understand how there can be a weaker variant of dualism, namely property dualism.[3] Property dualism eschews the notion of immaterial soul substances and maintains instead that the brain, a composite physical thing, possesses two fundamentally different sorts of property – mental features and consciousness in particular – that are non-physical in nature, as well as familiar physical properties such as mass, colour and texture. I shall have considerably more to say about property dualism in chapter 6.

2.2   Platonic dualism

The Greek philosopher Plato (*c*.427–347 BC) was a major exponent of dualism. Whilst he did not invent the theory, he was the first, as far as we know, to present written arguments in its favour. Plato believed not only in the survival of death by the soul, but also in its pre-existence before birth. In that state it was supposedly acquainted with the Forms – perfect, timeless, immutable essences or archetypes which, according to Plato, were the original patterns or templates of things. These exist in their own realm above the world of the senses, and are only apprehendable by the intellect after a rigorous training in mathematics and philosophy.

Plato claimed it was by their participation in the Forms that the ordinary, imperfect, changing and perishing things which we see around us are made to be the kinds of item they are. As well as the many individual things that exhibit beauty, for example, there is supposed to be the Form of the Beautiful, Beauty itself, by virtue of which the imperfect things of the world of the senses are made beautiful. The soul, according to Plato, resembles the Forms in being 'divine, immortal, intelligible, uniform, indissoluble, unvarying and constant in relation to itself'.[4] This description of the soul is taken from the *Phaedo*, a work in which Plato presents a variety of arguments in an attempt to demonstrate the soul's existence. Throughout many of these arguments it is reasonably clear that Plato conceives of the soul as a non-physical entity, and the person is identified with the soul. But Plato is not always consistent regarding the various things he says about the soul. For example, in one place in his dialogue the *Republic*, he speaks of the soul as 'the principle of life', roughly as that which makes living things alive. In this sense of the word, anything that is alive has a soul, by definition, because 'soul' is merely synonymous with 'being alive'. As such, the soul cannot be thought of as an entity, an individual person or agent, contrary to what Plato says elsewhere. In the *Phaedo*, Plato also says that the only activity intrinsic to the soul, and inseparable from it, is pure reasoning. This alone will survive when the soul separates from the body at death. However, it is not clear that the survival of the intellect means the survival of the person.

Plato had several arguments in support of substance dualism, but I will choose only one, which is taken from his dialogue, the *Alcibiades* I,[5] for examination. My reason for choosing to examine this argument is that it embodies a particularly seductive and common error whose exposure will save us from numerous other mistakes we might make when philosophizing about the nature of the mind.

Before I give details of the particular argument in question, however, it will be necessary to say a little more about what an argument is, and how arguments may be evaluated for their soundness or lack of it. There are two sorts of argument discussed in this book, inductive and deductive. Since inductive arguments are discussed in detail in chapter 8, sections 8.1 and 8.2, I will not say anything more about them here, our concern for the moment being solely with deductive argument.

In everyday life, the word 'argument' usually means having a row, engaging in a dispute, often heated. The present sense of the word is not like this. Essentially, in philosophy, an argument consists in trying to move rationally, or logically, from certain statements we call 'premises' in order to establish the truth of another statement, which we call the 'conclusion'. In a deductive argument that is valid, the conclusion logically follows from the premises. That is to say, if you affirm (put forward) the premises but deny the conclusion, you will formally contradict yourself. Contradicting oneself is a waste of time and to be avoided. It would be like giving money to someone with the right hand and taking it back with the left – nothing is accomplished. To make clearer what comprises a valid deductive argument, consider the following simple example:

> Premise 1: all women are mammals;
> Premise 2: all mammals are warm-blooded;
> Conclusion: therefore, all women are warm-blooded.

If you put forward (1) and (2), you must accept that the conclusion follows, on pain of contradicting yourself. It is, however, very import-ant to realize that validity has nothing whatsoever to do with the truth or falsity of the premises and conclusion, but depends entirely upon the structure of the argument. The argument above has the structure:

> Premise 1: all A are B;
> Premise 2: all B are C;
> Conclusion: therefore, all A are C.

Clearly, in this representation of the argument structure, we cannot say whether the premises or conclusion are true or false, because we have not said what A, B and C are. This helps to make it clear that validity depends solely upon the form of the argument, not what it actually concerns. It happens in the first example that both premises and conclusion are true. But consider:

> Premise 1: all pigs have wings;
> Premise 2: no creatures with wings can fly;
> Conclusion: therefore, no pigs can fly.

The argument is valid. The conclusion really does follow from the premises. But whilst the conclusion is true, both premises happen to be false. The problem is that arguments where either one, or all, of the premises are false, cannot provide any grounds for thinking their conclusions are true, even where those arguments are valid.

There is only one reliable way in which, just by examining the argument, you can be quite sure that conclusion has to be true. What conditions, do you think, have to be met?

Exercise 2.1

There are two conditions. You can tell the conclusion is true if, and only if:

1   The argument is valid.
2   All the premises are true.

Arguments can have more than two premises. An argument could have a thousand, or a million, even. But it only succeeds in establishing its conclusion if it is valid and if all its premises, without exception, are true. What I have said so far may not appear to amount to very much, but in fact it places an extremely powerful tool in our hands. If someone uses a deductive argument in their work, and we can extract it and set it out formally in the form of premises and a conclusion, we are then in a position to assess whether it succeeds by looking to see if, in the first instance, it is valid and, in the second, whether all its premises are true. If the argument fails either or both of these tests, then it has failed to establish its conclusion. This need not necessarily mean that the conclusion is false: there may be other independent grounds for thinking it to be true. But whether this is the case or not, we can still say that the argument does not prove what it is supposed to be proving – and that is a pretty devastating attack on anyone's argument!

The arguments I have outlined all concern classes of things, and this pattern of argument, which was invented by Aristotle, is called a syllogism. Not all deductive arguments take this form, but there is not enough space to go into the details here (interested readers can investigate the topic for themselves), though in subsequent chapters I do ask you to evaluate some examples of non-syllogistic deductive arguments.

It can often be quite difficult to extract arguments from philosophical texts and to state them formally. In the section which follows, I begin by describing informally the argument Plato gives in his dialogue Alcibiades I for the existence of the soul, and then provide a formal statement of it which I invite you to assess for yourself, using the guidelines I have provided above. (When evaluating the argument, look back at the details of how to do this: my own discussion follows the formal statement of the argument.) This kind of exercise, as you will see, occurs throughout the book, and should get you thinking for yourself.

2.3   A Platonic argument in favour of dualism

The argument goes like this: Socrates asks Alcibiades whether he uses speech in talking, to which the latter readily agrees. Socrates then runs through a number of other examples which are designed to establish the conclusion that the user of a thing, for instance a shoemaker, and the thing he uses, a cutting tool say, are numerically different from each other. Again, Alcibiades willingly accedes. Socrates then points out that a man uses not only his hands, but his whole body, and that therefore, just as a person is distinct from a tool he uses or an instrument he plays, so it follows that he must be distinct from his body. The argument may be stated more formally and runs briefly thus:

1 The user of a thing and the thing used are two numerically different and distinct things, i.e. two logical substances.
2 A person uses his or her body.
3 Therefore a person must be numerically different and distinct from his or her own body.

But if a person is different from his or her body, he or she must be a non-bodily logical substance, i.e. a soul.

Before reading on, look at Exercise 2.2.

What criticisms can you make of the argument above? Working alone, write them down, and then discuss the issue with someone else.

Exercise 2.2

The first premise can certainly and obviously be accepted as true if the thing used is a utensil such as a knife, or a musical instrument such as a harp or a piano. But, despite the fact that we speak of people using their limbs and bodies, do they use these things in the same sense in which they use a utensil or an instrument? We may well suspect a play on the word 'use' here. After all, someone may be told not to be so lazy but to use their mind – i.e. to apply their intelligence to a problem. But should this usage be taken to establish that a person is entirely different from their mind? Even a dualist is going to be stuck for an answer to this question if the person cannot be identified with their mind or soul.

I suggest we need to ask whether people stand in the same relation to their body and limbs, as they do to a tool they use, or an instrument they play. One reason to think that this cannot be the case runs as follows. When I use a chisel I do so by picking it up and grasping it in my hand. But when I use my hand, I do not have to pick it up and hold it – I simply move it. To put this another way, I can move my hand without having to do anything else first. I cannot, by contrast, just move a tool directly. I have to do this by doing something else – grasping it in my hand or mouth, blowing on it, thumping on the table until the vibrations cause the tool to roll off, and so forth. I cannot move the tool in the way I can move my own limbs. This strongly suggests that I do not stand in the same relation to my own limbs and body as I do to a tool which I use.

Continuing this line of thought, if, in the course of using a chisel, I make a slip and gouge my hand, we would ordinarily describe what has happened by saying that I have hurt myself. This is because my hand is a part of me, by contrast with the chisel which plainly isn't. A dedicated dualist, by contrast, would have to insist that this ordinary way of describing what has happened is mistaken. The dualist's preferred description of what occurred has to be that an injury was caused to my body, but not to me, because I am really an incorporeal soul. Moreover, non-physical things such as the soul cannot be injured by physical objects such as chisels. However, the dualist's insistence on this characterization of what took place can be seen merely to be begging the question in favour of dualism from the outset. The claim that a person uses their limbs and body in the same way that they use tools or instruments is similarly tendentious. We can recognize what is wrong with Plato's argument once we realize that it contains, in effect, a pun or equivocation on the word 'use'. In its literal use, the user of a thing and the thing used are two different things. But, unless the truth of dualism is assumed from the beginning, a person and his or her body are not two different entities. Consequently, I do not use my hands or body in the same sense in which I use a tool. The movement of a tool is the result of something else I do first, but the actions consisting in the movements of my hand and body when I move them are not the results of some prior actions which I perform. Of course, it is harmless to describe someone as using their limbs and body, just as long as we don't lose sight of the point that this represents a metaphorical, and not a literal employment of the word 'use'.

What underlies Plato's argument in the Alcibiades I is the fact that there are all kinds of ways of speaking in which a contrast of some sort is drawn between a person and their body, and these locutions can make it appear that the two must be different and distinct things. For example, we say that a person *has* a strong body, not that he or she *is* a strong body, and from this we might be tempted to argue that because there are cases in which the possessor of a thing and the thing possessed are genuinely two separate things, as illustrated by the usage 'Patrick has a powerful car', so the possessor of a strong body must be numerically distinct from the body that is possessed. However, it should be plain that this merely reprises the error which Plato commits in his dialogue with Alcibiades. After all, rather than saying that someone has a strong body, we can easily describe them instead as being physically strong, and this form of words carries no suggestion whatever that the person is an entity distinct from his or her body. Likewise, to borrow an example from Anthony Flew, to describe someone as flogging their protesting body over the line to win the race does not mean that the person in question must be a soul, literally wielding an incorporeal lash by means of which he or she urges a weakening body on to greater efforts. Such a description is merely a picturesque way of saying that the winner of the race made a great effort of will.

As Gilbert Ryle (1900–76) pointed out in *The Concept of Mind*[6] we should *not* be driven to draw from the 'absurdity of such collocations' the conclusion that a person is to be described as an association between a body and a non-body. The examples paraded above would enable us to reach that conclusion only if we were prepared to accept that the following argument established its conclusion:

1 Expressions that refer to persons and expressions that refer to people's bodies are not equivalent in meaning.
2 When one expression has a different meaning from another expression, this can *only* be because those expressions refer to, or name, different and distinct logical substances.
3 Therefore, persons must be logical substances, which are different and distinct from their bodies.

Now attempt Exercise 2.3 before reading my discussion of this argument.

Exercise 2.3

Are both the premises in the argument true or can either or both be rejected? Remember: given that the argument is valid (as this one is), the conclusion cannot be established if at least one of its premises is false. Decide whether the premises are true or false and write down your reasons. Then discuss the issue with someone else, before reading on.

Since the argument is valid, if we wish to reject the conclusion we must show that either, or both, premises are false. I think we can accept that the first premise is true, as the various examples already given demonstrate: there are numerous cases in which talk about a person and talk about his or her body are not equivalent in meaning. So if there is any fault with the argument, it must lie with the second premise. This is easily shown to be false, and one way in which this might done is as follows. Consider the following: the expression 'the Morning Star' has a different meaning from 'the Evening Star', but nevertheless these two expressions refer to one and the same entity, namely the planet Venus, and not to two different logical substances. A different kind of example that can also be used to expose the error under examination is provided by the statement 'I saw Patrick last night', which clearly has a different meaning from 'I saw Patrick's body last night'. The latter usage implies, as the former does not, that I saw Patrick dead. But again, this cannot possibly entail that in viewing Patrick's corpse I must therefore have been viewing an entity that is different and distinct from Patrick himself. When I see Patrick alive I see a living organism, a functioning human being. In seeing Patrick dead, I merely see the same organism which has ceased to function. There is nothing in these ordinary ways of speaking that can establish dualism, or even make it plausible. It is true, of course, that we commonly speak of dead people as having departed, as having deserted their bodies which are now empty shells. But these ways of speaking are merely figures of speech, and will only seem to lend support to dualism if one is already convinced of the truth of the doctrine in advance.

2.4 Cartesian dualism

After Plato, the most famous exponent of dualism was René Descartes (1596–1650). The fresh impetus Descartes gave to dualism was so strikingly original and compelling that the version he formulated is named after him and called Cartesian dualism.[7] The agenda for the modern debate on the nature of the mind was thus effectively set by Descartes in writings such as *The Discourse on the Method* (published in 1637) and the *Meditations* (published in 1642).

Cartesian dualism, like the Platonic variety, affirms that a person is one and the same thing as an incorporeal soul, an immaterial logical substance devoid of all features of material bodies and, in particular, extension, so that the soul has neither length, width or breadth, and thus occupies no volume of space. It is therefore, in principle, indivisible, so that it is logically impossible to have a half or a sixteenth of a soul. The indivisibility of the soul has been used as an alleged proof of its immortality on the grounds that only those things that can decay into parts are perishable.

Conceived of as a soul, a person is totally distinct and different in kind from his or her extended, space-occupying, physical body. Descartes refers to the soul as a *res cogitans*, a thinking thing. In the *Meditations* he spells out more fully what he means by this:

Thinking is another attribute of the soul; and here I discover what properly belongs to myself. This alone is inseparable from me. I am – I exist: this is certain; but how often? As often as I think; for perhaps it would even happen, if I should wholly cease to think, that I should at the same time altogether cease to be. I now admit nothing that is not necessarily true: I am therefore, precisely speaking, only a thinking thing.[8]

As this passage makes clear, thinking is not merely a feature the soul just happens to have, but its essential characteristic, or essence, a feature that is indispensable to it and makes it the kind of thing it is. Thus the soul cannot lose its essence without thereby ceasing to exist, which is why Descartes was prepared to embrace the extravagant claim that the human soul is always thinking, even in the womb.[9]

When Descartes speaks of thinking, he is using the term in a deliberately extended way to include not merely intellectual activities such as cogitation and reasoning, but even the experience of sensations of various kinds, as well as emotional states such as anger and jealousy. Descartes also mentions doubting, understanding, affirming, denying, being willing or unwilling, imagining and all forms of sense-perception as examples of thinking. Moreover, and crucially, the hallmark of the mental for Descartes is consciousness, and this means he would have regarded the very idea of unconscious or non-conscious mental states as a contradiction in terms. Descartes' emphasis on consciousness as the essential characteristic of mind is to be found in the following remark from his *The Principles of Philosophy*: 'By the noun "thought" I mean everything that takes place in us so that we are conscious of it, in so far as it is an object of consciousness.'[10]

By contrast with the soul, the body is *res extensa*, a thing whose essence, in common with other material things, is extension in space. The body is a complex, non-conscious machine, capable, unlike the soul, of divisibility into parts. Arrangements of matter, however complex, are incapable of thought and awareness. Only minds, conceived of as incorporeal non-physical souls, can possess mental features. The processes which take place inside the body can be explained in scientific, mechanical terms, and in viewing the body in this way, Descartes was laying the foundations for a scientific account of what makes living things alive. By contrast, Plato, as we saw in the *Republic*, sometimes claimed that the soul is the principle of life, that it is the soul which makes living things alive (see section 2.2) and this was later transmuted into a belief by some thinkers that living organisms were animated by a mysterious spiritual *élan vital*, or life-force, which lay beyond the scope of empirical investigation. A virtue of Descartes' way of looking at the matter is that it does away with mystery and makes the functioning of living things in principle explicable in terms of chemistry and physics. The corollary of Descartes' approach is that the body does not die because the soul departs, as Plato thought, but rather that the soul takes its leave because the body has stopped functioning.[11]

To summarize: for Descartes the soul is conscious, but incapable of extension, whereas the body, and matter in general, is extended but intrinsically incapable of consciousness and mentality.

2.5 Animals and machines

Only human beings have souls, Descartes maintained, and thus animals have neither thought nor consciousness. Animals, or the brutes, as Descartes sometimes referred to them, should be regarded as automata, albeit machines that are 'incomparably better arranged, and adequate to movements more admirable than is any machine of human invention'.[12] The last part of this remark makes it clear that Descartes thinks that it is impossible that we should be inflicting suffering on animals when we kill and eat them, because we would be doing these things merely to non-conscious machines, and hence we would be no more guilty of inflicting ill-treatment than we are when we send a car to the scrapheap.

2.5.1 Descartes' two tests for the presence of the soul

Descartes believed that the absence of the soul in animals could be established by two tests, which he outlines in his *Discourse on the Method*. Firstly:

> [Animals could] never use words or other constructed signs, as we do to declare our thoughts to others. . . . [Secondly,] while they might do many things as well as any of us or better, they would infallibly fail in others, revealing that they acted not from knowledge but only from the disposition of their organs. For while reason is a universal tool which may serve in all kinds of circumstances, these organs need a special arrangement for each special action; so that it is morally impossible that a machine should contain so many varied arrangements as to act in all the events of life in the way reason enables us to act.[13]

The first test hinges on the fact that we can use language and animals cannot. Descartes, anticipating Chomsky in the twentieth century, recognizes that true language-possession involves the ability to both understand and generate an indefinite variety of previously unencountered sentences and to be able to respond linguistically in an apposite manner across a whole range of novel situations. Thus, although you had doubtless never come across the sentences 'Perfume of embraces all him assailed. With hungered flesh obscurely, he mutely craved to adore' until you encountered them in James Joyce's *Ulysses*, you understood more or less instantly what they meant. Human linguistic response is not limited to a few set routines which might be reproduced in an unvarying way in entirely inappropriate circumstances, as when parrots which have been taught to swear utter obscenities with no comprehension of the meaning of the words they reproduce. This distinctive and unique human ability is, Descartes believed, one of those operations 'that depend on consciousness' and which 'are alone proper to us as men'.[14] Since Descartes is prepared to attribute consciousness only to the soul, it comes as no surprise that he thinks that only the presence of the soul can account for human linguistic ability.

Descartes' second test closely resembles the first, but appears to be designed to apply to non-linguistic behaviour instead. Human beings demonstrate an adaptability and creativity in their responses to new situations which is much diminished in the case of animals.

Descartes thus defies us to explain how it is that human beings can pass his two tests, whereas animals and machines cannot, unless dualism is true. Descartes would seem to be claiming that we will never be able to build a machine that can genuinely construct and understand sentences. Purely material beings, whatever their degree of sophistication and complexity, can never, in principle, be language-users and engage in genuine conversation and discourse generally. Fantasies of conversing computers and robots are just that, if Descartes is correct, and similarly, if any cognitive scientist is trying to build a machine which can engage in genuine discourse, then he is wasting his time and efforts as far as Descartes is concerned.

Before reading any further, look at Exercise 2.4.

How convincing do you find Descartes' two tests to establish dualism? Is there any reason, do you think, to suppose that human linguistic ability and range and adaptability of behavioural output and response, can only be explained by postulating the presence of a soul? Write down your reasons, and after discussion with someone else, read on.

Exercise 2.4

The essential objection to Descartes' tests was made by Baruch Spinoza (1632–77), who wrote: '[N]o-one has hitherto laid down the limits to the powers of the body, that is, no-one has as yet been taught by experience what the body can accomplish solely by the laws of nature, in so far as she is regarded as extension.'[15] What Spinoza says is entirely reasonable. Its implication is that perhaps one day we can look forward to an explanation of how language-acquisition and use are made possible, which will dispense with the need to invoke mysterious non-physical processes. In congruence with this hope, Noam Chomsky posited that each of us contains a LAD – a language acquisition device – and this presumably would consist of minute, highly complex physical structures and circuits in the brain. The challenge to describe such a system, let alone explicate its mode of operation, is one that still faces us today, however. But, in the face of this difficulty, to throw in the towel and conclude that the vehicle of our capacity to use language must somehow be incarnated in the ghostly paramechanical innards of the soul is not at all helpful. Souls, if they existed, would by their very nature lie beyond the scope of empirical investigation, and to assert that processes in the recesses of the soul alone can be invoked to explain language acquisition seems merely to mark a retreat into mystery.

2.6   The mind/body relation

The words on the VDU in front of me as I type this passage are appearing because I want them to, or, to put this another way, my desire to produce these words is helping to bring them about. This certainly looks like a causal explanation: a state of mind, my desire, acts as a cause to bring into being a physical chain of events, which includes, among other things, the physical movement of my fingers on the keys as an intermediate stage on the way to the production of the words on the screen. In this case, causality runs from mind to world. But, equally, the words on the screen are causing me to see them. Light is coming from the words, entering my eye and stimulating my retina and optic nerve, leading to a mental state consisting in my visual awareness of the words. The chain of causes and effects in this case runs from world to mind. Unless we are prepared to deny that the mind can affect the physical world, and in turn be influenced by it, some way of explaining how this is possible must be found. Since for Descartes mental states belong to the incorporeal soul, he has to find some way of explaining how the soul can bring about bodily events, and how happenings in, and to, the body, can be registered within the soul.

Descartes' solution was to conjecture that the soul operates through the pineal gland which is to be found in the limbic system in the middle of the brain. The soul supposedly gives the pineal gland a tiny push which is magnified by a chain of physical causes and effects, eventuating in a bodily movement, an action, such as my typing these words. Descartes conjectured that the nerves are like fine tubes containing what he called 'animal spirits'. These are not the non-physical ghosts of departed animals, but completely physical in nature, consisting supposedly of highly rarefied blood.

Why did Descartes choose the pineal gland as the seat of the soul? There were two principal reasons. Firstly, Descartes observed that the pineal gland is very light and mobile. This made it a suitably sensitive instrument which would be responsive to the minute pushes of the soul.

Secondly, Descartes believed that in ordinary perception we do not perceive external physical objects but images in the head to which these give rise. The two images coming from the eyes are supposedly fused together, and projected upon the surface of the pineal gland, much as if one had a miniature TV or film screen in one's brain. Seeing consists in the soul attending to the image projected upon the screen afforded by the pineal gland.

Before proceeding any further, look at Exercise 2.5.

Descartes exercises considerable ingenuity in describing a mechanism by means of which the non-extended, non-physical soul can affect the extended physical body, and be affected by it in turn. But can you see a problem with his account? Think about this on your own and then discuss it with another person.

Exercise 2.5

The difficulty that may have occurred to you is this: how can the soul, lacking all physical dimensions, possibly affect, and be affected by, the extended body? This would appear to be a difficulty in principle which no amount of neurophysiological ingenuity can circumvent.

In his Sixth Meditation, Descartes had another try at explaining psycho-physical causation. This attempt had its roots in Descartes' dissatisfaction with the pineal gland as the single point of contact through which the soul supposedly acts. Even if we grant, for the sake of argument, that interaction could occur through the pineal gland, the resultant model of how a person relates to his or her body is at odds with our experience, as Descartes realized. When we feel pain, for example, or the sensation of hunger, we feel the sensation in question in the hurt limb or in the pit of our stomach. We do not, as it were, merely perceive it detachedly and intellectually from a distance. An analogy makes this clearer. My car may be bumped and damaged as I am driving along, but I do not personally feel anything in the place where the damage occurs, although I may be able to see from my position inside the car that the wing, say, has been damaged. Similarly, if the water in the radiator runs low, it is not like the thirst I experience when I become dehydrated. I know I am dehydrated because I experience a sensation of thirst, but I only know the car is low on water when a red light on the instrument panel lights up or when I see steam rising from the bonnet of the car. If the soul interacted solely through the pineal gland, then it seems that my perception of damage to my body, or the fact that I am thirsty, would have to be like what happens when I see my car has been damaged by a bump or when I see the red warning light come on to tell me that the water level in the radiator is low. This is why Descartes, using a similar analogy to the car, says:

> I am not present in my body merely as a pilot is present in a ship; I am most tightly bound to it, and as it were mixed up with it, so that I and it form a unit. Otherwise, when the body is hurt, I, who am simply a conscious being, would not feel pain on that account, but would perceive the injury by a pure act of understanding, as the pilot perceives by sight any breakages there may be in the ship; and when the body needs food or drink, I should explicitly understand the fact, and not have confused sensations of hunger and thirst.[16]

To overcome the problem, Descartes proposed that bodily sensations like pain, hunger and thirst, which he calls confused modes of consciousness, should be explained as arising from 'the mind's being united to, and as it were, mixed up with, the body'.[17]

This alleged intermingling of the soul and the body creates what Descartes called a 'substantial union', and is essential to our human nature:

> [H]uman beings are made up of body and soul, not by the mere presence or proximity of one to another, but by a true substantial union ... If a human being is considered in itself, as a whole, it is an essential union, because the union which joins a human body and a soul to each other is not accidental to a human being but essential, since a human being without it is not a human being.[18]

What this means is that there is not the sharp division between the mind and the body which Descartes' early statement of dualism implies. Sensations seem to form a hybrid class intermediate between the pure acts of intellection of the soul, and the physical occurrences within the body. Both the physical and non-physical features of sensations are supposed somehow to be seamlessly integrated, and in this manner comprise the substantial union of mind and body of which Descartes speaks.

Now look at Exercise 2.6 before proceeding any further.

Can you see a problem with Descartes' suggestion that the substantial union between the soul and the body is constituted by the soul being, 'as it were, mixed up with, the body'? Work alone or in discussion with someone else and write down your answer before reading on.

Exercise 2.6

It should be plain that there is a serious obstacle to what Descartes is claiming. How can the soul, lacking all dimensions, be intermingled with an extended body? Contrast the intermingling of butter in a cake mix. What happens is that particles of butter become scattered throughout the mix and stick to the particles comprising it. But both the particles of butter and the mix fill a volume of space, hence there is no difficulty in understanding how they may be intermingled. Ultimately then, Descartes' attempt to explain how mind and body interact and together form a union, must be reckoned a failure.

2.6.1   Other attempts to account for the mind/body relation

Two well-known attempts to circumvent the problem of mind/body interaction were suggested by Nicholas Malebranche (1638–1715), to whom we owe the doctrine of occasionalism, and by Leibniz (1646–1716), who proposed the theory of psycho-physical parallellism.

According to the parallelist, the soul and the body are like two clocks wound up and synchronized by God so that appropriate correlations occur between mental and bodily events – for example, that injury to the body is accompanied by pain. But body does not affect mind, nor mind body: there is only the appearance and not the reality of interaction. Figure 2.1 neatly illustrates the theory. However, since God, too, is conceived of as a soul, how is he supposed to set the correlations up in the first place? It will not do to reply blandly that God is omnipotent and can do anything: the problem of how even a Divine non-extended substance could conceivably have an effect on the extended physical world remains.

Occasionalism also requires the intervention of God and is thus open to the same objection as parallelism. But it is a less elegant

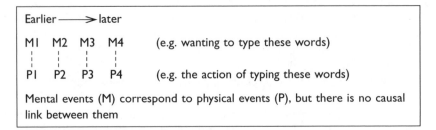

Figure 2.1   Leibniz's psycho-physical parallelism

theory, as God is represented as having to be present on each and every separate occasion to ensure that the right correspondences occur between mental and physical events. He is thus doomed to be an eternal busybody, unlike Leibniz's God, who merely winds up and synchronizes the mental and physical clocks at one go, and then retires, leaving things to take care of themselves.

2.7   Descartes' other arguments for dualism

One argument in support of dualism has already been discussed and dismissed, namely that the capacity to understand and use language is inexplicable in mechanical or scientific terms, requiring instead the ghostly paramechanical activities of the incorporeal soul. But Descartes has three other principal arguments, each of which will be examined in this section. The arguments are:

1   The argument from doubt.
2   The argument from clear and distinct perception.
3   The argument from divisibility.

The thrust of the first two arguments is something like this. I can call into question, or somehow imagine away, the existence of all my physical features. These features can thus in principle be separated from me, and cannot therefore be essential to what I am. Hence I can genuinely exist without them. But I cannot similarly call into question the fact that I am thinking and conscious, because as soon as I endeavour to do this, the very attempt will be self-nullifying, since questioning my own existence presupposes that I must exist and be conscious in order to engage in this activity.

2.7.1   The argument from doubt

The first argument, which may be labelled the argument from systematic doubt, is easily dismissed, as we shall shortly see. This argument results from Descartes' programme of trying to call everything into doubt in an attempt to discover what is certain and hence can serve as the rock-solid foundations of knowledge. At the beginning of the *Meditations*, Descartes resolves to reject not only all previous beliefs that are false, but also any that admit of the slightest doubt. But which beliefs can be called into doubt? Descartes recognizes that it would be an endless task to examine all of his beliefs one by one, and proposes instead to examine the foundations of what he has taken for knowledge. If these foundations are discovered to be wanting, then their rejection will mean the abandonment of all the beliefs depending upon them.

Descartes begins by noting that the senses have sometimes misled him regarding distant and minute objects and so he resolves never to put total trust in sense-experience again. But upon reflection he observes that surely there are many beliefs derived from the senses which it is impossible to doubt, such that he is presently seated in front of a fire wearing a dressing-gown. But has he not dreamed that he was so seated when in fact he was sound asleep in bed? Is it not possible that life could be nothing but a gigantic and systematic dream? Notice that if that were to be the case you could not even be certain that you had a body: the trunk and the limbs that you apparently see and feel might, for all you can tell, be a mere figment of the imagination. However, Descartes reflects that whether awake or asleep, some things, such as the logical truths that $2 + 3 = 5$ or that a square has four sides, obtain, so that at least these things can be known for certain. But can we not be mistaken even about these matters? Could it not be, Descartes supposes, that there is an infinitely powerful and cunning demon who causes him to be mistaken even about logical truths? Descartes does not literally believe in the existence of such a malignant spirit: the demon can be viewed as an imaginative device to lend force and persuasiveness to Descartes' sceptical doubts.

Descartes considers whether there might be a God whose existence it is impossible to doubt and who causes him to have the thoughts he is having. But, he quickly adds, it is surely possible that his thoughts, including the idea of God, are, in Hume's phrase, produced by the energy of the mind itself – in other words, it is merely Descartes himself giving rise to his thoughts and not an independently existing divine being. But if that is so, then at least it follows that he, Descartes, must be something. Now it cannot be that he is to be identified with a human body, because previously he had called into doubt the existence of an external world, including his own limbs and body. But if it is possible that, for all he can tell, he has no body and that its existence is merely an illusion, should he not be persuaded that he does not exist? However, to be persuaded that he does not exist, he must first exist in order to be so persuaded! Thus Descartes arrives tentatively at the first formulation of his famous principle *cogito ergo sum*, 'I think therefore I am'. Even if there is a malignant demon using all his power to deceive Descartes into believing there is an external world, including his own body, when there is no such thing, there is at least one thing he cannot deceive Descartes about, namely his own existence, because for Descartes to be deceived he must exist:

> Doubtless, then, I exist, since I am deceived; and let him deceive me as he may, he can never bring it about that I am nothing, so long as I shall be conscious that I am something. So that it must, in fine, be maintained, all things being maturely and carefully considered, that this proposition I am, I exist, is necessarily true each time it is expressed by me, or conceived in my mind.[19]

It is true that if Descartes is thinking, then he must exist in order so to think. But it is important to be clear exactly what can and cannot be established by reflection on this truth. For a start, it is not necessarily true that Descartes exists, since he might not have existed. Nor, even if there is such a person as Descartes, does this guarantee that he is thinking, as he might not have been. All that is true is that if Descartes is thinking, then he must exist in order to be thinking. But for anything to be in any state whatsoever, this means that the thing in question must first exist. In stating that Descartes is thinking, the existence of the subject of this statement is presupposed, so to go on to say that if Descartes is thinking then it follows that he exists amounts to a kind of repetition or tautology. But logical truths of this type do not tell us anything about the world, and, *a fortiori*, in this particular instance, anything about the nature of what is doing the thinking. As A. J. Ayer (1910–89) observed:

> If I start with the fact that I am doubting, I can validly draw the conclusion that I think and that I exist. That is to say, if there is such a person as myself, then there is such a person as myself, and if I think, I think. Neither does this apply only to me. It is obviously true of anyone at all that if he exists he exists and if he thinks he thinks. What Descartes thought he had shown was that statements that he was con-

scious, and that he existed, were somehow privileged, that, for him at least, they were evidently true in a way which distinguished them from any other statements of fact. His argument does not prove that he or anyone, knows anything. It simply makes the logical point that one sort of statement follows from another.[20]

Neither can reflections on the peculiarities of certain first-person thoughts or utterances establish anything about the nature of the person who gives vent to them. It is true that if I manage to utter, or to think, 'I exist', then clearly I must exist to have this thought, so that it would be incoherent for me then to suppose that, having succeeded in uttering or thinking 'I exist', it could turn out to be false at the time at which I express it publicly to others or privately to myself. And, conversely, if I utter or think, 'I do not exist', then plainly this statement must be false, since the very condition of its being made by me is that I am there to make it. But these features of first-person statements whereby if they succeed in getting made means they must be true at the time they are made, and which must be false if denied at the same time by the person who makes them, cannot possibly establish anything about the nature of the agents who produce them. The student who calls out 'Absent' when the register is called, or the person who replies 'Yes!' to the questions 'Are you asleep?' or 'Are you dead?' must be both be saying something false, but this obviously cannot establish that the persons in question must be non-physical substances.

Having supposedly established the truth of 'I think therefore I am' as the first principle of the philosophy he was seeking, Descartes went on to say:

> I then considered attentively what I was; and I saw that while I could feign I had no body, that there was no world, and no place existed for me to be in, I could not feign that I was not; on the contrary, from the mere fact that I thought of doubting about other truths it evidently and certainly followed that I existed ... From this I recognised that I was a substance whose whole essence or nature is to be conscious and whose being requires no place and depends on no material thing. Thus this self, that is to say the soul by which I am what I am, is entirely distinct from the body, and is even more easily known; and even if the body were not there at all, the soul would be just what it is.[21]

This argument may be formally set out as follows:

1   I can doubt that my body exists.
2   I cannot doubt that I exist.
3   Therefore I must be different and distinct from my body.

Having supposedly established the conclusion (3), Descartes then argues, firstly, that if he is different and distinct from his body, he must be non-bodily in nature, i.e. something lacking extension and consequently all physical features; and, secondly, because he cannot coherently call into doubt or deny that he is conscious, the one true property which inseparably belongs to him as an incorporeal substance is thought or consciousness.

However, can the argument establish in the first place that Descartes is an entity distinct from his body? The argument relies on a principle which later came to be known as Leibniz's Law. According to Leibniz's Law, if a thing A and a thing B are one and the same thing, then all the properties of A must be the same as all the properties of B. A consequence of this principle is that if there is at least one property or feature which A and B do *not* share, then A and B must be numerically different things. For example, if it is true that the building I am now standing in is in Oxford, and if it is also true that St Paul's Cathedral is in London, then I cannot be standing in St Paul's Cathedral.

In the argument above for the distinction between mind and body, Descartes has supposedly established that it is possible to doubt that one has a body, because the existence of one's body could be an illusion. But in trying to doubt whether one exists, one must exist in order to doubt, which means such doubt is not possible. We thus have something which is true of one's body, namely that its existence may be doubted, which is not true of 'I', oneself. Since one's body and 'I' differ in this respect, namely that the body's existence may be doubted, but the existence of 'I' may not, then, according to Leibniz's Law, it seems to follow that the person or consciousness cannot be identical with the body, but must be different and distinct from it.

Before continuing with this discussion, look at Exercise 2.7.

Exercise 2.7 Does Descartes' argument from systematic doubt succeed? Can you construct a parallel argument in which although one thing A can be doubted and another thing B cannot be doubted, nevertheless it is clear that A and B are one and the same? If such an argument can be produced, it can be used to reveal a flaw in Descartes' thinking. Work on this on your own and then discuss it with someone else, before reading on.

There are certain exceptions to Leibniz's Law. In the present instance it needs to be recognized that arguments that employ intentional mental verbs such as 'believe', 'doubt', 'know', 'imagine', 'dream' and so forth in their construction cannot succeed in establishing the non-identity of items. These mental states, it will be recalled (see chapter 1, section 1.3.5), exhibit the feature of 'about-ness', that is, they possess a representational content. Moreover, this representational content is *aspectual*, in that one and the same state of affairs can be represented under different aspects. When Oedipus married his mother, he did not recognize that she was his mother. He knew her only as the Queen of Thebes. Similarly, to adapt an example from Daniel Dennett, I might be known to all and sundry as an innocuous philosophy teacher, and not as the Mad Strangler. But nevertheless, I could still turn out to be the Mad Strangler. With these observations in mind, it is easy to formulate a parallel argument to Descartes' which plainly fails. Consider the argument:

1   Lois Lane knows that the reporter with whom she works is Clark Kent.
2   She does not know that the reporter with whom she works is Superman.
3   Therefore Clark Kent cannot be Superman.

Plainly something has gone wrong here, because an integral aspect of the Superman stories is that Superman *is* one and the same person as the superficially inept and unassuming Clark Kent. Why Leibniz's Law fails to hold is easily appreciated. Just because someone – in this case Superman/Clark Kent – is known under one description by Lois, it does not follow that she will know him under alternative descriptions. In knowing the man of steel under the aspect of Superman, it does not follow that Lois Lane will recognize this same man when he has cast off his cape and donned his owlish glasses. But the fact that she believes, mistakenly, that Clark Kent is not Superman, cannot establish that Clark Kent and Superman are not one and the same individual.

By this pattern of argument, then, Descartes cannot establish that he must be a non-bodily substance distinct from his body. Because, however, he believes he has established it, and thus managed to think away all his bodily features, leaving behind the sole attribute of think-ing or consciousness, he concludes not merely that he is a thinking thing – a conclusion that may be allowed – but that he is *only* a think-ing thing, i.e. a thing whose whole essence or nature consists in *nothing but* consciousness. Since I am now conscious as I write this, it follows that I am a conscious entity, i.e. consciousness is a feature of me. But it does not follow that *all* there is to me is consciousness, that this feature totally exhausts my nature. It might be that in order to think I have to be embodied and that certain complex physical processes need to go on inside me. Hobbes, a contemporary of

Descartes, made the essential criticism of this argument when he wrote: 'It may be that the thing that is conscious is the subject of a mind, reason, or intellect, and so it may be something corporeal; the contrary is assumed, not proved.'[22] Descartes' argument from doubt cannot show otherwise.

2.7.2 The argument from clear and distinct perception

However, in the Sixth Meditation Descartes had another argument for the distinctness of mind and body and the possibility of their separation, which is much harder to quash. The argument runs as follows:

> I know that whatever I clearly and distinctly understand can be made by God just as I understand it; so my ability to understand one thing clearly and distinctly apart from one another is enough to assure me that they are distinct, because God at least can separate them . . . Now I know that I exist, and at the same time I observe absolutely nothing else as belonging to my nature or essence except the mere fact that I am a conscious being; and from just this I can validly infer that my essence consists simply in the fact that I am a conscious being. It is indeed possible . . . that I have a body closely bound up with myself; but at the same time I have, on the one hand, a clear and distinct idea of myself taken simply as a conscious, not an extended, being; and on the other, a distinct idea of body, taken simply as an extended, not a conscious, being; so it is certain that I am really distinct from my body, and could exist without it.[23]

This argument requires some extended comment. As Anthony Kenny remarks, it was pointed out at the time by critics that,

> it does not follow from the fact that the human mind reflecting on itself does not perceive itself to be other than a thing which thinks, that its nature or essence consists only in its being a thing which thinks, in the sense that this word *only* excludes all other things which might also be supposed to pertain to the nature of the soul.[24]

This is reminiscent of Hobbes's remark quoted earlier. Kenny also points out that it is fatally easy to confuse the following two statements:

1 I do not notice anything else belongs to my nature or essence except thinking.
2 I notice that nothing else does belong to my nature or essence except thinking.

The fact that Descartes fails to perceive that anything else does belong to his nature or essence except thinking, does not mean that nothing else does so belong. Statement 2 does not follow from statement 1, but it is statement 2 that Descartes needs in order to establish that he is a thing whose whole essence consists in thinking or consciousness alone, partaking of no physical features whatsoever, and thus establishing that he can indeed exist separately and independently of his body.

It will help to state the argument formally before proceeding to a further assessment of it; it may be provisionally rendered thus:

1   I have a clear and distinct understanding of myself as a conscious, but not extended thing.
2   I have a clear and distinct understanding of my body as an extended, but not a conscious thing.
3   Therefore I can clearly and distinctly understand myself as a non-extended conscious thing apart from the extended body, and I can clearly and distinctly understand my body as an extended non-conscious thing apart from myself as a conscious thing.
4   Whatever I can clearly and distinctly understand can be brought about by God (as I understand it).
5   Therefore God can bring it about that I, as a conscious, non-extended thing, can exist apart from my extended, non-conscious body.
6   If God can bring it about that I and my body can exist apart, then I and my body really can exist apart.
7   So I really am distinct from my body and can exist apart from it. I can continue to exist as a non-physical consciousness independently of all my bodily features.
8   So my bodily features cannot be essential to my existence.
9   Therefore I must be a completely non-bodily thing which is essentially a conscious, non-extended thing, a *res cogitans*.

When you have studied this argument, look at Exercise 2.8 before reading any further.

Can you see a problem with the argument above? Assessing it is difficult, so I suggest you examine premise 3 very closely. It is ambiguous and can be interpreted to mean two things, only one of which will give Descartes what he wants, providing it is true (which it may not be).

Exercise 2.

As I have suggested in Exercise 2.8, a problem with the argument above is that the third premise is ambiguous. As M. D. Wilson suggests, Descartes could be claiming:[25]

a   I can distinctly conceive of my mind and body *separately* from each other.
b   I can distinctly conceive of my mind and body *as being separate* from each other.

Descartes does not see the difference between (a) and (b) and could be claiming either; he needs to establish the truth of (b), not (a). (a) could be true independently of (b), but (a) is too weak and will not give him the conclusion he wants, namely that the mind can exist independently of the body. To appreciate this, consider the following expansion of (a):

a1   I can form a conception of my mind, that is think about or reflect upon my mental features, without at the same time thinking about my physical features. For example, I could describe myself as emotionally fragile, stupid, slow-witted and imperceptive. These are all psychological features which make no mention of my physical characteristics. Equally, I could mention several of my physical features – short, bearded, blue-eyed, fat – without saying anything at all about my mental side. In this sense, the two conceptions can be formulated independently of each other. But this cannot show that I could exist mentally apart from my physical features.

To appreciate this, compare the extension and shape of a body. I can talk about the extension without reference to, or any explicit mention of, its shape, or talk about its shape without explicitly mentioning its extension. In that sense, the shape and the extension can be thought about, or conceived, independently of each other. But it by no means follows that the objects of these conceptions can be conceived to exist separately from each other. We soon realize this when we remember that what is extended must have some shape or other, however changeable, and that what has a shape must possess extension. The notion of a thing with a shape but lacking extension, and vice versa, is incoherent. Nevertheless, the logical impossibility of there being shape without extension or extension without shape need not prevent us from talking about extension without making any explicit mention of shape, or talking about shape without explicit mention of extension.

If Descartes is to stand any chance at all of establishing dualism by this argument, what he needs to serve as premise 3 is not merely that he can clearly and distinctly conceive mental features apart from physical features – that is, each *conception* can be held apart from, or independently of, the other – but rather that the *objects* of these conceptions, what the conceptions are about – in this case the mind and the body rather than the conceptions themselves – can be conceived to exist separately and independently of each other. In other words, instead of (a1), what Descartes needs is

b2   I can clearly and distinctly conceive of my mind as existing independently of, and separate from, my body.

This claim was attacked by one of Descartes's contemporaries, the philosopher Antoine Arnauld (1612–94). The essence of Arnauld's objection was that Descartes might believe that he can clearly and distinctly conceive of himself as a pure subject of consciousness capable of existing apart from the physical body, but actually he cannot form this conception. Suppose Descartes had argued instead that he could clearly and distinctly conceive that a Euclidean triangle had the property of being right-angled, without thereby clearly and distinctly conceiving that it obeyed Pythagoras's theorem, and that therefore it was possible for there to be right-angled triangles to which Pythagoras's theorem did not apply. This conclusion is unacceptable, since we know, and can easily show, that the property of being a right-angled triangle and the property of satisfying Pythagoras's theorem are logically connected. In a case like this, Descartes would be forced to conclude that he could not clearly and distinctly conceive what he originally thought he could. What appears to be conceivable at first glance turns out after further examination not to be conceivable at all, and hence not possible.

Descartes was not moved by Arnauld's objection. In his reply, he introduced, and made use of, the distinction between *complete* and *incomplete* beings. Descartes asks us to consider a moving body with a certain figure or shape. The distinction between motion and figure is a formal one, and it is possible to form a conception of motion without thinking of figure, and vice versa. Similarly, it is possible to form a conception of a triangle without thinking of it as obeying Pythagoras's theorem. By contrast, it is not possible to form a complete conception of motion apart from a thing that is moving, and, likewise, there cannot be a complete conception of a triangle to which Pythagoras's theorem does not apply. Hence, motion cannot exist apart from a moving thing, and a right-angled triangle that does not exemplify Pythagoras's theorem cannot exist.

However, in the case of body and mind none of this applies, Descartes maintains, because it is possible to form conceptions of body and soul as complete beings, or, at least, conceptions of body and soul which, if not *totally* complete, are at least *sufficiently* complete, to guarantee that it is possible for the one to exist apart from the other.

Descartes writes:

> But I completely understand what a body is merely by thinking of it as extended, figured, mobile, etc., and denying of it all those things which pertain to the mind; and vice versa I understand the mind to be a complete thing, that doubts, understands, wills and so forth, although I deny that any of those things contained in the idea of a body are in it.[26]

In other words, what Descartes is asserting is that I can form a distinct and sufficiently clear and complete concept of myself as a thinking thing without extension, and, equally, I can form a distinct and sufficiently clear and complete concept of my body as an extended thing without thought. The objects of these two conceptions – that is, what the conceptions are about or concern as opposed to the conceptions themselves – really do seem to be distinct and sufficiently complete in themselves. In conceiving of physical processes, I am thinking of events that are spatially located and occupy an area or volume of space. In the case of brain activity, brain scans can show blood-flows and neurological activity taking place in specific areas in the brain. The shape and volume of the area of the brain involved in neural activity can be measured, as can the frequency of nerve impulses down the nerves. This characterization of what goes on in the brain appears to be sufficiently complete for the state of affairs to exist just as it is described, with no further additions to it. On the other hand, we seem to be able to reach a sufficiently clear conception of the nature of mental features existing in their own right in complete independence of physical features.

But if my mind and body can be conceived of as complete things in themselves, that is, as including or borrowing no features from each other, then it is possible that these states of affairs can exist apart from each other; and since God can bring it about that what I clearly and distinctly conceive is possible, my mind and body really can exist apart from each other.

Thus Descartes writes:

Mind can be perceived clearly and distinctly, or sufficiently, so for it to be considered a complete thing, without any of those forms or attributes by which we recognize that body is a substance . . . a body is understood distinctly as a complete thing without those [features] which pertain to mind.[27]

It may be objected that this does not take account of the criticism that in noticing that all that seems necessary for one to exist is one's conscious experiences and awareness in general, this does not take account of what one fails to notice, and it could be that these overlooked features are physical and are just as essential to one's existence. But Descartes has his reply ready:

Surely where I have proved that God exists . . . who can do all that I clearly and distinctly know to be possible. For although much exists in me which I do not yet notice [at the particular stage of the Meditations he had reached] . . . yet since that which I do notice is enough for me to subsist with this alone [in other words, his conception of himself as conscious being], I am certain that I could have been created by God without other [attributes] which I do not notice.[28]

It will not do to reply to Descartes' argument from clear and distinct perception that the most it can show is that it is *possible* for mind and body to exist separately, and that it doesn't show that mind and body *actually* do exist independently of each other. This is because all Descartes needs in order to disprove materialism is the bare possibility of mind and body coming apart in the way he envisages. If it is genuinely conceivable that mental states should exist independently of physical ones, then physicality cannot be of the very essence of mental states, the *sine qua non* of their existence, and all attempts to reduce mind to matter must ultimately fail.

However, if Descartes' conclusion that the mind can exist separately from the body is to be resisted, then it seems that we must have recourse once again to an observation made earlier, namely that contrary to what he imagines, Descartes cannot genuinely form a distinct and sufficiently clear conception of himself as a purely thinking thing capable of existing separately from a physical body. He can apparently reach a clear and distinct conception of himself as a non-physical subject of consciousness, but only because he is ignorant of his true nature.

In claiming that we are nothing but non-physical minds, Descartes assumes that the way our conscious experience is presented to us sufficiently captures its nature to guarantee that we really can exist independently of all physical features. But is this really so? Once upon a time, the nature of sound was not transparent to us. No one knew that sound consisted of waves and that these required a medium in which they could be propagated. Only after experiments were done, such as evacuating the air inside a container in which a bell was ringing and observing that the sound gradually died away and ceased to exist when a vacuum was achieved, was it realized that it is of the very nature of sound to consist in waves in a medium such as air. Likewise, although at present we haven't the faintest idea of how consciousness might be identical with or depend on brain processes for its existence, it cannot be ruled out in advance that it is of the very nature of consciousness to have physical processes at its heart. Conscious entities, wherever they exist in the universe, might necessarily be physical arrangements of some sort or another, although at present we totally lack any plausible set of concepts or theories that might be employed to render transparent the identity of the mental with the physical, or, alternatively, its dependency upon the physical.

In his book on Descartes, John Cottingham makes a similar response:

> [I]t seems plausible to argue that although the concept of thought is quite distinct from the concept of brain-activity, thought is nonetheless a functional process, which cannot operate without some sort of hardware (either a brain or something analogous). Software engineers, to be sure, design their programs in purely abstract terms, without any reference to the physical world; but they know that for their programs actually to operate, they must be physically embodied (e.g. on a hard disk). For there to be an operating software program in the absence of a physical substrate is, ultimately, an incoherent notion: it is not just that it does not occur in our universe but that there is no possible world in which it is found (anymore than there is a possible world in which there are functioning digestive processes in the absence of some kind of physical organs capable of doing the job). If this is right, then however plausible it might appear at first sight to suppose it is logically possible for there to be minds existing apart from bodies, the notion turns out ultimately to be incoherent, and Descartes' argument thus fails.[29]

Cottingham's argument, however, assumes the truth of functionalism, the view that the mind is like a program run on the hardware of the brain, and, as we shall see in chapter 5, functionalism is deeply flawed as a theory of the mind. More appositely, functionalism cannot by itself establish the truth of materialism, since functions, as functionalists readily allowed, should be thought of as neither ghostly and mental, nor as physical processes, but as abstractions which are neutral between the two. Functions, it was allowed, might be instantiated in the ethereal hardware of immaterial substances and not only in material sets of arrangements. There may thus be possible worlds in which, even if functionalism turned out to give a true but incomplete picture of mentality, minds turn out to be immaterial after all. But, to return to the point made earlier, if it is possible that minds can sometimes exist independently of physical arrangements, a thoroughgoing reductionist materialism is going to be false.

2.7.3   The argument from divisibility

This argument may be briefly and formally laid out as follows:

1   The body is divisible into parts.
2   The mind is not divisible into parts.
3   Therefore the mind must be of entirely different nature from the body, i.e. it must be essentially non-physical.

   When Descartes considers his own mental states – for example, when he is in pain, or feeling angry or thinking about what he will have for dinner – he says that he can distinguish no parts within himself. But that should come as no surprise. Considered as the *states* of a subject, experiences cannot be split into halves or quarters, because it makes no sense to speak of states, whether mental or physical, as being composed of parts. Consider a non-mental example, a chemical compound, say nitro-glycerine, which is in a stable state. What this means is that its condition is such that it is not liable to explode without warning. Now the nitro-glycerine itself can be divided – various portions of it could be poured into different containers – but what could it possibly mean to describe its state of stability as being divisible? States are not divisible, but not for the reason that they are peculiar, simple, indivisible things, but rather because they are not things, not logical substances, at all. (We must guard here against the error I warned of earlier, the mistake of interpreting all nouns as if they acquired their meanings by naming substances. See section 2.1.) The same is true of capacities. Nitro-glycerine has the capacity to explode, but what sense could it make to speak of sharing out portions of this capacity, as opposed to the nitro-glycerine itself? Similarly, if, for example, a person possesses strength, or the ability to run very fast, we cannot speak of cutting their running ability or their capacity to lift heavy objects in half, as we might speak of dividing a piece of paper in two by using scissors or a paper-knife. Of course, a person's ability to lift heavy objects or to cover distance at speed may decline or even disappear, but this does not mean that it has ceased to exist because it has literally fallen into fragments as a nut shatters when we strike it a blow with a hammer.

We should not say, 'Bodies are divisible, minds are not', because, to borrow an expression of the philosopher Ludwig Wittgenstein, that makes the difference between minds and bodies look too slight. Wittgenstein invites us to compare the statement 'Three people cannot sit side by side on this bench; they have no room' with the statement '3 × 18 inches won't go into 3 feet'. These statements look very similar, but in reality they are very different. The first states a physical impossibility, the second a logical impossibility, something that is excluded by the concepts of 3 × 18 inches and 3 feet.

The statement 'Minds are not divisible' is like the second statement, not the first, and marks a conceptual impossibility, something that it makes no sense to say about minds, just as it is not meaningful to ask if the number 3 has parents. That the number 3 has no parents does not make it an orphan!

To reiterate: minds are not divisible, but not because they are some miraculous kind of hard, unsplittable, spiritual atom, but rather because the correlative concepts of divisibility and indivisibility have no application to mental states and capacities, owing to the fact that these are not logical substances, things capable of existing in their own right.

2.8 Problems for dualism

2.8.1 Possession of a mind is all or nothing

For the Cartesian, only human beings have minds in the form of incorporeal souls. Rationality and consciousness reside in the soul, hence animals should be regarded as non-conscious automata. But this makes the contrast between us and the rest of living creatures too stark. Given the facts of evolutionary biology, including, importantly, the growth in the size and complexity of the nervous system as we ascend the evolutionary scale, it is surely more plausible to regard possession of a mind as a spectrum reaching from creatures such as ants and slugs, which may have only the most rudimentary of mental lives, to the full panoply of mental states possessed by ourselves. Mindedness is a matter of degree, and not an all-or-nothing matter, as the dualist insists.

2.8.2   The brain is deprived of a function

If the existence of minds is ultimately nothing to do with what takes place in the brain and nervous system generally, why do we have such an immensely complicated organ, the most complex thing of which we know? Why do people suffer mental impairments if the brain is damaged, or experience altered conscious states when they take drugs, if the brain is not responsible for our mental lives? A dedicated dualist can resist this conclusion by insisting that the brain is merely like a transmitting station which relays the messages from the soul. Malfunctions of the mind or soul are only apparent; what is really happening is that the body is letting the mind down, either by not executing its commands or by carrying them out imperfectly. On this view, a person's inability to understand and produce speech when the speech centre of his brain has been severely damaged is merely the result of the brain no longer being able to translate the instructions from the soul. Purely within the soul itself, the ability to understand and generate language is left intact and undisturbed. This is precisely the line Descartes takes in a reply to one of his critics, Pierre Gassendi:

> [F]or from the fact that it [the soul] does not act as perfectly in the body of an infant as in that of an adult, and its actions can often be impeded by wine and other bodily things, it only follows that as long as the mind is joined to the body, it uses the body as an instrument in those operations in which it is usually occupied, not that it is rendered more perfect or less perfect by the body. . . . I have . . . often distinctly showed that the mind can operate independently of the brain; for certainly the brain can be of no use to pure understanding, but only to imagination and sensing.[30]

How plausible this response is, I leave readers to decide for themselves.

2.8.3   The homunculus fallacy

The term 'homunculus', which means 'little man' or 'manikin', is drawn from the early biologists who thought that each human sperm had a miniaturized human being inside it which enters the egg at conception and then gradually develops into a human foetus. The features essential to making up a human being had to be present and fully in place from the very start, according to the early biologists, because they had no conception of how a complicated living organism could gradually be formed out of what were originally non-living materials. But if a homunculus is postulated to explain how a fully fledged human being comes about, then the theory that makes use of such a device is vacuous or circular, because its explanatory base contains the very phenomenon for which it is supposed to be accounting.

The homunculus fallacy is evident in Descartes' attempt to explain perception by maintaining that the soul turns towards the pineal gland and inspects the images projected onto its surface as a result of impulses relayed from the outer sense organs. This model immediately invites the question of how the soul itself is supposed to perceive. Does it, too, have a ghostly counterpart mechanism to the material pineal gland inside it, by means of which it perceives? It will be obvious that embarking on this line of thought leads to a vicious infinite regress of perceiving agents within perceiving agents, like a series of nested Russian dolls, except that there can be no final doll at the core. In general, any psychological theory which attributes to the soul, or the brain, the very psychological features or abilities for which it is supposed to be accounting commits the homunculus fallacy.

2.8.4 The problem of counting souls

The most penetrating attack on Cartesianism, in my view, derives from the German philosopher Immanuel Kant (1724–1804). Descartes claims that one, and only one, soul is associated with, and acts through, a given human body. But, Kant asks, what is the Cartesian to say to the suggestion that, for all he can tell, a thousand such souls, or a million, all thinking the same thought, speak through an individual human being's mouth? Furthermore, over time why shouldn't a whole succession of soul substances be associated with a human being, each soul substance transmitting its states to the next member of the series in the same way that each member of a series of elastic balls, each ball being struck by and striking another ball in turn, transmits its momentum to the next ball in line, and so on throughout the series?

The point Kant is making fundamentally is this: How do you count souls? By what criterion or criteria is it decided at a given moment how many souls are present? How are we to tell when one soul finishes, so to speak, and we are getting on to the next one? In other words, how is one soul individuated, that is, told apart as a distinct and separate individual, from another soul at a given instant? In addition, how are souls to be told apart over time? How is the situation in which one and the same soul is encountered again after a lapse of time to be distinguished from the situation in which a qualitatively similar, but numerically different soul is encountered?

Kant's point is that if experience provides no grounds for distinguishing between the case in which the concept 'one and the same soul' is applicable, and the situation in which the concept 'qualitatively similar, but numerically different soul' may be applied, then we really have no concept of what we mean by one soul, and hence no concept of a collection of such individuals. But then we have no concept at all of the soul as an individual substance, and the notion of incorporeal substance has to be rejected as devoid of significance.

Contrast the case of billiard balls of a given colour. One billiard ball looks pretty much like another, and in practice it may be very difficult to tell them apart. But clearly, however closely resembling two or more such balls are, there must always remain one fundamental way in which they can be distinguished from each other, namely that no ball can occupy the space occupied by another ball at one and the same time. And, by extension of this principle, no ball can occupy the same successive spaces occupied by another ball at the same successive times. The spatial route traced by a ball throughout a given period of time must be unique to that ball. What applies to billiard balls applies equally to human beings thought of as embodied creatures of flesh and blood. However much Rosie resembles her identical twin Alice, she cannot occupy the same spot as Alice at the same time, nor the same places as Alice at the same moments over a period of time. Let us look at Exercise 2.9 before pursuing the matter any further.

Can you see a problem in trying to account for the identity of souls in the way in which we account for the identity of billiard balls and flesh and blood people? After working on this alone, discuss it with another person before reading on.

Exercise 2.9

The difficulty we come up with in this exercise should be very obvious. It is that incorporeal substances don't, by their very nature, occupy a unique area of space at a given time, and so this ground of identity cannot apply. But if this is so, we have no way of distinguishing one soul from the next, and this amounts to having to admit we have no clear and coherent concept of the soul. Kant points out that the mere fact of one's own self-consciousness will not help. In

the *Critique of Pure Reason* he writes: 'The identity of the consciousness of myself at different times is . . . only a formal condition
of my thoughts and their coherence, and in no way proves the
numerical identity of myself as a subject.'[31]

The point that Kant is making is this: it is necessarily true that, with
regard to any thought or mental state which is mine, it is indeed one
and the self same 'I' who has these experiences. (Kant once put this
by saying that with regard to those experiences that are mine, it must
be possible for the 'I think' to accompany those experiences.) But
although it is necessarily true that it is one and the same 'I' who is
conscious of all my thoughts and experiences as a condition of those
thoughts and experiences being *my* thoughts and experiences, this in
no way proves that what I ultimately am is a simple, non-composite,
incorporeal logical substance, a Cartesian soul.

To be able to demonstrate that, I would have to be able to specify
what features of my experience would license me applying and using
the concept of the soul. But to do that, experience would have to offer
me an object, discernible by the senses, which persists through time.
I must, in theory at least, be able to tell this object apart from other
similar objects at any given instant, and I must be able to re-identify
it over time. But, as I have tried to make clear above, this cannot be
done in the case of souls, even in the case of myself, since an incorporeal thing is an object of which I can, by definition, have no experience, because what lacks all physical features – and, in particular,
extension in space – cannot in principle be detected by the senses.
But, as both Kant and his predecessor Hume concur, concepts that
have no application within the realm of experience are empty of
content. Hence the concept of a person as a non-bodily incorporeal
soul would seem ultimately to be meaningless. By contrast, if we think
of people as the familiar flesh-and-blood entities we meet in the
street, then we can have a genuine and meaningful concept of a
person. This is because, thought of as embodied beings, we can always
ultimately distinguish one person from another at a given instant or
over a period of time, since they cannot occupy the same space at the
same time, or the same spaces at successive times. By this criterion, I
can tell Alice apart from Rosie, even though they are identical twins,
and, equally, both Alice and Rosie can tell me apart from other
people whom they meet.

This way of conceiving of persons finds its expressions in Kant's
words:

I may further assume that the substance which in relation to our outer
sense possesses extension is in itself the possessor of thoughts, and that

these thoughts can by means of its own inner sense be consciously represented. In this way, what in one relation is entitled incorporeal would in another relation be at the same time a thinking being, whose thoughts we cannot intuit, though we can indeed intuit their signs in the field of appearance.[32]

By this last phrase, Kant means that you cannot observe other people's thoughts directly, but you can see the signs of what people are thinking in the ways they behave, and in particular their facial expressions. He continues:

Accordingly, the thesis that souls (as particular kinds of substances) think, would have to be given up; and we should have to fall back upon the common expression that men think, that is, that the very same being which, as outer appearance is extended, is (in itself) internally a subject, and is not composite, but is simple and thinks.[33]

1 If mind and body affect each other, does this mean that mental states must really be physical states and that dualism is false?

2 What does 'I' refer to in the sentence 'I am feeling angry'?

3 Descartes concludes that if he is thinking, then he must exist as an incorporeal subject whose whole essence consists in thinking. But was he entitled merely to conclude that there are thoughts occurring?

4 Is it genuinely possible to conceive of mental states existing independently of physical states of affairs? What problems are posed by the notion of disembodied existence?

5 How is it that we are able to feel sensations in our limbs and bodies and not merely perceive them at a distance, like a pilot in a ship?

6 Must there be criteria for telling souls apart from each other, if the notion of the soul is to make sense?

Questions to think about

Suggestions for further reading

- Plato, *Phaedo, Meno,* the *Republic.* There are various editions of these dialogues available. They contain the main arguments for dualism, especially *Phaedo.* A good exposition and critique of these arguments can be found in A. G. N. Flew's *An Introduction to Western Philosophy* (London: Thames and Hudson, 1971).
- René Descartes, *Discourse on the Method, Meditations, Principles of Philosophy.* There are various editions of these works available.
- A famous attack on Cartesian dualism can also be found in Gilbert Ryle's *The Concept of Mind* (Harmondsworth: Penguin, 1973 [1949]), which has become a standard work to consult on this topic.

- John Cottingham's *Descartes* (Oxford: Blackwell, 1986) provides a clear and accessible introduction to Cartesian dualism as well as the main elements of his philosophy. See also Cottingham's *A Descartes Dictionary* (Oxford: Blackwell, 1993), for easy access to a wealth of fascinating details concerning Descartes' philosophy.
- Anthony Kenny, *Descartes* (New York: Random House, 1968) is another useful book which contains penetrating criticisms of Descartes' attempts to establish dualism, as well as a discussion of other aspects of his philosophy. See also Margaret Wilson's excellent study, *Descartes* (London: Routledge, 1978).
- Greg McCulloch's *The Mind and Its World* (London and New York: Routledge, 1995) provides a stimulating introduction to Cartesianism and the problems it raises.
- The clearest and most closely argued case for dualism amongst contemporary philosophers is probably to be found in John Foster's excellent *The Immaterial Self* (London and New York: Routledge, 1991), but the reader new to philosophy will find this very hard going.
- Much briefer and more straightforward is Richard Swinburne's *Is there a God?* (Oxford: OUP, 1996), chapter 5. See also his book *The Evolution of the Soul* (Oxford: OUP, 1986).
- A useful collection of extracts from the writings of the major philosophers beginning with the Greeks until the twentieth century on the mind/body problem is provided by A. Flew (ed.), *Body, Mind and Death* (Macmillan: Collier Books, 1964).
- *The Philosophy of Mind* by P. Smith and O. R. Jones (Cambridge: Cambridge University Press, 1986), as well as being a clear and accessible book on the philosophy of mind generally, contains a helpful section on dualism and its problems.

3

THE MIND/BRAIN IDENTITY THEORY

Objectives

> As a result of reading this chapter you should be able to:
>
> * provide a basic outline of the mind/brain identity theory;
> * explain the difference between an ontological and an analytical reduction of the mental to the physical;
> * explain the differences between type-type and token-token versions of the identity theory;
> * outline the evidence that can support an identity theory and understand the strengths of the theory;
> * explain and assess a number of objections to the identity theory.

3.1 A brief historical background

As we saw in the last chapter, dualism affirms that mental events can never be identical with physical events. Mental events are completely non-physical in all their aspects and consist in changes in the non-physical states of an immaterial entity, the soul.

The mind/brain identity theory denies what dualism affirms. The mind is not an entity separate and distinct from the brain. Put directly and simply, the mind is identical with the living brain and mental events just are brain events. There are no ghostly immaterial substances or events to constitute our minds. Everything, including your own consciousness and thoughts, is purely material or physical. The theory thus exemplifies materialism.

The mind/brain identity theory came to prominence in the early 1950s and 1960s and was advocated by philosophers such as U.T. Place, J.J.C. Smart and D. Armstrong, but materialism has had a very long history. The ancient Greek philosopher Epicurus (342–270 BC) graphically expressed the concept of materialism when he claimed: 'By convention colour exists, by convention bitter, by convention sweet, but in reality atoms and void.' All that ultimately exists are material atoms whirling in space. These come together, temporarily, to compose material things like the earth and its furniture, and physical organisms, including human and non-human animals. But in the vastness of eternity, everything is evanescent, fleeting, and all will go back to the void to re-form over slow aeons into new configurations of physical particles which again will eventually dissolve. For the dualist, life after death is a genuine possibility because as a logical substance the soul can exist in its own right independently of the body. But for the Epicurean materialist, the mind is fully a part of the material world, and ends when the rest of the body does. There is, however, no need then to fear death, because as a follower of Epicurus, the Roman thinker Lucretius (c.98–c.55 BC) piquantly put it, 'When we are there, death is not; and when death is there, we are not.'

Moving forward, in the last four hundred years a number of thinkers have reacted against Cartesian dualism and embraced materialism of different complexions. Thomas Hobbes (1588–1679) maintained that the notion of an incorporeal substance is a contradiction in terms, and also insisted that 'concepts and apparitions are nothing really but motions in some internal substance in the head'. John Locke (1632–1704) made the concession, daring and dangerous at the time, that God, if he so pleased, could superadd thought to the motions of matter. The atheist, Baron d'Holbach, in *The System of Nature* wrote of the mistake man made when:

> he conjectured he was not only a distinct being but that he was set apart, with different energies, from all the other beings in nature; that he was of a more simple essence, [i.e. the Cartesian soul] having nothing in common with any thing by which he was surrounded; nothing that connected him with all that he beheld.

Yet another materialist was Julien Offray de La Mettrie (1709–51), as the titles of his two books *Man a Machine* (*L'Homme machine*) and *Man a Plant* (*L'Homme plante*) boldly proclaim. La Mettrie argued that man is an evolutionary product of nature just like other animals – there is no sharp cut-off point between us and non-human animals, contrary to what Descartes averred. Human beings are essentially machines controlled by the neurology of the brain: 'Thought is so far from being incompatible with organised matter that it seems to me to be just another of its properties, such as electricity, the motive faculty, impenetrability, extension, etc.'

Like some of the forms of materialism outlined above, the mind/brain identity theory takes an uncompromising attitude towards belief in minds conceived of as non-physical in nature. Mental phenomena do not enjoy an existence over and above physical phenomena: they *are* physical phenomena. The identity theory exemplifies monism, *material* monism to be precise, because it says that only material substances and their states exist. It may also be said to exemplify physicalism.

Physicalism claims that human beings are fully material entities whose workings and properties may be completely explicated by the concepts and theories drawn from an ideally complete physics. There is no room for immaterial or supernatural interventions in the physical causal chains which run through a person's central nervous system, reaching from inputs in the form of physical stimuli through to behavioural outputs. Human beings are fully part of the natural physical world, not supernatural ghosts inexplicably linked to bodily machines. Whatever the mind is, it cannot be immaterial, and some account that locates it entirely within the natural world must be possible.

3.2 What the identity theory does and does not claim

It is important to be clear exactly what the identity theorists were and were not claiming when they said that mental states are brain states. To begin with, they were not saying that talk about mental states had the same meaning as talk about brain states. Suppose, to borrow a well-worn example from the literature, pains are theorized to be identical with C-fibres firing in the nervous system. Well, the identity theorists never wanted to claim that the sentence 'I am in pain' was synonymous with 'My C-fibres are firing'. To say 'I am in pain but my C-fibres are not firing' may be false, but it is not a contradiction in terms as it would be if both halves of the sentence were equivalent in meaning. The claim 'Pains are identical with C-fibres firing' is *not* like 'All trilaterals are identical with three-sided figures'. This is because 'trilateral' has the same meaning as 'three-sided figure', so that to describe something as a trilateral but to deny it is three-sided would be formally to contradict oneself. 'Trilaterals are three-sided figures' is analytically true, i.e. necessarily true by virtue of the meanings of the terms it contains, and can never be false. Hence all talk about trilaterals can be rendered without any loss of meaning into talk about three-sided figures. This is what philosophers call an analytical reduction.

3.3   Avoiding initial objections to the identity theory

In order to head off right from the start some prima facie objections to their claim, the identity theorists were very careful to point out that the identity they were asserting was not an analytic one.

One objection might run as follows: 'The meaning of talk about my mental states is completely different from talk about my brain states, so my mental states cannot possibly be identical with my brain states.' But, replies the identity theorist, from the fact that the meaning of talk about mental states is not the same as the meaning of talk about brain states, you cannot deduce that mental states cannot be brain states. Consider a parallel example: the meaning of the expression 'the Morning Star' is not the same as the meaning of the expression 'the Evening Star'. Quite obviously, the first expression means the star that appears in the morning, and the second means the star that appears in the evening. But this cannot mean the Morning Star is not identical with the Evening Star. In fact, the planet named by each of these expressions is one and the same throughout, namely the planet Venus. The non-synonymy of expressions flanking an identity sign does not automatically rule out the truth of the identity claim. 'The reporter who works with Lois Lane at the Daily Planet' does not mean the same as 'The man of steel'. Nevertheless, the reporter and the man of steel are identical, one and the same person, namely good old Clark Kent.

A related argument runs: 'I've been able to talk about my mental states for years without knowing anything about brain states, or even whether I have a brain or not. Therefore my mental states cannot be identical with my brain states.' The weakness of this argument is quickly exposed. I can talk about water without knowing anything about its inner constitution, but that cannot show it is not identical with collections of H_2O molecules. A nation of slugabeds, to borrow

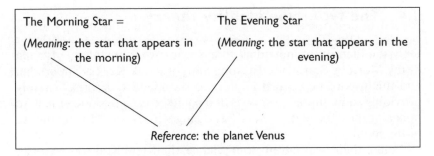

Figure 3.1   Meaning and reference

an example from J. J. C. Smart,[1] might know all about the Evening Star and absolutely nothing about the Morning Star, since they were sound asleep in bed when it was in the dawn sky, but this could not possibly show that the Evening Star was not one and the same entity as the Morning Star.

This all becomes clearer when the meaning of an expression is distinguished from its reference, what it happens to name or refer to. In the case of Venus, this distinction can be neatly illustrated with a diagram, as shown in figure 3.1. Clearly, it would be possible to talk about the Morning Star and enumerate any number of facts about it, and also to talk about the Evening Star and mention a number of facts about it, whilst failing to recognize that both realms of discourse had a common referent, and that we are in fact talking about one and the same object. This is what applies in the case of the mind and the brain, according to the identity theorist. In talking about physical brain events on the one hand and mental events on the other, we are actually talking, unbeknownst to ourselves, about one and the same set of events, describable in two different vocabularies. It thus appears that we know different sets of facts about two different streams of events, whereas the truth is that the facts relate to a single reality describable in both mental and physical terms. The basic error that underpins this argument against the identity theory is the attempt to discover the truth about reality on the basis of what one does or does not know. But this is a very poor basis indeed on which to reach substantive conclusions about the nature of the mind. If mental states were identical with brain states, the mere fact that one did not recognize that whenever mental states were referred to one was in fact also referring to brain states, could not possibly show that mind/brain identity did not obtain.

3.4   The type-type identity theory

Only the identity of individual things is involved in statements such as the Morning Star is the Evening Star, or Clark Kent is Superman, and this was of no special interest to the identity theorists, merely providing some simple examples that could be used to sketch the bare bones of the theory they were advancing with respect to the nature of the mind.

Taking their inspiration from science, their real goal was to make a case for the identity of classes of phenomena – namely, the identity of mental phenomena in general – with certain sorts of physical process in the brain. Scientists had achieved some spectacular successes in identifying one class of physical phenomena with another class, and the hope was that the same could be achieved regarding the identification of mental with physical phenomena.

To appreciate the significance of these advances it has to be remembered that before the advent of modern science the nature of diverse phenomena such as lightning, genes and water was not understood. At one time, for example, it was thought that lightning was thunderbolts hurled by the gods. Now we know that lightning is a pattern of electrical discharges. The first known Western philosopher, the ancient Greek Thales ($c.600$ BC), believed that water was a basic element out of which everything else is made. But scientific advances have shown that water is not an element, but a compound composed of hydrogen and oxygen. Genes were hypothesized to be whatever is responsible for the transmission of genetic features, but until Crick and Watson did their ground-breaking work in the twentieth century, no one knew that genes consist of encoded sequences of DNA molecules. Summarizing, we can see that these examples are illustrative of scientific identities, which may be expressed as shown in figure 3.2. The terms on the right-hand side of the equation are to be thought of as revealing the inner, hidden nature of the items on the left. Moreover, these identities obtain universally: they do not apply merely to individual, isolated instances, but to types. The type of stuff, water, is identical with the type of stuff, H_2O. The lightning flash I am now experiencing will not be the only lightning flash that is a pattern of electrical discharges. All lightning flashes, everywhere, at all times, will also be patterns of electrical discharges. The type of phenomenon known as a lightning flash is identical with the type of event consisting in a pattern of electrical discharges.

Like the scientific identities listed above, the type-type identity theory claims that each type of mental state will be identical with a

Water = H_2O
Lightning = a pattern of electrical discharges
Genes = encoded sequences on DNA molecules

Figure 3.2   Scientific identities

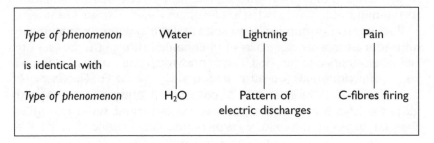

Type of phenomenon	Water	Lightning	Pain
is identical with			
Type of phenomenon	H_2O	Pattern of electric discharges	C-fibres firing

Figure 3.3   Type-type identity

given type of brain state. So, for example, every time anyone, anywhere, has a pain, their brain will be in a particular type of physical state, just as whenever and wherever someone encounters the type of stuff water, they will also be encountering the type of stuff H_2O. Which type of brain state will turn out to be identical with being in pain cannot be specified in advance, but will need to be discovered empirically by observing the brain states of people who are in pain. If a one-to-one correlation between being in pain and the existence of a given type of brain state is found in all observed cases, the advocate of mind/brain identity will argue that the best explanation of the correlation is the identity of the correlated items. A diagrammatic representation of type-type identity can be seen in figure 3.3.

3.5   The type-type identity theory and reductionism

As we have witnessed, the type-type theory rejects the analytical reduction of the mental to the physical. But it argues that it is reasonable to believe that events that fall under a given type of mental description must always also fall under the same type of physical description. Another way of putting this is to say that the meanings of mental and physical terms are different, but that their extensions – the states that fall under mental and physical concepts – exactly coincide. Put more precisely, the theory states that if a mental state M is identical with a brain state B, M can obtain only if B obtains, and B can obtain only if M obtains. Or, to put it more briefly, M obtains if, and only if, B obtains. This is exactly what we should expect if M is identical with B. To give an uncontroversial example, water is to be found in a given place if, and only if, H_2O is to be found in the same place. This is what philosophers mean by an ontological reduction – one group of phenomena that are apparently numerically different from another group of phenomena turn out to be just *one* set of existents and not two. The expression 'if, and only if' is known as a bi-conditional (because it contains two 'if's). The hope of the type-type theorist is that bi-conditional bridge laws – psychophysical laws – connecting given types of mental state with given types of physical state, will be forthcoming. An example of such a law, using the identification of pains with C-fibres firing, would then read: pain will exist if, and only if, C-fibres are firing in a human central nervous system. In other words, the firing of C-fibres is logically necessary and sufficient for M to occur.

What this is beginning to lead up to is the claim that not only are mental events identical with physical events, but that the mental properties by virtue of which mental events are mental will turn out to be identical with the physical properties by virtue of which physical events are physical. Mental concepts will remain non-synonymous with physical concepts, but the apparently different classes of property, mental and physical, which fall under each type of concept respectively, will turn out to be but a single class of property describable by means of two different vocabularies.

To make this clearer, compare the situation with regard to the properties of a gas. Talk about the temperature of a gas is not synonymous with talk about the average kinetic energy of its molecules. To deny that the temperature of a gas is identical with the average kinetic energy of its molecules may be false, but it is not self-contradictory. Nevertheless, the temperature of the gas is nothing over and above the average kinetic energy of its molecules. There are not two separate and independent sets of facts here – temperature facts and average kinetic energy of molecule facts – but one state of affairs describable in two different ways. In effect, what has happened in the case of the gas is a more or less smooth reduction of the macro-phenomenon of temperature to the micro-phenomena comprised by the behaviour of molecules. For such a reduction to be possible, there has to be, as a bare minimum, an exceptionless set of correlations between specific values for gas temperatures and specific values for average molecular kinetic energy. Unless there is a systematic relationship between these two sets of variables, such that we have good reason to believe that a given value of a variable can obtain if, and only if, a given value holds for the other variable, the prospect of a reduction of one phenomenon to the other is ruled out, because the absence of an invariant correlation opens the possibility that one phenomenon may vary independently of the other. The aim of reduction is to demonstrate that the true nature of the reduced phenomenon is provided by the base to which it is reduced. The true nature of the temperature of a gas is supposed to consist in facts about the average kinetic energy of its molecules, but this could not be the case if temperature varied independently of the gas's molecular kinetic energy.

The type-type identity theorist argues that mental properties will be reducible in a similar way, providing that an exceptionless set of correlations between a given type of mental state and a given type of brain state is forthcoming. It will then be reasonable to conclude that the painfulness of a pain, for example, is identical with the behaviour of certain sorts of neurons in the central nervous system, even though talk about pains is not equivalent in meaning to talk about the behaviour of neurons.

The kind of observation that gives hope to the type-type theory is instanced by the findings of PET scans – positron emission tomography – and MRI – functional magnetic resonance imaging. What investigation has revealed is that the exercise of certain mental capacities does involve distinctive regions of the brain, which 'light up' when specific mental functions are executed. For example, the areas of the brain that show increased activity when a person speaks and hears words exactly match the language areas identified by Broca and Wernicke at least a hundred years before the advent of modern scanning techniques. If the whole brain could be mapped in a similar fashion, showing a one-to-one correspondence between certain types of mental and neural activity, the case for the type-type reduction of the mental to the physical becomes stronger.

3.6   The token-token identity theory and the multiple realizability thesis

The type-type theory insists that each type of mental state will turn out to be identical with a given type of physical state and that there will be no exceptions to this rule. This makes it a very strong and demanding hypothesis. However, whilst we allow that water must always be H_2O, are we similarly constrained to accept that pain, for example, wherever and whenever it occurs, must be identical with C-fibres firing? Couldn't pain, on some occasions, in different people, or in animals, be identical with a different type of physical state? It is this thought, the idea that mental states could be multiply realized – that is, embodied in all different sorts of material arrangement, just as a computer program can be realized in a variety of mediums such as hard and floppy discs, silicon chips and so forth – that led to the demise of the type-type theory in the early 1970s, not long after it had been born.

The token-token theory took the idea mooted above and developed it into a major criticism of the type-type theory. To understand how it achieves this, however, I must first explain the difference between a type and a token. The distinction can be easily illustrated by reference to the expression 'type-type'. This expression contains four types of letter, namely 't', 'y', 'p' and 'e'. But each of these letters occurs twice in the expression: that is to say, there are two instances, or tokens, of 't', two tokens of 'y' and so forth. Clearly, if water considered as a type is identical with the type of stuff H_2O, then every individual instance or token of water, a pool of rainwater in my back-garden, for example, must be identical with an instance or token of H_2O. The type-type identity theory thus entails the identities of the tokens of the types in question. However, the converse does not obtain. Every token of a type of mental state could be identical with a token of a type of physical state, but it need not be the case that tokens of the same type of physical state must be involved on every occasion. Compare what is true in the case of watches. Every watch will be identical with some physical arrangement of parts, but clearly it would be ridiculous to claim that every token of the type 'watch' must be identical with a token of exactly the same type of arrangement of parts. Watches come in a variety of shapes, sizes and mechanisms, although at the end of the day they are all identical with material arrangements.

In the same way, every token of the thought-type 'Have I put the cat out?' will be identical with some token brain state or other, but it does not follow that it will always be identical with a token of the same type of brain state. Perhaps the token thought about the cat *in me* is identical with a token of the type of brain process in which C-fibres fire, but *in you* the same token thought is identical with a token of the type of brain process in which Z-fibres fire. In fact, even in me it is conceivable that tokens of the same type of thought might be

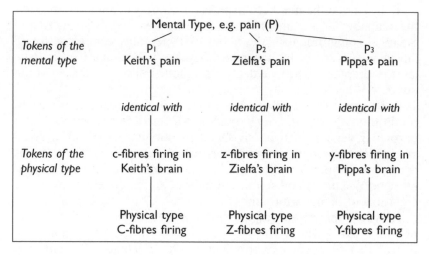

Figure 3.4   The token-token identity theory

identical with tokens of different types of brain process on different occasions. What happens in the case of stroke victims supports this point. A part of the brain is damaged and the victim loses the ability to walk. But then another part of the brain gradually takes over and the ability to walk is restored. The same could apply to thoughts. Whenever I thought about putting the cat out before my stroke, C-fibres would fire. However, my C-fibres were irreparably damaged by the stroke and now Z-fibres fire instead when I have the thought about the cat, these fibres having taken over the function of the original C-fibres. Figure 3.4 illustrates the token-token theory (lower-case letters represent tokens, upper-case letters represent types).

Which theory, the type-type or the token-token, is most likely to be true? (Of course, they could both be false if dualism is true, but we are not considering that possibility at the moment.) The plasticity of the brain, the fact that different parts of the brain may take over the functions discharged by other parts, counts strongly against the type-type theory. Besides, the type-type theory appears to be unnecessarily restrictive. Why should mentality be confined to human brains and human biology? Why shouldn't it be embodied in completely different physical systems such as the biology of whales, or aliens, or even the inorganic systems found in robots or androids? Only experience, and not philosophical theorizing in advance, can tell us whether these are genuine possibilities.

To insist that the mind can manifest itself only in human brains has been labelled as a manifestation of chauvinism, an unwarranted and fanatical commitment to the belief that mentality cannot be found anywhere except in human neurology. We will return to this issue later in chapter 5, when we deal with functionalism as a theory of the mind.

In response to the token-token theory it was argued that we can retain the type-type theory providing we restrict its scope, so that a particular version of it is envisaged to obtain only within a given species. Thus, pain in human beings will always consist in P-neurons firing, but in apes it will always be X-neurons, in cats it will invariantly be Y-neurons and so on, throughout all the different species of creatures or beings with minds.

However, there is no guarantee that even a species-restricted form of type identity will be true. As I remarked earlier, why could it not be true that when you and I think about the cat, totally different sorts of neurons fire in my case compared to yours? Going further, even in the case of a single individual, why, from moment to moment throughout that person's life, must it be the same type of neurons that are activated when that person has a certain type of thought? The token-token theory thus appears to be more plausible than the type-type theory. However, as we shall see when we come to examine objections to the identity theory, subscription to the token-token theory threatens to undermine the whole enterprise of identifying the mental with the physical.

3.7   Strengths of the identity theory

The identity theory, if some version of it can be made to work, is an attractive doctrine for a number of reasons. Firstly, it is a comparatively simple theory – mental states just are brain states. All else being equal, the simpler theory, which makes fewer assumptions and can get away with having to postulate fewer entities or properties, is the preferable theory. Unlike dualism, which has to posit both material and immaterial substances, and property-dualism, which has to postulate both non-physical and physical properties, the identity theory can make do with only physical things and physical properties.

Secondly, Descartes' problem regarding how the mind can affect the body simply disappears. If mental states just are brain states, then the problem of mind/body interaction is eliminated, because what initially looks like mental to physical causation turns out at the end of the day merely to be physical to physical causation. Physical events in the brain form part of a closed physical chain which extends from physical stimuli in the person's environment that impinge on the senses and cause changes in the person's brain, these in turn giving rise to a behavioural output which causes changes in the world beyond the person's skin. Whilst we do not fully understand physical to physical causality, at least we are exempted from the task of explicating how a non-physical substance with no dimensions could possibly have an effect on extended matter.

Thirdly, we are enabled to understand instantly why changes in the brain owing to injury, disease, operations and drugs are accompanied by alterations in mental functioning. In altering the brain, we are altering the mind, because the mind just is the brain. In a similar fashion we can also appreciate why increases in brain-size and complexity as we ascend the evolutionary scale are matched all the way up by corresponding increments in the sophistication of intellectual capacity and the richness of mental life.

3.8   Problems for the identity theory

Unfortunately we are not home and dry yet. There are a number of serious difficulties that the identity theory has to overcome, in any of its versions, if it is to be accepted as the solution to the mind/body conundrum. These difficulties are discussed at length in this section.

3.8.1   The mental and the spatial

The present objection to the mind/brain identity theory, which we will consider in fulfilment of a promise made in chapter 1, section 1.10, essentially takes its inspiration from Descartes, who divided the world into two mutually exclusive categories, the realm of *res extensa* – extended, space-occupying things – and the world of *res cogitans* – the domain of non-extended conscious things. The spatial location of brain processes can be specified with a high degree of accuracy. Scans can show in close detail those areas of the brain that become active when subjects are asked to perform various intellectual and practical tasks. But it appears to make no sense whatever to specify the location of a thought or an emotion. To claim that the thought 'Have I put the cat out' is located just behind one's eyes, or that a pang of jealousy can be found in the occipital region of the brain at the back of the head, is to talk nonsense. Moreover, whilst we can talk of brain processes as swift or slow, or molecular motions in the brain as straight or circular, it makes no sense to say this of my beliefs and feelings. Hence, mental states cannot be identified with brain processes.

This argument against the identity theory appears to succeed at one bound. In reality, however, it embodies certain confusions, which, when once made clear, render it much less conclusive. To understand what is wrong with it, we need to go back to the notion of a logical substance that was characterized at the start of chapter 2 (section 2.1). Logical substances are entities that can exist in their own right, independently of anything else, and it certainly makes sense to ask where in space these entities are located. The brain, as a composite logical substance, and the various parts of the brain, including all the micro-elements that comprise it, have a more or less specifiable location in space. Brain processes, consisting in the movement of logical substances such as molecules, also occupy a region of space: the movement of a group of complex molecules from one region in the brain to another could be tracked from one area to another, and their spatial route delineated. But, so the complaint against the identity theory goes, thoughts, sensations, emotions, beliefs and other mental states cannot be given a literal location in space, unlike regions and components of the brain, so there is no way the mental and the physical could turn out to be identical.

The objection, however, is based on a serious misunderstanding of the ontological status of the various mental items cited. By characterizing these items using noun-like expressions, it is fatally easy to think of mental states as logical substances. So conceived, it seems that these must have a specific location in space, along with other logical substances, yet when we attempt to say what the location is in the case of mental states, we end up talking nonsense. This in turn leads to the denial that mental states have any literal spatial location, and thus their identification with brain states, which do have a literal spatial location, is prohibited from the very start.

To appreciate what is wrong with this line of reasoning, however, we have to remember that pains, beliefs, thoughts and emotions (and mental states generally) are not logical substances. Although people have pains, thoughts, beliefs and emotions, this does not denote a relationship between two entities, a person on the one hand, and a belief or a pain on the other, but rather a condition of a single thing. We have a person who is feeling a pain, or thinking about something or believing that something is true. Now these things, necessarily, will be going on wherever the person happens to be. Kekulé was on the top of a bus when he thought about the structure of the benzene molecule, so that was where his thoughts about benzene occurred. Similarly, I was in my bed in the early hours of the morning when struck down by severe pains that heralded blood-poisoning some years ago, so that is where my pains occurred. To demand a more precise location for Kekulé's thoughts than the top of the bus where he was sitting, to ask where precisely inside him the thoughts were occurring, is already to make an illegitimate demand which amounts to no less than wanting to grant thoughts the status of logical substances. The same would be true even in the case of my pains, because although I might report intense pains in my side, it does not follow that there are things called pains which exist inside my body as nerves and muscles do. Rather, there is just me, an individual entity, in a condition of being in pain.

What this is leading up to is an amendment of the identity theory which can get round the original objection to it. This was first formulated by the American philosopher Thomas Nagel in a paper called 'Physicalism'. Nagel made the point that if the two sides of the proposed identity were adjusted so that they were to obtain not between a brain process and the occurrence of a pain or a thought, but rather between 'my *having* a certain sensation or thought, and my body's *being* in a certain physical state, then they will both be going on in the same place – namely, wherever I (and my body) happen to be . . . even if a pain is located in my right shin, I am having that pain in my office at the university.'[2] Once Nagel's adjustment is made, it will be apparent that the argument from the alleged non-spatiality of the mental against the identity theory loses much, if not all, of its force.

3.8.2   The symmetry of identity statements

The second difficulty for the identity theory which I shall consider is posed by the symmetry of identity statements. If A is identical to B, then B is identical to A. This means, to take an earlier example, that if the Morning Star is identical to the Evening Star, then, equally, the Evening Star must be the Morning Star. This will appear not only obvious but perhaps utterly trivial. However, the important lesson to learn is that because identity is symmetrical, we cannot argue that Clark Kent is really Superman (really, truly) but that Superman isn't really Clark Kent. Or, taking an example of a scientific identity, that water is really H_2O but that H_2O isn't really water.[3]

Before proceeding, look at Exercise 3.1.

Exercise 3.1

Try applying the symmetry of identity to the mind/brain identity theory. What result do you get? What do you think its significance is?

The upshot is that you cannot say that mental states are really only brain processes (really, truly) but that brain processes are not really mental states. To make this claim privileges the physical over the mental without justification. What it does, in effect, is to get rid of mental features in favour of brain features. It claims, effectively, that at the end of the day, there are only brain features. Mental properties and states have been neuralized, that is the mental has been assimilated and reduced to the purely physical. Of course, reading the identity statement from right to left leads to an equal and opposite absurdity, namely the error of mentalizing the brain. On this reading, brain processes are really only mental processes (really, truly) and the physical has been absorbed into the psychological.

Rather than privileging one side of the identity relation and trying to reduce the mind to the brain, or the brain to the mind, it would seem we must acknowledge that if mental events are brain processes, then they must have the physical properties that brain events possess. But equally we have to accept, by the symmetry of identity, that brain events have the mental properties by virtue of which the mental events with which they are identical are the kinds of event they are.

What should our response be at this point? Well, one thing we can be certain about in the Superman/Clark Kent case, and the water/H_2O example, is that we do not have two men on our hands, Clark Kent *and* Superman, and two kinds of stuff, water *and* H_2O, but only a single item in both cases. In the case of mind and body it seems that we must be prepared to accept that there are not two distinct streams of events, non-physical events taking place in the soul and physical events taking place in the brain, but only one set of events. In this way we can avoid a dualism of substances each with their disparate natures. Consider the question in Exercise 3.2 before reading any further.

Exercise 3.2

Given the symmetry of identity and its neutrality regarding both halves of the identity statement, what stream of events should we accept into our ontology: physical or mental? What are the reasons for your choice?

Evolution gives us a reason for privileging the physical. It seems reasonable to suppose that when the universe was first formed, there were no minds around but just particles whirling in space. After the planets had coalesced and the nuclear furnaces of the suns were lit, life gradually evolved. Eventually, after a certain level of physical complexity had been reached, mentality made its appearance. How it emerged we still do not know, but from the fact that I am addressing you now, we know that somehow it did. We also know that mental functioning is intimately bound up with what happens in the brain (see section 3.5). All this powerfully suggests that, contrary to what dualism claims, there is a one-sided dependence of the mental on the physical, that the physical, and not the mental, is what basically exists. Thus it seems not unreasonable to privilege the physical over the mental, to conclude that at the end of the day, in contradistinction to dualism, there are only physical and not spiritual immaterial substances.

However, even if we can give up positing two different kinds of substance or event, mental and physical, it seems we cannot avoid having to postulate a dualism of properties. As well as their physical properties, those brain states that are identical with mental states must, it seems, also have mental properties.

Another way to appreciate this is by reflecting that not all brain states are identical with mental states. There must be brain states that have absolutely nothing to do with consciousness – those states, for example, that govern the functioning of the autonomic nervous system. These brain states will possess only physical properties. But those that are identical with conscious, mental states must possess another layer of properties, namely mental ones, otherwise the identity of these brain processes with mental processes could not be asserted in the first place. What is emerging is that, colour it which way you will, we can escape a dualism of substances, but not a dualism of properties. Changes in a person's mental life will fundamentally involve physical changes or events in the person's brain and not events in a non-physical soul. However, these physical events will possess two distinctive kinds of property, physical and mental. Table 3.1 summarizes this position and contrasts it with dualism, illustrated in table 3.2 on the next page.

Table 3.1   The mind/brain identity theory

	E_1		E_2	
	Have I put the cat out?	C-fibres firing	Did I bring the cat in?	Z-fibres firing
One set of events (E) which can be given both mental and physical descriptions	Mental property	Physical property	Mental property	Physical property

Table 3.2   Dualism

Mental events in the soul	Mw	Mx	My	Mz
Physical events in the brain	Pa	Pb	Pc	Pd

3.8.3   Qualia, privileged access and the irreducibility of the mental

Another related argument which supports the position outlined in the last section runs as follows. In making an identity statement, there must be some features by means of which the items flanking the identity sign can be identified independently of one another, by means of which both halves of the identity can be pinned down, so to speak. Thus, Clark Kent is identified by his owlish glasses, his unexciting appearance and his bumbling manner. Superman is identified by his 20:20 vision, his alluring uniform and the way in which he speeds through the air unassisted. The features by means of which Clark Kent is picked out cannot be identified with the features by means of which Superman is picked out. Clark Kent's myopia is a different property from Superman's perfect vision.

Similarly, the features by means of which one's mental states are recognized are different from the features by means of which one's brain processes are discerned. I know I have a toothache because of the agonizing throbbing in my tooth. From looking at the X-ray photograph of it, I also know that my tooth is decayed and the nerve damaged. The agonizing throb is a feature that is quite distinct from the neurophysiological processes revealed by scientific investigation. I might notice the throb without noticing the physical processes (if I had no access to X-ray machines), or notice the processes without noticing a throb (if I'd been given an anaesthetic, or been hypnotized, say). What this overwhelmingly points to is that the throb cannot be identical with the physical properties of the damaged nerve.

Scientists could scan my brain as much as they like, but they would not discover merely by looking what it feels like to me to have a toothache. They won't, to put it another way, gain access to the qualia of my experience, which, as we noted earlier (in chapter 1, section 1.5), are available, in principle, only to me. Equally, if a film were made of my own brain's activity and at a later date I were shown the film, having forgotten in the meantime all about the occasion on which it was taken, even I myself could not tell purely from the observation of my own brain what I was thinking about at the time.

This helps to reaffirm the point made earlier in chapter 1, namely that whilst both the scientist and I have an equal access, in principle, to what goes on in our own and each other's brains, only I have access to the contents of my mind, unmediated by any process of observation or inference based upon more basic evidence. What this direct and immediate access reveals to me cannot, it would seem, be merely physical brain processes, otherwise, merely by observing my own brain processes on the film, I would automatically know what I was thinking about on the occasion in question. What I am aware of when I am aware of my own thoughts and sensations must, it appears, consist in features *other* than the public physical properties of brain processes.

In a public lecture given in London Thomas Nagel expressed the pious hope that one day a brain scientist might look into his brain and say of some process taking place in it: 'There! That's what Nagel's savouring the taste of his cigar looks like neurologically!' However, Nagel instantly went on to add that at present we haven't the faintest idea of how the taste of a cigar, felt subjectively and privately to him, could simultaneously be a physical process in the brain observable in theory by all. This recalls Leibniz's remark quoted earlier in chapter 1, section 1.1, namely, that if the brain were enlarged to the size of a mill and we were to enter it, we would observe only mechanical processes and nothing that could explain mentality and consciousness.

3.8.4   Intentional mental states

So far, the argument against the identity theory has turned on the non-reducibility of the private, subjective qualities – the qualia – of sensations. But by far the greatest bulk of the mental is comprised of intentional states which represent, or are directed upon, states of affairs other than themselves, including those that do not, and perhaps never did, exist. If intentional states are identified with brain processes, then the question instantly arises: how can physical states of the brain be about other states of affairs, including non-existent ones? The argument against the identification of the intentional with the physical can be stated formally thus:

1   Intentional mental states represent, or are about, states of affairs external to themselves, including states of affairs that do not – and perhaps never did – exist. For example, beliefs, desires, dreams, intentions, emotions, hopes, thoughts, as well as many other mental states, possess a representational content.
2   No brain states can possess a representational content.
3   Therefore intentional mental states cannot be identical with brain states.

Now look at Exercise 3.3 before reading any further.

Exercise 3.3   The argument outlined above is valid. Hence if the conclusion is to be resisted, either or both premises must be rejected. Which premises, if any, do you think should go, and why?

The argument is valid, and the first premise is undeniable, so if we wish to reject the conclusion some way must be found of rejecting the second premise. The thought that lies behind the second premise and can make it appear highly plausible is this: how is it conceivable that purely physical arrangements of particles in the brain should represent other states of affairs? How can collections of atoms in the void, so to speak, be about things other than themselves?

However, many philosophers nowadays would view this kind of response as merely begging the question against the possibility of a completely physical account of intentionality. Perhaps original underived intentionality can be physically explained and realized in purely physical systems. In support of this claim, consider the following case. We know that the kind of ring a tree lays down in a given year, its thickness and density, for example, depends upon what the weather is like that year. The correlation is easily established by cutting a tree down and comparing the nature of the rings with the weather records for different years. Thus we are enabled in the future, without consulting records, to establish what the weather must have been like in particular years, whether or not records were kept. The tree rings are, in the main, reliable indicators of the weather in past years. There is thus a sense in which tree rings contain information about the tree's external environment. The rings vary in a dependable and law-like way with changes in the tree's environment – that is, they causally co-vary. In a similar fashion, the internal states of a thermostat vary as a result of changes in the ambient temperature. Indeed, we build thermostats with this express purpose or function, so that switches can be activated when the internal state reaches a certain value in order to turn a heating system on or off.

Does causal co-variation amount to intentionality? Are the internal states of a thermostat *about* the ambient temperature? Can thermostats literally have beliefs about the ambient temperature, as some cognitive scientists have wanted to insist? Is a tree ring about the weather that was causally responsible for its character, and, hence, are purely physical systems such as trees the possessors of intentionality, a low grade of aboutness, admittedly, but aboutness no less?

Some philosophers, such as Michael Tye, Fred Dretske and Jerry Fodor,[4] are very sympathetic to this position, and thus reveal themselves as basically materialists in orientation. Others, such as John Searle, Galen Strawson and Dale Jaquette,[5] are more sceptical of the claims of the materialists. Searle believes that intentionality is an emergent, non-physical property of the brain, and would thus rule out tree rings and the internal states of thermostats, as instances of genuine intentionality. Any intentionality they possess derives from us, who assign interpretations to the internal states of these systems. Strawson would agree: in a world devoid of conscious life, there is no genuine aboutness, no genuine meaning. Dale Jaquette, in a similar fashion, regards intentionality as an explanatorily primitive and undefined concept: intentionality, he believes, is 'an ineliminable, irreducible, and mechanically non-replicable property' of the mind and this makes it 'a new category of entity in the material world. Mind emerges naturally from living matter in complex bio-systems at a comparatively late evolutionary stage. But, because of its intentionality, the mind is qualitatively different from non-mental, purely mechanical things.'[6]

As I remarked in chapter 1, section 1.4, it is beyond the scope of this book to delve further into this issue. It must suffice for me to say that I am inclined to side with Searle, Strawson and Jacquette: intrinsically, physical systems, purely in virtue of their physical features, do not possess underived intentionality. Intentionality appears to amount to more than physical causal co-variation and this begins to suggest that no purely physical theory can accommodate it.

3.8.5 Rationality and normativity

There is an even stronger argument against the possibility of providing a physicalist account of intentionality. It will be recalled from chapter 1, section 1.9 that because such states can be logically related to each other, they are subject to the constraints of rationality and normativity. Beliefs, for example, can conflict, and if we become aware of a conflict in beliefs then rationally we ought to give up either or both of them. We demand rationality of both ourselves and others, and it has been argued by the philosopher Donald Davidson that when interpreting the behaviour of others, we do so by trying to fit the intentional states we ascribe to that person – their intentions, desires, beliefs and so forth – into a coherent whole. Davidson agrees that people can be irrational, but irrationality depends for its existence upon a general background of rationality. 'To imagine a totally irrational animal', he says, 'is to imagine an animal without thoughts.'[7]

Davidson develops this line of thought further. He argues that the domain of the physical and the domain of the mental, where he has intentional states in mind, are subject to completely different over-arching constraints. An example of such a constraint in physical theory is provided by the principle of transitivity for length: if A is longer than B, and B is longer than C, then A must be longer than C. Should a principle like this be abandoned, then the coherence of physical theory is threatened. In this way, transitivity of length is a constitutive element of physical theory. The counterpart constitutive element in relation to the mental domain is what Davidson calls 'the constitutive ideal of rationality', an idea that we encountered a moment ago when speaking of the need to attribute a pattern of reasonably coherent and consistent intentional states to other people, on pain of forgoing the opportunity to think of them as persons, and to treat them accordingly.

Because the mental and physical are governed by such utterly different sorts of constitutive principle, Davidson believes that no wholesale matching of mental to physical states will be possible. Thus, strict psycho-physical laws connecting events under their mental descriptions with their physical descriptions will be ruled out. In other words, bi-conditional bridge laws of the sort mentioned earlier in section 3.5 will not be forthcoming, and with them any prospect of the reduction of mental to physical features as the type-type identity theory demands. Hence the concept of the holism of intentional states and the 'constitutive ideal of rationality' which governs their ascription constitutes yet another argument against the type-type identity theory.

3.8.6   Token-token identity and the prospect of reduction

We noted earlier (section 3.6) that the token-token theory appeared to be the more plausible alternative to the type-type theory. However, in addition to the objections that apply to identity theories generally, the token-token theory has to face some problems of its own.

The first problem the theory has to face is that although every token event which has a mental property will also have a physical property, there will be no systematic relationship between the type of mental event a token instantiates and the type of physical event it also exemplifies. To understand this more clearly, consider the properties of shape and colour. Every coloured object will have a shape and, equally, it is arguable, every item with a shape must possess a colour (I shall ignore the possibility of perfectly transparent or invisible objects). But there will be no systematic relationship between the properties of colour and shape, such that an object can be, say, rectangular if, and only if, it is red, or that an object can be blue if, and only if, it is round. Colours and shapes can vary quite independently of each other and are quite accidentally related. Hence there is no prospect of explaining colours in terms of shapes or shapes in terms of colours. The same would appear to be true of token-token physicalism as it has been characterized so far. There will be no systematic way of explaining why particular events co-instantiate concepts of a given mental type and a given physical type. The existence of the mental feature will be as apparently unrelated to the existence of the physical feature as are the colour and shape of an object to each other. That is why the thesis of token-token identity has been stigmatized by philosophers as not much of a physicalism because it does not allow physical states to play any explanatory role in accounting for the presence of mental states. The co-existence of mental and physical features has to be accepted as a brute, inexplicable fact, thus making token-token identity a difficult theory to embrace.[8]

However, there is reason to believe that this particular difficulty can be overcome by the invocation of what is known as the supervenience hypothesis. A full characterization of this proposal must wait until chapter 6, but its main thrust is that mental features depend for their existence on physical features in such a way that there can be no mental change unless there is a physical change. The converse does not apply, because tokens of different types of physical state could instantiate tokens of one and the same type of mental state. This is another way of stating the point made earlier, that mental states are multiply realizable in different types of physical state. Supervenience, if it can be made to work, at least has the virtue of bringing the mental and the physical into closer relationship with each other, and to that extent can overcome the stigmatization that we noted was levelled at the theory. However, supervenience and its attendant problems must wait until a later chapter.

3.8.7   Token-token identity and the impossibility of reduction

The token-token theory is not out of the woods yet, however. There is a powerful argument against it to the effect that the multiple realizability of mental states which token-token theory enshrines prohibits the wholesale reduction of the mental to the physical. To understand why this should be so, we need to recall that reduction of one set of phenomena to another appears to require the possibility of formulating bi-conditional bridge laws. A law of this sort, it will be remembered from section 3.5, requires that for a mental state M to be reducible to, and identifiable with, a physical state P, it must be the case that M occurs if, and only if, P occurs. Multiple realizability appears to breach this requirement. This is because M can be realized in an indefinite variety of physical states. In other words, a single physical state P is not necessary for M to occur: P1 or P2 or P3 . . . or Pn, may equally well do in instantiating M. Taken singly, either P1 or P2 or P3 . . . or Pn is sufficient for M to occur, but it is not necessary, yet the bridge law requires that any candidate physical state to which M is reducible should be both necessary and sufficient for the occurrence of M. Now pause to consider Exercise 3.4 before reading on.

Exercise 3.4   Can you see a possible response to the challenge outlined above? Think about this and discuss it with someone else.

The reductionist's response to the challenge is to maintain that a physical property can be found, or rather constructed, which can serve as the necessary and sufficient condition for M. All we need to do is to construct the disjunctive property *either* P *or* P1 *or* P2 *or* P3 . . . *or* Pn. The property is given the label 'disjunctive' because it specifies a number of alternatives linked by the logical constant 'or'. The bridge law will then read: M if, and only if, either P or P1 or P2 or P3 . . . or Pn.

However, there is a problem with this strategy. Look at Exercise 3.5 before continuing.

Exercise 3.5   Can you see a problem with the reductionist's response? Hint: think about what the features of properties are, and determine whether so-called disjunctive properties can qualify.

The problem with the reductionist's response is as follows. Even if P, P1, P2 and P3, etc. are properties when each is considered singly by itself, it does not follow that their disjunctive combination represents a genuine property. Properties are ordinarily thought of as marking points of resemblance, shared similarities, between particular items, yet P1, P2, P3, etc. might be quite radically different physical states, especially when we remember that such states need not be restricted to organisms but might even encompass the states of machines such as robots, computers or androids. At the very least, the possibility that mental states might be incarnated in arrangements other than those of carbon-based organisms cannot be ruled out in advance. But then the disjunction will contain such a heterogeneous collection of items that there will be no significant similarities between them, and thus it appears highly artificial to speak of them as constituting a single property. In addition, there is certainly not going to be a single scientific theory that can encompass such a miscellaneous collection of properties.[9]

Another problem posed for the reductionist is that it appears that in principle the disjunctive analysis could never be completed because, by its very nature, it is open-ended. If we try to complete the analysis, however, by adding on to the series P or P1 or P2 or P3, etc. the expression 'and any other physical state that instantiates M', then circularity is imported into the analysis by the mention of the mental term M. An analysis that contains the very mental term it is supposed to be eliminating by reduction to the physical plainly cannot do. Whether these difficulties for reductionism can be overcome ultimately, I leave the reader to pursue further.

A third severe difficulty for the token-token theory was pointed out by John Searle in his book *The Rediscovery of the Mind*.[10] According to the token-token theory, you and I could be in the same mental state – for example, thinking about what we will have for dinner – and yet our neurological states could be different from each other owing to the possibility of multiple realization of the mental by the physical. But what then is it that makes our differing brain states instantiations of one and the same pattern of thought? Look at Exercise 3.6 before reading my response to this question.

What answer would be returned by common sense to the above question in your opinion, and why would it be fatal to reductive materialism? What contrasting answer has to be given by the reductive materialist and why? Think about this on your own and if possible discuss it with someone else. Then compare my commentary below.

Exercise 3.6

The common-sense answer to the question posed in the last paragraph is that each token of a different type of neurophysiological state possesses the same type of mental property, namely the property of thinking about what there is for dinner, and that is why the different physical tokens are instantiations of the same type of mental state. It seems to me that this is the correct answer to the question and helps to constitute yet another reason for not subscribing to strict physicalism. Clearly, however, it is not going to satisfy the reductive materialist. The reason is that mental features cannot be cited to explain why tokens of different types of brain state are yet embodiments of one and the same thought pattern, because the ultimate aim of the identity theorist is to reduce mental features to physical features, to eliminate the mental, in effect, in favour of the material. Thus, as Searle points out, for the dedicated materialist, some non-mentalistic answer must be given, such as that the different neurological states execute the same function in the life of the organism. It is in just such a way that token-token physicalism and multiple realizability lead on to the most recent theory of the mind/body relationship, namely functionalism. However, we must wait until chapter 5 for a full exposition and evaluation of this latest take on the relation between the mental and the physical.

3.8.8   Kripke's argument against the identity theory

I have saved until near the end of this chapter the most complicated, and possibly the most powerful, argument against the mind/brain identity theory, which tells equally against both the type-type and token-token versions. The argument we will be examining is due to the American philosopher Saul Kripke, and is to be found in his book *Naming and Necessity*.[11]

   To understand Kripke's objection, we need firstly to recall the claim of the early identity theorists that the identity of the mental and the physical is a contingent and not an analytic truth. All that was meant by this was that it is not possible to tell merely by examination of the relevant identity statement whether it was true or not. The claim that mental states are identical with brain states, if true, is not true a priori, by virtue of the meanings of the terms flanking the identity sign. As we said earlier, talk about mental states is different in meaning from talk about brain states.

   Kripke argued, however, that if, as a matter of contingent fact, mental states are brain states, then they are essentially brain states. This is not to say that it is necessarily true that pain, for example, is physical. The difference between what philosophers call *de dicto* and *de re* necessity is vital here. *De dicto* necessity is a property of language, and analytic truths are an exemplification of it. *De re* necessity is a property of the world. Pain is necessarily physical and the necessity here is *de re* necessity, not *de dicto* necessity.

To understand why Kripke makes the *de re* claim that pain is necessarily or essentially physical, we must first look at the distinction that he draws between what he calls rigid and non-rigid designators. Kripke's own example of a non-rigid designator is the definite description, 'The first Postmaster General of the US'. This expression refers to Benjamin Franklin, who was, as it happens, the first Postmaster General. But plainly he might not have been, which means there is a possible world in which 'The first Postmaster General of the US' does not refer to Franklin but to somebody else. In general, all definite descriptions will be non-rigid designators and could refer to different individuals in different possible worlds.

By contrast, Kripke argues, the proper name 'Benjamin Franklin' (and proper names generally) is a rigid designator because it picks out the one and the same individual in all possible worlds – that is, it refers necessarily to Benjamin Franklin, and it is inconceivable that it might pick out someone else.

Now consider the name 'Lewis Carrol'. As a rigid designator, this necessarily picks out the same individual in all possible worlds. The name 'Charles Dodgson' also identifies the same person in all possible worlds. Now it would be possible that each of these names had picked out a different person from the other. So 'Lewis Carrol' could have referred to a particular individual who existed in all possible worlds, and 'Charles Dodgson' could have referred to another *different* individual who existed in all possible worlds. But although these names might have referred to different people, as a matter of fact they didn't, because, as is well known, 'Lewis Carrol' was the pseudonym which Charles Dodgson used when he composed his Alice books. Thus we can formulate the identity statement:

Lewis Carrol = Charles Dodgson

Each of the names flanking the identity sign is a rigid designator, so each name necessarily refers to the same individual in all possible worlds. The individuals so referred to might not have been numerically identical, but in this case they were, because it is true that Lewis Carrol *was* Charles Dodgson. This leads to an interesting result: there is no possible world in which the name 'Lewis Carrol' identifies an individual person who is not also identified by the name 'Charles Dodgson'. To put this negatively, there is no possible world, no conceivable set of circumstances, in which the reference of 'Lewis Carrol' could be different from the reference of 'Charles Dodgson'. Through-out all possible worlds, these two names must necessarily refer to one and the same individual person. So Lewis Carrol is not merely identical with Charles Dodgson, he is *necessarily* identical (in the sense of *de re* necessity) with Charles Dodgson, because there is no conceivable circumstance, no possible world, in which this identity does not obtain. To suppose otherwise would be like supposing that something, in this case the person known either as Lewis Carrol or as Charles Dodgson, could fail to be identical with itself, which is plainly an absurdity. By contrast with those identity statements in which the identity sign is flanked exclusively by rigid designators, an identity statement of the form,

Lewis Carrol = the author of *Alice in Wonderland*

can never be true in all possible worlds. This is because the expression on the right of the identity sign, 'The author of *Alice in Wonderland*', is a definite description. This means it is a non-rigid designator which may refer to different people in different possible worlds. The statement above is, of course, true, but it does not exhibit *de re* necessity, because it does not hold across the spectrum of all possible worlds. There may be a possible world in which the author of *Alice in Wonderland* was someone other than Lewis Carrol, say H. G. Wells instead.

Kripke extends the notion of a rigid designator to cover not merely proper names, but terms which name natural kinds, such as gold, chlorine, water and H_2O. Thus 'water' as a rigid designator picks out the same sort of stuff in all possible worlds. So does 'H_2O'. But 'water = H_2O' expresses a true identity, so that 'water' and 'H_2O' both refer to one and the same stuff in all possible worlds. Thus, although it had to be discovered empirically that water is H_2O and so was known solely on the basis of experience, unlike the analytic truths of mathematics and geometry which could be known independently of experience, the identity statement, 'water = H_2O', just like 'Lewis Carrol = Charles Dodgson', exhibits *de re* necessity – that is, there is *no* possible world in which 'water = H_2O' is false.

'Water = H_2O' is one of the scientific identities listed earlier in section 3.4. You will recall that in these kinds of statement, the term on the right is to be thought of as giving the hidden nature of the phenomenon referred to on the left. According to the identity theorist, the same holds true for the identity statement 'Pain = C-fibres firing'. But, as we have seen, according to Kripke this identity, like all other scientific identities, if true, must be true in all possible worlds.

In other words, there is no possible world we can conceive of in which pain is *not* identical with C-fibres firing, because the identity of pain with C-fibres firing is a *de re* necessary identity.

But this is precisely where the identity theorist comes unstuck, according to Kripke, because we can conceive of two possibilities. Firstly, it is possible to conceive of a situation in which a person has a pain but there are no C-fibres firing. All that is essential to pain is the way it feels. What may, or may not, be taking place neurologically is irrelevant, since all that is required is that if a sensation seems to you to be painful, then it *is* painful. There is thus a possible world in which pain occurs without the presence of C-fibres firing. In vain would an identity theorist protest: 'But what you feel cannot be pain, because your C-fibres are not firing'. The situation is precisely unlike one in which you see a colourless liquid in a jar and judge that it is water. Here you could be mistaken, because if the inner nature of the stuff in the jar is H_2SO4, and not H_2O, then the liquid is sulphuric acid and not water. What makes pain pain, however, is not some hidden, inner nature of which you may be ignorant, but simply the way it feels.

In case the point is not sufficiently clear, let me try making it another way. We know that water is identical with H_2O, and therefore according to Kripke it is necessarily (with *de re* necessity) identical with H_2O, so there is no possible world in which it is not H_2O. But cannot we imagine a world containing water which has the chemical formula XYZ? Kripke's response is that in a case like this one is not really succeeding in imagining water at all, but only some watery stuff which looks like water and behaves like water, but in reality is not water at all because its internal constitution is XYZ and not H_2O. In other words, contrary to what one thinks, one is not succeeding in imagining water apart from H_2O, because what one is imagining isn't water but something else. Now does the same stricture apply in the case of, say, pain? Can I succeed in imagining the occurrence of a pain without the occurrence of C-fibres firing? The identity theorist is committed, of course, to saying that I cannot, any more than I can imagine water without H_2O being present. What the identity theorist has to maintain is that, when I believe I am imagining pain in the absence of C-fibres firing, I am really only imagining a pain feel-alike and not pain itself, because the pain feel-alike does not possess the right inner constitution. But this is where Kripke wishes to make his essential point, namely that the case of water and the case of pain are radically different. All that is necessary for pain to be pain is that it feels like pain. There is not, and cannot be, any distinction between pain and pain feel-alike in the way that there is a distinction between water and water look-alike. You could have something that looked exactly like water, but nevertheless isn't water, because what it looks like is not essential to its being what it is, whereas its inner constitution, by contrast, is essential. But you could not have something that felt exactly like pain but which wasn't pain, because what is essential to pain being pain is simply the way it feels. So it seems that we genuinely can imagine pains occurring in the absence of C-fibres firing, and this means that pains are not identical with C-fibres firing. Similarly, we can imagine a world in which C-fibres fire, but there are no accompanying pains. That is to say, there are possible worlds in which the same sorts of thing go on in the brains of the creatures in those worlds as take place in our brains in this world, except, unlike us, those other beings are zombies without any vestige of mentality. Because mental states are not necessarily identical with brain states, since we can genuinely imagine the one without the other, they are not identical at all. This means the identity theory has to be rejected. Kripke's objection is fatal to both versions of the identity theory, the type-type and the token-token theory alike, and cannot be dodged by favouring the token-token theory at the expense of the type-type version.[12]

Kripke's contention that it is possible to conceive or imagine pain occurring without the presence of a corresponding brain state (or, indeed, any physical state whatsoever) is reminiscent of Descartes' argument in his Sixth Meditation (see chapter 2, section 2.7.2) – namely, that he can conceive of a situation in which it is possible for his mind to exist without his body. If that is the case, then, as I remarked earlier, there is the possibility that the mental can exist without the physical, and this means that any attempt to reduce the mental to the physical in the way the temperature of a gas is reducible to molecular motion cannot succeed. The temperature of a gas cannot exist without molecular motion because that, ultimately, is what the temperature consists in. But the possibility that mental states can occur without corresponding physical states being present means that ultimately the mental cannot be constituted by the physical. Thus a complete and thoroughgoing reductive materialism is, in the end, not achievable.

3.9   Eliminative materialism

Despite what appear to many philosophers to be overwhelming objections against reductive materialism, it will come as no surprise that it still has its champions. In this final section I shall briefly explain, and comment upon, the most radical form materialism takes today, namely eliminative materialism. What is distinctive about this theory is that it does not merely intend to show that when we talk about mental states we are really talking about brain states, but that we have to give up talking about mental states completely. Not only are there no mental items existing over and above physical items, but the very concept of the mental and the vocabulary through which it finds its expression have to be expunged from our habits of thought and speech. There is no worry regarding how the mental is to be reduced to the physical, because, according to the eliminative materialist, mental properties do not, and never did, exist. Once upon a time we spoke of goblins, witches, the planet Vulcan, calorific fluid, the ether, the mysterious 'powder of sympathy' which supposedly enabled longitude to be ascertained, and phlogiston. Now these terms no longer seriously figure in our vocabulary because we have realized that they refer to nothing. None of the items named by these terms exist, or ever existed. They are pure mythology, the result of muddled pre-scientific and pre-philosophical thinking.

The same fate awaits mental states. There are no mental states, only brain processes. We once imagined there were such things as mental states, including consciousness, but we were deluded. Really, there were only brain processes after all. Hence, this kind of identity theory is also known as the disappearance theory. One half of the identity, the mental half has, so to speak, been absorbed into the physical half (magicked away, one is tempted to say), and in the process has been abolished. Not only do mental states as traditionally conceived not exist, but we shall all do a lot better if we stop persisting in the habit of talking about them as if they did exist. Talk about mental states belongs to an outdated folk psychology (the term 'folk', with its associations of peasant simplicity and the bucolic, is intended to be mildly abusive), and we should instead embrace an up-to-date vocabulary couched in the terms of the latest biological, physical and psychological sciences. Mental terms and the items they allegedly refer to must be eschewed, and we must no longer speak of feeling pain or being wracked by jealousy, but talk instead of C-fibres firing or of circuits in the triune cortex discharging with spiking frequencies of various orders of hertz.

Look at Exercise 3.7 before reading my own views of eliminative materialism.

What is your response to the proposal of the eliminative materialist? How plausible a theory do you find it? After thinking about this issue on your own, combine with others to discuss it. Then read on for my response.

Exercise 3.7

From the tenor of my comments on reductive materialism throughout this chapter, it will doubtless come as no surprise to you to learn that I find the whole proposal of the eliminative materialist unbelievable and ridiculous. I believe that I can be more certain that I am conscious and enjoy a rich and varied mental life than I can be certain of the truth of any theory which attempts to deny the undeniable facts of my personal experience. The fact of my conscious experience is not a construction of theory akin to the early mistaken hypotheses of scientists, or the fantasies of mythologists, but constitutive of my very life as a human being. To deny these facts I would have to pretend I was anaesthetized!

Norman Malcolm, criticizing Katherine Wilkes's espousal of eliminative materialism in her book *Physicalism*,[13] trenchantly remarks, in response to her claim that in the future children will no longer say they have a headache but will report instead that their C-fibres are firing,

> What a marvellous solution! One expression is replaced by another. Would this *eliminate* sensation discourse? Not at all. For the new expression would not *take the place* of the familiar expression unless it were given the *same use*. For example, the first-person expression 'My C-fibres are firing' would not have to be used as an immediate expression of sensation, not as a hypothesis about what is going on in the speaker's brain, nor as a report of an observation made with the help of instruments. But then nothing would have changed except a bit of terminology.[14]

In other words, merely changing a bit of vocabulary won't thereby abolish the various conceptual distinctions between mental and physical states which we explored in chapter 1.[15]

It may be objected that this gives Wilkes rather short shrift. After all, she is a distinguished philosopher, who, together with other writers such as Paul and Patricia Churchland, has steadily advocated the elimination of mental terms and categories in favour of physical ones. Surely there must be more going for physicalism than I have indicated, if the thinkers I have just mentioned are willing to espouse it?

In reply I would say that for the reasons I have outlined above I can certainly appreciate the motivation of those who advocate eliminative materialism. Not only does its adoption simplify our ontology, but it neatly obviates the problem of how mind/body interaction is possible, together with the question of exactly how physical events in the brain could possibly produce such a different order of being as the phenomenon of consciousness. These are all extremely difficult and pressing issues.

However, the correct response to these issues, I believe, is to face them squarely, and not to sidestep them by throwing oneself into the arms of eliminative materialism. To deny that consciousness and other mental states exist is really, despite the extreme improbability of eliminative materialism turning out to be true, to opt for the easier route, for then one would be spared the hard task of fitting the mind into the physical world. On the contrary, the existence of consciousness should be taken seriously, and the issue of how mentality is to be explained and located within our world-view not balked. It is to these challenges that I shall be turning in later chapters.

Questions to think about

1   If my access to my mental states is privileged, but my access to my brain states is not, does this mean that my mental states cannot be my brain states?
2   'There are no logical objections to the mind/brain identity thesis.' Discuss.
3   Explain the difference between intrinsic and derived intentionality. Can a purely physical system possess intentionality?
4   Describe three features of mental states that are supposed to distinguish them from physical states. Do these features mean that mental states cannot be fully part of the physical world?
5   Explain the difference between type-type and token-token identity theories. What advantages, if any, does the token-token theory have over the type-type theory?
6   Is the multiple realizability of mental states incompatible with their ultimate reduction to purely physical states?
7   What reasons are there for thinking that although we can avoid a dualism of substances, we cannot avoid a dualism of properties?
8   Can thoughts be ascribed a literal spatial location in the brain?

Suggestions for further reading

- A seminal article is by J. J. C. Smart, 'Sensations and Brain Processes', originally published in *Philosophical Review* LXVIII (1959), 141–56, but available in many anthologies. Although it is more than forty years since it was written, this article is still very worthwhile reading because it sets forth the issues very clearly.
- A useful collection of articles, although it may now be out of print and only obtainable in university libraries, is C. V. Borst (ed.), *The Mind/Brain Identity Theory* (London: Macmillan, 1970).

- *Matter and Consciousness*, by Paul Churchland (Cambridge, MA, and London: MIT Press, 1988), provides a brief introduction to the identity theory and is helpful in getting a very quick overview.
- Another introduction to materialism, which is not too difficult, can be found in John Heil's *Philosophy of Mind: A Contemporary Introduction* (London: Routledge, 1998).
- For those who wish to delve more deeply, Cynthia MacDonald's *Mind/ Brain Identity Theories* (London: Routledge, 1989) goes into matters in considerable depth, but beginners may find parts rather heavy-going.
- Jaegwon Kim's *Mind in a Physical World* (Cambridge, MA: MIT Press, 1998) provides useful background. The first chapter 'The Mind/Body Problem; Where We are Now' traces the recent history of materialist thinking about the mind and is very helpful in providing a quick overview, whilst the last chapter takes a close look at reductionism. Another rather easier book by Kim, *Philosophy of Mind* (Boulder, CO: Westview Press, 1996), also contains good discussions of reductive materialism, as well as providing an overall view of various theories of body and mind.
- *Contemporary Materialism: A Reader*, edited by P.K. Moser and J.D. Trout (London: Routledge, 1995), contains an up-to-date collection of contemporary writings on materialism as does Howard Robinson (ed.), *Objections to Physicalism* (Oxford: Clarendon Press, 1993).
- David Chalmers, *The Conscious Mind* (Oxford: OUP, 1996) contains many interesting observations and discussions, but at 404 pages (including notes) is rather a marathon.

4

ANALYTICAL BEHAVIOURISM

Objectives

As a result of reading this chapter you should:

- understand the difference between psychological and philosophical or analytical behaviourism;
- understand the central claim of analytical behaviourism, namely that talk about mental states is equivalent in meaning to talk about actual and potential patterns of behaviour;
- understand the strengths of analytical behaviourism;
- understand Hempel's 'hard' version of behaviourism and the factors which motivated it;
- understand and appreciate the importance of avoiding circularity when attempting an analytical reduction of mental states;
- understand the difficulties Hempel faces in trying to provide a non-circular behavioural analysis of mental states;
- understand Ryle's 'soft' version of behaviourism and the factors which motivated it;
- understand Ryle's account of a disposition and be able to evaluate it;
- understand the difficulty behaviourism faces when trying to provide explanations of actions and behaviour in general;
- understand the difficulty behaviourism faces in accounting for the phenomenology of non-intentional states and its apparent privacy;
- understand why behaviourism cannot provide for first-person authority regarding the individual's knowledge of his own states of mind;
- understand why the possibility of pretence cannot show that behaviourism is false, but appreciate the strengths of the arguments from zombies and super-Spartans in achieving this goal.

4.1   Introduction

Dualism and the mind/brain identity theory share the assumption that the mind is a thing, a non-physical Cartesian substance, on the one hand, and the living brain, on the other. Analytical behaviourism challenges and rejects this presumption, in common with functionalism, which will be explored in the next chapter. Most straightforwardly and simply, analytical behaviourism maintains that statements about the mind and mental states turn out, after analysis, to be equivalent to statements that describe a person's actual and potential public behaviour. There is, on this view, ultimately no more to someone's mental states than certain overt patterns of behaviour he or she exhibits, or, in the appropriate circumstances, is disposed to manifest.[1]

Analytical behaviourism, if it can be made to work, has a number of strengths. These are:

Avoidance of the mind/body interaction problem   Firstly, it makes the nature of the relationship of the mind to the body perspicuous: the mind just is the behaviour, actual and potential, of the body. The mind does not cause the behaviour: it *is* the behaviour. Worries about the nature of the mind conceived of as an immaterial substance cannot arise.

The non-mysteriousness of the mental   There are no mysterious obscure mental properties to account for. Should a behaviourist be at all concerned about the relation of the mind to the brain, the problem reduces to the purely scientific one of which internal physical states are causally responsible for various patterns of behaviour. All speculation about how non-physical properties can emerge from underlying physical processes is rendered redundant.

Dissolving the problem of other minds   Cartesian dualism would appear to make knowledge of mental states other than one's own impossible. Mental states comprise a radically private realm to which only the person whose states of mind they are has access. Behaviourism sidesteps this difficulty, because in seeing someone's behaviour, we are witnessing their mind in action. Animals, too, may be granted minds, since animals exhibit a range of behaviours from the simple to the complex. In this way, the gulf that Cartesianism would place between us and the rest of the animal kingdom disappears.

However, against its strengths, there are a number of serious obstacles with which analytical behaviourism must contend, as we shall see later.

4.2 Analytical contrasted with methodological behaviourism

A much fuller characterization of analytical behaviourism remains to be given. However, before we can proceed it will be necessary to distinguish analytical behaviourism, which is a philosophical position, from behaviourism as it occurs in psychology. If this distinction is not drawn, it may lead to certain confusions, especially among those who have come to philosophy from studying psychology.

Behaviourism in psychology is not a theory regarding how talk about the mind is to be properly understood, but a method of doing psychology, a proposal as to how psychological investigations are to be carried out, hence its full characterization as methodological behaviourism. This approach to psychology is reflected in the fact that the discipline is often defined as the science of human and animal *behaviour*, and not as the study of human and animal *minds*. The idea is that anything that has pretensions to call itself a science must study what is public, because only what is public is capable of measurement and quantification and, even more importantly, verifiable by other observers and experimenters. The results of experiments must be reduplicable by other independent observers if they are to stand any chance of being accepted as viable theories in the so-called 'hard' sciences such as physics, and the same strictures are placed on psychological claims and theories.

Behaviourism in the hands of the American psychologists J. B. Watson and B. F. Skinner took the form of claiming that human behaviour was to be understood as a set of responses evoked by external stimuli. 'Internal' processes, whether in the form of physical brain events or mental events, were set to one side and it was claimed that knowledge of the external stimuli and the behaviour they caused was all that was needed to explain why people behaved as they did. Skinner, in particular, believed that the use of intentional terms in psychology committed one to believing in the existence of a homunculus, a little man in the head, and this leads to the familiar objection that appeals to a homunculus explain nothing, since the abilities and behaviour of the homunculus itself cry out for explanation (see chapter 2, section 2.8.3). Instead, then, of having recourse to a person's beliefs, desires and intentions in order to explain his behaviour, we are to account for it in terms of conditioned responses which have been reinforced by repetition and reward. A pigeon's behaviour can be 'shaped' by the reinforcement stimulus of a reward of food every time it makes a particular sort of movement, so that ultimately, by this means, it can be made to walk in a figure of eight. In the same way, the whole of human conduct is supposed to be explainable purely in terms of the reinforced stimulus-response relations produced by such operant conditioning.

Having completed this brief outline of methodological behaviourism, we must now return for a closer look at the philosophical variety that is our real goal.

4.3   Analytical behaviourism

The analysis of all talk about the mind into statements describing actual and possible behaviour is a form of reductionism, but it represents a different variety from the kind we encountered earlier in relation to the mind/brain identity theory. The mind/brain identity theorists never wanted to maintain that talk about mental states was equivalent in meaning to talk about brain states. Mental concepts were irreducibly different in meaning from physical concepts, of which talk about the brain and its states form a sub-class. But at the level of the items or states of affairs that fall under the concepts, the mind/brain identity theory alleges that there are no separate mental facts over and above physical brain state facts, the mental facts being constituted by the physical facts comprising the material operations of the brain. In the case of the identity theory, the situation is reminiscent of the relation between the temperature of a gas and the kinetic energy of the molecules comprising it. Temperature talk and kinetic-energy-of-molecules talk are not synonymous: it took empirical research to discover the identity of the two apparently different phenomena, not merely reflection upon, and analysis of, the meanings of words. Yet for all that, there are no temperature facts apart from, and over and above, kinetic-energy-of-molecules facts.

The analytical behaviourist, by contrast, insists that statements describing mental or psychological states can be translated, without loss of meaning, into statements describing possible and actual behaviour. The idea is that everything that can be said in the familiar vocabulary of sensations, beliefs, thoughts, consciousness and so forth can somehow be better, or more perspicuously said, in other, non-mental terms, namely behavioural descriptions. These behavioural descriptions are to be thought of as revealing the true nature of the mental. Analytical behaviourism resembles other forms of reductionism, for example, phenomenalism, which maintains that all talk about physical objects can be rendered in terms of the actual and possible experiences an ideal observer of the objects in question would enjoy. Talk about tables, to take a well-worn illustration of the thesis, is to be translated into statements describing actual and possible table experiences that a suitably placed ideal observer would have. Likewise, reductionism regarding statements about dreams denies that dreams are private experiences which occur to people when they are asleep at night, but are better understood as statements describing their waking experiences in the morning.[2]

It is important to realize, right at the start, that if these patterns of analysis are to stand any chance of success, then the terms comprising the analysis must not contain, or presuppose, any of the mental vocabulary that is being analysed, otherwise the analysis will be circular. In effect, it will merely be repeating itself.

In case this rather abstract point is difficult to grasp at first, I offer a comparison in Exercise 4.1, which you should consider before continuing.

I want to provide an analysis of the concept of a cause, to explain what it means to talk of cause and effect, and, accordingly, I offer the following formula: 'A is the cause of B' is to be analysed as 'B happens because of A'. Can you see why this attempted analysis will not do?

Exercise 4.1

I think it is very clear why the analysis given in Exercise 4.1 has to be rejected, because the second statement comprising the alleged analysis is merely a paraphrase of the first. That is to say, it makes use of the very concept of a cause that it is supposed to be analysing. To say 'B happens because of A' is merely another way of saying 'A causes B'. Matters would not be improved if, instead of the original suggestion, I offered 'B is the effect or result of A' Or even 'A makes B occur'. All these, I suggest, carry us no further forward than the statement 'A causes B', with which we began.

A famous analysis of causality by David Hume (1711–76) takes into account the need for the analysis of a concept or a phenomenon to be rendered in genuinely other terms if the analysis is to be informative and to produce a better and clearer understanding. Hume's first shot at 'A causes B' was 'Whenever A occurs, B follows'. Causality, to use Hume's own expression, is the constant conjunction of certain types of event, a regularity that we have discovered on the basis of repeated experience of one sort of event, in a given set of circumstances, invariably being followed by another sort. We cannot logically deduce an effect from its cause, or a cause from its effect. It is merely that the two sorts of event constituting the causal relation have been found, as a matter of contingent fact, to be related in this way. This has the further important consequence that if two events are causally related, it must be possible to identify each event in complete independence of the other. In other words, there must be descriptions of the events that carry no logical implications for the existence or nature of any other event. We shall return to this important point later in chapter 6, section 6.5, as well as in chapter 7, sections 7.3 and 7.4.

Although this first analysis of causation is not adequate, since it is possible to think of many examples where one sort of event is regularly followed by another sort but one does not cause the other, it is at least genuine and informative and does not make the cardinal error of merely repeating itself.[3]

A shorthand way of conveniently labelling this error, using some Latin tags, is as follows. The phenomenon to be analysed is called the *analysandum*, and the analysis of the phenomenon is called the *analysans*. But, on pain of circularity (and ultimate triviality), the *analysans* must not contain the *analysandum*. (A parallel error can occur with definitions: the *definiens* (the definition of a term) must not contain the *definiendum* (the term to be defined).) The programme of phenomenalism referred to above was ultimately judged by philosophers to be incapable of achievement, because it was discovered that, sooner or later, the *analysans* had to incorporate the very notion of a physical object, the *analysandum*, that it was supposed to be rendering in purely experiential terms.

However, to return to the main discussion, the challenge facing the would-be analytical behaviourist is to produce an analysis of mental terms using a non-mentalistic vocabulary which employs behavioural descriptions alone, containing no expressions that contain, or presuppose, any psychological concepts. But what exactly is a behavioural description?

4.4   Hempel's 'hard' behaviourism

An answer to this question, as well as an understanding of a possible motivation to adopt behaviourism, is supplied by the contribution of Carl Hempel to the debate. Hempel (1905–97), was a member of the

Vienna Circle, the logical positivists, who were chiefly active in the 1920s and 1930s. The logical positivists were much concerned with the nature of scientific knowledge and methodology, and had the achievement of some kind of scientific unity as one of their principal goals. For them, all genuine knowledge and explanation was ultimately to be understood on the model of the physical sciences. Psychology was to be unified with the 'hard' science of physics by reduction to it. This conception of knowledge was informed by, and a consequence of, the adoption of the verification principle. According to this principle, unless a statement could be verified empirically (the non-empirical analytic truths of logic and mathematics having been set to one side), it would have to be rejected as devoid of meaning, as literally empty of any significance. The statement in question did not have to be verified in practice, but only in principle. For example, we cannot as yet find out whether it is true that there are planets in the Great Andromeda Nebula because it is too distant. But we know the kinds of thing we would have to do to verify that there are planets there – build a more powerful telescope, send up a space-probe and so forth.

The verificationist theory of meaning had the following consequence. If statements about mental states are construed as concerning logically private states of affairs accessible in principle only to the possessor of those states, as dualism maintains, then statements about the states of minds of others cannot, even in principle, be verified by third persons. But then talk about other minds becomes meaningless. In fact, although one might claim that at least one could verify the existence and nature of one's own mental states, the positivists would probably disqualify this as genuine verification on the grounds that it is not open to a public, intersubjective check. Given, however, that talk about others' mental states as well as one's own, manifestly *is* meaningful, the only way this is achievable is if states of mind are understood to consist in what is indisputably verifiable, namely outward, public behaviour.

It is important, however, to understand what is meant by 'behaviour'. Look now at Exercise 4.2 before continuing.

Consider, firstly the statements (a) 'Martin raised his arm' and (b) 'Martin's arm went up'. These are not equivalent in meaning. Can you see the difference in meaning between these two statements?   **Exercise 4.2**

The reason for the non-equivalence of statements (a) and (b) in Exercise 4.2 is as follows. Statement (a) reports something that Martin did, an action he performed, presumably intentionally, and standardly with some purpose in mind. Statement (b) does not report something

Martin did; it merely describes the motion of Martin's arm through space, at best leaving it open whether or not the arm rising was a raising of the arm by Martin, and at worst implying that the motion of the arm was *merely* a motion, i.e. not something that Martin did. Statement (a) entails statement (b), but (b) does not entail (a). If Martin raised his arm, then it follows his arm rose. But if Martin's arm rose, it does not follow that he raised it. His arm might have moved for reasons quite unconnected with his agency. For example, an external reason for his arm moving might be that someone else raised it. Equally, there might have been an internal reason, a muscle spasm perhaps, or the random firing of the nerves that control movement.

This means that there are two distinct modes of behavioural description possible. The first is constituted by descriptions of what people do, of the actions they perform, and the deeds they accomplish through their personal agency. Let us call these, for ease of reference, agential descriptions. The second mode of description characterizes what occurs in terms of bodily movements, often, by implication and context, excluding these from the realm of action, but, at other times, leaving it an open question whether the movements really do comprise actions, or whether they should be viewed as mere bodily movements – 'colourless' bodily movements, to employ the useful expression of the psychologist C. L. Hull. 'Colourless' bodily movement descriptions could, in theory, be refined into sophisticated descriptions of matter in motion, employing the terms and concepts of mathematics, geometry and physics.

Thus, instead of saying, for example, that Suzanne clutched her cheek, we could say instead that a certain piece of matter of such-and-such dimensions (her hand and arm) were observed to move from one set of co-ordinates in space to another set of co-ordinates over a specified period of time. Similarly, rather than saying that someone smiled, we would have to say instead that a piece of flesh of certain dimensions underwent changes in its shape, characterizing these alterations in the language of mathematics and topology.[4]

You should now look at Exercise 4.3 before reading on.

Exercise 4.3   Can you see what mode of description Hempel must choose for his behavioural analysis and why? Give reasons for your decision.

At the risk of importing circularity into his proposed analysis, Hempel must confine himself to using descriptions of colourless bodily movements. This would also accord with his avowed aim of reducing psychology to physics. In line with this, Hempel wrote: 'We see clearly that the meaning of a psychological statement consists solely in the function of abbreviating the description of certain modes of physical response characteristic of the bodies of men and animals.'[5] It has to be said, however, that Hempel's attempted behaviourist analysis, when it appeared, of a psychological statement, 'Paul has a toothache', was less of a success, instantly violating the stricture that no analysis should contain the very terms it is supposed to be analysing. Hempel's proposed analysis comprised five elements:[6]

1   Paul weeps and makes gestures of such and such kinds.
2   At the question 'What is the matter?', Paul utters the words 'I have a toothache'.
3   Closer examination reveals a decayed tooth with exposed pulp.
4   Paul's blood pressure, digestive processes, the speed of his reactions, show such and such changes.
5   Such and such processes occur in Paul's central nervous system.

Conditions (3), (4), and (5) do not appear to be essential to an analysis of the meaning of the statement 'Paul has a toothache'. It could be true that Paul had a toothache, even if a physical examination revealed no decayed tooth and no changes in his blood pressure, digestive processes or nervous system. Conversely, the physical changes just described might occur, and yet Paul feels no pain. To be sure, this might be puzzling, but it would not be self-contradictory to conjoin Paul's truthful report that he had toothache with the denial that anything out of the ordinary was happening to his teeth or body. (After all, think of people who have so-called psychosomatic pains for which no obvious physical cause is forthcoming.) This is sufficient to show that (3), (4) and (5), cannot be part of what it means for Paul to have toothache.

    That leaves (1) and (2). In relation to (1) the problem is that terms such as 'weeps' and 'gestures' already imply the attribution of mental states to Paul. 'Weeps' implies that Paul is suffering some unpleasant experience (a more neutral description would be 'water is coming out of Paul's eyes'), and 'gestures' suggests hand movements made by Paul with the intention of indicating the place and intensity of the pain, and perhaps to get help and sympathy.

    In relation to (2), a further difficulty that infects the analysis is that it is clear that Paul cannot respond to the question unless he understands it. Moreover, he must affirm the words that come out his mouth, that is to say, he must know what the words mean and intend them to answer the speaker's question.[7] But understanding, knowing, affirming and intending are all behaviourally unanalysed mental terms. Lastly, Paul will only respond to the question in the way he does, if he wants to tell the truth. It might be that Paul is suffering, but not from toothache, and he wishes to conceal the real reason for his distress. But 'wanting' is again a mental or psychological term which the behavioural analysis is supposed to be eschewing in order to avoid the charge of circularity.

4.5   Specifying patterns of behaviour

A serious attempt to carry out the analysis of mental terms in a non-circular way has to face a number of difficulties. The first problem concerns which patterns of behaviour, characterized purely as bodily movements, the motion of matter through space, are to comprise the analysis. The root of the problem lies in the fact that there is no neat one-to-one correspondence between types of action and types of bodily movement. This is reminiscent of the difficulty that confronted the type-type mind/brain identity theorists: a given type of mental state might be identical with C-fibres firing in Keith's brain, but Z-fibres firing in Zielfa's brain or even P-fibres firing in Pippa's brain. Although every token of a type of mental state is identical with a token of some type of brain state, it is not necessarily one and the same type of brain state on every occasion: a token of a given type of mental state is multiply realizable in different types of brain state. So it is with actions. Every token of a type of action will be identical with a token of some type of bodily movement (movement includes stillnesses), but it is not necessary that each token of a given type of action must find its embodiment in exactly the same type of bodily movement on every occasion when it occurs.

Before reading on, consider the question in Exercise 4.4.

Exercise 4.4   Can you see the threat posed by the multiple realizability of actions to the behavioural analysis of mental states?

The threat suggested in Exercise 4.4 is that the analysis could never be carried through to completion. To see this, consider again the first two items in Hempel's purported behavioural analysis of 'Paul has a toothache'. Hempel translates this into 'Paul weeps, makes various sorts of gesture, and when asked what is wrong, utters the words "I have a toothache".' Well, Paul *may* do these things, but there is an indefinite variety of other things he might do instead which could equally count as behavioural expressions of the pain he feels. He might, for example, shout out, scream, reach for the whisky bottle, apply oil of cloves, sit there in grim silence or thump the bed. If he is a monoglot Frenchman, he will not utter the English words 'I have a toothache', but the French equivalent. On the other hand, if he is a Filipino, he might simply moan 'Agoy!' Remember: if the analysis is to be successful, it must mention all those types of behaviour, and only those types of behaviour, that are capable of constituting Paul's expression of pain. This suggests that, following Hempel's proposal, the analysis will look something like this:

Paul has the toothache = *Either* Paul is groaning *or* he is wincing *or* tears are coming out of his eyes *or* he is uttering the words 'I am in pain' *or* their various foreign equivalents *or* he is reaching for the whisky bottle *or* . . .

There are at least two things wrong with this analysis. Firstly, it appears that it could never be completed: there is an indefinite variety of things Paul might do. Secondly, the items on this list mention actions. But descriptions of actions are terms that implicitly refer to mental states and are prohibited from inclusion in the analysis. This means that each type of action-description in turn will itself need to be cast into a lengthy and complex disjunction of the various types of bodily movement through which the action could theoretically manifest itself. Thus it strongly appears that the analysis could never be carried through to a final conclusion.

Consider also that if the problem of specifying which behaviours are to constitute the analysis of a simple report of a sensation such as toothache looks hard, consider how much more difficult such an analysis would be to carry out when it needs to refer to the behavioural manifestations of a complex and abstract belief. Suppose I believe that no one as yet has been able to explain what consciousness is, and why it exists. How should this belief be analysed in behavioural terms? One obvious way, perhaps, is through my verbal expression of the belief by means of the utterance: 'I believe that no one as yet has been able to explain what consciousness is, and why it exists.' But we have already noted that such an analysis covertly contains mental items and therefore has to be rejected. Most importantly, however, it should be clear that there is a massively indefinite variety of ways in which I, or someone else, might express the belief about the intractability of providing an account of consciousness, and this means that the prospect of achieving a successful analysis recedes even further.

However, according to John Foster, this is not necessarily a conclusive objection. It may only show that 'in the case of at least some (and perhaps all) psychological statements, the linguistic items which make explicit their ultimately non-mentalistic content are of infinite length, thus showing that the content itself, in its fully analysed form, is of infinite complexity'.[8]

In so far as I understand him on this matter, what Foster is maintaining is that this does not mean that the notion of a non-mentalistic analysis of mental items is incoherent, just because, by its very nature, it could never be encompassed by us. All it shows ultimately, perhaps, are that there are things that we can say by means of a mentalistic vocabulary that we cannot manage to say purely by the use of a putative physicalist translation of that vocabulary.

Another obstacle to the analysis we need to consider is this: how are we to identify which types of colourless bodily movements are to be included in it, and which are to be excluded? There is nothing in the description of colourless bodily movements as such which provides a clue to their possible inclusion or exclusion in any particular pattern of behavioural analysis of a mental item. In other words, considered in themselves from the point of view of physical science, the various kinds of bodily movement form no natural or obvious grouping, such that we can read off from them which are to be included and which excluded from a behavioural translation of a particular mental state. It would appear that their identification can only be approached through the identification of the possible set of actions selected to comprise the initial stage of the analysis. The idea is this: think of which set of actions most plausibly could serve as the behavioural manifestations of a particular type of mental state. Then, reflecting upon these actions, try to imagine the gross bodily movements that would need to figure in their execution and those that would be excluded. For example, consider the action 'scoring a goal by kicking the ball into the net'. Movements of the leg of various types could figure in the analysis but not, say, movements of the head. However, what this is leading up to is that the identification of the movements has to proceed via the identification of the action. It is the action that gives the group of movements their unity, and it is only via the action that the grouping is identifiable and intelligible. But this means that the analysis relies upon an indispensable reference to a mentalistic item for its execution, and it was precisely all reference to such items that was to be excluded from the analysis on pain of circularity.[9]

4.6   Circularity and infinite regression

The actions we perform do not result from single mental states, but combinations of mental states. For example, suppose Manjit believes that the shop across the road contains cigarettes, but he has just given up smoking. Clearly, he will not cross the road with the intention of entering the shop and purchasing the cigarettes. On the other hand, if he hasn't given up smoking and wants to smoke, then this, in combination with his belief that cigarettes are to be found in the shop, will lead to him crossing the road.

With this in mind, let us suppose we want to analyse the mentalistic statement, 'Manjit wants a packet of cigarettes', behaviourally. How will the analysis proceed? We might try rendering this by saying that Manjit will go and buy some cigarettes. But clearly this is too simple. He won't do this if his intention to give up smoking is stronger than his desire to smoke, or if he believes he hasn't sufficient money to pay for the cigarettes, or that the shop is shut or temporarily out of cigarettes and so on. So it would appear that any attempt to spell out Manjit's desire for cigarettes purely in behavioural terms will involve a reference to other mental states, in this case a number of beliefs. But, fairly obviously, the analysis cannot be allowed to contain unanalysed mental terms such as 'belief', and some way of fleshing out what beliefs amount to in terms of behaviour will have to be found. The problem is that it appears that any attempt to spell out how Manjit is likely to behave, given that he believes the shop sells cigarettes, must involve a reference to Manjit's desires. His belief alone cannot motivate him to action, i.e. to behaving in a certain way. If Manjit is to cross the road and buy cigarettes, the belief needs to be combined not only with other beliefs but also with a desire for cigarettes. In fact, the matter is more complicated still, because Manjit's desire to buy cigarettes will only lead to action providing it is stronger than his other desires, such as the desire not to get knocked down crossing a busy street, or the desire to avoid crossing over into hot sunlight. Thus it appears that a behavioural analysis of a desire must involve a reference not only to other desires, but particularly to beliefs viewed as unanalysed mental items. And, likewise, a behavioural analysis of a belief must involve a reference not only to other beliefs but also to desires regarded as unanalysed mental items.

There are two circularities involved here, a larger one and a smaller one. The larger circularity is that no behavioural analysis may be allowed to contain unanalysed mental terms, and the problem is that however far we go in attempting to cash out mental items in terms of behavioural descriptions, a residue of unanalysed mental items will always be left, crying out for yet more behavioural analysis. It appears that this process will be unending, though arguably this does not ultimately compromise the analysis if Foster is correct.[10]

The smaller circularity consists in the fact that a behavioural analysis of a desire has to make use of the unanalysed notion of a belief, and the behavioural analysis of a belief has to make use of the unanalysed notion of a desire. Manjit's desire for a cigarette consists in, among other things, his crossing the road to the shop, given that he believes it sells cigarettes; and his belief that the shop sells cigarettes consists in, among other things, his crossing the road to the shop given that he desires a cigarette. In other words, the explanation of what it is for Manjit to want a cigarette involves a reference to Manjit's beliefs, and the explanation of what it is for Manjit to hold a belief about the availability of cigarettes involves a reference to Manjit's desires. Each half of the analysis takes in, as it were, the other half's washing.

However, it is arguable that this smaller circularity can be avoided. Sydney Shoemaker argues that the problem parallels the case of someone trying to give an account of what positive and electric charges are:

> Imagine someone whose beliefs about electric charge are summed up in the following sentence: 'Things with positive charge attract things with negative charge and repel things with positive charge; things with negative charge attract things with positive charge and repel things with negative charge; and negative charge can be induced in a rubber comb by rubbing it against wool.' And suppose he is asked to define 'positive charge' and 'negative charge' in terms of this set of beliefs. It might seem that there is no way he could do this without running into circularity, since each sort of charge is characterized in terms of its relation to the other.[11]

The solution, says Shoemaker, following a proposal by David Lewis, is to make use of the notion of a 'Ramsey sentence', so-called because it was invented by the Cambridge philosopher Frank Ramsey (1903–30). (We shall encounter the use of a Ramsey sentence again when we consider functionalism in chapter 5, section 5.5, where it is put to a similar purpose.)

A Ramsey sentence is constructed like this. The terms 'positive charge' and 'negative charge' are eliminated by being substituted by the terms 'properties F and G'. The original attempt to define positive and negative charge thus transforms into: 'For some properties F and G, things with F attract those with G and repel things with F; things with G attract things with F and repel things with G; and G can be induced in a rubber comb by rubbing it with wool.'

The phrase, 'For some properties F and G', which prefaces this definition, is another way of expressing what logicians call the existential quantifiers ∃(F) and ∃(G), which are to be read respectively as 'There are some things F such that . . .', and 'There are some things G such that . . .'. F and G do not mention the properties by name, and hence circularity can be avoided, since the terms being defined do not occur in the *definiens* of each definition (see section 4.3 if you have forgotten the meaning of this term).

4.7   Ryle's 'soft' behaviourism

In this section I want to say something about the importance of dispositions in analytical behaviourism, and I will approach this topic through a brief exploration of the work of Gilbert Ryle (1900–76), with whom the notion of a disposition is particularly associated. Ryle's behaviourism, in so far as it can properly be classified as behaviourism, is to be found in his book *The Concept of Mind*, first published in 1949.[12]

The motivation of Ryle's account of the nature of the mind is very different from Hempel's. Firstly, there is no evidence in Ryle's book that he subscribed to the verificationist theory of meaning outlined earlier. This is fortunate, as subsequent philosophical work on this issue has shown that verificationism is a dubious account of semantic content, fatally confusing being able to specify which state of affairs, if it occurred, would make a factual statement true with the quite different requirement of being able to tell whether or not the state of affairs in question does so obtain. Only the first of these two requirements can reasonably be viewed as spelling out what is essential for a factual statement to have significance.

Secondly, Ryle was no physicalist seeking to reduce psychology to physics. He was as suspicious of physicalist theories of the mind as he was contemptuous of Cartesian dualism, seeking to dissolve, rather than solve, the mind/body problem, by approaching the issue in a new way: '[T]he hallowed contrast between mind and matter will be dissipated, but dissipated not by either of the equally hallowed absorptions of Mind by Matter or of Matter by Mind, but in a quite different way.'[13]

In the introduction to his book, Ryle states that his avowed aim is to determine the logical cross-bearings of concepts of the mental, to enable people who can already talk sense *with* these concepts to be able, in addition, to talk sense *about* them, after the manner of the logical or philosophical map-maker who seeks to gain a synoptic view of the concepts by making clear their interrelations and the regulations governing their uses.

What this means, in practice, is that it is Ryle's aim to demolish the Cartesian conception of the mind as a ghostly non-physical entity existing over and above the familiar flesh-and-blood living human being, an entity whose states are supposed to be logically private in the sense explained earlier (chapter 1, section 1.5) to the individual whose mind is in question. However, it would be perfectly possible to repudiate dualism, without thereby being forced to abandon belief in the radical privacy of mental states, even while accepting that a commitment to dualism entails a commitment to acceptance of the privacy of the mental. Consequently, I shall consider Ryle's attack on these twin aspects of dualism separately.

Ryle's first aim is to repudiate utterly the Cartesian concept of mind as an immaterial substance linked in life to a corporeal machine, the body. Ryle characterizes this with, as he says himself, 'deliberate abusiveness', as 'The Dogma of the Ghost in the Machine.' It is, Ryle claims,

> entirely false, and false not in detail but in principle. It is not merely an assemblage of particular mistakes. It is one big mistake and a mistake of a special kind. It is namely a category mistake. It represents the facts of mental life as if they belonged to one logical type or category (or range of types or categories), when they actually belong to another.[14]

The mistake Ryle is thinking of is this. There are not, in addition to living human beings whose outward behaviour and inner workings are as public and open to scrutiny as the careers of trees, crystals and planets, ghostly entities called minds, whose inner 'paramechanical' workings are accessible only to the persons to whom those minds happen to belong. A person does not live through two collateral histories, the one consisting in outward public physical doings, and the other consisting in ghostly happenings on a private mental stage.

To illustrate the point he is making, Ryle offers what has become a famous analogy. We are to imagine a foreign visitor being shown around Oxford University. He visits the various colleges, the Bodleian Library, the laboratories, the Examination Schools in the High Street, the sub-faculty of Philosophy library and so forth. At the end of his tour, he says, 'Thank you very much. But unfortunately I have not yet been shown the university itself.' His mistake is obvious. He is thinking of the university as if it were a building itself, like the individual colleges or the examination school, and capable of existing independently of them, rather than realizing that the totality of what he has seen *is* the university.

The same mistake is evident, according to Ryle, in supposing that, in addition to the overt public performances of human beings, the purposeful, intelligent actions they carry out, and operations they engage in, there is something else, a non-physical entity called the mind, existing over and above the body, which is the true, hidden repository of a person's intellectual and mental repertoire.

In accordance with this, Ryle writes, in what is a pretty typical passage: 'Overt intelligent performances are not clues to the workings of minds; they *are* those workings. Boswell described Johnson's mind when he described how he wrote, talked, ate, fidgeted and fumed.'[15] In other words, for Ryle, Johnson's behaviour is not evidence that something is going on behind it in the secret recesses of Johnson's mind. Rather, Johnson's mental processes are manifest in his behaviour. His overt intelligent performances are not a substitute for workings of his mind, a mere stand-in, or proxy. Instead, they *are* those workings, fully open to public view and inspection.

It is thus not difficult to appreciate why Ryle should have been labelled a behaviourist. If mental processes are not ghostly concealed processes in an immaterial soul, and if the workings of a person's mind are identified with overt public performances, the reduction of mind to matter also having been repudiated, it is difficult to see what else the facts about a person's mental life could amount to, if not facts about his behaviour. (Another option would be functionalism – see chapter 5 – but this option was not open to Ryle, as the theory had not yet been invented at the time he was writing.)

Notice, however, that Ryle's behaviourism is a far cry from Hempel's ideal of rendering all descriptions of behaviour in terms of colourless bodily movements and the concepts of physics. Ryle is quite clearly not in the least worried that his analysis will be accused of circularity, because he is not attempting to reduce mental states to purely physical descriptions after the manner of the logical positivists. This is why Ryle's variety of behaviourism, by contrast with the 'hard' behaviourism of Hempel, has been labelled 'soft' behaviourism.[16]

4.8   Ryle and dispositions

Nothing very much has been said so far about the need to include descriptions not only of actual, but of potential behaviour in any proposed behavioural analysis of mental states, and to this we now turn. It would be highly implausible to maintain the thesis that mental states consist entirely in actual overt public behaviour, because this fails to accommodate the commonplace fact that people can be in all kinds of mental state without ever revealing these through their behaviour. For instance, at this moment there are all kinds of beliefs and intentions that I harbour, but someone observing me would not be able to tell exactly what beliefs and intentions these are. Even if I had a toothache, this would not necessarily reveal itself in my behaviour. For example, if I am at a concert and anxious not to spoil the enjoyment of others, I might well sit there and suffer in silence, no one being able to ascertain from my composure the agonies I am enduring.

To avoid this difficulty, the notion of a disposition to behave was invoked. This means that the behavioural analysis has to include not merely actual behaviour, but potential behaviour as well. For me to be described truly as having the toothache, it is not necessary that I should actually be groaning, clutching my cheek and so forth. Rather, it is enough that I am disposed to groan, clutch my cheek, etc. in the appropriate circumstances. In other words, it is to say that if certain conditions were fulfilled, then I would groan. The same applies to intentional states such as beliefs and desires. To describe me as believing that the moon is made of green cheese is not, improbably, to commit oneself to saying I actually am avowing this belief, but only that, in the right circumstances, I would avow it.

Ryle's way of making the point is to say that to have a belief is to have a tendency or to be prone to act in a certain way, and he goes on to explain this by using the examples of brittleness and solidity. To say that glass, for example, is brittle, is not to say it actually is shattering, but only that if it were struck, then it would shatter. Similarly, to describe sugar as soluble is to say that if it were placed in water, then it would dissolve. According to Ryle, for something to have a disposition is simply for a whole lot of hypothetical 'if . . . then . . .' statements to be true. In line with his denial of mental states as events different in kind from, and concealed behind, behaviour, Ryle is anxious to emphasize that to have a disposition is *not* to be in a certain kind of state: 'To possess a dispositional property is not to be in a particular state, or to undergo a particular change; it is to be bound or to be liable to be in a particular state, or to undergo a particular change when a particular condition is realized.'[17] Before reading on, look at Exercise 4.5.

How plausible do you find Ryle's claim that having a disposition consists simply in a set of hypothetical 'if . . . then . . .' statements being true, providing the appropriate conditions are realized? Consider your response and discuss it with someone else before reading my comments.

Exercise 4.

Most philosophers would now agree that there is more to a disposition than what Ryle claims it to be. The reason that glass has a disposition to break when struck – the explanation of its brittleness – is to be found in facts about its underlying micro-structure. If the micro-structure were to be altered in an appropriate manner, as when glass is annealed, then its tendency to shatter when struck is much reduced, or even removed, as in the case of toughened glass. By parity of argument, to have a belief (or any other mental state) is not merely to be inclined to behave in a certain way, but to be in an inner state, which may, in the appropriate circumstances, manifest itself in outward behaviour. However, once the propriety of thinking of beliefs and other mental states as inner causes of outward behaviour has been allowed, behaviourism has been abandoned.

This critique of Ryle's refusal to countenance dispositional mental states as consisting in anything more than tendencies to behave in particular ways, leads to another important criticism of behaviourism. The essence of the objection is this: it is a commonplace that we explain why people exhibit the behaviour they do in terms of their states of mind. For example, a sharp pain makes me cry out. The realization that I've left my keys in the door leads me to turn round and go home. The desire for some cigarettes, coupled with the belief that the shop over the road sells them, explains why I cross the road.

But if the pain, the realization and the desire are all to be rendered in purely behavioural terms, then how can they be appealed to in order to explain my behaviour, since this will amount to attempting to explain one bit of behaviour in terms of another bit. It will be tantamount to the futile task of trying to explain behaviour by reference to itself. Items that explain behaviour cannot, so to speak, be on the same level as the behaviour they are invoked to explain. Rather, they must be conceived of as the underlying causes of the surface behaviour in question, i.e. they must themselves be non-behavioural in nature.

The point was well made by Hilary Putnam when writing about what we mean when we attribute a disease such as multiple sclerosis to someone. It is plausible to say that 'Normally people who have multiple sclerosis have some or all of the following symptoms' is a necessary (analytic) truth. In other words, it is part of what we mean by 'multiple sclerosis' that normally it gives rise to certain symptoms. But, it must be emphasized, this does not mean that talk about the disease, multiple sclerosis, can be translated, without loss of meaning, into talk about the symptoms of multiple sclerosis. This would be analogous to the error the analytical behaviourists make when they try to render talk about 'pain' in terms actual and potential pain-behaviour. The error that underpins both these attempts is the mistake of trying to make *causes* logical constructions out of their *effects*. But pains and diseases are causes of behaviour and symptoms respectively, and cannot be reduced to, and constructed out of, their effects.[18]

4.9   The denial of the subjective 'inner' features of mental states

One of the strongest objections to behaviourism derives from out-raged common sense. Because of its insistence on reducing mental states to patterns of outward behaviour, or dispositions to engage in such behaviour, behaviourism effectively denies the existence of the 'inner' aspects of mental states, their qualia. But obviously there is more to having toothache than groaning and clutching one's cheek, or even being disposed to do so. When one goes to a dentist or takes some aspirin, the aim is not merely to prevent oneself from behav-ing, or being disposed to behave, in a certain way, but to get rid of the unpleasant sensation, the pain one is experiencing. It is for this reason that behaviourists were accused of feigning anaesthesia. Accounting for sensations in behavioural terms comprises a particu-larly intractable difficulty, because it is of the essence of sensations to possess a phenomenology. In short, there is something it feels like to have an itch, or pins and needles in your foot, or an ache in the shoulder. These all involve consciousness: there is something it is like to undergo such experiences.

   The experience of visualizing something in 'the mind's eye' is also peculiarly difficult to account for in behaviourist terms. We unhesi-tatingly think of this experience as consisting in private mental imagery, which frequently does not, and does not need to, manifest itself in outward behaviour. But in his anxiety to repudiate the exis-tence of inner states, Ryle writes:

[A] person picturing his nursery is, in a certain way, like that person seeing his nursery, but the similarity does not consist in his really looking at a real likeness of his nursery, but in his seeming to see his nursery itself, when he is not really seeing it. He is not being a spectator of a resemblance of his nursery, but he is resembling a spectator of his nursery.[19]

Before reading my response to Ryle's account, look at Exercise 4.6.

How plausible do you find Ryle's account of what it is to picture one's nursery to oneself? What criticisms can you make of this account?

Exercise 4.6

What Ryle is maintaining is thin and unconvincing. To begin with, how could I resemble a spectator of my nursery if I were lying in bed, undressed, in the dark, engaging in a spot of nostalgia, by visualizing my nursery to myself? Besides, as I have already remarked, the experience of visualizing my nursery is a prime example of the sort of case where we would want to say that a private episode of consciousness, not capturable in terms of outward public behaviour, is integrally involved.

4.10   The denial of first-person knowledge and authority regarding mental states

We allowed in the first chapter (section 1.7) that there are occasions when it seems that others know our own minds better than we do ourselves, temporarily requiring us to adopt a third-person perspective from which to make an assessment of our state of mind. But for most of the time, and especially as regards non-intentional states such as sensations, we are in the best position to say what we are feeling or thinking. Moreover, we can describe our sensations, or avow our beliefs or intentions, without having to go through any process of finding out what these are through observation or inference from more basic data. In particular, I do not need to observe my own behaviour in a mirror or on a video in order to be able to say what I believe or how I feel. Behaviourism, by making my mental states a matter of how I behave, reverses all this, and leads to jokes such as: 'One behaviourist meets another on the street. You feel fine, he says to the other. How do I feel?' Or one behaviourist says, after making love to another: 'It was great for you. How was it for me?' To this, we may add the further observation that if there were nothing more to being in pain or holding a belief than behaving or being disposed to behave in a certain way, we would have the absurd consequence that a person would have to wait until he or she exhibited the appropriate behaviour before being able to report his or her state of mind.

4.11   Can the possibility of pretence show that behaviourism cannot be correct?

It might be said that behaviourism cannot be correct because a person could be merely pretending to feel pain. That is to say, there might be plenty of pain-behaviour but no corresponding pain. How then can pain be identical with pain-behaviour, since one can occur without the other? The behaviourist, however, has a comeback. The point of the example is to show that there can be behaviour without a corresponding mental state – in this case pain – and hence there must be more to mental states than merely behaviour. However, whilst there are independently good reasons for thinking this con-clusion to be true, it does not seem that it can be established on the basis of the possibility of pretence. Pretence implies the presence of an intention to pretend, and this intention, the behaviourist might argue, can be analysed into the mock pain-behaviour that constitutes the pretence. To put this another way, it is true that the pain-behaviour cannot be identified with pain, for the person is feeling none. But the pain-behaviour can still be identified with *some* state of mind, the behaviourist can contend, namely the more complex mental state of intending to pretend. Hence the argument from the possibility of pretence cannot show what it was intended to show, namely that, despite an abundance of behaviour, no mental states are present, and thus behaviour cannot constitute mental states, contrary to what behaviourism maintains.

The possibility of zombies, however, which was discussed briefly in chapter 3, section 3.8.8, is sufficient to establish the falsity of behav-iourism. Zombies are physically just like ordinary human beings, except that they lack a mental life. They behave to all intents and purposes just like human beings, but they lack any consciousness or knowledge of the motions their bodies are making. In other words, zombies exhibit all the right sorts of behaviour as far as an external observer can tell, but, nevertheless, mentality is entirely absent. This does appear to be an intelligible fantasy, unvitiated by internal contradiction, and if this is indeed so, then behaviourism has to be rejected on this ground alone.[20]

The falsity of behaviourism would also be demonstrated by the converse possibility, namely the presence of mentality in the absence of any behavioural manifestations. Hilary Putnam has devised the following thought-experiment to provide a convincing case for this possibility. We are to imagine a race of super-Spartans or super-Stoics who constitute a community in which the adults have the ability to suppress successfully all involuntary pain-behaviour. Although they sometimes admit that they are in pain, they always do this in calm, well-modulated voices, even if they are suffering the torments of the damned. Neither do they groan, scream, wince, sweat nor grit their teeth. They admit it takes a great effort of will to do this, but they have important ideological reasons for behaving in the way they do, and they undergo years of training to achieve the right standard of behaviour in the face of pain. It might be argued that the lack of pain-behaviour will only be found in adults who have been suitably conditioned, and that non-adults will exhibit unconditioned pain-reactions, thus giving the ascription of mental states to the community a toehold. However, in response to this objection Putnam elaborates the fantasy further. We are to suppose that after several millions of years, the super-Spartans begin having children who are born fully acculturated, speaking the adult language, sharing opinions about their society and also the beliefs about not giving any signs that one is in pain, unless it is by verbal report in a calm, unanxious and unconcerned manner. There are, then, no unconditioned pain-responses in this community, yet it would be crazy to take the position that because there is a total absence of natural, unconditioned pain-behaviour, the super-Spartans cannot have the capacity for experiencing pain to them.

Putnam also asks us to imagine super-super-Spartans, who inhabit the X-world. These people have been super-Spartans for so long that not only do they not evince unconditioned pain-behaviour, but they have begun to suppress all talk about pain. X-worlders do not admit to having pains, and pretend not to know either the word 'pain' or the experience to which it refers. Nevertheless, they do have pains and know that they do. Putnam concludes:

> If this last fantasy is not, in some disguised way, self-contradictory, then logical behaviourism is simply a mistake. Not only is the second thesis of logical behaviourism – the existence of a near-translation of pain into behaviour talk – false, but so is even the first thesis – the existence of 'analytic entailments'. Pains are responsible for certain kinds of

behaviour – but only in the context of our beliefs, desires, ideological attitudes, and so forth. From the statement 'X has a pain' by itself no behavioural statement follows – not even a behavioural statement with a 'normally' or a 'probably' in it.[21]

The most extreme example of mental states without behaviour is provided by the possibility of disembodied existence. It might be argued that only a limited range of experiences could be ascribed to disembodied persons, since they would not have bodies in which to feel pains, or eyes with which they could see. But there is no reason why it should not seem to such people that they had bodies and eyes, even though they did not, and that it seemed to them that they were feeling pains in these imaginary bodies and were having visual experiences as a result of the operations of their imaginary eyes. It is arguable that Descartes' argument from clear and distinct perception (see chapter 2, section 2.7.2), as well as Kripke's argument against the identity theory (see chapter 3, section 3.8.8), do succeed in establishing the possibility of disembodied mental states – that is, that even if such states cannot exist in this world, there is a possible world in which they do, and this is all that is needed to prove that analytical behaviourism is false.

Questions to think about

1   In your opinion, does behaviourism offer a clear and satisfactory solution to the mind/body problem?
2   Can behaviourism account for the existence of an inner mental life with no behavioural manifestations?
3   Could there be super-Spartans who feel pain but never exhibit pain-behaviour?
4   Do zombies represent a genuine possibility?
5   When I say 'I have an itch', am I describing something that is private to me?

Suggestions for further reading

- A clear and excellent introduction to analytical behaviourism can be found in Stephen Priest's book, *Theories of the Mind* (London: Penguin, 1991).
- An even brisker account is available in Paul Churchland's *Matter and Consciousness* (Cambridge, MA: MIT Press, 1984).
- One of the very best discussions can be found in Jaegwon Kim's *Philosophy of Mind* (Boulder, CO: Westview Press, 1996). This is very useful for beginning students who wish to go further.
- John Foster's treatment of behaviourism in his book *The Immaterial Self:*

A Defence of the Cartesian conception of the Mind (London: Routledge, 1991) is extremely rigorous and thorough. Not recommended for beginners, but very useful at a later stage.

- Peter Smith and O.R. Jones provide a stimulating and clear discussion of behaviourism in their book *The Philosophy of Mind* (Cambridge: CUP, 1986). It is highly recommended, especially for beginners.

5

FUNCTIONALISM

Objectives

As a result of reading this chapter you should:

- understand what a function is and what it means to characterize the mind as a function;
- understand the difference between metaphysical and psycho-functionalism;
- understand what computational or Turing machine functionalism is;
- understand some of the strengths of functionalism;
- understand the following objections and arguments to functionalism: liberalism; Chinese mind argument; Chinese room argument; arguments from inverted and absent qualia;
- understand what homuncular functionalism is, and the difficulties it faces;
- understand Jackson's argument against physicalism and be able to make some evaluation of it.

5.1   Introduction

Like analytical behaviourism, functionalism rejects the notion of the mind as an entity, a logical substance, whether this is thought of as a soul or, alternatively, as the brain. Functionalism, as the name implies, conceives of the mind as a function. But what is a function? An easy way to understand this is to think of a thermostat. The function of a

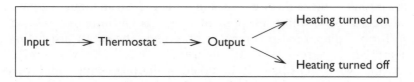

Figure 5.1   Function of a thermostat

thermostat is to regulate the temperature of a room or a building. It takes a certain input in the form of the ambient temperature and then, depending on how the thermostat has been set, it does either of the following: (1) it turns the heating system on because the room is too cold; (2) it turns the heating system off because the room is too warm. This is diagrammatically represented in figure 5.1. As the diagram helps to make clear, the function of a thermostat is what it does, the task it executes or the role it discharges. If you were in the market for a thermostat, it is the function that would be the focus of your interest. How the thermostat does what it does, what its internal arrangements are like to enable it to carry out its job and what it is made of are usually of secondary interest to the ordinary consumer, if of any interest at all. What actually goes on inside the thermostat is the concern of technical specialists, especially if it fails to function efficiently or stops working completely. The lesson I wish to draw from this example is that a clear distinction can be drawn between:

- the function of a thing – i.e. what job it performs;
- what set of arrangements enables the thing to discharge its function.

As soon as you start thinking about functions, myriads of examples suggest themselves. Artefacts of various kinds discharge functions: mousetraps, carburettors, telephones and computers. Human and animal biology also yield many instances of functions: think of the functions of the heart, the kidneys and the eye. And, lastly, human beings, both singly and collectively, discharge functions – for example, the roles of Queen, Prime Minister, Parliament, the Judiciary and so forth. In all these cases a sharp distinction can be drawn between the job that the artefact, the organ and the person (or the people) do and the material or formal arrangements that enable it to be carried out. More abstractly, the notion of a function can be illustrated mathematically. Consider the function $y = x^2$. Different values of the variable x – the input – are transformed into the output – the value of y – by being squared. So an input of 2 yields an output of 4, whilst an input of 12 yields an output of 144, and so forth. Compare also computer programs. The set of instructions comprising a program – an algorithm, as it is known – which specifies what steps have to be taken in the processing of information, is clearly also an example of a function. Data are entered into the computer which then, according to the particular algorithm being employed, transforms this data into an output.

Reflection on these examples in the light of the distinction between a thing's function and the arrangements which enable the function to be carried out, leads to the realization that functions, by their very nature, are multiply realizable. That is, one and the same sort of function can be carried out by an indefinite variety of arrangements. We might say that one and the same function can be embodied or incarnated or realized or instantiated in different sorts of arrangement. If the thermostat breaks down, I could take over its function, boring though it would be to sit in a room all day turning the heating on and off. If someone suffers heart failure, then a mechanical heart can be fitted to pump blood around the body. And if the Queen dies, the monarchy will not come to an abrupt halt, because Prince Charles can step swiftly into Her Majesty's shoes.

The point I am leading up to is that a function can be specified abstractly, and in complete independence of whatever it is that enables the function to be discharged. Quite clearly, the function cannot be identified with the material arrangements that make it possible, or with the person who discharges the role, as these may change and yet the function continues to be executed. Consequently, it would be wrong to conceive of the function as a physical thing or process. But if the function is not physical in nature, does this mean it is non-physical after the manner of the Cartesian soul? Is it like a ghostly soul-substance? I suggest we desist from thinking of functions in this manner, lest we overpopulate the universe with abstract entities and also generate the pseudo-problem of how functions relate to, and interact with, physical things. A function is best conceived of as neither physical nor non-physical. It resists classification into either category, a conclusion, as we shall see later, that chimes in with what many functionalist philosophers have had to say about the nature of functions.

However, although functions are not identical with the arrangements that embody them, they require some kind of embodiment or other if they are to be carried out. If the function of delivering petrol to the engine is actually to occur, some set of arrangements must be in place for this to happen. Without an embodiment of some kind, nothing can or will happen. Carburation would remain merely an idea in the inventor's mind, something on paper that in theory could work, but which won't take place until a carburettor is actually constructed and fitted.

5.2   Metaphysical functionalism

What happens if we try applying a functional analysis to mental states, say a particular type of mental state, a pain? Suppose we take our cue from the example of the thermostat. The function of a thermostat is to take a certain input and to transform it into a certain output. Well, perhaps pain can also be conceived of in the same way. What typically happens when someone experiences a pain is that damage occurs to some part of their body, pain is experienced, and as a result the person winces and groans or rubs the affected part, having in the meantime attempted to remove him- or herself from whatever is causing the pain.

Put more formally in functional terms, a pain can be functionally specified as comprising an input in the way of tissue damage, an output in the form of pain-behaviour – wincing, groaning and so forth – and a relation to other mental states – typically, it provokes a desire to be rid of the pain. Naturally, as a mental state itself, the desire to be rid of the pain will also need a functional specification (see figure 5.2). At this level of analysis, the specification of mental states is

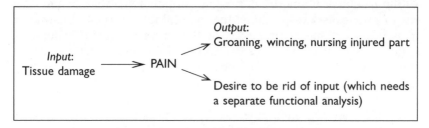

Figure 5.2   Functional specification of pain

highly abstract. Once we have characterized the mental state in terms of inputs, outputs and relations to other mental states, we have provided an exhaustive description of it: the mental state, conceived as a function, comprises nothing more than the system of relations described in terms of inputs, outputs and other mental states, which in turn are also functionally analysed. This kind of functionalism, in which the mental state is specified purely formally, is generally known as metaphysical functionalism, although it is sometimes called plain functionalism. This formal specification is arrived at purely by philosophical analysis and trades on our common-sense understanding of what mental states are. It is supposed to be the expression of a conceptual truth, something that is necessarily the case and could not be otherwise.

5.3 Psycho-functionalism

However, this leaves open the question of what set of arrangements enables the function, formally specified, to be executed, and this cannot be gathered from knowledge of the function alone. It is perfectly possible to appreciate what thermostats, hearts and monarchs do without having the faintest idea of how thermostats and hearts are constructed, or who the monarch actually is. From the point of view of the metaphysical functionalist, the mind is a black box, as the psychologists call it, mediating between inputs and outputs, but opaque as regards what actually takes place within it. It works all right, but how it works is unknown.

Now although there are functionalists who, in theory, are willing to allow that what is in the black box is something non-physical in the shape of ghostly soul, the function being discharged by processes within its ethereal innards, in practice all functionalists are materialists or physicalists, maintaining that mental functions are incarnated in neurophysiological processes in the brain and central nervous system. They argue that since the notion of the soul is highly dubious (see chapter 2, section 2.8.4), only the second materialist alternative is a realistic option. Nevertheless, providing that the idea of nonphysical souls makes sense, the first option represents a genuine possibility, because metaphysical functionalism is neutral between a materialist and an immaterialist metaphysics. The function itself, as I was at pains to stress earlier, is classifiable as neither nonphysical nor physical, and can never be strictly identified with the system of arrangements that happen to instantiate it, whatever the nature of those arrangements ultimately turns out to be. Indeed, the neutrality of metaphysical functionalism was perceived as an advantage by materialists, precisely because it did not foreclose the

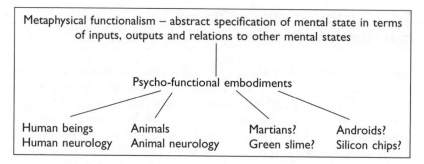

Figure 5.3   Metaphysical and psycho-functionalism

possibility that the function could be discharged by purely material sets of arrangements.

No amount of philosophical theorizing or speculation alone will reveal what neurophysiological mechanisms are responsible for embodying pain as a functional state. This is a matter that requires empirical investigation. This is the project of psycho-functionalism, the job of spelling out the details of what has come to be called the causal occupant of the functional role. In human beings, as we have said, this will consist in processes in the human nervous system. But psycho-functionalists, not forgetting their metaphysical roots, were willing to go further and allow that it is conceivable that mental functions may also be embodied in other quite different sorts of physical arrangement. If there are Martians whose heads contain the traditional green slime, then it is possible that mental functions may be executed by this slime. But, equally, if there are androids such as Data in Star Trek, then mentality may find its embodiment in the chips comprising a silicon brain. The diagram in figure 5.3 sums this up.

Functionalism is thus well placed to circumvent the objection that played a major role in seeing off the type-type mind/brain identity theory, namely that it is grossly implausible to insist that a given type of mental state is always and everywhere identical with a given type of brain state. Indeed, the functionalist theory, partly inspired by the rise of computer science, was expressly designed to accommodate the objection and, in so doing, nullify it. It would appear to secure all the advantages of materialism without ever strictly having to identify with this position, since functions are not reducible to the material arrangements that make them possible, contrary to what the mind/brain identity theory affirms.

5.4   Computational or Turing machine functionalism

The whole purpose of computers is to compute functions. That indeed is how a computer may be defined. It is a device that is designed to take a certain input and transform it, according to a set of instructions, step by step, into an output. (Obviously I'm thinking of digital computers here. I leave aside analogue computers such as neural nets, which work on an entirely different basis.) As John Searle has often reminded us, in any given age the latest technology has been seized upon as a model for the mind. The ancient Greeks, Searle reports, thought that the mind resembled a catapult. Leibniz, as we saw (chapter 1, section 1.1), envisaged the mind as a mill. Whilst in the twentieth century, for the physiologist Sir Charles Sherrington (1857–1952), the mind was like a telephone exchange. Small wonder then, in this age of computing and information processing, that minds have been conceived of as natural computing devices which take information in the form of physical or sensory stimulation and process it into a behavioural output.

How do computers compute functions? An algorithm is a procedure, a method of computing a function. It consists in a finite number of discrete steps, which have to be taken if the values that comprise the input to a function are to be transformed, step by step, into the output of the function. Each step to be taken is specifiable in a definite, clear and unambiguous way, which does not require any special insight or feat of imagination.

To understand this more clearly, consider the following example. Suppose you empty your pockets of coins and put them down randomly in rows, just as they come to hand. Suppose, further, that your rows of coins turn out to be as shown in table 5.1. If I now asked you to put these pieces in order, from the highest to the lowest denomination, you would very rapidly pick up the £2 coin, then the £1 coin which you would place below it, then the 50p piece and so forth. If I were to ask you how you did this, you would probably just say that you could recognize the value of each of the coins and, knowing this, it was a simple matter to put them in order. But the request I made to you to arrange the coins from the highest to the lowest is not an order we can give to a computer. We can't just say to the computer, as we can to a human being, put the pieces in order and then seriously expect the computer to respond. The basic instruction – and obviously it would have to be in a programming language – to enable the computer to carry out the task would be something like this.

Table 5.1

Row	Coin
1st	£2
2nd	2p
3rd	50p
4th	20p
5th	1p
6th	10p
7th	£1
8th	5p

Table 5.2

Row	Coin
1st	£2
2nd	50p
3rd	20p
4th	2p
5th	10p
6th	£1
7th	5p
8th	1p

Compare the magnitudes of the coins in the first two rows of the table. If the magnitude of the coin in the first row is higher than that of the coin in the second row, leave both coins where they are; otherwise, move the coin in the second row to the first row. In the case in question (see table 5.1), it is obvious that the coins will be left untouched. Now repeat this procedure with the coins in the second and third rows. In this case the 50p piece will move to the second row and the 2p piece will move into the third row. Now compare the coins in the third and fourth rows and carry out the same procedure. Do this all the way down until rows seven and eight have been compared. Table 5.2 shows the order of the coins after carrying out this procedure just once.

Clearly, as we can see in table 5.2, the coins are still not ranked from the highest to the lowest denomination, but the computer could be instructed to run through the procedure again, and in fact as many times as necessary until no further alterations to the positions of the coins needed to be made, when the program can terminate (in fact, it takes three more run throughs – try it!). It would be incredibly tedious and time-consuming for a human being to go through this procedure every time coins or columns of figures had to be put in order, say when listing students' examination marks. But what I have described, in effect, albeit somewhat simply and crudely, is an algorithm, a series of discrete steps, which a non-intelligent, non-understanding, mindless device such as a computer could take to transform randomly ordered denominations of coins into an ordered list, going from the highest to the lowest value of the denominations.

I must now introduce the idea of a Turing machine, named after the mathematician Alan Turing (1912–54), a mathematical genius who, among other achievements, broke the Nazi's ENIGMA code during World War Two. A Turing machine is not an actual machine, but a blueprint for a possible machine. Basically, such a machine is a way of explicating how algorithms can be computed. The machine consists of a tape divided into squares, and a device, a tape-head, that can write a symbol in a blank square or overwrite an existing symbol, one symbol per square only. The tape-head can also read the symbols on the tape. The tape can be moved from right to left, and left to right, but only one square at a time. The machine is also capable of being in either of two internal states, which I shall call S1 and S2. There are just four things the machine can do: move the tape either left or right; write a symbol on the tape; erase a symbol on the tape; change its internal state from S1 to S2 or S2 to S1. What the machine actually does in operation is specified by what is called its machine table. The machine table consists of a list of instructions that specify what the machine is to do. The general form of the instructions will be that if the machine is in state S1 and reading a certain symbol, X, then it will either write or erase a symbol, stay in state S1 or change to state S2, and move the tape either left or right. A simple and perspicuous example of this procedure, which also illustrates how a Turing machine can add 1 to an existing number, is provided by Tim Crane in his excellent book, *The Mechanical Mind*.[1]

Crane asks us to imagine that numbers can be represented by simple strokes, such as the chalk-marks a prisoner might make on the wall of the cell to count off the passing days. So ||||| means 5, || means 2, | means 1 and so forth. These marks can be written on a tape – one mark per square – and different groups of numbers can be separated by zeros thus:

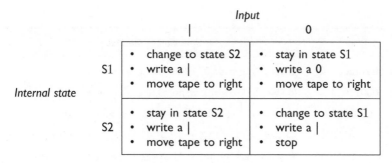

Figure 5.4   Machine table

... 000|||||000|000|||||| represents the sequence of numbers 5, 1, 7 ...

The dots show that the tape goes off in both directions indefinitely.

What we now need is a machine table which specifies what the machine is to do in order to add 1 to an existing number – see figure 5.4. Suppose the machine is now presented with a tape with a 2 on it, so it will look like this (remembering that 2 will be represented by 2 vertical strokes):

0   0   0 | | 0   0   0

The machine has to perform a very simple operation, namely to add 1 to this number by following the instructions given in the machine table. It starts off in S1 reading the first symbol on the extreme right of the tape. The instruction in the table says that the machine is to write a 0, stay in S1, and move the tape one square to the right. This it does, and still being in state S1 it encounters another 0 in the column next to the extreme right, so once again it writes a 0 and moves the tape one space to the right. As the tape moves from left to right and the machine follows the instructions in the machine table, what we get at each step is shown in table 5.3 (the line under the figures indicates which square the tape-head is reading and ∧ stands for the tape-head, which remains fixed as the tape moves square by square to the right). At (f), the machine is in state S2 when it encounters a |. The machine table instructs it to write a |, change back to state S1 and then stop. What is now on the tape are three and not two vertical strokes, representing the number 3. In this way, by moving

Table 5.3

Tape	Operation of machine
(a) 00011000	In state S1, reads 0, writes 0, moves tape to right
(b) 00011000	In state S1, reads 0, writes 0, moves tape to right
(c) 00011000	In state S1, reads 0, writes 0, moves tape to right
(d) 00011000	Changes to state S2, reads 1, writes 1, moves tape to right
(e) 00011000	Stays in state S2, reads 1, writes 1, moves tape to right
(f) 00011000	In state S2, reads 0, writes 1, changes to state S1, stops
(g) 00111000	In state S1: reading on tape has changed, machine has stopped

Direction of movement of tape ⟶

the tape one square at time and writing or erasing a symbol, the machine has added 1 to 2.

Adding 1 to 2 is a very simple operation, but if this computation can be done by a Turing machine, then in theory any function capable of computation by following an algorithm (a series of simple, discrete steps) can be done on such a machine. To be sure, to execute other operations, such as multiplication, division, factorials and so forth, the set of instructions comprising the machine table will have to be more complex, but in principle there is no barrier to devising more complex tables. Of course, the numbers in real computers are not represented by a series of vertical strokes as in the example given above, but are written in binary code: $1 = 1, 2 = 10, 3 = 11, 4 = 100$, etc., but the principles of operation of the Turing machine stay the same.

Turing machine tables can be used to carry out all sorts of function, not purely mathematical ones. An example (provided by the philosopher Ned Block[2]) which you will frequently encounter in the literature on functionalism is that of the Coca-Cola machine. What we want is a machine that will take 50p pieces and £1 coins and will do four possible things: (1) deliver a bottle of Coke if a £1 coin is inserted or if two 50p pieces are inserted; (2) do nothing if only one 50p piece is inserted; (3) deliver a Coke if another 50p piece is added to the one already inserted; (4) deliver a Coke and 50p change if £1.50 is put in the machine by mistake. Figure 5.5 illustrates how the machine table will look. The machine table describes the functions the machine carries out, depending upon:

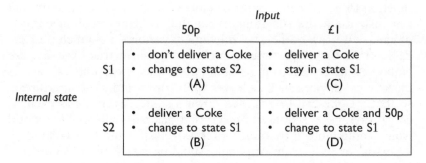

Figure 5.5 Machine table for a Coca-Cola machine

1 Its internal state: state S1 or S2.
2 Inputs into the machine:
    (a)   a 50p piece;
    (b)   a £1 coin (or total of £1 made up of two 50p pieces);
    (c)   a 50p piece and a £1 coin (or £1 made up of two further 50p pieces).

There are four possible ways, (A), (B), (C) and (D), in which the machine can behave depending upon what a customer does. These are:

(A)   The machine is in state S1. A customer inserts 50p. Nothing comes out of the machine, but internally it goes into state S2.
(B)   The machine is in state S2, a 50p coin having been inserted. Suppose the customer then inserts another 50p. The machine delivers a Coke and then goes back into state S1, to await the arrival of another customer.
(C)   The machine is in state S1. A customer inserts a £1 coin. The machine delivers a Coke and stays in state S1 to await another customer.
(D)   The machine is in state S2 because 50 pence has just been inserted. A £1 coin is then inserted by mistake. The machine delivers a Coke and a 50p piece and then goes back into state S1.

    The functional state of the machine is defined, and exhausted by, the description of inputs, internal states and outputs, as displayed in the machine table given in figure 5.5. The functional state as described by the machine table is abstract and purely formal, which means that it exemplifies the metaphysical functionalist level of analysis. For the function to be executed, it needs embodiment in some medium that can instantiate the functions. What the realizing medium consists of can, as we saw earlier, be indefinitely various in character. In the case of the Coke machine it might comprise instructions that are embodied in an electronic system, or in the operations of various mechanical devices such as levers which open and close apertures – so that a Coke can be released down a shute, say. It could even, as Block says, be a 'scattered object' that has parts all over the world which communicate by radio. Alternatively, it could be executed by a person, or by a team of people, standing inside the machine and following the set of written instructions which define the machine table.

How does all this relate to functionalism as a theory of the mind? Well, the proposal is simply that we conceive of the human mind as an enormously complex machine table, incarnated in the neurological processes of the brain. Like Coke machines, human beings take inputs in the form or sensory and perceptual information, and output them in the form of behaviour. For example, information is received through your eyes that the bull in the field you are crossing is about to charge. This information is processed in your brain and a behavioural output results, namely that you run for the gate. (The implementation of a different part of the mental machine table might, alternatively, mean that you stand your ground if, for example, you've had experience in handling bulls before and know how to cope with emergency situations involving them.)

As I have remarked already, the machine table comprising the human mind would be incredibly complex, but for the Turing machine computational functionalist that is how human beings function internally. Doubtless, the table comprising human (and animal) mentality would contain systems within systems, arranged hierarchically, beginning at the lowest or most basic level with the simplest elements that cannot be broken down into simpler functions, and becoming increasingly more complex as the hierarchy is ascended, until the final and complete functional structure may be discerned. Such complex systems are exemplified by the organization charts of large companies, which detail the functions and internal structures of various departments together with their relationships to other departments, so that the aims of the company as a whole may be carried out. Machines, too, consist of sub-systems, which enable the various functions of the machine as a whole to be served. In her book *Physicalism*, K. V. Wilkes uses the example of a washing machine to illustrate the point.[3] Washing machines need systems that will allow water egress (input), and will discharge the water after washing has taken place (output). They require a system to agitate the drum in which the washing is done, and a means of heating the water. Nowadays, they have a programming system to enable different sorts of wash routine to be carried out. Each of these systems can be broken down in turn into other components and functions. The inlet pipe, for example, will consist of a valve which operates electronically to open and let a measured quantity of water enter the machine. In turn, the valve will have various components, until finally the physical elements that cannot be broken down into smaller functional units are reached.

In the case of human beings, these simpler elements, it may be conjectured, will be the molecules (and ultimately the atoms) which make up the nerve cells that help to constitute the brain and central nervous system. At higher levels we will find such structures as the hippocampus, which is responsible for the laying down of long-term memories, or the lateral geniculate bodies, which act as a staging-post for the transfer of neural impulses from the optic nerves to the occipital region of the cerebral cortex, which is known to deal with visual perception. In this way, computational functionalism offers us an information-processing model of the mind which can explain our abilities. It cannot, after all, be by magic – pixie dust in the synapses – that we possess the capacities we do for face recognition or the use of language, for example. The computational theory of the mind offers us our best chance yet of understanding why human beings are the creatures they are. Or so the computationalists claim.

5.5 Functionalism and reductionism

Like analytical behaviourism, functionalism is reductionist. That is to say, it attempts to explicate the nature of mental states in a non-mentalistic vocabulary by reducing them to input/output structures. As Sidney Shoemaker remarks:

> [F]unctionalism . . . is the doctrine that mental, or psychological terms, are, in principle, eliminable in a certain way. If, to simplify matters, we take our mental vocabulary to consist of names for mental states and relationships . . . the claim will be that these names can be treated as synonymous with definite descriptions, *each such description being formulable, in principle, without the use of any of the mental vocabulary.*[4]

The question, however, is how this is to be done without running into circularity, that is, without using the very terms that functionalism is supposed to be analysing away. How, to take the example given earlier of someone seeing a bull charging and as a result running away, are the inputs and outputs to be captured in non-psychological terms? The expression 'seeing a bull charging' explicitly attributes a state of mind, a perceptual state, to the individual concerned. 'Running away' ascribes an action to the person and thus implicitly attributes desires and beliefs. Unless some way can be found of describing these inputs and outputs in a way that manages to avoid characterizing them mentally, the functional analysis will be vitiated by the importation into it of the very terms it was seeking to eliminate.

Fortunately for the functionalist, a method by means of which the employment of mental terms could be avoided when characterizing inputs and outputs was found. The technique employs a device we encountered on page 118, a 'Ramsey sentence', named after Frank Ramsey, who is credited with its invention. To see how it works, suppose the person who sees the bull in the field and starts running is called Ron. Then we can say that Ron has the belief B that the bull is going to charge at him because of his perception P that it is moving rapidly in his direction, and this, together with his desire D not to be mauled, causes him to take the action A of running for the gate. B, P, D and A are all terms that directly or indirectly attribute mentality to Ron. How can the input P, the internal states B and D and the output behaviour A all be rendered in non-mental terms?

We could begin by referring to the belief B merely as 'something', some state or other that results from perception P and which, together with desire D, causes action A. Naturally, at this stage the process of Ramseyfication is not complete, as the sentence still contains mental terms. The next step is to replace another mental state term, D say, by the expression 'something else'. We can now say that there is something, some state that resulted from the perception P, which together with something else, another state, causes action A. Clearly, the aim is eventually to replace both P and A with expressions that avoid characterizing them mentally. The expressions 'something' and 'something else' are clumsy, however, and if a large number of different sorts of mental state are involved, we shall soon run out of suitable expressions for them. What philosophers do is to replace mental terms such as P, B, D and A with variables such as w, x, y and z, and put what is called an existential quantifier in front of them. The existential quantifier, $(\exists w)$, which is always followed by a variable, as some of you may already know from studying logic, is to be read: 'There is a w such that . . .'.

Applying this technique to the original sentence and replacing only the perception of the bull, P, with w, we get: $(\exists w)$ (Ron has w and w causes the belief B, which together with the desire D leads to action A). Further substitutions of variables for the mental state terms B, D and A yields: $(\exists w)\ (\exists x)\ (\exists y)\ (\exists z)$ (Ron has w and w causes x which together with y causes z). In this way the causal relations between input, internal states and output are captured without using any mental vocabulary, thus avoiding circularity in the analysis.

5.6 Strengths of functionalism

Functionalism has a number of strengths:

1   It avoids behaviourism's error of identifying mental states with actual and potential outward behaviour, but it also escapes from postulating mysterious non-physical soul substances beloved of the dualist. In addition, because functions, by their very nature, are multiply realizable, it is not committed to an implausible type-type mind/brain identity. In this way it also avoids the chauvinistic stance of narrowly insisting that mental states can exist only as the states of human brains.

2   Thinking of a mental state in terms of its typical causes and effects fits in well with our common-sense view of the mind.[5] A pain, as we saw, can be thought of as that kind of mental state that typically results from tissue damage and causes pain-behaviour plus a desire to be rid of the pain.

3   The problem of mind/body causation disappears. We cannot say that pain, thought of as an entity or a state existing independently of pain-behaviour, brings that behaviour about. Pain is the whole functional state characterized in terms of inputs, outputs and relations to other mental states, themselves analysed functionally. Behaviour is not caused by pain; rather, one might say it is a constitutive part of the total functional state which counts as being in pain. Naturally, in human beings pain-behaviour will be caused by events in the central nervous system, but these events alone cannot be identified with pain. These events help to constitute the embodiment of the function by means of which a certain input in the form of tissue damage gets converted into a certain output in the form of wincing and groaning. It is the entire system of relations between inputs and outputs and other functional states which comprises being in pain, not some stage or aspect of that process.

5.7   Problems for functionalism

Despite its strengths, functionalism faces a number of serious difficulties, which I will consider in this section.

5.7.1   Liberalism

If chauvinism unfairly restricts mentality to human nervous systems, liberalism is too bountiful in the attributions of mentality it is prepared to make. The essence of the liberalist position is that any system that is functionally equivalent to a human mind must itself be allowed to have mental states. Yet it is possible to find many examples, often bizarre, where it is totally implausible to attribute mentality.

The two crucial aspects of the mind which functionalism seems unable to capture are: (1) the subjectivity and privacy of mental states such as sensations, their qualia in other words; and (2) the intentionality or 'aboutness' of the propositional attitudes such as beliefs, desires and emotions. Two arguments – in particular, Ned Block's so-called Chinese mind argument and John Searle's Chinese room argument – have emerged to demonstrate functionalism's inability to deal with qualia and intentionality. This can be summarized diagrammatically – see figure 5.6.

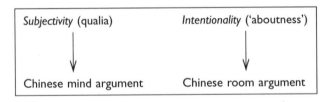

Subjectivity (qualia)	Intentionality ('aboutness')
↓	↓
Chinese mind argument	Chinese room argument

Figure 5.6

5.7.2   The Chinese mind argument: the problem of absent qualia

The Chinese mind argument may be explained in the first instance by reference to the homunculi heads argument. The homunculus (plural 'homunculi') fallacy was explained in chapter 2, section 2.8.3.

The idea, you will recall, is that if you try to explain some mental process such as vision by postulating an agent, perhaps in the form of a soul, in the brain that scans the visual input from the eyes, you end up with a vacuous or circular account, because you then have to explain how this agent sees. A vicious infinite regress of souls within souls threatens.

Ned Block appropriates the notion of a homunculus in order to articulate the following objection to functionalism.[6] We are to imagine a human body outwardly just like our own but internally very different. Its sense-organs are connected to a bank of lights in the head, and further connections to motor-output neurons are made via a set of buttons. Inside the head is a group of little men, or homunculi. A group of these homunculi are designated G-men because they carry out operations on what we can call a G-square, which constitutes just one square of the complex machine table that describes you. (Remember the simple machine table above consisting of four squares that functionally characterizes a Coca-Cola machine.) Imagine that a card is posted on a bulletin board in the head, and it turns out to have a 'G' written on it. This tells the G-men to get ready. An input light, say I_1, goes on, and this causes a little man to go and press an output button O_{200} and change the card on which 'G' is written to an 'M'. In other words, the little men in your head implement the machine table which functionally characterizes you, just as a team of people might stand inside the Coca-Cola machine and implement the machine table for it. In this example, 'G' and 'M' correspond to the internal states of the machine which were characterized as S1 and S2 in the case of the Coca-Cola machine.

Would it be plausible to suppose that this team of little men, considered as a group, enjoys subjective experience? It seems strongly counterintuitive to suppose that it would. The objection might be raised: but doesn't each of the little men enjoy awareness, and so perhaps experience is present after all? The objection misses the point of the example. What is internal to the little men is irrelevant, the question being: do the little men, simply by virtue of carrying out the function of changing G squares to M squares, that is, by acting as the causal occupants which discharge the functional role that is being modelled, thereby collectively as a group enjoy qualia? Again, it seems even clearer that they do not. Moreover, whatever is substituted for these little men will not introduce qualia either. Block at one point supposes that perhaps we are all flea-heads and that tiny trained fleas play the role of the G-men. But still this will not introduce qualia. It might be argued: but if you have qualia and it turned out then that you were a flea-head, you would have to agree that flea-heads can, after all, possess qualia. This argument, however, begs the question in favour of flea-heads having qualia. If I can be sure that I have qualia – and surely I can – then this, together with Block's thought-experiments, suggests that I just could not turn out to be a flea-head or to have regiments of little men in my head.

Block drives home the point he is making with the even more extravagant example of the Chinese mind, which has become something of a minor classic in the literature dealing with functionalism. We are now to imagine that the Chinese government has been converted to functionalism and that, in order to enhance their international standing, the entire one billion inhabitants of China have been provided with two-way radios that connect them with other people and with the artificial body described in the previous example. The bulletin board in the head is replaced by satellites which can be seen from all over China. The system of the billion people communicating with each other, together with the satellites, constitutes a huge artificial external 'brain'.

Such a system could be functionally equivalent to a human being, say you or me. But would it thereby enjoy the qualia that you or I do? Again, the answer must be no. The same objection may be raised as in the case of the homunculi-headed robots: surely the Chinese mind would have qualia because of the neural signals of the Chinese citizens composing it. However, these signals would not count as inputs to the system because what is to count as an input is stipulated by the person who specifies what the system is. As Block says, the signals would no more be inputs than would a tape jammed by a saboteur between the relay contacts in the innards of a computer.

The essential point that Block wants to make with all his examples is that something could be functionally equivalent to what is supposed to take place in the case of human minds, and yet for all that lack any vestige of mentality. There is nothing it is like to be the Chinese mind, considered as a whole, nor do all the individuals who comprise it have a collective understanding of what is going on. The Chinese mind is, therefore, at the end of the day, no mind at all.

5.7.3 Inverted qualia

Essentially the same point – that functionalism is leaving something important out in its attempt to account for the mind – can also be made by reference to the possibility of inverted qualia. You will recall from chapter 1, section 1.5, Wittgenstein's beetle-in-a-box metaphor. Each of us has what we call a beetle in our box but, since no one can look in anyone's else's box, it is possible that the boxes contain completely different sorts of thing, or even nothing at all. Applying this to the mind, is it not possible that the colour that I experience when I see a marigold is the colour that you experience when you see a violet, and vice versa?[7] It might even be, going further, that your whole colour experience is inverted with respect to my own, that when I see red, you see green, when I see yellow, you see blue, and so forth. Naturally, when you and I see a red object, we will both say it is red, and when decorating a house, for example, we will both do things such as ensure that the red wallpaper matches the red carpets, that only red candles are bought for Christmas decorations and so forth. However, suppose it turned out that, unbeknownst to both of us, you had had colour inverters inserted in your eyes at birth, so that all along red wallpaper, carpets and candles have looked to you as holly and Christmas trees have looked to me? The inputs can also give rise to the same internal states – say, beliefs – in both your case and mine. Thus we will both be caused to believe, and judge as a result, that pillar-boxes are red, even though in your case pillar-boxes will look the colour that I would call green. We will also both agree that fir trees are green, together with the grass, even though both of these look to you the colour that I would call red. If someone asks either you or me to choose something that matches the colour of the grass, we might both choose a spray from a fir tree, or pick a leaf from a beech tree, even though internally these things look to you what I would call red.

What this demonstrates is that we can have two systems, you and me, which are functionally equivalent in terms of inputs and outputs (the photons entering our eyes, our decorating the house for Christmas), yet differing in their mental states. The contents of your visual experiences and beliefs are different from mine, but this is something that functionalism is failing to discriminate. To make what I am saying quite clear, the same point can be expressed in another way, using the example of pain. It is perfectly possible to imagine a mental state that fulfils the same functional role that pain normally fulfils, yet internally does not feel like pain to its possessor, and so does not qualify as pain, because what is essential to pain being pain is simply how it feels. The moral seems clear. There's more to life mentally than functionalism.

5.7.4 Absent qualia revisited: what Fred knew and Mary didn't know

Although functional states cannot strictly be identified with physical states, they find their embodiment in such states, non-physical substances and properties having been rejected. To that extent, functionalists are materialists. There is no more to us internally than brains and central nervous systems, which take a physical input through the senses in the form of photons and sound-waves, for example, and then convert that input in various ways into an output, in the form of behaviour – gross bodily movements (and stillnesses). What this somewhat stark picture suggests is that once scientific investigation has worked out the neurophysiological details of how inputs are transformed into outputs, the task of explicating the nature of the mind has been completed. To put this another way, according to the materialist or physicalist, if we could know all the physical details, all the physical facts known through sciences such as physics, chemistry, biology, etc., about what takes place within us when we think, imagine, perceive, believe, suffer pain and so on, to include all possible types of mental states and activities, then we would know everything there is to know about us. A complete physical story of our functioning, covering what goes on in our brains and central nervous systems, is a complete story simpliciter. Similarly, if we now imagine this knowledge to be extended beyond what occurs to, and in, our bodies, a complete physical account of reality is, for the dedicated physicalist, a complete account, full stop. Once we know (assuming we could) all the physical facts and all the explanations, models and theories employing just those facts (and none other, for there are none other), then our knowledge would be complete.

This claim has been powerfully challenged by Frank Jackson in two much-debated, and deservedly famous, papers, 'Epiphenomenal Qualia' and 'What Mary Didn't Know'.[8] Jackson asks us to imagine someone, Fred, who has the best colour discrimination on record. Not only can he distinguish colours as well as anyone alive, but he can also make discriminations that no one else in the world can. When everyone else looks at ripe tomatoes, they see but one colour. The colour of all tomatoes is exactly alike to them. Not to Fred, however. To Fred, the colour of tomatoes falls into two distinct classes, red^1 and red^2, but although out of courtesy to us Fred talks of red^1 and red^2, to him these colours are not shades of a single colour at all, but are as different from each other as marigold is from violet. When Fred is given a pile of tomatoes, he can unerringly sort them into two piles, each pile composed of numerically the same identical fruits, again and again, the tomatoes having been mixed up between the various sortings. Moreover, investigation of Fred's optical system reveals that it can separate out two groups of wavelengths in the red part of the spectrum, just as ours can when we distinguish red from green. It seems it has to be granted that Fred really can see at least one more colour than the rest of us can, and this sets us wondering what it would be like if we could do this ourselves. If our nervous systems could be altered so that they were just like Fred's, then presumably we, too, would be able to distinguish tomatoes in the way that Fred can, and we might wonder what our experience of seeing tomatoes *after* our nervous systems had been adjusted would be like compared to what it was like *before* the change took place.

Unfortunately, however, we are not going to be able to acquire Fred's ability, because medical technology is not advanced enough to enable surgeons to make the appropriate alterations to our nervous systems. Thus we are left in the dark about what it would be like to see two totally different colours of tomatoes when before we saw only one. It may be supposed that we have a complete knowledge of what goes on physically in Fred's brain and nervous system, as well as a complete knowledge of the atomic structure of the surfaces of ripe tomatoes, of the properties of light waves and so forth, but none of this is going to give us the experience of seeing the two different colours that Fred sees. In relation to Fred, we are like the inhabitants of the country of the blind in relation to the one person in their community who can see.

The point of this story is this. Although we know everything there is to know physically about what goes on in Fred's case and ours, Fred knows something we don't know, namely that tomatoes that look uniformly the same colour to us actually form two groups with two different colours. This implies that physicalism leaves something out, namely what these colours look like to an experiencing subject who can discriminate them. In other words, the materialist picture of the world is not a complete picture, full stop. It is only a complete physical picture. But there is more to the complete picture than the physics; there is also the non-physical, mental aspect evidenced by Fred's experience of seeing two colours where we see only one.

Jackson makes the same point, using the example of Mary, a brilliant scientist who has always lived alone in a completely black-and-white room, and forced, for some reason, to investigate the world via a black-and-white TV monitor. (We will suppose, somewhat artificially, that she cannot even see her own hair and body, so that she really is excluded from experience of all colours except black and white.) Mary specializes in the brain mechanisms that deal with vision and has acquired a knowledge of all the physical details that perception involves. She knows which wavelengths stimulate which parts of the brain, and how these ongoings ultimately lead to the person in question uttering the words 'The sky is blue'. Mary, we may suppose, can see the sky on her monitor, but to her it just looks black, or various shades of grey and white.

One day, Mary is released from her room, or given a colour television. She looks at the sky and at tomatoes and exclaims: 'So that's what blue and red look like to all those people who I've only ever been able to see on my black-and-white monitor.' Does Mary learn anything new, anything she did not know before her release? It seems we are forced to conclude that she does. Before, she knew everything physical that was going on when people (and herself) saw colours, but now she has learned something new, namely what the experience of colour, previously denied to her, is like. Again, it seems to follow that the knowledge or information she subsequently acquires cannot be merely knowledge of, or information about, the physical, because that knowledge was complete before her release.[9]

You should now look at Exercise 5.1 before reading any further.

Exercise 5.1   Without looking below, try setting out Jackson's argument against physicalism using two premises and a conclusion. Then read on.

Jackson's argument can be displayed thus:

1   Mary (before her release) knows everything physical there is to know about other people.
2   Mary (before her release) does not know everything there is to know about other people (because she learns something about them on her release).
3   Therefore, there are truths about other people (and herself) which escape the physicalist story.

You should now consider Exercise 5.2.

Exercise 5.2   Can you see any way of attacking Jackson's argument and showing that its conclusion is false? Try this in discussion with others – it is quite difficult to achieve.

Paul Churchland has offered what he calls 'a conveniently tightened version' of the argument, thus:[10]

1   Mary knows everything there is to know about brain states and their properties.
2   It is not the case that Mary knows everything there is to know about sensations and their properties.

3 Therefore, applying Leibniz's Law (see chapter 2, section 2.7.1), sensations and their properties are not identical with brain-states and their properties.

Bearing in mind Jackson's argument and Churchland's version of it, you should now look at Exercise 5.3.

Exercise 5.3

Do you agree that Churchland's version accurately captures Jackson's argument? Can you suggest any other criticisms of it? After you have thought about this, read my comments below.

Firstly, if Jackson's argument amounts to no more than we have suggested above, Churchland would have demolished it. It parallels the case of the slugabeds (chapter 3, section 3.3), who know all about the Evening Star and its properties, but nothing about the Morning Star and its properties (because they are in bed when it appears in the morning sky), this supposedly leading to the conclusion that The Morning Star ≠ The Evening Star (because the Evening Star supposedly has a property, namely being known about by the slugabeds, which the Morning Star lacks). As we saw, this no more establishes the non-identity of the Morning and Evening Stars, than the fact that Lois Lane knows that the man she works with is Clark Kent but not that the man she works with is Superman, proves that Clark Kent is not Superman.

But Jackson argues that Churchland has not accurately represented his position. He reminds him that the whole thrust of his original argument is that Mary does not know everything about brain-states and their properties because she does not know about the qualia, the experiences of colour, associated with them. She knows everything physical about them from her achromatic perspective, but learns something new in addition to what is known physically when she experiences colour for the first time. As Jackson remarks, rhetorically, 'What she knows beforehand is *ex hypothesi* everything physical there is to know, but is it everything there is to know? That is the crucial question.'[11]

As part of his criticism, Churchland also pointed out, accurately, that Jackson's argument equivocates on the word 'know'. What Mary knows before her release can be called, following Bertrand Russell's distinction, 'knowledge by description', whereas the knowledge she acquires after her release, when she experiences colour directly for the first time, is 'knowledge by acquaintance'.[12] However, this is not germane, and does not refute Jackson's claim. *How* Mary knows what she knows is not to the point, but *what* she comes to know, however she comes to know it. She does acquire new knowledge after her release, something she did not know before, and since what she knew before was everything there was physically to know, she comes to know something the physicalist picture leaves out.

It has also been argued by David Lewis and Laurence Nemirow that on her release Mary does not learn anything new at all.[13] She merely acquires a new representational or imaginative ability. However, whilst it is true that she acquires new abilities – she can, for example, perfectly sort vegetables by colour, something she was very bad at in her bleached-out former existence – and she can now also imagine what her room would look like lined with crimson wallpaper – are these new abilities *all* she acquires?

Jackson argues that if Mary thought to herself that since her release she had learned something about other people's minds she did not know before – namely, what it was like to experience colours – and then subsequently received a lecture about whether we really can know that minds other than our own exist, she might start to worry that perhaps, after all, she hadn't acquired the knowledge about other people she thought she had. Suppose later she succeeded in quieting her scepticism and concluded that she did know something new about other people following her release after all. What then, Jackson asks, was she vacillating about – her abilities? Surely not, but about whether she had acquired new information, facts that she had now known before her release: '[H]er representational abilities were a known constant throughout. What else then was she agonising about than whether she had gained factual knowledge of others? There would be nothing to agonise about if ability was *all* she acquired on her release.'[14]

Does Jackson's argument succeed? It seems to me that it does. But here I must leave it up to you to decide for yourselves.

5.8 The Chinese room and the problem of absent intentionality

Not only can functionalism not capture qualia, it is alleged, it cannot accommodate another main characteristic of mental states either, namely intentionality, the capacity of the propositional attitudes to be directed upon a propositional content, to represent the other states of affairs, even those that never existed.

To establish this conclusion, John Searle employs an example that has probably become even better known than Block's Chinese mind analogy: the Chinese room. Searle's argument, like the argument in section 5.7.4, is aimed at overturning metaphysical functionalism. The point Searle wants to make is that merely by instantiating a program or by implementing a machine table, a computer cannot possess genuine thoughts and understanding. A genuine thought possesses intentionality – it has the feature of being about some state of affairs other than itself. As Searle puts it, a genuine thought has a meaning, a semantic content. Likewise for beliefs, emotions, intentions and desires. But the operations performed by a digital computer do not mean anything to it, and do not have a content for it. The words being displayed on the VDU screen as I type this out mean something to you and me, but they do not mean anything to the word-processor itself because an essential ingredient is missing in its case which is not missing in ours, namely consciousness. Unlike us, in the case of the computer there is no one at home. The computer which displays on its screen the message 'Hello Keith' when I type in my name, is neither greeting, nor referring to, me. Nor would any amount of sentences a computer types out to the effect that it has certain beliefs, fears, intentions, wants, hopes and so forth mean that it literally does have those beliefs and other intentional states in the sense that a human subject does.

To demonstrate this conclusion, Searle asks us to imagine that he is in a room which he cannot leave. Chinese characters are posted in through a slot on one side of the room. Searle's task is to match these incoming characters with others that are specified in a rule book. Thus when Searle receives say, a squiggle-squiggle, he looks up in the book the character it is to be paired with, say a squoggle-squoggle, and passes this character out through a slot on the other side of the room. Given that Searle-in-the-room has no prior understanding of Chinese, there is no way, merely from this pairing procedure, that he could learn it. To him, the incoming and outgoing characters are merely meaningless doodles, not words. To the Chinese speakers outside the room these characters are meaningful. The characters posted in may constitute questions in Chinese and the characters posted out may represent answers to these questions. The point of Searle's thought-experiment is that Searle-in-the-room is imitating what goes on in the CPU of a computer and this formal symbol manipulation cannot lead to any kind of understanding of the characters that are being manipulated. Merely by virtue of instantiating a program in this manner, a computer is not thereby led to an understanding of Chinese any more than Searle-in-the-room is.

Matters are not helped if we imagine a miniaturized, homunculus Searle inside the titanium skull of a robot with the character-input effected by television cameras and the output symbols serving to make the motors inside the robot move its arms and legs. The inputs Searle receives from the robot's sense-organs and the instructions that are passed to its motor apparatus will still mean nothing to Searle-in-the-robot. The symbols that are manipulated by Searle-in-the-robot do not suddenly acquire meaning simply because Searle is now inside something that can move around the world and which can receive its inputs and transmit its outputs in technologically sophisticated ways. Inside the robot, Searle is still only formally manipulating symbols, and hence, Searle claims, any path to semantics remains blocked.

In this example Searle was willing to grant that even though computer programs lack a semantics as far as the computer or the formal symbol manipulator in the Chinese room is concerned, they do at least possess a syntax, that is, there are rules governing the ways in which symbols can and cannot be combined. The Chinese room argument appeared early on in Searle's 1984 Reith Lectures, published subsequently as *Minds, Brains and Science*.[15] But by the time Searle had written *The Rediscovery of the Mind* in 1992, he had taken the more radical step of not merely dismissing semantics from computational systems, but syntax as well.[16] The Chinese room argument showed that semantics is not intrinsic to syntax. But now Searle insists that syntax, as well as semantics, is not intrinsic to the purely physical events that take place inside the computer. Both semantics and syntax are relative to human beings who design and use computers and assign interpretations to the inputs and outputs from these machines. In themselves, the inputs and outputs have neither semantic nor syntactic features. It follows then, as Searle points out, that nothing is intrinsically a computer. Thus, even if it could be shown that certain natural processes can be interpreted as instantiating certain functions, it would not follow that those processes could be described as computing those functions. That is something added by a human interpreter. To take a concrete example, the output from a transformer can be characterized as the differential of the alternating or changing current, but the transformer is not literally using the differential calculus to convert the input into the output. Rather, we assign the computational interpretation to the inputs and outputs of the transformer: the interpretation exists purely relative to us. Similarly, the motions of the planets in their orbit can be computed using Kepler's laws of planetary motion, but the planets themselves are not carrying out any computations.

Now what goes for the innards of an electronic computer goes equally well for the brain, Searle points out. The brain also cannot be viewed as carrying out computational functions and should not, contrary to what some authors have claimed, be seen as a 'syntactic engine'. 'Computational states', Searle says, 'are not discovered within the physics, they are assigned to the physics.'[17] The physical processes that go on inside a system such as a computer or the brain function as real causes, but the functional or computational inter-pretation we assign to such processes is not intrinsic to the system but merely something projected on to it from the outside. Conse-quently, the computational interpretation of the physical processes has no real existence, and therefore no causal powers, as it exists only in the eye of the person assigning the interpretation to the system.

The point Searle is making can also be put in terms of systems that genuinely do follow rules and those that do not. If we go back to the Coca-Cola machine for a moment and imagine that inside the machine there is actually a person collecting money and giving change and bottles of Coca-Cola in return, then it is true that the person is consciously following rules for carrying out the functions of the machine. The sentence 'If £1.50 comes in through the slot, give a coke and 50p change' has a meaning for the person, and it is a con-sequence of the person understanding this meaning and deciding to follow the instruction it represents, that the change and the bottle of Coke are delivered. In this way, the semantic and syntactic features of the sentence figure as genuine causes which help to explain the person's behaviour.

But now suppose that the person inside the machine is replaced by a conventional mechanism of mechanical or electronic gates and chutes and so forth. In delivering a Coke, does this machine follow rules in the way that a person standing inside the machine does? The answer must be no. The machine looks as if it were following rules, but in fact it cannot really be following rules because, lacking con-sciousness, it has no understanding of what is going on when a coin comes through the slot and various mechanical processes take place which ensure that a bottle of Coke comes out of the machine. We can and do speak of the machine giving change and delivering Coke to people, but this way of speaking does not impute genuine actions to the machine and has to be understood merely as a metaphor. The machine does not intentionally give you a Coke, or unintentionally omit to give you any change. Its operations cannot be described as either intentional or unintentional. The lack of change would be described as due to a mechanical or electrical defect in the operation of the internal mechanism. This is because the machine has no view-point, no first-person perspective. There is nothing it is like to be a Coke machine, unlike us and bats.[18] All that is occurring in its case are certain mechanical processes to which we, as outside observers, assign a meaning.

A nice example which also illustrates the point is provided by Anthony Kenny in his book *The Metaphysics of Mind*.[19] Compare a piano and a pianola. When a pianist plays a piece of music, this is because he is assigning a meaning to the notes on the musical score, that is, he is following certain rules for the production of the music. But these notes could be represented by holes in a pianola roll and the piece of music produced purely mechanically by setting the roll in operation. To the pianola, the holes don't mean anything in the way that the notes on the score mean something to the pianist. The holes in the roll are not symbols or sets of instructions. But the notes on the score are, because these symbols were set up by conventions to represent certain sounds. These conventions were set up by human beings who can use symbols, for whom symbols have a meaning, because human beings possess consciousness and intrinsic intentionality. In the case of the non-conscious pianola, any understanding we attribute to it is merely a derivative, as-if intentionality: the holes in the pianola roll are not symbols and possess no semantic content, no meaning or significance for the pianola. Following out the consequences of Wittgenstein's view that the meaning of symbols is not to be conceived of as sets of private images in the head, but as consisting in publicly checkable uses of the symbols, Kenny adds:

> If my brain were as deterministic as an electronic computer, so that its entire output could be predicted from the inputs it receives, that would not suffice for anyone to be able to predict the thoughts that I will have. For what gives meaning to any kind of output of my brain – whether channelled through action, speech, or writing – is something quite external to it, just as what gives meaning to the output of a computer is external to it. What gives meaning to my physical activities, what makes some of the sounds and gestures I produce into symbols, is my power to be a participant in the social activity of language – an activity which is impossible outside the context of the co-operation of others.[20]

5.9   Homuncular functionalism

Searle believes that the only way of endowing the physical processes that take place in computers with a semantics and a syntax is by putting a homunculus, a conscious experiencing agent who possesses genuine underived intentionality, into the system. This is not a problem in the case of the PCs which you can buy in a shop, because each one comes equipped with a homunculus which can interpret the inputs and outputs – you! If it is then insisted that computers themselves have intrinsic intentionality, the only way in which this seems possible is by putting the homunculus inside the computer. It then only needs the brain to be thought of as a computer with a homunculus sitting inside it interpreting the various neurological ongoings and endowing them with a semantics and a syntax for us to arrive back at the full-blown homunculus fallacy described earlier.

The American philosopher Daniel Dennett has proposed a bold response to this claim. There is nothing wrong with postulating homunculi just as long as these homunuculi are stupider than the person whose intelligent behaviour and understanding the homunculi are invoked to explain: 'If one can get a team of relatively ignorant, narrow-minded, blind homunculi to produce the intelligent behaviour of the whole, this is progress.'[21]

A person can be thought of as a set of sub-systems arranged hierarchically, just like the washing machine characterized by K. V. Wilkes earlier in section 5.4. As one descends the hierarchy, the homunculi become progressively less and less intelligent until, at the very bottom layer, homuncularity and the intentionality that it implies, are completely discharged from the system. The genuine understanding and rule-following which we attribute to other people at the normal everyday level are to be understood as the product of the functioning of the complex set of stupider sub-systems. In other words, ultimately what takes place at the higher levels – what we label as genuine understanding and rule-following – can be explicated in terms of the behaviour of the lower-level elements to which we feel no inclination to attribute intentionality. According to this picture, there is really no such thing as the intrinsic intentionality of which Searle and Kenny speak, because it will have been reductively decomposed into the actions and interactions of progressively simpler and more basic non-intentional elements. As Searle remarks, 'All of the higher levels reduce to this bottom level; the top levels are all just as-if.'[22]

The problem with a reductive strategy of this type is that one is left with the feeling that none of it adds up to awareness or understanding on the part of the human being who is being decomposed into progressively stupider sub-systems. In response to this, Dennett has suggested the analogy of a large organization in which all the various workers and departments execute their lowly functions, while a press secretary represents what is going on to the external world. Unfortunately, the analogy limps, because organizations as a whole are not conscious or self-conscious. In addition, the importation of a press secretary, what might be called a Master Homunculus, who collates the work of all the stupider homunculi in the more lowly positions and represents it to the outside world, simply raises the question of how in turn the Master Homunculus itself is aware. The idea of a such an homunculus, it is interesting to note, is not new, as it can be found in the work of William James, written more than a hundred years ago: 'Every brain-cell has its own individual consciousness, which no other cell knows anything about . . . There is, however, among the cells one central or pontifical one to which our consciousness is attached.'[23] James himself was, however, quick to dismiss the theory, not only because it leads to a vicious infinite regress of homunculi, but also because there is no evidence that there is anything like a pontifical cell in the brain: 'There is no cell or group of cells in the brain of such anatomical or functional pre-eminence as to appear to be the keystone or centre of gravity of the whole system.'[24]

Questions to think about

1 Is Searle really claiming, ultimately, that arrangements of matter, however complex, will never be capable of thought and consciousness?
2 Can a physicalist explain fully what is going on when someone is sent off for committing a foul in football?
3 Is a 50p piece just a physical object?
4 Do qualia really exist?
5 If a function is neither mental or physical, what is it?

Suggestions for further reading

- An excellent collection of articles on functionalism and related matters is William Lycan's *Mind and Cognition* (Oxford: Blackwell, 1990). The collection includes Daniel Dennett's attempts, against Frank Jackson, to get rid of qualia, to 'quine' them out of existence – see 'Quining Qualia', pp. 519–47.
- See also Dennett's *Consciousness Explained* (Harmondsworth: Penguin, 1991) for views which lean towards physicalism and eliminativism.
- Tim Crane's *The Mechanical Mind* (Harmondsworth: Penguin, 1995), is one of the clearest introductions I know to Turing machine functionalism and associated issues.
- D. B. Mitchell and F. Jackson, *Philosophy of Mind and Cognition* (Oxford: Blackwell, 1996) is excellently clear and comprehensive.
- J. Searle, *The Rediscovery of the Mind* (Cambridge, MA: MIT Press, 1992) is very readable and polemical.

- Try also Searle's *The Mystery of Consciousness* (London: Granta Books, 1997). This is good knock-about fun – but serious – featuring very lively exchanges between Searle, Dennett and David Chalmers. Very accessible and well worth reading.
- M. Davies and G. W. Humphreys (eds), *Consciousness* (Oxford: Blackwell, 1993) is a useful collection.
- Good discussions and attacks on various materialist theories of mind can be found in G. Madell, *Mind and Materialism* (Edinburgh: Edinburgh University Press, 1988).
- A comprehensive collection of articles grouped in different sections, with clear introductions to the sections by Rosenthal himself, can be found in D. Rosenthal (ed.), *The Nature of Mind* (Oxford: OUP, 1991).

TAKING CONSCIOUSNESS SERIOUSLY: NON-REDUCTIVE MONISM

Objectives

As a result of reading this chapter you should:

- understand what is meant by non-reductive monism;
- be able to state the supervenience doctrine and give some account of the features of supervenience;
- be able to explain Searle's 'solution' to the mind/body problem and give criticisms of it;
- be able to appreciate some of the problems faced by non-reductive monism;
- understand why McGinn thinks we will never be able to explain how the brain gives rise to consciousness, and be able to criticize this position;
- appreciate a Humean-based approach to the problem of consciousness.

6.1   Introduction

So far, we have examined the following theories of the mind and found them to be wanting: the identity theory, in both type-type and token-token versions; eliminativism; analytical behaviourism; and functionalism. The main problem with all these theories, which are either avowedly materialist or materialist in inspiration, is that they fail to take consciousness seriously, either by making no room for it, or by explicitly denying its existence.

Substance-dualism at least allowed full-blooded reality to states of mind conceived of as non-physical in nature. But the problems with dualism are numerous, as we have seen, and include among them two that are particularly intractable. The first of these is the question of how incorporeal souls are to be individuated and identified over time: the unavailability of such criteria alone appears to deal a death-blow to substance-dualism. The second issue is how souls are supposed to enjoy a causal commerce with the body when the two entities that are supposedly causally related are so utterly different in nature from each other. Explaining how a non-extended entity could causally interact with an extended one proved an insuperable difficulty for Descartes, and remains one to this day.

6.2 Property dualism and non-reductive monism

To what theory of the mind/body relationship, then, can we now turn? What appears to be required is a theory that can tread a middle path between radical materialism and strong dualism, a theory which, on the one hand, does not seek to deny the fact of mentality by reducing states of mind to the purely physical but, on the other, does not turn the possessors of mental states into incorporeal Cartesian ghosts, impotent to affect the world.

A candidate that appears to fit the bill is provided by property dualism. Property dualism, which was described briefly in chapter 2, section 2.1, exemplifies non-reductive monism. It is non-reductive because it does not insist that mental properties are nothing over and above physical properties. On the contrary, it is willing to allow that mental properties are different in kind from physical properties, and not ontologically reducible to them. It is clusters and series of these mental properties which constitute our psychological lives. On the other hand, property dualism dispenses with a dualism of substances – material substances and immaterial substances. There are only physical substances and physical events, hence it is a form of monism. But these physical substances and events possess two very different kinds of property, namely physical properties and, in addition, non-physical, mental properties, hence the title of the theory. In the version of property dualism that I will be putting forward for inspection, these two sorts of property do not merely happen to co-exist, bearing only an accidental relationship to each other. Instead, there is a one-sided dependence of the mental on the physical, a relationship that has become known in the literature surrounding this topic as the supervenience relation. A fuller characterization of supervenience is provided in the next section.

6.3   The supervenience doctrine

In recent philosophy of mind, Donald Davidson is a good representative of the kind of non-reductive monist position I have just sketched. As we saw in chapter 3, section 3.8.7, Davidson denied that the wholesale reduction of the mental to the physical was possible. Bridge laws connecting events under their mental descriptions with those events described physically were ruled out, and Davidson embraced a version of token-token identity theory. For Davidson, events are to be thought of as concrete, non-repeatable particulars, on a par with logical substances. Since he rejected substance dualism, there were no purely mental events, but only physical ones. He maintained, however, that these physical events not only had physical properties by virtue of which they were physical, but irreducibly mental properties as well. In this way he came to espouse non-reductive monism.

But merely to assert that event tokens had irreducible mental properties as well as physical properties was felt to be deeply unattractive, as it left the relationship of the mental properties to the physical properties unexplained (see chapter 3, section 3.8.6). Are we supposed to accept, as a brute fact, that these two kinds of property co-existed as features of events, the one not explicable in terms of the other, as an object might just happen to be both red and square, these features bearing no intrinsic or explanatory relationship to one another?

To get over this difficulty and to bring mental properties into closer relation to physical properties, without reducing them to, or identifying them with, physical properties, Davidson proposed the following relationship between the two kinds of property. Mental properties, he said, supervene on physical properties. Translated literally, this unfamiliar and frankly obscure word means 'to arrive on top of'. The essential idea is that one phenomenon, the supervenient phenomenon, appears 'on top of' a more basic phenomenon to which it owes its character and existence, the subvenient, basal phenomenon.

Davidson's own explanation of supervenience runs:

> Although the position I describe denies there are psycho-physical laws, it is consistent with the view that mental characteristics are in some sense dependent, or supervenient, on physical characteristics. Such

supervenience might be taken to mean that there cannot be two events alike in all physical respects but differing in some mental respects, or that an object cannot alter in some mental respect without altering in some physical respect.[1]

This characterization of supervenience is extremely brief. Indeed, as Jaegwon Kim has remarked, it sounds in the context of Davidson's work almost like an after-thought, a throw-away remark.[2] Nevertheless, in the light of the enormous amount of ink that has since been spilt over supervenience, it still manages to capture what is essential to the supervenience relation. Davidson's characterization of supervenience, together with remarks drawn from the context in which it appears, appears to have three elements.

Irreducibility   Supervenient phenomena, or facts, are not reducible analytically, by definition, or ontologically to subvenient facts or phenomena. Supervenient phenomena exist over and above subvenient basal phenomena. In the context of the token-token theory certainly, even if not in some other broader characterizations of supervenience, mental properties cannot be reduced by definition to physical properties, nor ontologically reduced, contrary to what the type-type identity theory maintains.[3] Davidson's explicit distinction between mental and physical properties in the passage above supports this characterization of the supervenience relation.

Co-variation   Supervenient phenomena are determined by, and co-vary with, changes in the underlying subvenient base. This means that there can be changes in the supervenient phenomena if, and only if, there are corresponding changes in the subvenient basal phenomena. The converse does not obtain: a change in the subvenient base does not necessarily mean a change in the supervening features. In the case of the mind/body relationship, the reason why the physical can change without the mental changing, is supplied by the multiple-realizability thesis leading to token-token identity – one and the same type of mental state is realizable in a variety of different types of physical arrangement (see chapter 3, section 3.6). Another way of spelling out what co-variation means is to say that two individuals cannot differ in their supervenient properties unless there is some difference in their subvenient features. In other words, if two individuals exactly resemble each other in their subvenient features, they must be indiscernible with respect to their supervenient properties. An exact molecule-for-molecule physical duplicate of you must exactly resemble you mentally.

Dependence   Supervenient phenomena emerge from, and are dependent for their existence upon, subvenient basal phenomena. They also owe their particular character to the basal phenomena. This dependence is asymmetric. In the context of the token-token identity theory, the existence of the mental and its features are determined by the physical. The primacy accorded to the physical in this theory makes it clear that it is a weak form of physicalism. The physical is given prime importance, but without going so far as to reduce the mental to the physical, or to eliminate the mental in its favour. Hence this particular application of supervenience yields non-reductive monism or property-dualism. There are two distinct kinds of property, physical and mental, but ultimately the mental is there only because of the physical (compare my remarks on evolutionary theory, chapter 3, section 3.8.2), and cannot alter independently of it.

Supervenience, as described above, can be summed up in a diagram – see figure 6.1. However, this probably all sounds rather abstract, so an example may help. The features of supervenience, as defined above, are all satisfied by Plato's famous 'simile of the cave' in the *Republic*. In this, Plato represents non-philosophers at the lowest stage of cognition – imagination – by prisoners chained up in a cave from birth so that they can only see the cave wall in front of them. Behind the heads of these prisoners is a curtain-wall, behind which there is a fire. Between the fire and the curtain-wall men are walking and carrying all sorts of objects on their heads. The shadows of these objects are cast by the fire on the wall of the cave directly in front of the prisoners. The shadows are not genuine logical substances capable of existing in their own right, but depend for their existence upon physical objects and the fire, as regards both of which the prisoners are ignorant. The prisoners play a game trying to predict the

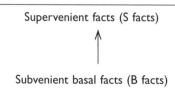

Supervenient facts (S facts)

Subvenient basal facts (B facts)

- S depends for its existence on B;
- S can change but if, and only if, B changes;
- but B can change without it necessarily being the case that S changes.

Figure 6.1   Supervenience

order of appearance of the shadows and, if any regularities in appearances were discovered, they might well conclude that earlier shadows were causing the occurrence of later shadows. This would be a mistake as, quite clearly, the existence of the shadows and their sequences is determined entirely by the physical objects (and the fire) casting the shadows. The shadows are distinct from the physical objects casting the shadows and irreducible to them. Any attempt at reduction would be incoherent, as it would entail identifying a shadow with the object of which it is a shadow.

Plato's simile also illustrates co-variation. The shadows can change if, and only if, the physical objects and the light casting the shadows alter in some way – i.e. if the objects move or the light moves. Moreover, two exactly similar physical objects orientated towards the light behind them in an identical way, and the same distance from it, must cast the same type of shadow. (Strictly speaking, the objects would have to be sequentially in the same position, since two objects cannot occupy the same space at the same time.)

6.4 Why does supervenience obtain?

The nature of the supervenience relation has been spelt out formally. But why should a pair of phenomena be related in this manner? If, and when, supervenience does obtain, what is the reason? A leading exponent of supervenience, Jaegwon Kim, whose work I referred to earlier, has pointed out that the bare invocation of the supervenience relation does not by itself explain why supervenience holds. Supervenience, maintains Kim, is not a theory of the mind/body relation on all fours with the other major theories we have surveyed, but leaves open the precise reason why the mental supervenes on the physical.

Probably the most straightforward answer to this question is that the supervenient phenomenon is causally dependent upon the subvenient phenomenon, but the subvenient base has to be conceived of as a sustaining cause that needs to operate continually in order to keep the supervenient phenomenon in existence. (A possible analogy here is with a fountain of water which must continually flow to sustain a ping-pong ball in the air.) Certainly, in the case of the shadows on the wall in Plato's cave, it is clear that the relation between the light source and the objects, on the one hand, and the shadows, on the other, is one of causal dependence. Take away the light and the objects and you take away the shadows. It's as simple as that.

However, if supervenience is weakened to exclude the dependency condition spelt out above, so that only the features of irreducibility and co-variation remain, then Leibniz's psycho-physical parallelism (see chapter 2, section 2.6.1) illustrates this modified form of supervenience. The mental and the physical form two complete and disparate systems, so one cannot be identified with the other. Mental changes co-vary with physical changes (though, equally, physical changes co-vary with mental changes). But from the very nature of parallelism, neither realm, the mental nor the physical, can have the slightest effect on each other, merely occurring, as they do, owing to the initial action of God in synchronizing the mental and physical clocks.

The philosophy of mind is not the only area in which the notion of supervenience has been employed. In his book *The Language of Morals*, R. M. Hare appealed to the notion of supervenience when he maintained that moral evaluations supervene on underlying non-moral facts.[4] Hare agrees with Hume that no amount of non-moral facts can ever logically entail the existence of any moral evaluations, so there is no logical dependency of the evaluative on the factual. But the factual determines the moral in the sense that any change in a moral evaluation of a situation requires some change in the facts comprising that situation. Hare provides the example of a moral judgement on the life of St Francis to illustrate the point:

> Suppose that we say 'St Francis was a good man'. It is logically impossible to say this and to maintain at the same time that there might have been another man placed in precisely the same circumstances as St Francis, and who behaved in them in exactly the same way, but who differed from St Francis is this respect only, that he was not a good man.[5]

Moral evaluations are not reducible by definition or analysis to the non-moral facts; to suppose otherwise would be to commit the error of ethical naturalism, which attempts to reduce value-judgements to factual statements. However, it cannot be said that non-moral facts cause moral evaluations. The reason the relation holds in this case, as Burwood, Gilbert and Lennon make clear, is that 'The relation between moral properties and natural ones is built into our moral vocabulary. Someone has not grasped the practice of giving moral justifications if they don't accept the requirements of the supervenience relation.'[6] In other words, someone does not understand what it means to justify an action morally if they do not appreciate that a change in a judgement requires the mention of a change in the morally relevant non-moral facts, and that exactly the same moral judgements must apply in those cases, like that of St Francis above, where all the non-moral facts that ground the judgement are relevantly similar.

In a similar fashion, the aesthetic features of works of art have been said to be supervenient upon the various physical features that help to comprise artworks. That is why there cannot be an aesthetic difference between, say, two paintings, unless there is some difference in the underlying properties that the aesthetic features of the paintings supervene upon. What exactly constitutes the basal subvenient features of an artwork is a complex issue, which we cannot pursue further here. (It appears that it can include non-observable, historical properties such as coming from the hand of one person rather than another, as well as directly observable features.) But unless there is *some* difference between whatever the basal features are in the case of two paintings, the aesthetic features of the paintings, and their value as works of art, must be the same.

It seems to me that unless and until the reasons why the supervenience relation holds in particular sorts of cases can be made clear, it must remain of limited value in explicating the relationship between the mental and the physical. That is, of course, assuming that it actually does hold between mind and body, something Descartes, who believed that the physical body and the incorporeal soul could go their own ways in glorious independence of each other, would have flatly denied. In contradistinction to Cartesianism, however, it seems not unreasonable to maintain that the physical is ontologically more basic, and that whilst there might be physical phenomena without mental phenomena, evolutionary theory (see chapter 3, section 3.8.2) gives every reason to believe that, as a matter of fact, there would not be minds without complex arrangements of matter to give rise to them. There may be possible worlds in which mental states exist which are not produced by underlying physical processes. That possibility, it would seem, cannot be logically excluded. In the actual world, however, it is true that as far as we can tell, mentality would not be there were it not for the right kinds of physical features to give rise to it.

6.5   Searle and the mind/body problem

In typically robust fashion, John Searle grasps the nettle of the relationship between the mind and the body with both hands. According to Searle, the solution to the problem is extremely simple and has been available for many years. Here is the solution: brains cause minds. More precisely, says Searle, mental phenomena are caused by neurophysiological processes in the brain and are themselves features of the brain. This is what Searle calls 'biological naturalism': '[m]ental events and processes are as much part of our biological natural history as digestion, mitosis, meiosis, or enzyme secretion.'[7]

To digress briefly, the point of the word naturalism is to signal that mental events are fully part of the natural world, and not in some sense beyond it or outside it – i.e. not non-natural in some sense, and certainly not supernatural. Their existence and character is, in principle, fully explicable in terms of worldly, natural occurrences. Naturalism is therefore not a million miles apart from the project of physicalism, the goal of explicating everything ultimately in terms of the concepts and theories drawn from the natural sciences (see chapter 1, section 1.4).

However, returning to the exposition of Searle's views, Searle proceeds to spell out in more detail what he means when he calls mental phenomena features of the brain. He is not content merely with saying that these phenomena are properties of the brain, but asserts instead that they are both caused by, and realized in, the microstructure of the brain, specifically the neuronal structure. In an attempt to make the meaning of this claim as clear as possible, Searle uses an analogy. Take water, he says. We are all familiar with the behaviour of water at the ordinary macro-level of everyday objects. We know its wet feel, its odourlessness (if it's pure), the fact that it can be drunk, that it takes up the shape of the inside of the container in which it is held and so forth. But why does water behave as it does? The answer is to be found, says Searle, at the micro-level, when we understand that water is composed of millions of individually invisible water molecules made up of two hydrogen atoms and one oxygen atom (H_2O). The same is true in the case of solids. Once again, the surface behaviour of something like carbon can be understood in terms of its micro-structure. Diamond and graphite are both composed of carbon atoms, but whilst diamond is the hardest substance of which we know, graphite is soft and soapy. Why? Because the atoms in graphite are arranged in a plate-like form, enabling one plate to slip smoothly over another, whilst diamond atoms are arranged octahedrally, forming a rigid structure that cannot easily be penetrated.

As we have seen, Searle maintains that these macro-, surface features, are caused by the behaviour of the underlying micro-elements. This is where I must register my first disagreement. If we have learnt anything at all from Hume's analysis of causation (see chapter 4, section 4.3) it is this, namely that a causal relation can only obtain between what he called 'distinct existences' between what we can call discrete particulars. These particulars do not have to be logical substances, though logical substances certainly qualify, but they must comprise distinct states of affairs. Thus, the smile on my face, though not a logical substance but a modification of such a substance, might cause you to feel happy. Your happiness also is not a logical substance, being a state of you, but it is a discriminably numerically different state of affairs. I might smile without you feeling happy, and you might feel happy even if I don't smile. The two states of affairs could exist independently of each other and consequentially can be identified independently of each other.

Bearing in mind Hume's analysis of causation, look now at Exercise 6.1 before reading on.

Can you anticipate the objection that can be levelled at Searle's claim that the behaviour of the micro-structure of water causes its behaviour at the macro-level?

Exercise 6.1

The objection is that the relation between the behaviour of the micro-structure and the behaviour at the macro-level is too close for causality. It seems to me that the behaviour at the macro-level is identical with the behaviour of the molecules at the micro-level. There are not two phenomena here, the micro-behaviour and the behaviour of a numerically different phenomenon at the macro-level, but one single phenomenon viewed from two perspectives. Imagine observing water rippling in a tank with the naked eye. You then start viewing the same water through a microscope and it looks completely different. Suppose the magnification could be increased without limit. There would then come a point, in theory, where you would no longer see the ripples, but the individual molecules swimming around in the tank.

It is true that there are two levels of description here, but one cannot speak of a level of description causing another level of description because descriptions are not non-linguistic events or states of affairs. As part of language, descriptions may be logically related to each other. For example, one description may logically entail another description or logically contradict it. If you are an only child, for example, this must entail that you have no brothers or sisters. To maintain otherwise leads to a formal contradiction. You cannot, logically, be an only child yet have a (natural, non-adopted) sister. But logical relations between descriptions, which can be discerned by reason alone independently of experience, are not causal in nature, because cause and effect are related contingently. Conversely, causal relations can obtain between events or states of affairs, but not logical relations. Cause and effect are related contingently as a matter of fact and are only discoverable on the basis of experience. If a cause and an effect appear to be logically related, this is only by virtue of how they are described. Logical relations cannot hold between non-linguistic states of affairs or events which comprise each half of the causal relation.

It is true that a knowledge of the micro-structure of things can be used to explain their macro-properties, but this is not a cause and effect relation in the ordinary Humean sense of cause, as outlined in chapter 4, section 4.3. Rather, we understand the behaviour of water at the macro-level when we understand how water is composed, what goes to make it up. We cannot say that the micro-features cause the macro-features, because they are constitutive of the macro-features. The micro-features just *are* the macro-features viewed very, very close up. It makes no sense to talk of one causing the other, because that would be tantamount to saying that a phenomenon is the cause of itself, and this is plainly an absurd position to adopt.

It is important to be very clear about this because it seems to me that Searle muddies the waters here by introducing a non-standard conception of causation. Searle acknowledges that it is correct to say that solidity might be defined as the lattice structure of the molecular arrangement, but he claims it is not really an objection to the analysis he is proposing. He then maintains that we can say, indifferently, either that solidity just is the lattice structure of the system of molecules and that, so defined, solidity causes resistance to touch and pressure, or that solidity consists of higher level features such as rigidity and resistance to touch and that it is caused by the behaviour of elements at the micro-level.

I must immediately disagree. The macroscopic feature of solidity, and the feature consisting in the lattice structure of the behaviour of molecules at the micro-level, are one and the feature described in different terms. Hence the micro-feature cannot cause the macro-feature, because causes must be distinct existences. I will return to this observation in the context of the mind/body relationship later.

The second term Searle uses to characterize the relation of the mental to the physical – 'realized in' – is, as I remarked, puzzling. Searle explains that at the level of the individual water molecule, you will not find liquidity. You cannot say of individual molecules that they are liquid. Liquidity is only to be found when there is an aggregate of molecules. However, this is not really surprising as the liquidity just is the behaviour of an aggregate of molecules viewed from the macro-level.

What about consciousness? Again, as Searle is keen to stress, you cannot point to a single neuron and say 'that is conscious'. But what about the behaviour of a whole collection of neurons, the entire functioning brain? In this case, a moment's thought reveals that the analogy with water breaks down. The more closely you peer into the brain, the more you will see of the movement of molecules and chemical transactions, but you will not suddenly stumble across consciousness. This is because, as I have said several times in earlier chapters, consciousness does not appear to be a public phenomenon equally accessible to all observers, but something radically private to the individual whose consciousness it is, something comprised from a purely first-person subjective view. The behaviour of molecules, on the other hand, is something public, which can be apprehended from a third-person point of view.

This is why I find Searle's claim, that mental phenomena are realized in the structure of the brain, puzzling. This is something he asserts frequently in early writings on the mind in his books *Intentionality* (1983) and *Minds, Brains and Science* (1984), For example, he says in the first of these books that the feeling of thirst is localized in the hypothalamus and that visual experiences are right there in the brain where the firing of a vast number of neurons at literally millions of synapses have brought them about.[8]

We could examine the workings of Searle's hypothalamus as much as we liked, as well the processes in his visual cortex (the part of the brain associated with, or responsible for, vision), but we will not come across Searle's thirst or visual experiences. Indeed, to suppose we would find visual experiences literally in Searle's head commits the homunculus fallacy. It would amount to postulating an inner miniaturized Searle who watches a neural television screen in his head.

If necessary, look back to chapter 3, section 3.8.1 to refresh your memory on the difference between mental states and brain processes, and then look at Exercise 6.2.

What other error does Searle make in attempting to locate thirst and visual experiences in the brain?

| Exercise 6.2 |

The attempt to locate thirst and visual experiences literally is illustrative of another flagrant error. In locating thirst, for instance, so precisely in the hypothalamus, Searle, I contend, has illegitimately elevated thirst to the status of a logical substance, that is, to genuine thinghood. Once this reifying move has been made, it becomes legitimate to demand precisely where in space the thing, or cluster of things, is. If the things in question are neurons, the demand to know their precise location is allowable. This is because they become basic particulars, logical substances, and their identities, unlike the identities of grins and smiles, do not logically depend on anything else. A grin or a smile, by contrast, is a logically dependent particular. It is the particular grin or smile it is by virtue of the identity of the person whose grin or smile it is.

The same is true in the case of visual experiences or thirst. As logically dependent particulars, these owe their identities to the persons who are having visual experiences or feeling thirsty. Plainly we do not come across these experiences floating loose and separate about the world and then have to look to see who owns them. Rather, we learn to talk about thirst and experiences as states or conditions of living people. But then, conceived of in this way, the only answer to the question 'Where is the person's thirst?' is to say that it is wherever the person happens to be, out on a hot country walk, for example. Thirst, as a state of a person, cannot be located any more precisely than this.

If we do not grasp this point, then we might conjecture that my thirst is, for example, in my throat. But while it is true to say that I feel thirsty because my throat feels parched or dry, it would be very odd to say that I feel thirst in my throat, and even odder to say that my throat feels thirsty. It is I who feels thirsty because I haven't drunk any water, and as a result my throat feels dry. Make no mistake, it is I, the person, who has a dry feeling in his throat. The throat by itself doesn't feel anything. How could it, since it is not a person but merely a part of my anatomy. The greatest oddity of all would be to locate thirst literally in my brain, as Searle does. This would result in the nonsense that my brain feels thirsty.

In saying all this I might be accused of being unfair to Searle. When he says that thirst and visual experiences are realized in the micro-structure of the brain, this might merely be a way of claiming that these mental phenomena are really only physical phenomena, that at the end of the day these states consist in nothing more than the behaviour of neurons describable in a purely physicalist vocabulary. However, we can tell from reading Searle that this cannot possibly have been his real intention because he explicitly rejects any commitment to reductive materialism, as we shall shortly see.

This repudiation of reductive materialism, especially in Searle's early work, was not, perhaps, always as clear as it might have been. The claims that thirst and visual experiences are right there in the brain could, as we witnessed, have been interpreted as an indirect advocacy of the identity of the mental with the physical. However, by the time *Searle and His Critics* was published in 1991, Searle himself was making very clear his disavowal of radical materialism.[9] In that book, in a reply to the Australian identity theorist David Armstrong, Searle wrote (and it is essential on this occasion that I quote at length to make the point quite clear):

> Armstrong thinks that if a property is causally supervenient on the behaviour of the elements of its microstructure then it ought to be ontologically reducible as well. On his view, higher lever supervenient properties like solidity and consciousness, because they are subject to the sort of causal reduction involved in causal supervenience, are for that reason ontologically reducible as well. For Armstrong solidity, consciousness, and Intentionality are all in the same boat as heat: there is nothing there in addition to the behaviour of the micro elements. Now that is emphatically not my view and I believe it is mistaken. Supervenience, however strict, does not entail reductionism. From the fact that a property is supervenient on the behaviour of lower level elements it simply does not follow that there is nothing there except the behaviour of the lower level elements. In the case, for example of consciousness, we have a supervenient, but nonetheless non-reducible property. That, indeed, is the difference between, for example, heat and consciousness. Consciousness is a separate and non-reducible property and in that sense it is, I guess, emergent.
>
> Indeed, by agreeing with me that certain features such as liquidity and solidity are emergent, in this sense, it seems to me Armstrong is committed to denying their ontological reducibility because by saying the property is emergent we are saying there is a separate phenomenon there, even though the phenomenon may be entirely causally supervenient on other phenomena. Causal reduction, yes; ontological reduction, no.[10]

This passage makes Searle's commitment to non-reductive materialism abundantly clear. Mental properties such as consciousness and intentionality are ontologically distinct from physical properties such as heat, and not ontologically reducible to the behaviour of purely physical micro-elements, as in the kinetic theory of gases, for example. In the opinion of many philosophers, this commits Searle to an acceptance of a dualism of properties, to the view that as well as its physical properties, such as colour, mass and extension, the brain possesses the non-physical feature of consciousness.

However, Searle vigorously and repeatedly denies that he is a property dualist. To accept dualism, even property dualism, according to Searle, is:

to deny the scientific worldview we have painfully achieved over the past several centuries. To accept dualism is to conclude that we really live in two quite different worlds, a mental and a physical world, or at the very least that there are two kinds of properties, mental and physical. I hope I have made it clear . . . that I think one can accept the existence and irreducibility of consciousness as a biological phenomenon without accepting the ontology of traditional dualism, the idea that there are two metaphysically or ontologically different sorts of realms we live in, or two different sorts of properties in the world.[11]

This passage, which is taken from near the end of *The Mystery of Consciousness*, sits very uneasily, however, with Searle's cheerful acceptance at the start of the book:

[W]e don't have anything like a clear idea of how brain-processes, which are publicly observable, objective phenomena, could cause anything as peculiar as inner, qualitative states of awareness or sentience, states which are in some sense 'private' to the possessor of the state . . . how could these private, subjective, qualitative phenomena be caused by ordinary physical processes such as electrochemical neuron firings at the synapses of neurons.[12]

The tenor of this passage, perhaps contrary to Searle's intentions, is to imply that there is an explanatory gap, incapable of being bridged or closed, between what takes place physically and publicly and what takes place mentally and privately. If the mental were physical, then presumably it would not be radically private and subjective. Indeed, an integral part of what it means to classify some phenomenon as physical, as opposed to non-physical, is surely that it is public and objective and not apprehendable from a purely first-person subjective perspective. If Searle's position is not property dualism couched in other words, then I am afraid I do not know what it is. Despite his continual harping on about consciousness and intentionality being biological, natural phenomena – a very reasonable position in the light of the difficulties with full-fledged substance dualism – I believe Searle should gracefully accept that he is, at the end of the day, a property dualist.

A virtue of Searle's version of non-reductive monism is that he makes it quite clear that the reason the supervenience relation holds is because the physical causes the mental. In fact, Searle suggests that the term 'supervenience', and the idea of any *novel* relation it denotes, can be dispensed with, because it no longer does any work in philosophy once the existence of bottom-up, micro- to macro-causation, is recognized:

The formal features of the relation are already present in the formal sufficiency of the micro-macro forms of causation. And the analogy with ethics is just a source of confusion. The relation of macro mental features of the brain to its micro-neuronal features is totally unlike the relation of goodness to good-making features, and it is confusing to lump them together.[13]

If Searle is right, and the postulated supervenience of mental features on physical features is really only another way of talking about the causal dependence of the mind on the body, then the examination of the strengths and weaknesses of this theory is made more straightforward. Searle's claim that physical processes cause mental occurrences seems an eminently reasonable one, and it is therefore on this basis that I shall continue to make my assessment of property dualism as a theory of the mind.

6.6   Three problems for property dualism

Property dualism poses three major problems. These run as follows:

1   What is the nature of the non-physical mental properties which collectively make up our mental lives and which are supposedly given rise to by physical processes in the brain?
2   To what extent can we explain, and understand, how physical processes in the brain can give rise to non-physical states of mind?
3   How can property dualism, and the causal dependence of the existence of the mental on the physical, avoid leading straight to epiphenomenalism, the claim that the causation runs one way only, from the brain to the mind, and not from the mind to the brain, thus making the mind an impotent and non-contributing spectator to what takes place in the world?

In the remainder of this chapter I will attempt to deal with the first two questions. The third, which takes us back to Descartes' problem of how the mind, conceived of as a soul, could affect the body, requires a longer treatment, as we will see.

6.6.1   What is the nature of mental properties?

Our first question asked: what is the nature of the mental properties which collectively make up our mental lives?

Here, we are led straight back to Descartes, who was surely right in maintaining that an essential aspect of our mental life is consciousness, our consciousness of things around us as well as our own internal states. Shorn completely of any vestige of consciousness, our mental lives have effectively ceased to exist. Even though, as we noted, there can be beliefs, desires, intentions and so forth of which we are not aware at a given moment, these states can normally be recalled to consciousness when required, this ready accessibility to consciousness constituting an integral feature of them.

But the answer that consciousness is integral to the very existence of our mental states, still does not tell us what consciousness is. So our next question has to be: what is the nature of consciousness or awareness itself? Responses to this question have included remarks such as 'Consciousness is like jazz; if you gotta ask what it is, you ain't never gonna know' or 'Consciousness is like the Trinity; if you can explain what it is, you haven't understood it.' I think the serious point behind these remarks is that in one sense we all do know what consciousness is, purely from the fact that we are conscious. We all know what is it like to see, hear, smell, touch and taste things; to experience sensations and emotions; to think thoughts and to reminisce. In short, we know that there is something that it is like to be us, to use Thomas Nagel's phrase,[14] and in that sense we know what it is to enjoy or endure consciousness. If, on the other hand, we don't know what it is like to be conscious, there is no one who can tell us, and, indeed, it would be pointless for anyone to try, since an essential condition of their succeeding is that we already are conscious, otherwise we could have no awareness or understanding of what they were trying to tell us. What more then is there to say about what consciousness is, since how, as experiencing beings, could we fail to know what it is?

But, it will doubtless be objected, the question asked not for *examples* of consciousness, but a *definition* of it. In other words, the demand was that we should be able to spell out in other terms that do not contain, overtly or covertly, the term 'consciousness' or its equivalents, precisely what consciousness is. This presupposes that a reductive analysis of what consciousness consists in is possible. The danger is, however, that if we accept this presupposition and then fail to come up with convincing details of what comprises consciousness, couched in other concepts, it will then appear that we have failed to understand properly what consciousness is.

Now look at Exercise 6.3 before reading on.

Exercise 6.3   Is it possible to define consciousness? Can you provide a non-circular definition of consciousness that will satisfy the formula: A being may be truly described as conscious if, and only if . . .?

My response is to reject the presupposition that an analytical reduction analysis of consciousness is possible. (Given the main thrust of the argument of this book, it goes without saying that I do not think an ontological reduction is possible either.) I do not believe, though I do not see how I can strictly prove the claim to anyone who remains unconvinced, that consciousness, to adapt the words of the philosopher Bishop Butler (1692–1752), is what it is and not something else. The notion of consciousness is logically primitive or basic, i.e. it cannot be broken down into simpler, more basic terms or components. Consequently, it is not possible to provide a non-circular analysis of what consciousness is, and this is tantamount to saying that no analysis is possible at all. Synonymous terms can be provided, and various examples of states where consciousness is integral to their very existence can be provided, as in the instances given above, but it does not seem possible to decompose consciousness into more basic states of affairs, or to provide a more basic description of what consciousness is, using other terms.

6.6.2   How do physical brain processes give rise to mental features?

The question of what consciousness *is* – to which I have suggested no question-begging answer will, or can, be forthcoming – must be kept completely distinct from how consciousness is caused. Even if we cannot spell out in other terms what consciousness is, that is no reason at all for concluding that we will not be able to explain one day how consciousness is brought about by the physical mechanisms that underpin it. In fact, with every detail that we uncover about how the brain functions, there is every reason to think that we will eventually be able to give the underlying physical causes of consciousness, and thus understand how it depends upon the physical for its existence.

However, there are philosophers who would immediately accuse me of misguided optimism in making this claim. According to this way of thinking, even if I succeeded in identifying those brain events whose occurrence appeared to be essential for the existence of consciousness, I still wouldn't have really explained how consciousness is brought about by physical processes in the brain. To put this another way, suppose I could switch on and off the physical processes in the brain upon which consciousness appeared to depend. I switch the processes off, and the person slumps unconscious. I switch them on again, and the person recovers and wakes up. All over the world, let us suppose, various scientists put this theory to the test, and all agree that certain complex brain events, described in very close physical and chemical detail, would seem to be essential for there to be consciousness. Well, according to the objection I am about to outline, even if all this took place, we still wouldn't have achieved a proper understanding and explanation of how the physical causes consciousness.

The basis of the objection is this: physical occurrences do not just appear to be different from consciousness; they are utterly different, so utterly different in fact, that it is inconceivable how the physical could produce the mental. It is not difficult to sympathize with this position. I think it would be true to say that we have a strong, overwhelming intuition that there is a fixed gulf between the material and the mental, which not only forever prohibits their identification, but in addition renders an account of how one gives rise to the other out of the question. How is the water of the brain turned into the rich wine of consciousness, to borrow Colin McGinn's striking metaphor.[15] The accumulation of neurophysiological details, it seems, will never render transparent their relation to mentality, much less demonstrate that consciousness and neurology are but two names for a single phenomenon.

McGinn pessimistically believes we will never crack the problem of how consciousness emerges from brain activity. He argues that our sensory and cognitive constitution forever debars us from gaining the necessary insight into how the mind/body knot is tied. Our failure to understand how consciousness is related to neuronal events is a failure in principle because of the limits of our experience and the corresponding limitations on the concepts we can acquire. As a result, it is likely that we will forever be precluded from solving the mind/body problem.

Hume's theory of how we form concepts helps to illustrate the approach McGinn is making. According to Hume, concepts are supposed to be faint images derived from more vivid sense impressions. Our senses respond to only one small part of the electromagnetic spectrum – we cannot see radio waves, for example. So we have no genuine concept of the colour of radio waves on Hume's theory, because there is no impression of sense from which to derive the appropriate concept. By contrast, we can see roses, so we do know what is meant by describing a rose as red. By parity of argument, there may be other features of the universe that we are not in a position to detect but, *ex hypothesi*, we cannot possibly say what these are. Not being capable of having experience of these features, we could not, on a simple empiricist theory such as Hume's, form any concept of them. But then, any explanatory theories which employ these concepts would not be accessible to a Humean mind. Taking this line of argument to its conclusion, we can say that there may be creatures who can form concepts and theories unavailable to us, either because their perceptual apparatuses are different from ours, and/or because they are in general cognitively different from us.

Unless we believe in magic and the miraculous, there presumably must be *some* theory that can explain how conscious states are caused by brain states. But it might be the case – and in fact the very intractability of the mind/body problem and the difficulty of conceiving what an explanation of consciousness in terms of brain processes could conceivably look like suggest it indeed is the case – that these theories are simply unavailable to us because they employ concepts we cannot acquire. Thus, as McGinn puts it, there may be some property of the brain which would enable us to account naturalistically for consciousness could we but grasp the nature of that property. However, if there is such a property, McGinn maintains, there would seem only to be two possible avenues that would give us access to it.

One is through our own experience of consciousness. Unfortunately, as McGinn points out, consciousness does not seem able to help because reflection upon, or inspection of, our own phenomenal states provides no clue whatsoever as to how such states can depend upon, and be given rise to, by the brain. We all know what it is to be conscious quite independently of any knowledge of what goes on in our brains, or even without knowing that we have brains. Reflection on the fact of our conscious experience gives us, so to speak, no window on any physical processes that might be involved in giving rise to it, or in constituting it.

The other possible avenue to understanding is through brain research and neuroscience in general. But here again we draw a blank, essentially for the same reason given by Leibniz (see chapter 1, section 1.1). I can look into your brain, but I will not thereby be able to discern what you are thinking: all I will see, in Leibniz's words, are 'parts which push and move each another, and never anything which could explain perception'.[16] Enlarging on Leibniz's remark, McGinn writes:

[B]ecause the senses are geared to representing a spatial world . . . they essentially present things in space with spatially defined properties. But it is precisely *such* properties that seem inherently incapable of resolving the mind/body problem: we cannot link consciousness to the brain in virtue of spatial properties of the brain . . . Consciousness does not seem to be made up out of smaller spatial processes; yet perception of the brain seems limited to revealing such processes.[17]

David Chalmers agrees with McGinn:

[The problem] lies in the overall explanatory strategy. These [physicalist] models and theories are simply not the sort of thing that could explain consciousness . . . Any account given in purely physical terms . . . will yield only . . . structure and dynamics. While this is enough to handle most natural phenomena, the problem of consciousness goes beyond any problem about the explanation of structure and function, so a new sort of explanation is needed.[18]

There is no denying that McGinn's and Chalmers's suggestions can exercise a powerful appeal. Given the utter disparateness of the phenomena in question – public, objective, extended brain processes that exemplify matter in motion, on the one hand, and private, subjective, non-extended modes of consciousness to which the concepts of motion and rest have no application, on the other – it does appear difficult to understand how the essentially mechanical could give rise to the essentially non-mechanical.

Nevertheless it seems to me that McGinn and Chalmers are wrong in viewing the issue in this way. The mind/body relationship is hard to understand, to be sure, but the approach taken by both these thinkers makes it harder to understand than it needs to be. In short, their way of conceptualizing the difficulty puts an understanding of the issue permanently out of reach, turning a difficult problem into an insoluble mystery.[19]

What motivates McGinn's approach is the desire, it seems to me, to make crystal-clear how the physical gives rise to the mental. Put this way, the demand seems eminently reasonable, until we turn our attention to what such an account is supposed to look like. It appears that what McGinn is after is that we should somehow render transparent how material processes cause the mind, and this may be interpreted in turn as the demand that it be shown how, given the occurrence of certain sorts of physical event, certain sorts of mental event *must* occur. What he wants, by his own admission, is to find some natural feature or property of the brain which, if only we could grasp its nature, would reveal itself as the mechanism by which means mechanical motion is transformed into conscious thought. At the moment, the emergence of mind from matter has to us the appearance of a miracle, but at the same time we know it can be no miracle and that there must be a rational explanation. Our difficulty is that we simply cannot understand how the conjuring trick is worked, because we lack an insight into the nature of the hidden link between physical processes and conscious experience.

It is the belief that there must be such a link which is the source of McGinn's mistaken view of how we are to attain an understanding of the physical causes of consciousness. What McGinn hopes to achieve, in effect, is to exhibit the necessary connection between the physical and the mental, the missing, hidden and secret nexus, which, if only it could be laid open to our eyes, would reveal in an instant how the mental must necessarily and inevitably arise from underlying physical activity. But this search for such a nexus is a wild-goose chase. The search for a necessary connection, a mysterious glue that shows how the phenomenon of consciousness is linked to, and emerges from, brain activity, is fruitless, because all closer and closer scrutiny of a causal relation can ever reveal is more links in the chain, i.e. more events that are causally related to each other. A category mistake is in evidence here. The causal relation is not itself an event or an object. However many events are discovered in a causal chain, none, in principle, could count as what we are looking for. At the end of the day all we will discover is that certain sorts of event regularly follow other sorts of event, and that a true statement describing a causal relation between an event of type A and one of type B will entail a counterfactual conditional which states that if A were not to occur, then neither would B. Any mysterious necessary connection between the events, the glue that binds them together, not only would not, but in principle could never, be found. The search would be recursive. It would be like looking for a featureless substratum underlying all perceptible qualities. Whatever was stumbled upon in the search would turn out merely to be another perceptible quality, previously unobserved. In just the same way, the hidden nexus we are seeking, which is supposed to illuminate how the physical causes the mental, and renders completely transparent and intelligible how the one is the result of the other, would merely retreat before us like a will o' the wisp.

What both McGinn and Chalmers seem unable to accept is that it could turn out to be the case that complex physical processes just do give rise to conscious states, and that there is no hidden mechanism featuring as yet undiscovered properties of the brain to be uncovered which will render transparent the causal link between matter and mind. This inability to accept that there is no hidden mechanism manifests itself, in the case of Chalmers, in his claim in the passage quoted above, that 'Any account given in purely physical terms . . . will yield only . . . structure and dynamics.' But why must this be so? What Chalmers is claiming is that an effect must be like its cause if

the causal relation is to be possible and any explanation which uti-
lizes it is intelligible. The unstated assumption is that if consciousness
is totally different in character from brain processes, then it cannot
possibly result from such processes, and that there must be some mysterious mediating link between the physical and the mental which
explains how the latter can result from the former. But there is
no warrant for this conclusion, as a famous passage from Hume
demonstrates:

> [I]f you pretend ... to prove that ... a position of bodies can never
> cause thought; because, turn it which way you will, 'tis nothing but a
> position of bodies; you must by the same course of reasoning conclude,
> that it can never produce motion; since there is no more apparent con-
> nection in the one case than in the other.[20]

In other words, prior to experience, anything could be the cause of
anything. A person might, by a simple wish, extinguish the sun or
control the planets in their orbits. The world does not work in this
way, but there is no contradiction in supposing that it might. Similarly, complex physical processes might give rise to thought and
consciousness; the possibility cannot be ruled out in advance and
independently of experience of how the world actually works. In fact,
from everything we know about the way mental sophistication
matches neurological complexity as we ascend the evolutionary scale,
together with a wealth of well-documented evidence of the effects on
mentality by damage to the brain, or the taking of drugs, it is more
than reasonable to suppose that the physical does give rise to the
mental. How it achieves this, however, is ultimately no more mysterious then how *any* cause gives rise to its effect. If physical to mental
causality seems unaccountable, then equally so must physical to
physical causality. There is, as Hume points out, no more connection
discernible in the one case than in the other. Since, I assume, McGinn
and Chalmers are not especially concerned to try to fathom the secret
of how one physical event leads to another, they have no reason to
look for some mysterious ingredient that will supposedly lay bare
how the physical brings the mental into being. There is, as I have tried
to explain, no such ingredient to be found, and to demand that one
should be produced is a false ideal of what it means to explain one
phenomenon in terms of another. It is the hankering, the craving, for
a special insight into how the brain produces the mind which is the
error that motivates McGinn's and Chalmers's approaches, for there
is no such special insight to be had, other than by discovering, through
careful and patient scientific investigation, what physical states of the
brain consciousness actually does depend upon.

If we compare physical to mental causality with physical to physical causality, we cannot complain that we have some special understanding of how one physical event gives rise to another physical event, which we lack in the case of how one physical event gives rise to a mental event. This is because all we ever observe, even in the case of physical to physical causality, is a certain type of event following another type of event and exemplifying a counterfactual dependence upon it. We commonly experience one physical event bringing about another physical event, as when a stone smashes a window. But, equally, we all know from our own experience that physical to mental causation occurs, as when a pin causes us to feel pain, or the sight of a bull in a field we are crossing causes an adrenalin rush and makes us run for the gate.

Explanations of how one thing causes another thing must eventually come to an end. We cannot continue citing links in a causal chain. Sooner or later we will reach the last link, and if it is then asked why the event in question was produced by another event, we shall be forced to acknowledge that this is just how things happen. This applies equally to both physical to physical causation and physical to mental causation. An understanding of how certain brain processes produce certain states of mind can ultimately amount to no more than this. The search for a mysterious nexus between mind and matter is a quest for a chimera, and only leads to mystification.

6.7 Conclusion

In the last part of this chapter I have dealt with the question concerning to what extent we can explain how consciousness, and mental states in general, are caused by physical processes. I have suggested, taking lessons from Hume's account of causation, that there is no reason to think that our comprehension of this matter need ultimately be in any way inferior to the understanding we have in the case of causal explanations of a variety of occurrences where mentality is not involved.

But the theory that the brain causes the mind is not home and dry yet. A number of philosophers have thought that if the mind is produced by the brain and depends for its existence upon it, then this must unavoidably lead to an unacceptable epiphenomenalism, the view that the mind is impotent and constitutionally unable to make a causal difference to the world. A discussion and critical evaluation of this problem forms the content of the next chapter.

Questions
to think
about

1 What is meant by 'supervenience' and does it lead straight to epiphenomenalism?

2 Can consciousness be defined?

3 How plausible do you find Searle's claim that mental states are caused by, and realized in, the brain?

4 Must a non-reductive monist deny that disembodied existence is logically impossible?

Suggestions for further reading

- Jaegwon Kim's *Mind in a Physical World* (Cambridge, MA: MIT Press, 1998) looks in detail at reductive materialism and the problem of mental causation.

- See also Kim's *Supervenience and the Mind* (Cambridge: CUP, 1993), which will tell you all you ever wanted to know about varieties of supervenience. The book includes very thorough and rigorous discussions from one of the leading experts on supervenience.

- For lively discussions of the main issues of consciousness, read Michael Tye's *Ten Problems of Consciousness* (Cambridge, MA: MIT Press, 1995).

- Essential reading is David Chalmers's *The Conscious Mind* (Oxford: OUP, 1996). It includes very detailed discussions of all the main issues, but it is rather long and involved.

- Owen Flanagan's *Consciousness Reconsidered* (Cambridge, MA: MIT Press, 1992) is a lively and accessible book, which covers many of the important issues currently being debated.

- In *Kinds of Minds* (London: Weidenfield and Nicolson, 1996) Daniel Dennett looks at the emergence of mind from an evolutionary perspective.

7

PSYCHO-PHYSICAL CAUSATION

Objectives

As a result of reading this chapter you should:

- be able to supply some examples of causal relations between mental and physical events;
- understand what epiphenomenalism claims and how the doctrine can be criticized;
- understand why reasons for actions have been denied the status of causes, and have a critical appreciation of Donald Davidson's response to this claim;
- understand the main elements of Davidson's causal theory of intentional action;
- have a critical appreciation of Davidson's anomalous monism and why it has been thought to lead to epiphenomenalism.

7.1   Introduction

This chapter concerns itself with the problem of psycho-physical causation. How, in other words, is it possible for the mind to affect the body? In everyday life we do not doubt for a moment that our mental states do affect our physical states, yet explaining how this is possible has proved extraordinarily difficult. In what follows I want to set the problem in the context of recent philosophy of mind and action, looking principally at the work of Donald Davidson in this area and, to a lesser extent, that of Jaegwon Kim.

Firstly, I shall provide a sketch of Davidson's theory that desires and beliefs that are cited as the reasons for actions can be the causes of those actions. I shall then explain how, out of these early theorizings on this issue, Davidson was led to develop a theory called anomalous monism – the meaning of this term will be fully explained shortly – and why a number of philosophers believe that this theory commits Davidson to epiphenomenalism.[1] Epiphenomenalism is the thesis that mental states are causally inoperative and that, contrary to our common-sense view of things, the mind never makes a causal difference to the world. Having attempted to determine whether Davidson may be let off the charge of being an epiphenomenalist, I shall then contrive a rather briefer exposition and evaluation of Jaegwon Kim's contribution to the issue of psycho-physical causation.

7.2   Psycho-physical causation

Let us begin by reminding ourselves of some of the ways in which we believe the mental and the physical exert a causal influence on each other. Consider the following sentences, which exemplify the different ways in which mental and physical states may be causally related:

1   The sudden sharp pain in his side made him cry out involuntarily (*mental to physical*).
2   The pain in his chest became so intense that for moment he thought he was having a heart-attack (*mental to mental*).
3   When John saw how upset Mary was by what he had said (*physical to mental*), he felt intensely sorry (*mental to mental*), and decided to apologize then and there (*mental to physical*).
4   'All his life he had regarded the syllogism he had learned while studying Kiesewetter's Logics: "Caius is a man, men are mortal, and therefore Caius is mortal" as being true only in respect to Caius, not to himself. Caius was a man, a man in the abstract sense, and so the syllogism applied to him: but Ivan Ilyitch was not Caius, and not a man in the abstract sense' (*mental to mental*).[2]

These examples require some brief explanation and commentary.

(1) exemplifies the case where a bodily sensation, a mental event, causes a piece of behaviour that is not an action but a reaction, some-

thing involuntarily forced out of a person. The pain is the reason why the person cries out, but not the person's reason, i.e. not the reason the person has or adopts for behaving as he does. The notion of adopting a reason and deciding to act upon it, does not apply in this case, where no action is involved.

(2) and (4) exemplify mental to mental causation but in different ways. (2) is akin to (1). Just as the pain in the person's side gives rise to the involuntary cry, so the pain in his chest momentarily causes him to panic. The thought that he might be having a heart-attack comes over him unbidden. In (4), however, the movement from the thoughts expressed by the statements 'Caius is man, men are mortal' to the thought 'Caius is mortal' is a logical step which Ivan Ilyitch is happy to take with respect to Caius, but cannot bring himself to take in his own case because of the prospect of his own annihilation. When we think logically we try to see the implication of a collection of statements and allow ourselves to be guided by that. The movement from thought to thought exemplifies not merely a causal, but a rational process, and in some sense is under our control.

The most complex case is represented by (3). A physical state of affairs in the world – Mary's being upset, crying and so forth – helps to cause John's perception that she is upset (physical to mental). This realization in turn causes him to feel sorry, and this mental state leads to a desire to apologize (mental to mental). The desire is backed by an unstated belief that apologizing will heal the offence and restore Mary's spirits to equilibrium. As a result of the desire to make amends and the belief that an apology is the right way to achieve this, John acts accordingly (mental to physical).

Committed epiphenomenalists must deny that mental states have any efficacy at all in these examples. They will allow, naturally, that the physical gives rise to the mental, but not that the mental can cause physical occurrences, or even play a part in bringing about other mental states. Bearing this in mind, look at Exercise 7.1 before proceeding any further.

What is your response to the threat of epiphenomalism? Consider your reaction and then read my response below.   **Exercise 7.**

Epiphenomenalism is a deeply repellent doctrine for a number of reasons. Firstly, our own first-person experience as agents testifies strongly against it. If I cross the road to buy some sweets in a shop, the reasons for my action will mention my beliefs and desires. I crossed the road because I wanted some sweets and because I believed I could get some in the shop opposite. If I had not wanted some sweets, or if I had believed that none were to be found in the shop, then I would not have crossed the road. (We will assume I did not have some other reason for crossing the road.) This certainly looks like a causal explanation of what I did, even down to entailing the contrary-to-fact conditional (which has been taken as the hall-mark of causal explanation), stating what would have happened if, contrary to what in fact did happen, I had not wanted the sweets or had not believed the shop contained any.

Secondly, we extend to other people what we believe obtains in our own case, namely, that their desires and beliefs also operate to explain and cause their behaviour, which in turn brings about other changes in the world. In fact, we have only to look around to witness the innumerable differences that human minds have contributed to the order of things – their creation and preservation as well as their destruction and decay. Again, epiphenomenalists must deny the truth of all this. For them, our everyday ways of speaking about human agency must represent a huge assembly of mistakes, a systematic illusion that states of mind make a difference, causally, to how things are.

Thirdly, a further peculiarity of epiphenomenalism is that if anyone believed it were true, and wished to say so, they would not be able to, because their desires and beliefs would be causally inactive. Paradoxically, anyone who believes that epiphenomenalism is true, and manages to say so, abandons the doctrine in the very act of asserting it. The assertion of a belief presupposes that the belief itself, together with a desire to communicate it, have given rise to the outward verbal expression of it.

I share the view of many thinkers that we can be more certain from our own experience that epiphenomenalism is false than that it is true, even if metaphysical speculation can make it appear so. The best attitude to epiphenomenalism, perhaps, is that recommended by Tyler Burge, who has aptly remarked that it can be viewed as a minor form of scepticism, which, whilst in practice no one can take seriously, is nevertheless useful in sharpening up our thinking about the nature of mental and physical relations.[3]

Epiphenomenalism poses the challenge of how best to explain our ordinary common-sense intuitions that the mind does make a difference to the way the world is. Compare epiphenomenalism with solipsism. No one seriously embraces solipsism, or scepticism of the sort that maintains that we cannot know that there is a past, or that the laws of nature will continue to operate in the future just as they do at present. But the sceptic, in posing queries about whether we can know what we unreflectively believe what we do know, plays a valuable role in alerting us to the need to justify our intuitions.

7.3   Reasons for actions as causes

How are Davidson's views on the explanation of actions supposed to lead to epiphenomenalism? To explain this, I need first to provide a quick sketch of Davidson's theory that reasons for actions are causes. In a seminal paper, 'Actions, Reasons and Causes', Davidson maintained that the reasons people mention to explain and justify what they do standardly function as the causes of those actions.[4] On the face of it, this may seem uncontroversial. After all, if a person's reasons for their actions are not the causes of the actions they rationalize, how else could they conceivably be related? John apologized to Mary. Why? Because he saw he had hurt her feelings, wanted this not to be the case and believed saying he was sorry would repair the damage. As we noted earlier, this certainly looks like a causal explanation, even down to entailing a counterfactual conditional: if either John had not wanted to apologize, or if he had not believed that apologizing would do any good, or both, then he would not have apologized. The occurrence of John's action is conditional upon the existence of the appropriate combination of desire and belief, and this provides a strong reason for thinking that it is a causal explanation. Why should we not, then, in default of a more plausible theory, accept that an agent's reasons for his or her actions are the causes of those actions?

One reason was supplied by analytical behaviourism, kept alive by neo-behaviourist elements in the philosophy of Wittgenstein. A major problem with behaviourism is that by depriving mental states of an inner status by reducing them to patterns of actual and possible behaviour, they can no longer be invoked to explain behaviour, including actions, since that would be tantamount to trying to explain a piece of conduct in terms of itself. Yet it seems clear that the examples (1)–(4) which I have provided above are all genuine instances where behaviour is brought about by underlying mental events.

A committed Wittgensteinian, such as Norman Malcolm, who had turned his face resolutely against the Cartesian conception of mental states as inner and private, was forced to deny that desires could be causes of actions.[5] Malcolm gives an example of two people playing chess. One player asks the other, 'What caused you to make that move?' and the opponent replies, 'Nothing caused me. I wanted to make that move.' Malcolm claims that this answer demonstrates that the opponent's move cannot be caused in the standard Humean sense of cause. Before continuing, pause to look at Exercise 7.2.

Exercise 7.2 Do you agree with Malcolm's claim? Consider your own response and then read on.

Malcolm is surely mistaken here. It is true that 'What caused you to make that move?' can be glossed as 'Who, or what, made, or forced, or impelled, you to make that move?', in which case the reply, 'Nothing made or forced me, it was my own decision which led to my making that move' is appropriate. But this response merely excludes a certain *sort* of causation of the move, namely, that in which some kind of compulsion or constraint is visited upon the agent. In the example given, this constraint is envisaged as emanating from an external source in the shape of another person or persons. But quite clearly, the chess player in question might have been suffering from some kind of psychological compulsion or irresistible impulse.

However, the key point that needs to be made against Malcolm's claim is that when constraining or compelling causes are absent, this does not mean that the chess player's action lacked *any* kind of cause at all. Malcolm's argument cannot show that when the person made the move just because he wanted to, thinking it to be the best strategy, his desire did not play a causal role in the generation of his action. Unsurprisingly, Malcolm does not give up so easily. He has a different style of argument, which is founded upon considerations regarding what it would be natural and easy to say about such cases as the one under examination. Thus, Malcolm writes:

> If B can be said to be giving the cause of his move, we obtain the following consequence: it could not be said that B's making that move was 'the effect' of his wanting to disconcert his opponent! Just imagine B saying, 'My making that move was the effect of my wanting to disconcert A'! A different example may help us to see this point: if I want to climb a cliff to see what is up there, and do climb it for that reason, it cannot be said that my climbing the cliff is 'the effect' of my wanting to climb it in order to see what is up there – even though the latter can be said to be 'the cause' of my climbing the cliff. These examples show that when the cause of a person's doing X is his reason for, his purpose in doing X, then his doing X is not 'the effect' of his reason or purpose. Philosophers have been mistaken in assuming that in all cases when Y is the cause of X, X is the effect of Y.[6]

The trouble with this style of argument is that it is heavily and unjustifiably dependent on so-called 'ordinary language philosophy'. It is true that the locutions Malcolm cites have a certain unnaturalness and stilted air about them, but so momentous a conclusion as that desires and purposes cannot possibly serve as causes in essentially a familiar Humean sense cannot rest upon such a slender basis. As an alternative to the ponderous expression Malcolm attributes to B, we can imagine B saying instead, 'I made that move *because* I wanted to disconcert A'; and it is equally natural to interpret B's words as giving part of the cause of his action. The other contribution to the genesis of the action will be made, of course, by B's belief that making the move he did would suffice to upset A.

Malcolm's second claim is even less satisfactory. He wants to insist that my climbing the cliff cannot be said to be the effect of my wanting to climb it and see what is up there, even though my wanting to climb the cliff can be said to be the cause of my climbing it. According to Malcolm, philosophers have been mistaken in thinking that when Y is the cause of X, X can always be described as the effect of Y. This claim sounds distinctly odd. But presumably Malcolm wants to reconstrue it, reinterpreting it to mean that X is the non-causal outcome of Y. Frankly, however, I cannot understand how X can be the outcome of Y, and yet not be caused by Y. There is a strong appearance of self-contradiction on Malcolm's part here.

Ordinary language is perhaps the first word on these matters, but it is by no means the last. Playing the same game as Malcolm, why should we not say that a person's climbing a particularly dangerous cliff is the outcome, the result, of a burning desire to prove that nature could be conquered by the efforts of a man? If the overcoming of the cliff was the result of the man's ambition, then surely the ambition helped to bring about the climbing of the cliff? If the man had not wanted to climb the cliff, if he had lacked the ambition to climb it, then he would not have climbed it (I leave aside the possibility that someone forced him to climb it). This strongly resembles the counterfactual statement, 'If the electric fan had not been plugged in, then you would not have received an electric shock from it.' Both these statements conform to Hume's second definition of cause in his first *Enquiry concerning Human Understanding*: 'If A had not been, then B had not existed', and are as fully causal as one could wish for. Furthermore, just as something might intervene to stop the fan from giving you an electric shock – a break in the power cable perhaps – so something might disrupt the causal chain reaching from desire to climb the cliff to the actual climbing of it – a sudden onset of illness perhaps.

Malcolm invokes another well-known argument to try to prove that desires and intentions cannot be causes, namely, the claim that there is a conceptual connection between a desire or intention and what it is a desire or intention to do. This violates Hume's stricture that causes and effects must be distinct existences and merely contingently, not logically, connected. But this objection is easily over-come once the details of Davidson's account of how reasons explain actions have been given, as we shall shortly see.

Davidson calls a reason that explains why an agent acted as he did a rationalization. A rationalization has two components. Firstly, it jus-tifies or rationalizes an action by mentioning a desire or pro-attitude (a favourable attitude) towards the action as described in a certain way, and a belief by the agent that the action satisfies that descrip-tion. As Davidson himself puts it: 'R is a primary reason why an agent performed the action A under the description D, only if R consists of a pro-attitude towards actions with a certain property, and a belief of the agent that A, under the description D has that property.'[7] Thus John apologized to Mary because he wanted to make things right again, and he believed that by apologizing he would do just that. Sec-ondly, in saying that John acted as he did because of what he wanted and believed, Davidson's claim is that the 'because' gives the causes of John's action, the desire and belief which together give rise to the action.

In explaining one physical event in terms of another, where no per-sonal agency is involved, the causal aspect of the explanation is pre-served, but the justificatory element has no place. When we explain why a kettle boiled by mentioning the gas flame that heated the water, we give the cause of the water's boiling, but we do not ra-tionalize or justify why the water boiled, since a flame is not a per-sonal agent. Conversely, the justificatory aspect of an explanation may be preserved, but the causal element may be missing. This is what happens when someone invents a reason in order to justify his or her action. For example, consider again the self-deception of Conrad's *Lord Jim* (see chapter 1, section 1.7). Jim tells himself that the reason he did not go to the rescue of two men swept overboard was that he thought he would enlarge his knowledge of the hearts of men by not going to the rescue. In giving himself this reason for his action, his aim, unacknowledged even to himself, was to palliate his failure to act, to let himself off the hook, as the saying goes. What makes this a *mere* rationalization, and not the genuine reason why he did not go to the rescue, is that the explanation does not mention a causally operative reason. The real cause of Jim's inaction was far less noble, namely, that he was terrified and did not want to risk his own skin, a reason he will not, or cannot, acknowledge to himself. And even in those cases where both the justificatory and the causal element are present, it is implicit in Davidson's characterization of a primary reason, as we have partially seen, that John's reason for apologizing to Mary will only justify his action under the description 'giving an apology' and not under some other description. Suppose Mary interprets John's action as a piece of pointed sarcasm designed to give offence. Then John's desire to put things right with Mary, together with his belief that an apology would serve the purpose, are the causes of his unintentionally offending her. But they do not rationalize or justify his action under the description 'giving offence'.

An argument against Davidson's view that rationalizations are causes of actions runs something like this: all true singular causal statements entail causal laws; it is only as tokens or instances of certain types of event that one event may be said to be the cause of another. To put this another way, according to Hume, any causal relation has to be viewed as an instance of a general regularity in nature. Thus if a token event a of the event type A caused a token event b of the event type B, there must be a backing causal law describing how events of type A typically cause events of type B under certain conditions. But there is no law of the sort 'Whenever people like John want to put things right with people like Mary, and believe they can do it by apologizing, they say they are sorry.' Rationalizations of actions cannot be sharpened up into statements of precise laws on the basis of which predictions can be made.

Moreover, it has been argued that laws must be true as a matter of fact, and not merely by virtue of the terms they contain. That is to say, statements that describe laws of nature must be synthetically, not analytically, true. But rationalizations of actions seem to be true by definition and, as it were, help to explicate what we mean by terms such as 'want' and 'believe'. Thus, if someone wants a packet of cigarettes more than he wants anything else, and believes that he can get one in the shop across the road, then, unless he changes his mind at the last minute, isn't killed in a road accident and so forth, he will cross the road to the shop. If he was not prevented from going to the shop but didn't go, we would conclude either that he had given up the desire for cigarettes or that it had been outweighed by a stronger want – not to die of lung cancer for example – or that he no longer believed that cigarettes were to be found in that shop. We reach this conclusion merely by reflecting on the meanings of the terms 'want' and 'believe'. It is an integral part of what it means to say that an agent wants a thing X and believes that by a-ing he can get X, that unless he is prevented, has other overpowering wants, changes his mind and so on, then he will perform action a. In other words, there seems to be some kind of logical or conceptual connection between rationalizations and the actions they explain which precludes them from being instances of laws, and hence in turn prevents them from being causes of actions.

Before proceeding to the next section, look at Exercise 7.3.

<table>
<tr><td>Exercise 7.3</td><td>The claim that there is a conceptual connection between actions and the reasons for actions which prevents reasons being causes has been debated for many years. Can you see any ways of solving this problem? Discuss your ideas with someone else before reading further.</td></tr>
</table>

7.4   Davidson's response: the causal theory of intentional action

Davidson has a response which, if successful, can get round both objections outlined above. According to Davidson, analyses of causality must proceed on two different levels. At the lower level, singular causal statements describe a causal relation which holds between particular events. This causal relationship holds between the events regardless of how the events are described. For example, consider the sentence, 'Striking the match on the side of the match-box caused the match to burst into flames.' The event described as 'the striking of the match' is causally related to the event described as 'the match bursting into flames'. It is the events themselves that are causally related, not the descriptions of the events (cf. chapter 6, section 6.5). Because the causal relation does not hold between linguistic entities but between the events themselves out there in the world, causal relations between events are said to occur at an ontological level. Because the causal relation obtains between events and not between descriptions of events, it holds, as I said a moment ago, regardless of how the events are described. By contrast, different descriptions of events are different by virtue of singling out different properties of those events, and so Davidson can be seen as maintaining that it is not by virtue of how events are described, or by virtue of the properties picked out in those descriptions that events are causally related, but merely by virtue of the fact that one event, a, is causally related to another event, b.

However, we must distinguish a higher level of causality, namely that at which causal explanations are given. Causal explanations employ what has become known as the deductive-nomological model of explanation, which is prevalent in the sciences. This model consists of a deductive argument with two premises.

The first premise consists of a statement of a law which describes the cause and effect relation that holds between certain classes of events. Davidson emphasizes that such laws are what he calls strict laws, by which he means two things:

1   It is a true general statement that contains no 'other things being equal' clauses. The regularity that it states holds universally and without qualification. In effect, it treats the universe as a closed physical system (cf. chapter 3, section 3.1).
2   It supports counterfactual statements. A counterfactual statement states that if a cause had not occurred, then neither would its effect. This means that an effect does not merely follow a cause, but is dependent for its occurrence on the cause. This makes the law as deterministic as nature can be. In other words, the notion of the dependency of the effect on the cause helps to capture the idea that the cause is naturally necessary for the effect to occur.

The second premise consists of a singular statement which describes the occurrence of the event that is the cause. Putting these two statements together in an argument, we can deduce the occurrence of the effect as the conclusion of the argument. This model of explanation has the pattern:

1   If certain initial conditions C1, C2, C3 . . . Cn obtain, then event E will occur. (C1, C2, C3, etc., comprise the conditions that have to be fulfilled if the event E is to follow.) This is a statement of the causal law.
2   And in this instance C1, C2, C3 . . . Cn do obtain. (Singular statement asserting that the initial conditions described in (1) above do obtain.)
3   Therefore E will occur.

To put this less abstractly, suppose there is a physical law which states how much a certain type of metal, say copper, will expand if it is heated through one degree centigrade. (This law states the coefficient of linear expansion for copper.) With regard to a particular piece of copper that has been heated through one degree centigrade, we can deduce that it will have expanded by the amount specified in the law. The model of explanation will run as follows:

1   If copper is heated through one degree centigrade, then it will expand by so many fractions of a millimetre (causal law).
2   This piece of copper has been heated through one degree centigrade.
3   Therefore this piece of copper will have expanded by the amount stated in the law.

What is deduced is not the event itself, but a statement (3) which describes the event, and it is deduced from two other statements (1) and (2). This is why Davidson maintains that causal explanation obtains between statements which describe events, and not between the events themselves, as these are non-linguistic entities. For causal explanation to be possible, everything hangs upon how the events are described. Suppose, for example, that my fountain pen is made of copper. Then, although it is true that my fountain pen will expand by so many fractions of a millimetre if it is heated through one degree centigrade, a statement to the effect that my fountain pen was heated through one degree centigrade cannot be substituted for (2) in the explanation above if the conclusion (3) is logically to follow. The explanation,

1   If copper is heated through one degree centigrade, then it will expand by so many fractions of a millimetre.
2   My fountain pen was heated through one degree centigrade

cannot yield the conclusion,

3   My fountain pen expanded by a certain fraction of a millimetre

because the law is couched not in terms of what happens to fountain pens but only in terms of what happens to copper. Thus it can be seen that with regard to causal explanations that employ laws, the possibility of giving an explanation depends on how the events are described. By virtue of being made of copper, my fountain pen will expand by so many fractions of a millimetre if heated through one degree centigrade, and, under the description that it is copper, the deduction that it will expand when heated can be made. But under the description, 'the present which was given to me on my 21st birthday', no deduction again is possible, even though it is true that when heated through one degree centigrade the present which was given to me on my 21st birthday will expand by a certain fraction of a millimetre.

Davidson claims that all singular causal statements will be backed by laws, but that this does not mean that the descriptions which figure in the singular causal statement will necessarily be the same as those that occur in the statement of the laws. His claim implies, however, that there must be descriptions of the events that figure in singular causal statements which instantiate causal laws, even if we are not aware of what those descriptions are. This is commonly the case. To use one of his own examples, high winds may bring about the collapse of a bridge, but there are no laws describing causal relations between winds and bridges. Nevertheless, at some level there will be laws using concepts that can be used to characterize the movement

of air and the collapse of structures on the basis of which the collapse
of bridges on particular occasions can be explained and predicted.
Davidson makes the point that singular causal statements must be
backed by causal laws in the following way:

> It may mean that 'A caused B' entails some particular laws involving
> the predicates used in the descriptions 'A' and 'B', or it may mean that
> 'A caused B' entails that there exists a causal law instantiated by some
> true descriptions of A and B. Obviously both versions of Hume's doc-
> trine give a sense to the claim that singular causal statements entail
> laws, and both sustain the view that causal explanations involve laws.
> . . . Only the second version can be made to fit most causal explana-
> tions; it suits rationalizations equally well.[8]

Davidson can use the distinction between singular causal statements and causal explanations to avoid the second objection –
namely, that a person's reasons for his or her actions cannot be causes
– in the following way. The second objection, it will be recalled, said
that the fact that explanations of actions in terms of the agent's
desires and beliefs turned out to be necessarily true ruled out those
explanations as causal explanations, because for events to be related
as cause and effect they must be distinct existences, neither of which
logically entails the occurrence of the other. Davidson's response is
to point out that how an event is described can make it seem that it
is logically related to another event and hence cannot serve as a
genuine cause. What we need to realize is that it is only descriptions
of events that are logically related, not the events themselves. The fact
that an event can be described in terms that logically link it to its
effect cannot show that the events in question cannot be related as
cause and effect. To see this, take any singular causal statement, such
as, 'Putting the kettle on the gas-flame caused the kettle to boil.' The
action described as 'Putting the kettle on the gas-flame' can easily be
redescribed 'as the cause of the kettle boiling'. If this redescription is
then substituted back into the original singular statement, we get:
'The cause of the kettle boiling caused the kettle to boil.' But
although this statement is analytically true, it does not rule out the
putting of the kettle on the gas-flame as the cause of the kettle
boiling, because the logical relation obtains purely by virtue of how
the two events are described. At the level of events conceived of as
non-abstract particulars, these still count as distinct existences, and
thus can stand in a causal relation to each other.
    A good illustration of the same point is provided by the example
of substances described as poisonous. To describe something as a

poison is to characterize it in terms of its typical effects – the sickness and possible death it brings. It is thus analytic to say that, all being equal (e.g. no antidotes were administered earlier), a poison causes death and sickness; if it did not typically bring this effect about, it would not be a poison. But poisons can be described in other terms, which show that their relation to their effects is purely contingent after all. Sodium cyanide typically causes sickness or death if ingested in significant amounts, and the statement that sodium cyanide causes sickness or death is not necessarily true, but obtains purely as a matter of fact.

Furthermore, just as causes are sometimes described in terms of their typical effects, so effects are sometimes characterized in terms of their causes. It is analytic to say that boiled eggs were produced by boiling, and that cooked meals resulted from cooking. Nevertheless, the boiling of the egg or the cooking of the meal were causally responsible for the boiled and cooked state the egg and the meal respectively end up in. Other descriptions of the internal changes that result when food is cooked can be found which mean that under those descriptions there is no longer any appearance of a logical link between the cooking of the food and the state the food finally ends up in.

Those descriptions of desire and intentions that specify which desires and intentions they are – individuating descriptions – are like the description of something as a poison, in that such descriptions imply what typically comes about as the result of having the particular desire or intention in question. An intention to mow the lawn will, all things being equal, result in the lawn's being mowed. This is indeed what it means to have an intention to mow the lawn, rather than some other intention, and not to give it up, have it frustrated by interfering factors and so forth.

However, according to Davidson, the intention and the action to which it leads, in this case mowing the lawn, must have descriptions under which they may be seen to instantiate a strict law. Since Davidson thinks that only strict laws are physical laws, this means that desires, intentions and the beliefs that also rationalize particular actions must all have physical descriptions. Thus, Davidson writes:

> The laws whose existence is required if reasons are causes of actions do not, we may be sure, deal in the concepts in which rationalizations must deal. If the causes of a class of events (actions) fall in a certain class (reasons) and there is a law to back each singular causal statement, it does not follow that there is a law connecting events classified as reasons with events classified as actions – the classifications may even be neurological, chemical or physical.[9]

7.5   Anomalous monism

We are now in a position to examine Davidson's position that has become known as anomalous monism. I shall outline the thesis by stating the propositions which are constitutive of it, and then comment on each of these.

1   Mental events cause physical events.
2   If two events are causally related, then there must be a strict physical law under which they can be subsumed. (Strict laws contain no *ceteris paribus* clauses, i.e. no other 'things being equal' clauses, and are part of a closed system, so whatever can affect events within the system must itself be included in the system.) To put this another way, cause and effect must have descriptions under which they instantiate a strict physical law.
3   There are no strict psycho-physical laws. That is, there are no strict bridging laws connecting mental events under their mental descriptions, with physical events under their physical descriptions. What this amounts to, in effect, is a rejection of the type-type identity theory which seeks an ontological reduction of mental events to physical events (cf. chapter 1, section 1.9, and chapter 3, section 3.8.5).

7.5.1   Commentary

The first proposition outlined above represents Davidson's rejection of epiphenomenalism. Mental events can, and do, function as causes. They make a difference to what happens physically in the world: a person's reasons for their actions are the causes of those actions.

The second proposition in section 7.5 has become known in the literature surrounding this topic as the principle of nomological causality. Davidson does not argue for this position but is content to point out that it has seemed to be true to many philosophers, Hume and Kant notably among them. Since, according to the first proposition, mental events are causally related to physical events, there must be a strict law under which such events can be subsumed, and this must be a physical law, so there must be a physical description of the mental event under which it can figure in the strict physical law. So mental events must be physical events. This is the thesis of event monism. Contrary to what dualism affirms, there are not two sorts of event, those that are purely physical, and those that are purely mental. Rather, all events are physical events, but some physical events will also possess mental descriptions. According to the third proposition in section 7.5, mental events cannot be systematically reduced, either by analytical or ontological reduction, to physical events, so there will not be any strict psycho-physical causal laws relating the mental, described as the mental, to physical events.

Davidson's reason for rejecting the ontological reduction of the mental to the physical is that the propositional attitudes – beliefs, desires, intentions and so forth – are holistic, and this places a normative constraint on the attribution of these attitudes to other people. There must, he claims, be a large degree of coherence among the attitudes, otherwise we would be trying to imagine a totally irrational being and this would be equivalent to thinking of an animal without thoughts: 'To the extent that we fail to discover a coherent and plausible pattern in the attitudes and actions of others we simply forgo the chance of treating them as persons.' There is no counterpart of this constitutive ideal of rationality in physical theory, and hence there can be no wholesale systematic reduction of the mental to the physical that the type-type identity theory requires.

It is in the impossibility of this kind of reduction that the anomalousness of the mental, its unlawlikeness, consists. Because there cannot be psycho-physical laws, mental events can be neither explained nor predicted in purely physical terms. Someone might know the entire physical history of the world, yet they would not be able to explain or predict a single mental event, even though every mental event would necessarily fall under some physical description or other. Davidson's rejection of the reduction of the mental to the physical on a type-type basis, together with his insistence that mental events must have physical descriptions, entail that he holds some version of the token-token identity of the mental with the physical. In order to explain the relation between the mental features of physical events and the physical features of those events, Davidson espouses supervenience. To say that the mental is supervenient on the physical is to make the modal claim that there can be no events that are alike in all physical respects but differ in some mental respect (see chapter 6, section 6.3). Thus, if a person's mental state changes from M1 to M2, this means that there must be some change in the physical states upon which M1 and M2 supervene. Likewise, no two persons' mental states could be different, according to the supervenience hypothesis, unless there is a difference in the subvenient physical bases that ground those mental states.

7.6   Objections to anomalous monism

The first objection we shall consider derives from Jaegwon Kim, who says that Davidson's position commits him to the view that 'events are causes or effects only as they instantiate physical laws'.[10] But this, Kim maintains, amounts to claiming that mental events are causally efficacious only by virtue of their physical features and not their mental ones. The mental does not cause anything else qua mental; it is not *as* the mental that it has a causal role to play, but only because of its physical properties under which it alone can be seen to be the instantiation of a strict physical law which all true singular causal statements must instantiate. Hence, anomalous monism leads straight to epiphenomenalism. Kim's objection is complicated, so before reading on, pause, and look at Exercise 7.4.

Is Kim right in claiming that Davidson is committed to maintaining that the mental properties of physical events are causally impotent, and that therefore the mind makes no causal difference to the world?

Exercise 7.4

Davidson dismisses Kim's objection. Causal relations for him hold between events, non-abstract particulars, regardless of how they are described. He is not committed to the view that only by virtue of its properties can one event be the cause of another: 'Given this extensionalist view of causal relations, it makes no literal sense . . . to speak of an event causing something as mental, or by virtue of its mental properties, or as described in one way or another.'[11] He also puts it another way: 'Events instantiate a law only as described in one way rather than another, but we cannot say that an event caused another only as described.'[12] The fact that all mental events have physical descriptions makes them fully part of the physical world, on Davidson's theory, but it would be wrong to insist that they can function as causes only in so far as they have physical properties. What properties events do or do not happen to have is irrelevant to their causal powers, as far as Davidson is concerned. In this way, he sidesteps the question of whether mental events cause physical bodily events by virtue of their mental properties or by virtue of their physical properties by disallowing the dilemma to be foisted upon him. For him, there is no dilemma to confront. Mental events are not mere epiphenomena, but this has nothing to do with what features, mental or physical, such events possess.

This, however, is strongly counterintuitive. Consider an event consisting in an explosion, which kills several people. Perhaps when the explosive goes off it emits a red, rather than a greenish, glow. The mere colour of the explosion considered by itself, we would want to say, is a feature or property of the explosion that is causally irrelevant to its devastating effects, which depend upon other more pertinent properties such as forces generated when the chemical detonates, the temperatures reached by the explosive gases and so forth. In other words, it seems reasonable to conclude that some properties of events, but not others, play a causal role in bringing about certain other events. The suspicion that Kim has voiced regarding the role of the mental in anomalous monism cannot, then, be entirely dismissed. There must, I submit, on the basis of what Davidson has said so far, remain some residual doubt about the role of the mental if, in order to figure in a causal law, it must attract a physical description.

A second worry is that if mental events are caused by underlying physical events, and owe their existence and features entirely to those events, then it is difficult to see how mental events can have separate and independent powers of their own. If M is the mental event which supervenes upon a physical event, P, it is questionable that causal powers can emerge at higher levels. 'There are', writes Kim, 'no new causal powers that magically accrue to M [the mental event] over and beyond the causal powers of P [the physical state upon which M supervenes]. No new causal powers emerge at higher levels.'[13]

Searle is alert to this difficulty, but with characteristic sang-froid argues that it can easily be overcome:

> [T]he fact that mental features are supervenient upon neuronal features in no way diminishes their causal efficacy. The solidity of the piston is supervenient upon its molecular structure, but this does not make solidity epiphenomenal; and similarly, the causal supervenience of my present back-pain on micro-events in my brain does not make the pain epiphenomenal.[14]

You should stop to consider Exercise 7.5 before reading on.

Exercise 7.5   Do you agree with Searle? Look back to chapter 6, section 6.5 to refresh your memory on this question.

Unfortunately for Searle, his proposal will not work. The supervenience of the solidity of the piston on its micro-structure does not parallel the supervenience of pain on cerebral micro-events. The reason harks back to something I pointed out in my discussion of Searle in the last chapter, namely that, unlike the liquidity of water, the solidity of the piston is not a distinct and separate phenomenon from its micro-structure. The solidity of the piston is constituted by

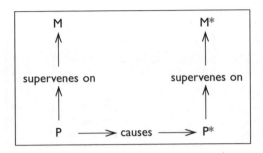

Figure 7.1   Mental/physical supervenience and physical causation

its micro-structure. It is that very structure viewed from a macro-scopic perspective. In the case of the solidity of the piston, the identity theory is true. The solidity is the micro-structure, just as the temperature of a gas is the mean kinetic energy of its molecules. The reason that the solidity of the piston is not epiphenomenal is that its solidity/micro-structure is, without doubt or ambiguity, fully part of the physical world. The solidity just is the physical micro-structure, and hence it is unsurprising that it cannot be classified as epiphenomenal (see chapter 6, section 6.5).

By contrast, the phenomenon of consciousness, by Searle's own admission, is a separate and distinct phenomenon from the physical micro-events that gave rise to it. Those micro-events are part of an objective, third-person, public and spatial realm, the physical world. Consciousness, on the other hand, is a subjective, first-person, private phenomenon. Applying Leibniz's Law (see chapter 2, section 2.7.1), we are forced to the conclusion that consciousness cannot be identical with micro-physical events, but must be seen as a separate and different sort of occurrence.

A closely related and very considerable difficulty is posed by the thesis that the physical world is causally closed and that mental and physical causes do not overdetermine their effects. However, to make the import of this objection clear, some explanation will be required (see figure 7.1). A physical event, P, a brain event of some kind, is causally sufficient to give rise to another brain event, P*. In other words, the physical world is causally closed: all physical events have physical causes which are sufficient to bring about those events. This, as we noted, forms a central plank of anomalous monism. At the same time, a mental event, M, e.g. a sensation of pain, supervenes on P. P determines the existence and character of M, and M cannot change unless P does. For Searle, as we have seen, the supervenience relation is just causality: P causes M. Kim disagrees with this characterization

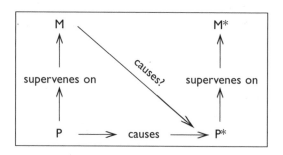

Figure 7.2   Over-determination?

of supervenience, but in this context the disagreement between Searle and Kim is not a material one. M* supervenes on P*, which determines the existence and character of M* and lets M* equal a desire to be rid of M, the pain.

In everyday life we would account the pain, M, as at least part of the reason why M*, the desire to be rid of the pain, comes into being. In other words, M plays a causal role in bringing about M*. However, it seems clear from figure 7.1 that the real reason M* exists is not because of M, but solely because of P and P*. P acts to bring about P*, and P*, in turn, is the supervenient cause of M*. M* follows M, but only because at the subvenient base level P gives rise to P*. M plays no causal role in the generation of M* – it only appears to. All the real causal work is done at the physical subvenient level. M and M* are mere epiphenomena, dangling on the coat-tails of P and P* and making no causal difference to the world.

But, it might be suggested, even though P is causally sufficient to bring about P*, why should not M also be part of the cause of P*, and in this way play an indirect causal role in the generation of M*, thus avoiding relegation as a mere epiphenomenon? Why should figure 7.1 not be modified as shown in figure 7.2. The claim that is now being made is that P* is overdetermined by P and M. That is to say, both P and M operate as separate and independent causes to bring about P*.

Having looked carefully at these claims, and at figures 7.1 and 7.2, consider Exercise 7.6 before reading on.

Exercise 7.6   What is your response? Can an event such as P* be brought about by two separate and independent causes?

Philosophers have been very chary of accepting that a single event can have two independent causes, both of which singly are sufficient to bring that event about. Their intuition has been that given an event, C, and two postulated causes, A and B, there are only three genuine possibilities available. Firstly, A but not B was the cause of C. Secondly, B but not A was the cause of C. Thirdly, neither A nor B was the cause of C. (For the purposes of this discussion, this last possibility can be discounted.)

To begin to appreciate why causal overdetermination has been rejected, consider the following example. A man is about to be burnt at the stake. Wishing to ensure that he does not suffer, one of his friends drops a small tablet at his feet. This tablet, when ignited, will give off highly poisonous fumes, which will kill the person who is to be burnt very rapidly just as the flames begin to lick around his feet. If the tablet does not work for some reason, then the man will be burnt to death. Alternatively, if the tablet does work, he will be dead long before the flames have any significant effect on him. Both the tablet and the flame, considered singly and separately on their own, are causally sufficient to kill the man. But now suppose someone claims that the man's death was the result of both the flames and the poison operating together. This is where we are likely to protest: he cannot have been killed by both of these agents. It must have been either one or the other. If it were the poison, then the flames can be excluded as being the cause. And likewise, if it were the flames, then the poison is ruled out as the reason for the man's death.

A formal demonstration of the point being made can easily be provided once we remember that any true causal statement must entail a contrary-to-fact conditional. In other words, if X is the cause of Y, this means that if X were not to occur then Y will not occur. Let us apply this to the present case and see what the outcome is:

1   If the flames are the cause of the man's death, then were the flames not to occur, the man would not die.

However, in the case where the poison operates, the man does die after all, so the contrary-to-fact conditional stating what would have happened if the flames had not occurred is false.

On the other hand consider:

2   If the poison is the cause of the man's death, then were the poison not to work, the man would not die.

However, if the flames burn the man, then he does die after all, so the contrary-to-fact conditional stating what would have happened if the poison had not worked is false. (1) and (2) cannot be true simultaneously. If (1) is true, then (2) must be false, and if (2) is true, then (1) must be false. In other words, (1) and (2) cannot operate as separate and independent causes. The man's death cannot be overdetermined: it must either have been caused by the burning, or by the poisoning, but not by both.[15]

Applying this to the problem of psycho-physical causation, if P really is causally sufficient to bring about P*, then, if overdetermination is rejected, there is simply no room left in which M can operate. The problem could be solved if M could be ontologically reduced to P, that is, if the pain could be identified with neural events in the person's brain. But then what becomes of the experience of pain, and consciousness in general, if these mental phenomena are made out to be nothing more than physical and chemical events in the head? Reducing mental phenomena to purely physical states certainly prevents those phenomena from being causally inactive. It brings them totally inside the physical world and makes them fully a part of a closed physical causal system. But this is only achievable by denying the distinctive fact of consciousness, which is an unacceptable consequence. Certainly, it is not an option that Searle himself can take in the light of his rejection of materialist reductionism.

Another option would be to abolish the supervenience relation between the mental and the physical, so that the mental does not depend for its existence or character on the physical. But this might seem an even more unattractive choice, for it amounts to allowing that there can be purely non-physical mental events that can be just what they are in complete independence of the physical world. In other words, we are led straight back into the arms of substance dualism with all its attendant difficulties.

If the mental supervenes upon the physical, which seems a very reasonable belief, and if this is taken to exclude materialist reduction, then I am afraid, for the reasons given, that I cannot see how states of minds can escape turning out to be epiphenomena. My own experience, on the other hand, tells me that this cannot be so, and that my own and others' mental states make a clear causal difference to the world. How these two positions are to be reconciled, I cannot yet see. I can only commend the problem to you.

Questions to think about

1 Can reasons for actions be the causes of those actions, as Davidson claims?

2 Must all singular causal statements be backed by causal laws?

3 Davidson denies that he is committed to claiming that it is only by virtue of their physical properties that one event causes another, but is he correct?

4 If the mental properties of events are epiphenomena, then how can an agent's reasons justify and explain his or her actions?

5 Can epiphenomenalism be proved false?

6 If mental states are caused by brain states, can there be genuine top–down causation from the mental to the physical?

Suggestions for further reading

- Carlos J. Moya's *The Philosophy of Action: An Introduction* (Cambridge: Polity, 1990) is an excellent way into questions concerning the nature of agency, the will, whether reasons for actions can be causes, anomalous monism and Davidson's contributions to this area of philosophy. Highly recommended for its clarity and comprehensiveness.

- Donald Davidson's *Essays on Actions and Events* (Oxford: Clarendon Press, 1980) is a classic of its kind, but the reader new to Davidson will have to be prepared to work hard.

- Both the following books by Jaegwon Kim contain useful discussions of mental causation: *Mind in a Physical World* (Cambridge, MA: MIT Press, 1998) and *Philosophy of Mind* (Boulder, CO: Westview Press, 1996).

- John Heil and Alfred Mele (eds), *Mental Causation* (Oxford: Clarendon Press, 1995) is a useful and up-to-date collection, but tough-going.

- S. Evnine, *Donald Davidson* (Cambridge: Polity, 1991) is a very clear introduction to Davidson's thought. Unfortunately, it may now be out of print.

- I. Thalberg, *Perception, Emotion and Action* (Oxford: Blackwell, 1977) contains good discussions of Davidson's thesis that reasons for actions are causes and the problem posed by wayward causal chains.

8

THE PROBLEM OF OTHER MINDS

As a result of reading this chapter you should:

- understand how the problem of other minds arises;
- understand the difficulties posed by attempting to solve the problem by inferring, deductively or inductively, the existence of such states from a person's behaviour;
- understand the argument from analogy for other minds, and its weaknesses;
- understand Wittgenstein's attack on the Cartesian conception of how mental terms acquire their meanings;
- be able critically to assess Wittgenstein's positive criterial account of how mental terms acquire their meanings and to evaluate its contribution to our understanding of the other minds problem;
- be able critically to assess P. F. Strawson's attempt to solve the problem of other minds.

8.1 Introduction

The bulk of this book so far has been concerned with the meta-physics of mind. Metaphysics deals with what kinds of thing exist, and what their existence or being consists in. Thus a central question has been what the nature of the mind is. More specifically, our investigation has concerned what is the ontological status of mental states as well as the subjects or possessors of such states. The focus of this chapter, by contrast, is on the epistemology of mind. Epistemology is that branch of philosophy which deals with questions such as what it is to know something, what kinds of thing we can know, and how. The particular concern of this chapter is whether, and how, each of us can know of the existence of minds other than our own.

Let us begin by remembering that a recurring theme in the philosophy of mind is the privacy of the mental. Recall, for example, the argument that if a person's mental states are radically private but their brain states are publicly accessible, then by Leibniz's Law (see chapter 2, section 2.7.1) mental states cannot be identified with, or reduced to, brain states. This argument embodies a picture of the mind we have largely inherited from Descartes. I make the qualification 'largely' because it seems to me that many people who have never even heard of Descartes and are unacquainted with his philosophy of mind subscribe to something like his view of the mind as a radically private realm, an inner landscape or theatre, accessible only to the owner of the mind in question.

If, however, mental states really do possess a radical privacy, or logical privacy as it has come to be called, which shields them from public scrutiny, then it appears that there must forever be a doubt as to whether anyone can ever really know what is occurring in another person's mind, or even, as the limiting case, whether anyone other than oneself actually has a mind. By contrast, there is no parallel problem concerning the existence of other brains. With regard to physical events such as brain processes, I could in principle observe what is taking place in your brain, just as you could observe directly, or find out with the use of a device such as an electro-encephalogram which measures the brain's electrical output, what is occurring in mine. I have no special means of finding out what is happening in my brain which is denied to you, just as you have no special means of finding out what is taking place in your brain which is denied to me. Our access to our own, and to each other's brain processes, is symmetrical. Neither of us possesses any special privileged access to what is going on in our brains which is denied to the other. However, if the picture Descartes offers us is correct, our access to the contents of our own minds, and to each other's minds, is asymmetrical, the individual person possessing a privileged access that is unavailable to others. It is the doctrine of privileged access which makes room for doubt about the existence of other minds, a doubt that is excluded in the case of other brains, which are directly observable by all and sundry.[1]

The problem of the existence of other minds never usually strikes us in everyday life. We unhesitatingly attribute states of mind to other human beings; the possibility that what we take to be other people might in fact be mindless zombies not only never crosses our mind, but would be dismissed out of hand as a ludicrous possibility by most people if it did. But why are we so certain that other minds exist and, crucially, on what basis?

That basis, it would seem, can only be the behaviour that other people exhibit, namely what they say and do. In my own case I do not need to observe my behaviour in a mirror in order to be able to know what I am thinking and feeling, neither do I need to make any inferences from more basic evidence as to my mental state. I am able to know directly and non-inferentially my own state of mind. But in your case it seems that I know, if I know at all, what your mental state is solely on the basis of your behaviour. How else could I know, if not from observation of your behaviour, the state of mind that lies behind it?[2]

The problem, however, is this. Mental states, on the one hand, and items of behaviour, on the other, cannot, it seems, be identified with each other, despite the efforts of analytical behaviourists to reduce mental states to patterns of behaviour. Those efforts, as we witnessed in chapter 4, failed. Mental states stubbornly refused to be reduced to behaviour, leading to the conclusion that the two could exist completely separate from each other. Just as there could be behaviour without any corresponding mental states, so there could be mental states in the absence of any behaviour. But, given that mental states are different and discrete from items of behaviour, by what process of inference is it possible to go from statements describing a person's behaviour to statements describing their state of mind, since the meanings of the two classes of statement appear to be utterly different from each other?[3] Talk about the mental, in accordance with the Cartesian model of the mind as a private theatre, is talk about what is radically or logically private. Talk about behaviour is talk about what can be publicly witnessed. Moreover, mental states are conceived of as the underlying causes of behaviour. To attempt to identify mental states with the behaviour they are invoked to explain, would be to seek to equate causes with their effects. But, as Hilary Putnam has pointed out, '*causes* (pains) are not logical constructions out of their *effects* (behaviour)'.[4]

If mental states could be identified with behaviour, there would be no need to infer the existence of such states from behaviour. No pattern of inference would be involved or required. In witnessing a person's behaviour, one would literally be witnessing their state of mind. But because states of mind cannot be identified with behaviour, it would appear that some kind of inference from the one to the other must be involved. What is the nature of this inference?

There are only two types of inference available to us, deductive inference and inductive inference. The hallmark of deductive inference is that in a valid deductive argument the conclusion of the argument is logically entailed by its premises. That is to say, if the premises are asserted but the conclusion denied, a formal contradiction results. This is because the information contained in the conclusion is already contained in the premises. Deductive arguments are not ampliative: no information or meaning can be extracted from the conclusions of these arguments that is not already contained in their premises. But this means that we cannot deductively infer people's mental states from their behaviour. Before reading on, consider the question posed in Exercise 8.1.

Can you see why deductive inference is blocked in this case? Think about this on your own for a few minutes and then discuss the issue with someone else before reading my commentary below.

Exercise 8.1

The difference between the meanings of behavioural statements and those attributing mental states rules out the possibility of passing deductively from statements describing behaviour to those describing mental states. As we have seen, since talk about mental states is not equivalent to talk about behaviour, any attempt to move from purely behavioural premises to a conclusion attributing a non-behavioural item such as a mental state would represent an attempt to put more into the conclusion than is contained in the premises.

8.2 Induction and the argument from analogy

The use of deductive inference in passing from behaviour to mental states having been ruled out, we are left with induction. The hallmark of inductive inference is that the conclusion goes beyond what is logically entailed by the premises. In other words, this pattern of inference is ampliative. It takes the form 'All the As observed hitherto have been Bs', therefore 'All the As there are will turn out to be Bs'. Clearly there is more information contained in the conclusion than in the (single) premise. This is why to assert the premise but deny the conclusion does not amount to a contradiction. The conclusion does not contain in a different form the information contained in the premise, but goes beyond it, by contrast with what happens in the case of deductive arguments.[5] An example of an inductive inference might run as follows. It has been observed that if people who are asleep are woken up when their eyes are moving rapidly under their lids, they report that they have been dreaming. Let us suppose that this has been found to happen in all observed cases. On this basis, the inductive inference is made: 'Whenever people's eyes move rapidly while they are asleep, they are dreaming.' Quite clearly, the conclusion makes a much larger claim than is made by the premise, which only claims that in cases observed so far is there a correlation between eye movements in sleep and dreaming.

How might inductive inference be applied to the problem of other minds? Well, it might be argued that whenever a certain type of behaviour is observed, the same type of mental state is observed to occur at the same time, thus providing inductive grounds for the claim that whenever that type of behaviour occurs, it will be accompanied by the same type of mental state. Notice, however, that just as in the dreaming/rapid eye movement example, for an inductive argument about the existence of other minds to get going, correlations must first have been established between the occurrence of a certain type of behaviour and the presence of a certain type of mental state. Now how does this correlation get established in the first place? Consider this question as you look at Exercise 8.2.

Exercise 8.2   Can you see the difficulty in establishing a correlation between the presence of certain kinds of mental state and certain patterns of behaviour in the case of other people?

The difficulty should be fairly obvious. The correlation cannot be set up because the mental states of other people cannot be observed. All that one can observe in the case of others is their behaviour. Whether there are mental states behind such behaviour cannot be assumed. It is the very existence of these states which is the question at issue.

There is, however, just one case in which a correlation between a mental state and a pattern of behaviour can be discovered, namely one's own. Suppose I notice that whenever I feel sad, I cry. I then conclude that whenever I see you cry, the same correlation holds, because you are very much similar to me outwardly in appearance and behaviour as well as biologically similar to me. It is only in my own case that I am directly acquainted with my sadness – as an inner private mental state. In your case I can only be acquainted with one-half of the correlated phenomena, namely your outward public behaviour. Nevertheless, by analogy with my own case, it seems inductively reasonable to conclude that the outward public phenomenon of crying is accompanied by a private inner sadness in your case as well as mine. This argument was stated by the philosopher John Stuart Mill in the nineteenth century in this way:

> I conclude that other human beings have feelings like me, because, first, they have bodies like me, which I know in my own case, to be the antecedent condition of feelings; and because, secondly, they exhibit the acts and other outward signs, which in my own case I know by experience to be caused by feelings.[6]

To make this quite clear, the situation is rather like one in which I pass down a street at night and see shadows on the window-blinds of houses showing people apparently sitting down to tea. I cannot enter these houses to check if that is what is really going on, but eventually I come to my own house. There, outlined on the blind, is my wife apparently sitting down to tea. Accordingly, I enter the house and see with my own eyes directly that she is indeed sitting down to tea. Having established the correlation between the shadows on the blind and what is taking place within in my own case, I then conclude that, by analogy with my own case, the same must be true of all the houses I have passed on the way to my own home.[7] With this example in mind, consider Exercise 8.3.

Can you see an important difference between the problem of other minds and the problem of what is taking place in other houses? Does this difference create a problem for the attempt to establish the existence of other minds by analogy with my own case?

Exercise 8.3

The illustration using the blinds does not quite capture the problem of other minds, for the following reason. Were I to be in any doubt regarding my inductive inference about other people sitting down to tea when characteristic shadows appear on the blinds, I could always resolve it by entering other people's houses and seeing for myself. But this is only possible because the interiors of other people's houses are not private, in the sense of closed to me, and so I could look inside if I wished. However, if mental states, by contrast with what goes on in houses, are logically private, then I can never check the accuracy of my inductive inferences, since nothing will ever be able to count as gaining a direct access to the mental states of others. This has been felt to be a serious weakness of this kind of argument. I can be sure of the correlation between a certain type of mental state and a certain type of behavioural pattern only in my own case. How then can I blithely conclude that what is happening in all other cases is similar to my own, if my own case is all I have to go on? It seems wildly irresponsible to generalize from a single case, my own, to that of other people. Moreover, as we have seen, I never have the opportunity of discovering if my induction is correct, since I can never directly come to know the mental states of others.

The argument from analogy has also been accused of chauvinism. If we know by analogy with the human form and human behaviour that there are minds other than our own, won't this apply only in the case of other human beings and not in animals, since the latter do not resemble human beings? But then we will be led by a different route to the conclusion that Descartes reached, namely that animals are not minded. There is also a worry that we may fail to attribute mentality to human beings who are abnormal in some way, and accordingly treat them inappropriately. It seems to me that this criticism overstates the case. Animals, from the very nature of the case, do not have human faces, for example, but they do have faces nonetheless. Their limbs are different from ours, but nevertheless they are recognizable as limbs. Likewise, their internal arrangements may differ from our internal arrangements but the various organs – heart, liver, lungs and, perhaps most importantly, the brain and nervous system – are all recognizably similar to ours. If the argument from analogy does warrant us in attributing mental states to other people, then it equally warrants us in ascribing mental states to animals. Not, to be sure, the same range and complexity of mental states as in the case of the human species – we don't, for example, attribute contrition to a cat, or moral indignation to a dog or a lizard – but that is entirely what we should expect in the light of the restricted range of behaviour that animals exhibit by comparison with human beings, and especially in view of the fact that animals lack the capacity for language.

8.3   Wittgenstein's attack on the argument from analogy

Wittgenstein has attacked the twin conceptions of mind and meaning which Cartesianism enshrines. For Descartes, terms describing a person's states of mind acquire their meanings by naming logically private inner states. The nature of the state named determines the meaning of the expression which refers to it. Since only the person whose states they are can be acquainted with them, only that person can know the meanings of the various terms used to talk about those states. It would thus be entirely possible that what I mean by the word 'pain' and what you mean by the same word is entirely different. As Wittgenstein's analogy of the beetle-in-the-box made clear, the nature of the inner state named by 'pain' in my case could be entirely different from the nature of the inner state named by 'pain' in your case (see chapter 1, section 1.5). We could never actually find out, because I cannot be acquainted with your states of mind and you cannot be acquainted with mine. In fact, if all the items that fall within the purview of my experience are private to me, all the words I use might have entirely different meanings from the words used by other people. The realm of private objects comprising *their* experience could be totally different from the realm of private objects comprising *my* experience. We could all therefore be speaking our own logically private languages, but none of us is able to discover what other people mean by their words, since those words acquire their meanings purely by naming things with which only those others can be acquainted. You will recall that the eighteenth-century philosopher John Locke was aware of this consequence of Cartesianism when he conjectured that the idea of a colour put into one man's mind by a violet might be the same in quality as the idea of a colour put into another man's mind by a marigold, and vice versa. Both would agree that violets were violet and that marigolds were gold, and yet the one would mean by 'violet' what the other meant by 'gold', and vice versa. In other words, with respect to each other, the colours they experience when they look at violets and marigolds would be inverted, so that the meanings of the words 'violet' and 'gold' for each of the men would also be inverted, since words derive their particular meaning from the private experiences of each individual. However, whether this is really so, and not merely a possibility, can never be discovered, since neither person can exhibit to the other the private exemplars of colour which furnish colour words with their meanings (see chapter 5, section 5.7.2, note 7).

This is the point of departure for the argument from analogy. I know what I mean by the words I use to talk about my own mental states, since I uniquely am directly acquainted with the states which give the terms in my private mental vocabulary their meanings. The problem is whether I can ever know that there are other beings like myself who similarly enjoy mental states and can talk about them in the way that I do. The essence of Wittgenstein's attack is that the starting point presupposed by the argument from analogy is not a possible one. I cannot acquire a mental vocabulary in the splendid isolation constituted by the logically private contents of my mind and then try to argue by analogy that others must have the same as I have. To take the second point first, one prong of Wittgenstein's attack runs as follows. I am trying to establish, on the basis of analogy, the existence of mental states other than my own, but Wittgenstein questions what the expression 'mental states other than my own' can possibly mean if such states lie beyond any possible experience of them. The problem parallels the puzzle of how I can know there is an independently existing external world, if all I can be acquainted with is my own private world of mental images or sense-data. It is not so much that I cannot know that there is an external world, but rather what can the words 'external world' mean if they answer to nothing I could possibly experience? For concepts to be meaningful, it must be possible to recognize or state those conditions which, if fulfilled, would license the application of the concept to the state of affairs in question. But if I can never be acquainted with the external world, or with other minds, there is nothing conceivable to which such terms could apply, and this would seem to entail that such terms are devoid of significance. Concepts without intuitions, that is, without possible experience-situations to which they can be applied, are empty, as Kant famously said in his *Critique of Pure Reason*.[8]

It might be thought that this objection can be easily dodged. To be able to suppose intelligibly that someone else is in pain, I do not need to be directly acquainted with that pain. All I need to do is to suppose that when that person feels pain, he or she feels what I feel when I feel pain. Here the second prong of Wittgenstein's attack comes into play. He points out that if I had learnt the meaning of the word 'pain' only from my own case, as the argument from analogy presupposes, then pain will mean, in effect, 'sensation that *I* feel'. The fact that it is I, and no one else, who is feeling the pain will enter into the very definition of what pain is. But if that is true, then it will be incoherent to suppose that other people have pains. That is none too easy a thing to do, says Wittgenstein with deliberate ironic understatement, for it will amount to trying to conceive of a sensation I do *not* feel on the model of a sensation I *do* feel. If an integral part of the meaning of pain is the sensation that *I* feel, then the supposition that there could be pains not felt by me, but by somebody else, will be self-contradictory.

The point had already essentially been made by the great German logician, Gottlob Frege (1848–1925), who had written:

> If every thought requires a bearer, to the contents of whose consciousness it belongs, then it would be the thought of this bearer only and there would be no science common to many, on which many could work. But I, perhaps, have my own science, namely a whole of thought whose bearer I am and another person has his . . . No contradiction between the two sciences would then be possible and it would really be idle to dispute about truth, as idle, indeed almost ludicrous as it would be for two people to dispute whether a hundred mark note were genuine, where each meant the one he himself had in his pocket and understood the word 'genuine' in his own particular sense.[9]

8.4   The other minds problem and the impossibility of a logically private language

Wittgenstein's misgivings about the argument from analogy, which we have just discussed, represent preliminary skirmishes. The main attack is reserved for the idea that the meanings of words, including terms that refer to mental states, could be radically or logically private. According to the Cartesian, I can form a conception of my own mental states, I can name them and silently soliloquize about them, but I can never be sure of the existence of the mental states of others. On the contrary, Wittgenstein maintains that if the mind did comprise an inviolably private realm whose contents were accessible only to the person whose mind it is, then it would be impossible for a person to acquire and use mental predicates, that is, general terms and concepts that are used in classifying and describing the mental economy. In other words, Wittgenstein is claiming that from a purely private first-person perspective, talk about the mind, even one's own mind, is not possible. Rather, ascriptions of mental states to oneself – first-person ascriptions, as they are known – are only possible because a mental vocabulary has been acquired in association with ascriptions of mental states to other people, so-called third-person ascriptions. In other words, although it might seem to us that we acquire and learn to use a mental vocabulary initially from our own private first-person perspective, a vocabulary that we then wonder if it can be applied to other beings, this is an illusion. Even in the case of the words that we use to describe our own mental states, these words must have originally acquired their meanings and been learnt in essentially a public social context (cf. chapter 1, section 1.8). The very possibility of first-person ascription of mental states, if Wittgenstein is right, presupposes other-ascription – that is, the attribution of mental states to third persons. Mental concepts cannot be private in nature, and learnt and applied in the logical privacy of one's own mind. If this is correct, then any approach to the problem of other minds which, like the argument from analogy, starts from a conception of the mental as radically private to the individual, and, from this perspective, tries to justify belief in the existence of other minds, must be flawed. Before I reveal the fine details of Wittgenstein's attack on the notion of a logically private language, it may be helpful to provide a brief summary, point by point, of his general strategy for attacking the Cartesian conception of meaning discussed above:

1   Cartesianism assumes that solipsism – the view that only I and my mental states exist – is a possible state of affairs. There may be no world outside my mind. Only I and the private mental items making up my experience might exist.

2   But, so the Cartesian argues, even if solipsism is true, the person can still use language to think and to formulate the sceptical doubt, namely 'Is it not possible that only I and my mental states exist?'

3   But this assumes that someone can speak a language only he or she can understand because the words of this language refer to the logically private states of his or her mind.

4   Wittgenstein attacks this assumption. A language conceived of as in (3) above is a logical impossibility. Words, including terms for one's own mental states, can only acquire their meanings via a reference to things in a public, shared world.

5   So the very possibility of formulating the sceptical, solipsistic doubt entails there must be a public world for the words the person uses to formulate the doubt to have acquired their meanings in the first place. This means that terms for mental states must, equally, have a public meaning and an application in the public domain, thus entailing knowledge of other minds.

6   Thus, Cartesianism, and the private internalist theory of meaning it entails, is not a possible viewpoint to adopt. Even to formulate the Cartesian perspective presupposes its falsity.

8.5   The details of Wittgenstein's attack

Wittgenstein mounts two major offences against the idea that words, including the names of mental states, could acquire their meanings in the way presupposed by Cartesianism. Firstly, he attacks the notion of an inner ostensive definition, a definition by means of a kind of logically private inner pointing which is supposed to endow words with their meanings. He then concentrates on demonstrating that language as a rule-governed activity is not possible if meanings are supposed to be logically private. Beginning with the first objection, let us look more closely at Wittgenstein's attack on the notion of private ostensive definition.

8.5.1   Inner ostensive definition

To define a word ostensively is to define it by an act of showing or pointing. For example, someone asks me what 'griffin' means, and I explain the term by pointing at a picture of a griffin, as represented say, by the Esher College logo. By pointing out the type of object to which the word 'griffin' applies, the hope is that the other person will come to understand what the word means. Words cannot always be defined in terms of other words, otherwise we shall simply end up going round in a circle. There must be some words that acquire their meanings by direct reference to the world, to non-linguistic reality, so that it seems that ultimately we cannot escape having to give ostensive definitions.

   Giving a definition of what the word 'griffin' means by pointing at the Esher College logo is an activity that takes place in a public world, since everyone can see the logo. But now suppose we are trying to define a mental state such as a pain. If pains, like other mental states, really are inner and private, as Cartesianism maintains, then the act of ostensive definition is supposed to take place in the logically private, self-contained, solitary world of my mind. I point the mental finger of my concentration, as it were, at the pain, and say to myself, in order to fix the meaning of the word, 'That's what I will mean in future when I use the word "pain" to describe to myself how I am feeling.' A consequence of this theory as to how I learn to describe my own states of mind is that no one else can find out what I mean by 'pain'. In this way, as I give myself private inner ostensive definitions of my private states of mind, I invent my own logically private language, a language that I can understand but which other people cannot.

8.5.2   'Tove' and the impossibility of private ostensive definition

Wittgenstein attacks the idea that ostensive definition can be accomplished in the radically private manner outlined. In the *The Blue and Brown Books*[10] he asks us to imagine what happens when someone is supposed to give an ostensive definition of the word 'tove' (chosen because it is not a word in English), by pointing at a pencil. Wittgenstein's point is that this act of pointing could be interpreted in all sorts of ways; it *could* mean:

'This is a pencil'
'This is round'
'This is wood'
'This is one'
'This is hard'

Of course, someone could ask 'Which do you mean?' Do you mean that the shape is tove, or the type of thing it is, or just that one is tove? But in order to ask this question and to understand the answer, the person must already have a language. In fact, even for someone to understand these words as constituting demonstrative sentences and not questions, or exclamations, or the calling out of names, the assumption has to be made that the person has a language. But Wittgenstein does not want to make this assumption. His concern is with how language is possible in the first place. How does a person acquire the concept of the colour of an object as opposed to its shape, or, alternatively, the kind of thing it is as opposed to its being that particular individual. Here it is tempting to say that when the private linguist gives himself a private ostensive definition of, say, the colour of a thing, he just somehow concentrates on the colour, or 'means' the colour as opposed to meaning some other feature. We are tempted to think of the mind, Wittgenstein says, as a mysterious non-physical mechanism which can bring about effects that no mere material mechanism can accomplish, and that the ostensive definition is fixed accordingly by some peculiar, occult, mental act. Wittgenstein writes:

Point to a piece of paper. – And now point to its shape – now to its colour – now to its number (that sounds queer). – How did you do it? – You will say that you 'meant' a different thing each time you pointed. And if I ask how that is done, you will say you concentrated your attention on the colour, the shape, etc. But I ask again: how is *that* done?[11]

Before reading on, consider the questions posed in Exercise 8.4.

How is ostensive definition possible? How does one mean the colour rather than the shape? How do the meanings of colour and shape words ever get established in the first place?

Exercise 8.4

The answer basically is because of shared activities in a public social world. Wittgenstein gives the following example of how the meaning of a word like 'blue' might become established:

Suppose, however, someone were to object: 'It is not true that you must already be master of a language in order to understand an ostensive definition: all you need – of course! – is to know or guess what the person giving the explanation is pointing to. That is, whether for example to the shape of the object, or to its colour, or to its number, and so on.' – And what does 'pointing to the shape', 'pointing to the colour' consist in? Point to a piece of paper. – And now point to its shape – now to its colour – now to its number (that sounds queer). – How did you do it? – You will say that you 'meant' a different thing each time you pointed. And if I ask how that is done, you will say you concentrated your attention on the colour, the shape, etc. But I ask again: how is *that* done?

Suppose someone points to a vase and says 'Look at that marvellous blue – the shape isn't the point.' – Or: 'Look at the marvellous shape – the colour doesn't matter.' Without doubt you will do something *different* when you act upon these two invitations. But do you always do the *same* thing when you direct your attention to the colour? Imagine various different cases. To indicate a few:

'Is this blue the same as the blue over there? Do you see any difference?' – You are mixing paint and you say 'It's hard to get the blue of this sky.'

'It's turning fine, you can already see blue sky again.'

'Look what different effects these two blues have.'

'Do you see the blue book over there? Bring it here.'

'This blue signal-light means...'

'What's this blue called? Is it "indigo"?'

You sometimes attend to the colour by putting your hand up to keep the outline from view; or by not looking at the outline of the thing; sometimes by staring at the object and trying to remember where you saw that colour before.

You attend to the shape, sometimes by tracing it, sometimes by screwing up your eyes so as not to see the colour clearly, and in many other ways. I want to say: This is the sort of thing that happens *while* one 'directs one's attention to this or that'. But it isn't these things by themselves that make us say someone is attending to the shape, the colour, and so on. Just as a move in chess doesn't consist simply in moving a piece in such-and-such a way on the board – nor yet in one's thoughts and feelings as one makes the move: but in the circumstances that we call 'playing a game of chess', 'solving a chess problem', and so on.[12]

One of the points Wittgenstein is making is that these activities take place in a public setting. It is through these kinds of activity, and multifarious other ways, that the grammar of words such as colour words becomes established. There is also the hint in this passage, developed elsewhere in Wittgenstein's writings, that the acquisition of concepts and language presupposes a background of customs and activities. To begin to appreciate the point, consider the situation of someone who does not know what a chess king is. It might be thought that to make this clear all we need to do is to get hold of a chess king and show it to the person, pointing at it whilst uttering the words 'That is a chess king.' Suppose further that this person has never heard of, much less ever played, a game before – not just chess, but any game at all. I think it will be obvious that the attempt to tell him what a chess king is will mean nothing at all. Even assuming he understands that we are trying to tell him what the object is called, the most he might conclude is that a chess king is a piece of wood shaped in a certain manner. On the other hand, if he has learnt simple board games by watching, or perhaps by trying out games for himself, then when we pick up the king and show him the various moves it can make, he might gradually begin to understand its use. But this is only because, as Wittgenstein says, the place for his gaining the understanding is already prepared. This preparation of the place for the learning of the use of a piece in a game is what Wittgenstein refers to as 'stage-setting'. It presupposes that there are practices and customs consisting in 'playing games', and it is by acquaintance with, and involvement in, these kinds of activity that the concept of different sorts of games is acquired. On this foundation, an understanding of new and unfamiliar games, and moves and strategies can be built. But none of these resources or involvements is available to the Cartesian self imprisoned within the private circle of its own consciousness.

Wittgenstein's criticisms of how words are supposed to acquire meanings for the Cartesian go very deep, and I can only indicate briefly here the direction in which they run. It has to be remembered that for Descartes, and for philosophers such as Locke and Hume who were strongly influenced by him, experience comprises a series of mental images, secured within the fastness of the private realm of the mind. This is a very thin conception of experience. Private images are presented to the person, who is essentially an inert spectator passively viewing the passing show. The images that come from the senses are strong and vivid. From these images fainter copies are supposed to be derived, and these constitute concepts that serve as the meanings of words. But this conception of meaning is deeply flawed, and numerous criticisms have been made of it by Wittgenstein. For reasons of space, however, I shall limit myself to providing only four.

Firstly, mere acquaintance with a thing that falls under a concept does not amount to, or guarantee possession of, the concept. Acquaintance with a particular chess king will not by itself guarantee the acquisition of the concept of a chess king, an understanding of what the expression 'chess king' means. To acquire the concept, as I attempted to explain earlier, one must be an agent actively involved in a public world and its practices. The mere passive registration of images will not amount to possession and mastery of the concepts in question. In this connection Wittgenstein remarks: 'Do not believe that you have the concept of colour within you because you look at a coloured object – however you look. (Any more than you possess the concept of a negative number by having debts.)'[13]

Secondly, Wittgenstein argues that the meaning of a word cannot consist in an object or thing, even if that thing is thought of as a mental item, such as an image. To help us understand this criticism, Wittgenstein asks us to imagine that the mental image that is supposed to constitute the meaning of a word – the concept it expresses – is replaced with a painted sign. The original sign – the word – is dead, and the image is supposed to bring it to life, to breathe meaning into it. But a painted sign is just as dead as the original sign. Thinking of the sign not as painted but as a mental image does not miraculously explain how it can be about anything else. It is just the occult character of the mental image that you need, says Wittgenstein. In thinking of the concept that constitutes the meaning of a word as an image, you are thinking of the meaning as if it were just another object which accompanies the word. But if the original object is dead,

Figure 8.1

so is the one you add to it. The meaning of a word cannot therefore consist in an associated object, even a private mental one. We have to get right away from thinking of meaning in these terms, and think of it instead as the use to which it is put, the function it has in language, in a shared public world.

A third, related criticism points out that an image does not bear its interpretation on its face. Images are not self-interpreting. When we look at the image in figure 8.1 (Wittgenstein's image), what do we see? What does it represent? Many people will say that it represents a man with a stick walking up a hill. But does it? Suppose I suggest that it is actually a man with a stick sliding down a hill backwards? In fact, it might not even be an image of a man at all, but a cross-section through a piece of wood or some other piece of stuff, the brain perhaps. This last suggestion may seem a strange one, but there is a part of the brain that resembles a sea-horse, hence its Greek name, the hippocampus (its function concerns the laying down of long-term memories). If the image is supposed to constitute the meaning of a word, as Descartes and Locke assert, then we cannot use language to explain what the image means, because that will be arguing in a circle. The deep point for which Wittgenstein is arguing is that the meaning of a word is supposed to fix or determine its use, but an image cannot fix or determine use because its application cannot be read off from it. There is an indefinite variety of ways in which an image might be used or applied, hence an image cannot determine its application. In the *Blue Book*, Wittgenstein writes: 'As part of the system of language, one may say, the sentence has life. But one is tempted to imagine that which gives the sentence life as something in an occult sphere, accompanying the sentence. But whatever accompanied it would for us just be another sign.'[14]

The image with which a word is associated, the idea the word stands for in the mind, cannot dictate how the word is to be used, because the image, like the word with which it is associated, is itself just another sign, and the application of signs is not intrinsic to them. To appeal to yet another sign in order to make clear how the image is to be applied merely recapitulates the error of thinking of signs as self-interpreting. Any interpretation of a sign, says Wittgenstein, 'still hangs in the air along with what it interprets, and cannot give it any support. Interpretations by themselves do not determine meaning.'[15]

How meaning is to be determined is a large and complex topic, which I cannot go into here. It will suffice for our present purposes to recognize the negative conclusion, namely, that whatever meaning consists in, it cannot be comprised by signs or images, even if these are supposed to exist in the ghostly occult recesses of the mind.

A fourth criticism put forward by Wittgenstein argues that images have no syntax. Sentences have a syntax, which specifies how words can and cannot be combined and in what order. In other words, there are rules governing the combinatorial possibilities of words, and how words are combined determines the meaning of the sentence in question. Furthermore, the word order is important in determining whether a statement has been made or a question asked, as in 'This is a cat' and 'Is this a cat?'. But what rules could conceivably govern the combinatorial possibilities of images, and how could the order in which images are arranged determine what is meant? A row of images could mean anything or nothing. At the moment on my desk there are arranged in order: my reading light, my image scanner, my glasses, my VDU, my watch, my computer mouse and my printer. But this array does not assert or deny anything. Common experience shows it to be merely a conventional arrangement of items which a person engaged in word-processing might have on their desk. If I put my glasses on the right rather than on the left of the VDU, or if I take them off the desk, what difference does this make? Shuffling the items around on my desk and perhaps removing some altogether is precisely unlike making permitted changes to the word order in a sentence, or adding words in or taking words out, in order to alter the meaning of the sentence.

8.6   The impossibility of private rule-following

The point of ostensive definition was to fix the meaning of a word. Once the definition of the word in question has been fixed by reference to a private mental exemplar, a token instance of a particular type of thing, the word can be used over and over again to talk about the kind of thing in question. In this way people can construct a kind of dictionary in the privacy of their imagination. When I have a pain, say, I look inwards and, by pointing the inner finger of my attention, I call the sensation 'S'. Later, I have an itch, which, in a similar way, I call 'T', and later still, a tickle, which I call 'U'. Table 8.1 sets out simply how the 'dictionary' is thus constructed. The idea is that when I have, say, ❏ again, and I wonder what to call it, I can refer to this table in my imagination and say 'Ah yes – my mental state has the character ❏, and this correlates in the dictionary with 'S', so I must currently be feeling "S".'

Table 8.1   The 'dictionary' in the private world of the mind

Word	Mental state (non-linguistic item)
S	❏
T	◆
U	●

But, says Wittgenstein, for this procedure to work, I must remember correctly what 'S' stands for, otherwise I shall use 'S' wrongly. A sign that I could use in any way I want cannot count as a word. It has to be possible to draw a distinction between using a term correctly and using it incorrectly, between genuinely following a rule for its use and mistakenly thinking a rule is being followed. But the difficulty, as Wittgenstein points out, is that these distinctions cannot be drawn in the private world of the mind. Whatever is going to seem to me to be right will be right, and that only means that we cannot speak about something being right here. When using 'S', I have to be able to remember correctly that 'S' does indeed mean ❏, otherwise, in naming my current sensation 'S', I shall be mistaken. But how can the distinction be drawn between the situation in which I really do remember that 'S' means ⊔, and that in which it merely *seems* that I remember correctly? If Wittgenstein is right, this distinction does not hold in the situation we are envisaging. In the private world of the imagination no independent check on whether I am using a word correctly according to a rule is possible. The distinction between really following a rule and only seeming to collapses, and can therefore have no application. It would be no use appealing from one memory to another to justify whether one's usage of a term were correct or not. That, remarks Wittgenstein, would be like buying several copies of the same morning paper in order to verify that a story in it is correct. Without the possibility of an independent check on the usage of a term, attempting to define a word by a private ostensive definition is an empty ceremony which accomplishes nothing. Hence the notion of a logically private language turns out to be, as Wittgenstein puts it elsewhere, a piece of nonsense in disguise. This in turn means that the Cartesian programme of systematic doubt cannot even get started. Descartes cannot begin from within the closed circle of his own private consciousness and start wondering whether there is an independently existing public world. For the question even to be formulated, the existence of a public social world within which alone language is possible has to be assumed.

8.7   How do mental terms acquire their meanings?

How does all this relate to the problem of other minds? As I hope I have already partly made clear, the first point that needs to be stressed is that, according to Wittgenstein, one cannot learn the names of sensations and other mental states from one's own case. The acquisition of language to talk about one's own states of mind, and indeed the states of minds of others, is not possible from a purely first-person, private perspective. How then is it possible?

The answer, unsurprisingly, is from a third-person, public viewpoint. Even the ascription of mental states to oneself by oneself, based upon, as it seems, a purely private first-person basis, is made possible only because mental terms acquire an application and a use essentially in a third-person framework. At this stage, this sounds suspiciously like analytical behaviourism, which maintained that all talk about the mind could be rendered without remainder in terms of actual and possible displays of outward, public behaviour. But Wittgenstein denies that he is a behaviourist in disguise. What then do the details of his account look like? There are two main strands to it.

The first claims that behaviour serves as the criterion against which the attributions of mental states to someone, either others or oneself, are to be evaluated for correctness. The other claim is that mental terms do not *describe* behaviour, but gradually come to *replace* it. The emission of moans is not equivalent to issuing a description of one's pain; rather, it is a natural manifestation or expression of that pain. Gradually, however, this manifestation of pain is replaced, firstly with exclamations such as 'ouch' and then with sentences such as 'It hurts' or 'I am in pain'. Let us look at both these claims in depth before attempting some evaluation of them.

8.7.1   The criterial approach

To begin with, the notion of a criterion needs some explanation. 'An "inner process"', says Wittgenstein, 'stands in need of outward criteria.'[16] This has been interpreted by many commentators to mean that terms for mental states are made possible, i.e. meaningful, only because there are behavioural criteria governing their use. Behaviour provides the measure against which a person's usage of mental words can be assessed for correctness or incorrectness. To count as a correct usage, a term such as 'pain' has to fit in with the rest of the person's behaviour in the right kind of way. If I cut myself, and moan and grimace, and then announce that I have a tickle, others can correct me and point out that I should have described myself as being in pain instead.

By contrast with the ascription of pain to others, ascription of pain to oneself is often said to be 'criterionless'. What this means is that I attribute pains to you on the basis of your behaviour, but in my own case I clearly do not need to observe my own behaviour to be able to report accurately how I feel. Nevertheless, it is insisted, even in the case of self-ascription, the links with the behavioural criteria for the ascription of pain are not lost. If my criterionlessly ascribed mental state does not cohere with appropriate behaviour on my part, then I have got the self-ascription wrong. In other words, even though I do not need to make use of any criteria to ascribe pain to myself, criteria in the form of my public behaviour are always available against which the rightness or wrongness of my self-ascription can be checked.

You should consider the question raised in Exercise 8.5 before reading on.

Does Wittgenstein's account of how mental terms are possible lead straight to behaviourism? Doesn't it really come down to the claim that what being in pain really means, after all, is behaving in a certain sort of way?

This is where matters become very difficult. The usual response here on the part of a number of philosophers is to focus on what it means to call a person's behaviour a criterion of their being in a certain mental state. In response, it has been said that a behavioural criterion constitutes an essential part of a mental term, but the meaning of the term is not exhausted by the behavioural description. Sometimes this is put by saying that the criterion is non-inductive evidence for the existence of the mental state. The point of calling it non-inductive is to indicate a deeper kind of link than merely the contingent association between behaviour and mental states presupposed by the argument from induction. On the other hand, there is not a straightforward relation of logical entailment between behaviour and mental states. It does not logically follow that if a person is behaving in a certain way, then they must be in a certain kind of mental state. The notion of a criterion, on the interpretation of Wittgenstein we are considering, is supposed to offer a middle way between these two positions. As Oswald Hanfling puts it:

> According to [the Wittgensteinian argument] . . . criteria can constitute evidence that is stronger than mere induction. . . . On the other hand, this evidence is not strict in the manner of deductive entailment, so that the advocate of this view can freely admit – what it would be absurd to deny – that there may be pain-behaviour without pain.[17]

We are also told, by the distinguished commentator Peter Hacker, that 'the criteria for being in pain do not entail that the person is in pain. They are logically good evidence, which is, in certain circumstances, *defeasible* [i.e. can be defeated]. But if not defeated, the criteria confer certainty.'[18]

This appears to be claiming that, normally, it follows logically from the satisfaction of the criteria of being in pain that pain is present, but that there can be special circumstances in which the criteria fail to license this inference. The advocate of criteria, it seems, wants to borrow from the best features of deduction and induction, but to discard what is likely to prove embarrassing to an account of how knowledge of other minds is possible.

Before proceeding any further, pause to consider Exercise 8.6.

Exercise 8.6   How intelligible do you find the idea of a criterion as just outlined? Discuss this with others before reading on.

The notion of a middle way, a *via media*, between strict logical deduction and non-logical induction, has made some critics feel uneasy. It appears to be a way of wanting to have your cake and eat it. Critics are wont to argue that there is no logical room for such a middle way. Deduction and induction, as forms of inference, divide up the entire field between them, leaving no space into which a third form of inference can be inserted. But then the problem of other minds as traditionally conceived – that is, how we can go from behaviour to knowledge of the mental state underpinning it – reasserts itself. We are left once again with the choice between a deductive inference from behaviour to mental states and an inductive inference, and neither of these, as we have seen, is adequate to provide the knowledge we seek.

It has also been claimed by, for example, Galen Strawson, that Wittgenstein's views do lead to analytical behaviourism after all. Strawson asserts that once it is allowed that behaviour must play a crucial role in enabling mental terms to acquire their meanings, it is difficult to prevent a slide into anti-realism about the meaning of mental terms:

> [O]nce one has accepted the W [Wittgensteinian] theorists' argument that reference to publicly observable occurrences enters essentially into any satisfactory account of the meaning of the word 'pain', it may be hard to see how one can stop the slide into the view that reference to publicly observable occurrences is all that enters into any satisfactory account of the meaning of the word 'pain'.[19]

The basic idea behind anti-realism is this: the meaning of a statement is given by its assertibility conditions, that is, by that set of circumstances which, if they were satisfied, would license the application of that statement to those circumstances in order to make a true assertion. For the Wittgensteinian, the assertibility conditions that govern the application, and hence the meaning, of a statement about a state of mind consist in behaviour in certain circumstances. It should be clear that this position is essentially reductionist: mental states are constituted entirely by outward behaviour. Strawson has admirably criticized the Wittgensteinian position when he argues that a three-step argument is involved in the reduction of mental states to behaviour. We go from how we can tell that someone is in a given mental

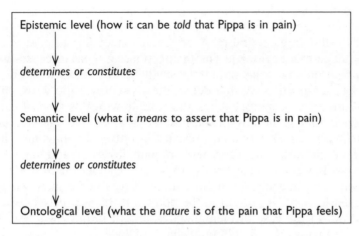

Figure 8.2   Neo-behaviourism

state to the position that how we tell determines what we mean by attributing the state in question, and this in turn fixes the nature of the state. Epistemology determines semantics, which in turn determines ontology. This is illustrated in figure 8.2.

Dedicated Wittgensteinians deny, as we have seen, that they are committed to a slide into behaviourism in this fashion. However, for reasons of space and time, I can take the debate no further here, although I hope I have helped you in the promotion of your own thinking about this difficult issue.

8.7.2   Mental terms replace behaviour

What are we to make of Wittgenstein's other suggestion, namely, that sentences such as 'I am in pain' gradually come to replace natural expressions of pain? One problem is that sentences have different properties from natural expressions of pain, so it is hard to see how one can be the extension or the replacement of the other. Sentences have truth-values; they have tenses; they can be negated; they can stand in logical relations to each other; and they can also comprise a component of hypotheticals – e.g., if I were to be in pain, then I should . . ., etc. None of these features can apply to natural expressions of pain, moaning, for example.

A second problem concerns what it means to say that natural pain-behaviour, and the first-person ascriptions of pain that allegedly come to replace it, are expressions or manifestations of pain. The obvious way to interpret this is to say that my wincing and moaning are manifestations of my pain because my pain gives rise to them. In other words, a non-behavioural private mental state, being in pain, causes outward pain-behaviour, just as an infection, e.g. measles, causes spots to appear on a person's skin. It is usually by this outward manifestation of measles that we first detect the presence of the virus within us. In the case of mental states, the trouble with this kind of explanation is that it already presupposes that there are mental states present which manifest their presence in outward behaviour. There is a fatal difference between being in pain, however, and having the measles. If we are uncertain as to whether spots on the skin are measles, we can check up in more direct ways to determine whether the measles virus is present in the body. But this is precisely what is ruled out in the case of mental states, except in our own case. The sceptic can always maintain that what look like natural and acquired manifestations of mental states are in reality no such thing. Behaviour appears to indicate an underlying mental cause, but in reality there is no such cause, because what we take to be a normal person is actually a zombie.

There are philosophers who maintain that Wittgenstein cannot be accused of failing to provide a solution to the problem of other minds, because he never set out to solve this problem in the first place. Thus, Oswald Hanfling writes:

> It is sometimes thought that Wittgenstein's solution, or attempted solution, of the other minds problem, is one of his main contributions to philosophy. Yet it would be difficult to point to a statement of the problem in his main work, let alone a 'solution' of it by means of criteria. In the private language argument, as elsewhere in the Investigations, his main concern is about meaning rather than knowledge; the argument is an investigation into the limits of language.[20]

In so far as Wittgenstein did produce a solution to the other minds problem, Hanfling maintains that it is to be found in his remark that 'If we are using the word "know" as it is normally used (and how else are we to use it!), then other people very often know when I am in pain.'[21] This remark has to be understood in connection with another claim of Wittgenstein's, namely, that it makes no sense for me to say that I know that I am in pain. This is because in my own case there is no room for doubt or error, since my claim is not founded upon any evidence and no pattern of inference is involved. The very possibility of doubt and mistake are thus excluded, and hence it would be tempting to say that in one's own case, with regard to many kinds of mental state, one cannot fail to know. But, says Wittgenstein, where nothing can ever count as failing to know, then nothing can count as success. It would be better, then, to say that with regard to one's own pains and other sensations, neither the concept of knowing that one has them nor the concept of failing to know that one has them applies. 'I know that I am in pain' consequently says no more than 'I am in pain'; the words 'I know' add nothing new to the sentence.

In the case of other people, however, whilst there is sometimes room for doubt and error regarding their state of mind, and hence a lack of knowledge regarding it, in other cases the grounds for doubt and error are missing, and in those cases I can meaningfully and truly say that I know what the mental states of those others are: 'I can be as *certain* of someone else's sensations as of any fact. . . . "But if you are *certain*, isn't it that you are shutting your eyes in face of doubt?" – They are shut'[22] There are cases where no doubt can enter in. Doubt, like knowledge, requires grounds, Wittgenstein reminds us in *On Certainty*.[23] The bare possibility that an attribution of a sensation to another person could turn out to be false cannot constitute a ground for doubt. A person in a workshop, or in a traffic accident, lies scream-ing on the ground, covered in blood due to horrendous injuries. Might this all be prearranged and faked? There will be circumstances in which this possibility just cannot be entertained, where, as Wittgen-stein says, one does not close one's eyes to doubt because, by the nature of the case, they are already shut: 'Just try – in a real case – to doubt someone else's fear or pain.'[24]

I imagine, however, that this response will not satisfy everybody. To be sure, in everyday life sceptical questions about belief in the existence of the external world, of the causal efficacy of mental states and the problem of the existence of other minds do not arise. But this does not mean that such questions cannot be pressed philosophically. In trying to provide a rational justification of induction, Hume admit-ted that someone might say that his everyday practices belied his doubts. In other words, he accepted that he did not take a sceptical attitude to induction, which he relied upon a thousand times a day, never doubting, for instance, that the sun would rise in the morning or that he would not step off into nothingness instead of familiar solid ground once he left his room. However, as Hume remarked, the observation that he is not a sceptic outside his study is all very well, but what he wanted, if he could possibly find it, was a rational justi-fication of induction.

Similarly, in everyday life we might find it impossible to doubt that someone was in pain, but this still does not explain how we could acquire knowledge of others' states of mind. Mental states, it was granted, are not identical with behaviour. In the case of other people, we are directly acquainted with their behaviour, not their mental states. A sceptical gap thus opens between knowledge of someone's behaviour and knowledge of the mental states that allegedly lie behind it. Since neither deductive or inductive reasoning can apparently bridge this gap, and since its elimination by reducing mental states to behaviour is unacceptable (see chapter 4, section 4.8), we still appear to lack a solid foundation for rejecting scepticism about other minds.

8.8   P. F. Strawson's attempted solution to the other minds problem

A Wittgensteinian-inspired account of how mental terms acquire their meaning and use, which contains many of the features we have discerned above, is to be found in the work of Peter Strawson in his book *Individuals*. It will be instructive to look briefly at this approach before I bring this chapter to an end.

A key passage in *Individuals* runs as follows: 'It is a necessary condition of one's ascribing states of consciousness, experiences, to oneself, in the way one does, that one should also ascribe them, or be prepared to ascribe them, to others who are not oneself.'[25] In other words, self-ascription is possible only because other-ascription is possible. Self-ascription can only take place if other-ascription can occur. This appears, on the face of it, to solve the problem of other minds at one stroke. Unless I can attribute states of mind to others, I cannot attribute states of mind to myself. But this means I cannot begin from my own case – that is, by attributing mental states to myself and then wondering whether they can be ascribed to others. Only if they are already ascribed to others, or at least I am prepared to ascribe such states to others, can I form the concept of my own mental states. Having argued for this position, Strawson then spells out how other-ascription is possible: 'One can ascribe states of consciousness to oneself only if one can ascribe them to others. One can ascribe them to others only if one can identify other subjects of experience. And one cannot identify them only as subjects of experience, possessors of states of consciousness.'[26]

The thought here is that if people are conceived of as purely mental in nature, like Cartesian souls, one would not be able to ascribe mental states to them. The reason is twofold. Firstly, as we noted in chapter 2, if people are conceived of as incorporeal souls, then we have no way of distinguishing one soul from another. But then we cannot form the concept of the individual subject of mental states. The general principle underlying this is that for a concept to be meaningful we must be able to specify those features of our experience which, if fulfilled, would license the application of the concept. But since we cannot have any experience of incorporeal souls we have no way of applying the correlative concepts of numerically the same soul, and numerically a different soul. Thus we do not really know what we mean by one soul, or many souls (since many is a collection of ones).

Secondly, if we are to be able to attribute features – mental states – to these souls, we must be able to specify those experience-conditions that would license the application of the mental state in question. But again, if these states are empirically undetectable because they are non-physical in nature, then we cannot specify the conditions which, if fulfilled, would license the ascription of the particular mental state in question. What Strawson is implying, and later makes explicit, is that we have to conceive of people as material entities. Their unique occupancy of space then enables us to distinguish one subject of experience from another. However much two or more people resemble each other, they cannot occupy the same space at the same time, so we always have a firm ground for distinguishing one person from the other (see chapter 2, section 2.8.4). The fact that people have physical characteristics also makes possible the ascription of mental states to them. It is their publicly observable behaviour which supplies the ground – or, as Strawson says, the logically adequate criterion, a term that is reminiscent of Wittgenstein – for the ascription of various states of consciousness to them. Thus we reach the same conclusion as we did in the case of our discussion of Wittgenstein, namely, that third-person ascriptions make possible first-person ascriptions, and are logically indispensable to them. This position is quite clearly the reverse of Cartesianism. For the Cartesian, one is able to ascribe mental states to oneself purely by being uniquely and privately acquainted with one's own states of mind. No acquaintance with, or knowledge of, anyone else's states of mind is presupposed or necessary for self-ascription. Even if there are no other states of mind, the Cartesian will maintain that at least you can be acquainted with, and ascribe to yourself, your own mental states.

How successful is Strawson in attempting to defuse the problem of other minds in this way? George Graham, in his excellently clear *Philosophy of Mind: An Introduction*, identifies two difficulties.[27] Firstly, Graham thinks that because ascribing mental states to others is done on the basis of observation of their behaviour, an advocate of Strawson's theory or the closely related theory of Wittgenstein will have difficulty in avoiding some form of logical behaviourism. This objection we have encountered before, having been set out by Galen Strawson.

Graham's second objection is that Peter Strawson's argument begs the question: it assumes in advance that it must be true that other people have minds – i.e. that mental terms may truly be ascribed to other people. But that, of course, is the very point at issue.

The point Graham is making was probably most clearly set forth by A.J. Ayer in *The Concept of a Person*.[28] Ayer's key criticism of Strawson's argument is that even if one did make, or was prepared to make, or even had every reason to believe one was justified in making the ascription of a mental state to another putative person, it still would not follow that the ascription was true, i.e. that the alleged other person really was in the mental state ascribed, or indeed any kind of mental state at all.

To illustrate the point he is making, Ayer imagines the fantasy of a child, kept from any contact with human beings, at least in his early years, who is brought up by automata which resemble and behave just like human beings. These automata are so constructed that when, for example, the child hits them, they cry out or retaliate, and when he asks them questions, they respond by shaking and nodding their heads. The child is instructed in the use of language and in other forms of behaviour by a voice from a loudspeaker. In this way he learns the names of the objects in the room in which he is kept, his own name and pronouns and demonstratives. The voice also teaches the child the words that describe his own mental states and he also learns how to distinguish seeing from imagining, and memories of real events from memories of dreams. The voice stresses the similarities between the automata and the child, always speaking of them as if they, too, were conscious, and the child finds that the different states of consciousness attributed to the machines fit in with certain general patterns of behaviour they exhibit and with changes in their behaviour. In this way the child comes to attribute mental states to himself as well as to the automata. In other words, he satisfies Strawson's condition that he is ready to ascribe mental states to a range of other similar beings, as well as to himself. In short, he acquires, and learns to operate with, the concept of a person. Clearly, however, all the attributions of mental states that he makes, and is quite happy to make, to the automata, are false, since the automata are mere mindless machines. This is an important consequence of the thought-experiment. As Ayer himself puts it:

> The example shows not only that one might be able to ascribe experiences to oneself, whilst being invariably mistaken in ascribing them to

others, but also that the criteria which are taken to be logically adequate for ascribing experiences to others may determine no more than that some locution is correct, that in such and such conditions this is the proper thing to say; it does not necessarily follow that what is said is true.[29]

Ayer continues:

There is no warrant for assuming his concept of a person is not the same as ours ... It is not that he has a different concept of what it is to be conscious, or that he applies the concept incorrectly, but that he just happens to be in a situation where the things which he has every reason for thinking to be conscious are not really so. If he were an infant philosopher, he might begin to wonder whether his companions really did have experiences in the way that he did and infer that they did from their resemblance to himself. Or perhaps if he were struck by some stereotyped quality in their behaviour he would rightly conclude that they did not. Whichever conclusion he came to, his scepticism would not be senseless. How could it be if it were actually justified?[30]

It would appear then, that Strawson's argument does not provide a way of overcoming scepticism about other minds, and neither, sadly, do the other attempts to solve the problem canvassed above. This is a disappointing conclusion, and hopefully it is mistaken. It does, however, have the look and feel of one of the perennial issues in philosophy, and I believe it is likely to go on perplexing generations of thinkers to come.

1 What are the strengths and weaknesses of arguing from one's own case to the existence of other minds?

Questions to think about

2 If mental states were identical with brain states, would the problem of other minds be identical with the problem of other brains?

3 Does knowledge of one's own mind depend upon knowledge of other minds?

4 Could scientific advances ever make it possible:
   (a) to feel someone else's pain?
   (b) directly to see someone else's thoughts?

5 'Joy, distress or amusement are not hidden behind the face that manifests them, but visible on it. What we so misleadingly call "the inner" infuses the outer. . . . We see friendliness or animosity in a face and do not infer its presence from the disposition of facial muscles (which we could not even describe).' (Peter Hacker, *Wittgenstein* (London: Phoenix, 1997), p. 43.)

How is Hacker's remark to be interpreted, and do you agree with it?

6   What is meant by describing behaviour as a criterion for the existence of mental states? How convincing do you find the criterial account of the meanings of mental terms? Does it ultimately lead to neo-behaviourism?

Suggestions for further reading

- D. Locke, *Myself and Others; A Study in Our Knowledge of Other Minds* (Oxford: Clarendon Press, 1968) is extremely useful if you can find it, but it may be out of print.
- Especially useful for its discussion of the possibility of a logically private language and the viability of the distinction between the 'inner' and the 'outer' is M. McGinn's *Wittgenstein* (London: Routledge, 1997).
- If you want to get a quick grasp of Wittgenstein's thought, including especially the Private Language Argument, read A. Kenny, *Wittgenstein* (London: Allen Lane, The Penguin Press, 1973).
- One of the very best introductions to Wittgenstein's Philosophy of Mind can be found in P. Hacker, *Insight and Illusion* (Oxford: Clarendon Press, 1972).
- Also by Hacker is *Wittgenstein* (London: Phoenix, 1997), which is short and snappy with interesting and provocative remarks on the problem of other minds.
- M. Budd, *Wittgenstein's Philosophy of Psychology* (London: Routledge, 1989) gives a systematic investigation of Wittgenstein's views on the nature of the mind. It is essential reading.
- The following works are also worth looking at: C. McGinn, *Wittgenstein on Meaning* (Oxford: Blackwell, 1984); G. Graham, *Philosophy of Mind: An Introduction* (Oxford: Blackwell, 1993); A. J. Ayer, *The Concept of a Person* (London: Macmillan, 1963); A. Bilgrami, 'Other Minds', in J. Dancy and E. Sosa (eds), *The Blackwell Companion to Epistemology* (Oxford: Blackwell, 1992).
- A. Avramides, *Other Minds* (London and New York: Routledge, 2001). Ten years in the writing, this book gives an admirably lucid and thorough discussion of the issue.

PERSONAL IDENTITY AS PHYSICAL CONTINUITY

Objectives

As a result of reading this chapter you should:

- understand the difference between qualitative and numerical identity;
- understand the difference between how we tell that a present person is numerically identical with a past person and what is constitutive of a person's identity over time;
- understand the difference between reductionist and non-reductionist theories of personal identity;
- understand the physical continuity theory and how one of its versions, the bodily continuity theory, may be attacked using the thought-experiment of brain transplants;
- understand that continuity of the brain is more plausible than continuity of the body as a necessary condition of personal identity;
- understand how the thought-experiment of brain fission leads to the view that survival without identity is possible.

9.1   Introduction

The final two chapters of this book are devoted to the subject of personal identity. The present chapter introduces the problem of what constitutes personal identity and focuses on physical continuity as an account of it. Chapter 10 examines the contrasting claim that psychological continuity is what is most important for our identity over time, balancing this account with a retrospective of the place and importance of physical continuity in achieving a satisfactory theory of personal identity.

The problem of personal identity may be broached initially in this manner. What makes a present person – let us call him Shaun – at time t1 one and the same person as Shaun at an earlier time, t0? Shaun, let us suppose, was born about nineteen years ago. Since that time he has changed considerably from the infant mewling and puking in his mother's arms. He was born practically hairless, but now he has a fine head of lank, black hair. His fingernails then were short, unpainted and stubby. Now they are long, slender and painted black (after the latest fashion). In one sense, Shaun is no longer the person he was. His features have changed considerably over the nineteen-year period. Nevertheless, Shaun at t1 and Shaun at t0 are one and the same person. So Shaun, it would appear, both is, and is not, the same person. The contradiction expressed in this last statement is, however, only apparent. This is because the statement contains two quite different notions of identity and sameness. Hence there is no collision in meaning when asserting that Shaun both is, and is not, the same person.

Philosophers mark the distinction between these two senses of 'same', by saying that qualitatively, Shaun is not the same person as he was. However, numerically, Shaun at t1 is identical, one and same, as Shaun at t0. To make sure the distinction between numerical and qualitative identity is clear, consider the following examples.

Qualitative identity If one thing is qualitatively identical with another thing, then it exactly resembles that other thing. For example, your car is exactly like mine. You own a Vauxhall Cavalier, and so do I. Your car looks exactly like mine and has all the same features, e.g. fuel-injection system, electric windows and so forth. If your car were destroyed, mine would still exist, and vice versa. Identical twins also furnish a ready-made example: Felipe and Pedro are so similar that usually I cannot tell which one I am teaching without looking at the class list (thankfully they are in different classes!).

Numerical identity If one thing is numerically identical with another thing, then really we have one thing on our hands, and not two things. We own one and the same Vauxhall Cavalier. I go out in it on Mondays, Wednesdays and Fridays. You go out in it on Tuesdays, Thursdays and Saturdays. We both go out in it on Sundays. If the car is destroyed, we both simultaneously become carless. Other cases illustrate the point. The slugabeds, as you will recall from chapter 3, section 3.3, thought that the Morning Star and the Evening Star were two quite distinct celestial bodies. Nevertheless, they turned out to be one and the same object, namely the planet Venus. King Oedipus married his mother, but he did not do this knowingly and intentionally because he did not know that Queen Jocasta was one and the same person as his mother. The police little suspected when they captured Mr Hyde that they were in fact arresting Dr Jekyll, who had been hideously transformed.

In relation to the topic of personal identity, the interest of philosophers is in numerical, not qualitative identity. So, to return to our opening question, what does the numerical identity of a person over time consist in? What makes Shaun now one and the same person as he was then?

9.2   The metaphysics and epistemology of personal identity

Before we go any further, however, a further distinction needs to be made. In asking what makes Shaun now numerically identical with Shaun then, I am not merely asking how I tell that Shaun is one and the same person that I taught last week. In the normal case I can tell that the student I am teaching now is one and the same person that I sent to the library last week, on the basis of his physical appearance, his bodily features, the sorts of clothes he habitually wears and his distinctively shaped and coloured fingernails. But, clearly, none of these features is constitutive of Shaun's identity. That is to say, none of these features is essential to Shaun today being one and the same person as Shaun yesterday.

The balding, fat, red-bearded, pale-nailed, middle-aged man who stands before me in twenty-five years could still be the lean, black-haired, beardless, black-nailed Shaun I taught many years before. And, conceivably, even if I had taken Shaun's finger-prints while he was a student, and, comparing them with my 44-year-old visitor's twenty-five years later, found they did not match, this would not be sufficient to prove that the visitor was not Shaun. Perhaps, with some nefarious purpose in mind, he had surgically had his finger-prints altered. Perhaps, even, through some natural biological process, his finger-prints had undergone alteration, just as the rest of his appearance had. It is, after all, merely a contingent fact, and not a logical necessity, that people's finger-prints do not significantly change over time and also that no two individual's prints are qualitatively exactly the same. If it had turned out that everyone's finger-prints were qualitatively identical, which logically could have been the case, then finger-prints could not serve as a useful, but fallible, means of establishing identity. We would have to have recourse to some other criterion – DNA, for example. How, in practice, we tell whether or not a person at time t1 is one and the same as someone at time t0 cannot yield an answer, then, to what the identity of a person consists in, what is essential, logically or conceptually, to the person's identity and not merely contingently a convenient sign of it.

What makes Shaun now one and the same as Shaun then is a metaphysical concern about the nature of the identity of persons, what is logically indispensable to it, and not merely an epistemological issue as to how we tell that the person we are encountering now is one and the same as the person we encountered earlier. The fallible evidence to which we appeal in trying to settle issues of personal identity does not tell us what is logically constitutive of the identity of persons over time. In answering that question, we need to spell out the necessary and sufficient conditions for a person at t1 to be one and the same as a person at t0. In other words, we need to complete the formula: 'Shaun at t1 is one and the same person as Shaun at t0 if, and only if . . .'.

The notion of necessary and sufficient conditions can be clarified by means of some simple examples. A necessary condition of something's being a horse is that it is warm-blooded, but plainly this is not sufficient, as many things are warm-blooded which are not horses – birds, for instance. A condition may be sufficient, but not necessary. For example, it is sufficient to be British that you were born in Britain of British parents. But it is not necessary, since British citizenship can be acquired by naturalization or marriage. What then would a statement of the necessary *and* sufficient conditions for British nationality look like? Well, perhaps something like this: a person is a British citizen if, and only if, they were born in Britain of British parents, *or* they have acquired British nationality through naturalization, *or* they have married someone British, *or* . . . *or* . . . (I don't know precisely what these other conditions are). The satisfaction of any one of these conditions is sufficient to make someone British, but none, taken singly, is necessary, since the satisfaction of one of the other conditions would have done equally well instead. However, the list of alternatives considered as a whole is necessary in that at least one out of all the various alternatives has to be satisfied. It does not matter which, but it has to fall within this list of alternatives and not outside it. In this sense, the list of alternatives – what philosophers call a disjunction – is a necessary condition (cf. chapter 3, section 3.8.7)

9.3   Reductionism and non-reductionism

The assumption of the previous section was that there is something that is constitutive of personal identity – that is, there is a way of spelling out in other terms, which make no use of the concept of personal identity itself, what it consists in. To make this assumption is to embrace a form of reductionism, to commit oneself to the belief that the concept of personal identity can be rendered, without loss of meaning, in terms of other concepts. You will recall that an analogous move was made by analytical behaviourists (chapter 4, section 4.3) when they alleged that everything we want to say about the mind could be captured by talk about actual and possible behaviour.

However, there are philosophers who disagree that the concept of personal identity is analysable in the manner proposed by the reductionists. These philosophers – non-reductionists – maintain that the concept of personal identity is primitive and unanalysable, subscribing to Bishop Butler's dictum that 'Everything is what it is, and not something else.' A major problem for analytical behaviourism was that it involved circularity: any attempt to translate talk about mental states into talk about behaviour ended up having to import into the analysis the very notion of a mental state that it was purporting to analyse. Similarly, so non-reductionists about personal identity claim, any purported analysis of the concept will inevitably, at some point, need to have recourse to the unanalysed notion of one and the same person that it is seeking to analyse. We will return to non-reductionism in relation to personal identity later.

9.4   Reductionist theories of personal identity

Throughout this book we have seen that, by contrast with ordinary physical objects such as rocks, trees and artefacts, human beings are viewable from both first- and third-person perspectives. From the third-person, objective viewpoint, human beings are living physical organisms whose internal workings and external behaviour are open to public scrutiny and observation. But people also have a first-person, private, subjective perspective on the world, which does not seem to be accessible to others. This epistemic contrast between first- and third-person perspectives also finds its expression in the differing ways in which we make judgements about the identity of others, by comparison with the judgements we make about the identity of ourselves.

From the third-person perspective, I know that Shaun is one and the same person I taught last week, because I have good reason to believe that the living flesh-and-blood human being before me now is physically continuous with the person I taught then. I could, naturally, be mistaken. A Shaun lookalike could have been substituted for the original Shaun, so that were I to trace the path of the lookalike back through space and time, I would find that it did not coincide with the space/time track traced by the original Shaun. However, not only is the substitution of a lookalike unlikely in the extreme, but were I in any doubt that such a trick might have been pulled, I could always ensure that I never let Shaun out of my sight from last week's to this week's lesson. Practically, this would be very difficult, but in principle it is achievable. In a case like this, how I tell that Shaun now is one and the same as Shaun then, and what it means to say that Shaun now is one and the same as Shaun then, would appear to coincide. Shaun's identity over time consists in the physical continuity through space and time of a living human body. This is the common-sense answer that many would return to the question of what constitutes personal identity, and, as far as it goes, it appears to be correct.

But what about my own case? Before reading on, think about this and the question posed in Exercise 9.1.

Exercise 9.1   How do I know that it was indeed I who taught Shaun last week, and that it wasn't some other teacher who stepped in and took the class?

The short answer is that I remember being here teaching Shaun last week. I have a good memory and distinctly remember coming into this room and teaching Shaun last week. In a case like this, I have access to knowledge of the identity of the person who taught Shaun – namely myself – from a first-person, non-observational perspective. I recall the experience of being here in the classroom teaching Shaun, and that's how I know that it was indeed myself, one and the same person who is recollecting now, being in the classroom a week ago. The question 'I distinctly remember teaching Shaun last week, but was it me that taught him at that time?' is pointless. If I really do remember, then I now must be one and the same person that did the teaching of Shaun then.

The situation is totally unlike the one in which a person steps into my shoes for a week. In a case like this, whilst looking round the staffroom, I might conceivably misidentify the teacher who took my classes, thinking mistakenly it was the person in the corner, whereas in reality it was the person by the door. Of course, I might have been under some kind of delusion when I claimed that I taught Shaun last week. For a start, I might have done some teaching, but the person I taught might have been the Shaun lookalike mentioned earlier. Or, more radically, it might turn out that I could not possibly have taught Shaun last week, because I was at home with the flu and the illness caused some weird memory delusion or amnesia. Nevertheless, the possibility of these mistaken memories does not alter the fact that, when I really do remember, I can know 'from the inside', i.e. from a first-person perspective and non-observationally, that I now am one and the same person as the person who taught Shaun last week. Other people cannot know in this way. Their only way of knowing is through observation of the living human being, Keith Maslin, who has existed physically and continuously from last week to this week, tracing a publicly verifiable unbroken path through time and space.

We are now in a position to appreciate that these two ways in which a person's identity may be known have given rise to two major theories of what constitutes personal identity. The first of these is the physical continuity theory to which I have already partially referred. A person now is one and the same as a past person, because the present person is physically continuous with that past person. The philosopher Bernard Williams, in an article written in 1956–7, makes use of the physical continuity criterion of identity.[1] He imagines a case where two men, Charles and his brother Robert, both make memory claims that fit very closely with what we know of the life of Guy Fawkes, as well as exhibiting similar personality traits to Fawkes. Are we to conclude that Fawkes has somehow returned to life in the person of one of these brothers? If we do, we will have to try to settle which one is Fawkes. Think carefully about this and look at Exercise 9.2 before continuing.

How would we settle which person, if any, was Fawkes?

Exercise 9.2

The answer would be supplied, claims Williams, if we discovered which of the two brothers, Charles or Robert, was physically continuous with Fawkes. Only the person who traced one and the same continuous track through space and time as Fawkes may be identified with him.

The second theory is the psychological continuity theory. According to this, what is important to the identity of a person over time is not the identity of the person's body or, indeed, any physical part of their body, such as the brain, but the continuity of their mental life, namely, the continuity of memory, character traits and intellectual and artistic abilities. Imagine a person whose memories and character traits, as well as their abilities, right down to being to eat, walk and talk, were completely wiped out by drastic tinkering with the person's brain. According to the physical continuity theory, we would have one and the same person on our hands after the wipe as we had before the destruction of all memories, character traits and abilities. This is because, physically, the person's body and brain after the drastic brain surgery are one and the same as the body and brain before the operation. But we need to ask: would it really be one and the same person, contrary to what the physical continuity theory maintains? If, after the wipe, the person gradually acquired the abilities to walk and talk, developed new character traits totally unlike the old person and started laying down a whole new set of memories, would it really be one and the same person now as the one before the brain surgery, despite having one and the same body and brain?

Considerations such as these have led some philosophers, starting with John Locke in the seventeenth century, to maintain that personal identity can be analysed in terms purely of the continuity and connectedness of a person's mental life, and that, ultimately, bodily identity and physical continuity are irrelevant. Remember that the physical continuity theory and the psychological continuity theory, despite their obvious and radical difference, both belong in the reductionist camp, the one maintaining that personal identity consists in certain more particular facts about bodily or physical identity, the other asserting that personal identity is to be spelt out in terms of memory and other psychological relations. We will now look at the first of these theories before turning to the psychological continuity theory in chapter 10.

9.5   The physical continuity theory

At its simplest, this theory maintains that a present person is one and the same as a past person if, and only if, the person in question has one and the same body today as he had yesterday. In more detail, what this means is that Shaun's body must have existed continuously over the period of time in question. In other words, it must meet the same criterion for identity over time as ordinary physical objects, namely, spatio-temporal physical continuity – the capacity to trace a unique continuous track through time and space. But here we must be careful. Suppose Shaun undergoes radical surgery in which his arms and legs are detached and then sown back on. Is Shaun's body one and the same after the detachment and reattachment of the limbs? It would surely seem to be so. Consider another possibility. Shaun is quick-frozen and then cut into quarters. After a time these quarters are put back together again and then thawed out, Shaun awakening from the operation apparently unperturbed. Is Shaun's body one and the same as it was before the quartering?

Before reading on, look at Exercise 9.3 and consider your reaction to the questions posed above.

Is the numerical identity of Shaun's body preserved, despite the quartering and the reassembly of the parts? What arguments can you devise to support and attack this claim?

Exercise 9.3

I believe there is reason to suppose that the identity of Shaun's body is preserved. In case anyone should doubt this, consider the situation in which I want to go biking in some distant part of the country but do not want to reach this far-off region by having to cycle there. Since my bike won't fit in my car, I disassemble it, load it in the boot and reassemble the machine once I reach my destination. Is the bike reassembled one and the same as the disassembled bike? It would be crazy to suppose it is not. The disassembly and reassembly of Shaun's body in its frozen state, after which it is thawed and resumes normal functioning, is, I contend, in principle no different from the disassembly and reassembly of the bike.

The identity of Shaun's body over time is also not disturbed by the fact that the body is continually renewing itself. As time passes, Shaun sheds dead skin cells and loses various particles from internal parts as his organs age. In fact, we are told by scientists that, over a period of time, all the molecules in Shaun's body change. Nevertheless, because the change is gradual, one and the same body continues to exist. Compare the case of Theseus' ship in the famous ancient Greek puzzle concerning identity.

Theseus has an oak ship composed of a thousand seaworthy oak planks, but he has seen a teak ship, and he fancies one of those instead. Consequently, he has one oak plank at a time removed from his ship and a teak plank inserted to take its place. It takes one minute to remove an oak plank and replace it with a teak plank, so after a thousand minutes Theseus' ship is composed entirely of teak. To be sure, it has changed a great deal qualitatively. It was made entirely of oak and now it is made entirely of teak. But arguably it is still numerically one and the same ship, because throughout the changes in the matter composing it, its form – that is, its organizational structure and the function that the structure serves – are continuously preserved. The identities of many things are like this: trees, buildings, clubs and organizations generally: although their constituent parts gradually change, their numerical identities are not lost. Despite a complete change in the students, the staff and even conceivably all the buildings, the Esher College of the future will be one and the same as the Esher College of today, because of the continuous preservation of the organization and function of the college in spite of radical, but gradual, alterations.

There are some changes, however, which it seems would destroy the numerical identity of Shaun. Consider the following scenario. Shaun enters a molecular disintegration device. His body is broken down into its constituent molecules, which are then scattered to the four winds. Later, by some pure fluke, a body that is qualitatively just like Shaun's body at the moment of dispersal is reconstituted out of the original molecules, the right sorts of molecule going to exactly the same sorts of location they occupied before separation. Would this new body be one and the same as the old body which was destroyed? It appears it would not. When the molecules are scattered, they go on existing as individual things and retain their identities, but the identity of the body they used to comprise is lost. This is because the organizational structure, which is essential to Shaun's being the individual entity or logical substance that he is, is not preserved when his body is decomposed into the micro-elements that comprise it.

It seems to be a sound metaphysical principle that one logical substance cannot have two beginnings. Consequently, even after all the molecules have been gathered up and assembled into a body that is qualitatively identical to Shaun's old body, that new body will still not be Shaun's old body, despite being made of the same matter that comprised Shaun's original body, and despite being qualitatively indistinguishable from it.

Suppose, less radically, that Shaun's biological molecules were replaced with inorganic molecules, which, after being gradually absorbed into the various organs, were able to discharge exactly the same functions that had been discharged by the original organs before the gradual replacement of their parts. In other words, Shaun's body ends up something like the body of an android. Is it one and the same body after these changes? This is much harder to settle. The fact that the same functions are discharged inclines us to say that it is one and the same body. On the other hand, can we meaningfully speak of a human body any more, once it consists entirely of inorganic parts? Radical change of this type, it is arguable, does destroy the identity of the body. I leave the reader to decide this for him- or herself.

9.6   Physical continuity and brain transplants

Even if some kind of physical continuity should turn out to be a necessary condition of personal identity, it clearly is not sufficient for it. If Shaun lies dead on the floor before me, then, considered as a mass of organized physical matter, Shaun dead has one and the same body as he did when he was alive. But the existence of Shaun's dead body cannot provide for the sameness of the person between yesterday and now, because the person is no longer there. Although we speak of dead persons, strictly we no longer have a person on our hands, but an ex-person, a corpse, what is left over of a former person. For the continuity of Shaun's body even to stand a chance as being necessary for Shaun's identity over time, it seems we must specify that the body in question is the body of a living organism. Yet even the continuity of a living body and brain still cannot be sufficient for the preservation of Shaun's identity. This is shown by the possibility of total amnesia which we discussed earlier (section 9.4). Although a human being who suffered this would have one and the same living body, it appears that radical mental discontinuity would rule out the identity of the person before and after the amnesia.[2]

Locke's way of accommodating this possibility was to draw a distinction between a man – that is, a living human being – and a person. Outwardly, after total amnesia, we would have one and the same man, i.e. one and the same living human organism. But viewed internally, we would have to say that what has happened is that one person has ceased to exist owing to the total memory wipe, and that another one has begun as new memories begin to be laid down. In other words, we have two persons inhabiting one and the same body successively, one after the other.

Having drawn the distinction between the concept of a human being and the concept of a person, Locke was also alive to other possibilities in which it would be necessary for the two concepts to part company. Thus it would be possible to envisage a situation in which two persons inhabited one and the same human body more or less consecutively. Locke imagines a case in which there was a day-person who could remember what had happened on past days, but not past nights; and a night-person who, conversely, could remember events that had occurred in the night, but not the day. This, it appears, amounts to two distinct, incommunicable streams of consciousness, manifesting themselves through one and the same body. But if that is a possibility, then it is also possible that one stream of consciousness should manifest itself through two human bodies. Lastly, although we do not think of parrots as persons, is it not possible that there should be a very rational parrot, just like the rational horses in *Gulliver's Travels*? If so, would we not be forced to concede that parrots and horses might also count as persons?

The reason why the distinction between the concept of a human being and the concept of a person may strike us as odd is as follows. Firstly, the only persons of whom we presently know are human beings. Secondly, since cases of multiple personality are far and few between, the bulk of our experience bears out the fact that if we have one living normal adult human being in front of us, then we have just one person before us. In other words, the entities that fall under the quite different concepts of a human being and a person respectively normally coincide. Let us be quite clear about this. The concept of a person is not equivalent to the concept of a human being. If it were equivalent, then talk about non-human persons would be a contradiction in terms. But the mere imaginability of life-forms that are not human, yet qualify as persons, such as the various assorted characters in the science fiction series *Star Trek*, helps to establish the non-equivalence of the concepts in question. Similarly, it is possible to conceive of human beings who, unfortunately, have ceased to be persons, such as accident victims in permanent comas on life-support machines.

I said earlier that physical continuity might turn out to be necessary for personal identity. But what precisely is meant by physical continuity? It is natural to interpret this to mean that a person now is one and same as a past person if, and only if, that person has one and the same body now as he or she had then. To put this another way, what lies behind my judgement about the identity of my student, Shaun, who furnished the example with which I opened this chapter, is the entirely natural assumption that the person before me now that I call Shaun is physically continuous with the person I called Shaun in the past.

If I were in any doubt that the person before me now was an impostor, a mere lookalike, I could in theory trace the path of the individual before me now back through time and space to see if it led to the person I called Shaun last week. If it did, we would conclude that the Shaun before me now is indeed one and the same person whom I taught last week. If, alternatively, the path of the person before me now did not lead back to Shaun whom I taught last week, we would have to conclude I had a replica of the original Shaun before me now. This is represented diagrammatically in figure 9.1.

However, a radical objection to this theory was envisaged by Locke in his thought-experiment concerning the prince and the cobbler. If, said Locke, the soul of a prince, carrying all the memories of the prince's life and his character traits and abilities, were to enter the body of a cobbler, and the cobbler's soul were to enter the prince's body, everybody would agree that the person whom we formerly thought of as the prince was now in reality the cobbler, and vice versa.

An updated materialist variant on this theory was supplied by Sydney Shoemaker.[3] We are to envisage two people, Brown and Robinson, who are having brain operations which involve their brains being removed from their skulls and then replaced again. Unfortunately, Brown's brain is mistakenly inserted into Robinson's head, and Robinson's brain is put into Brown's head. The latter patient dies, leaving the person with Robinson's body containing Brown's brain, as shown in figure 9.2.

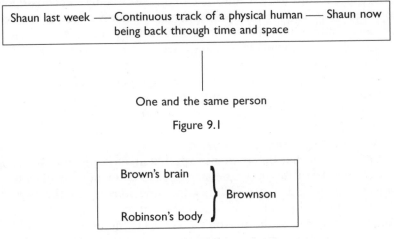

Shaun last week —— Continuous track of a physical human —— Shaun now
being back through time and space

One and the same person

Figure 9.1

Brown's brain
}
Robinson's body
Brownson

Figure 9.2

Following Shoemaker, let us call the resulting individual Brownson. Brownson, it seems reasonable to suppose, will receive a severe shock after he has recovered. Upon looking in the mirror he will see not what he is expecting to see, namely, Brown's face looking back at him, but Robinson's face instead. It seems likely that he will discover he has Robinson's body and not his own original body. When Brownson is asked about where he was born, what job he does, and who his wife and friends are, everything he says, we would expect, will match Brown's life, not Robinson's. Moreover, his personality and abilities will also correspond to Brown's, not Robinson's. In such a situation it would be hard to avoid the conclusion that Brownson is Brown and not Robinson. Brown has had a body-swap, or, to put it another way, virtually a whole body transplant, with the exception of Robinson's brain.

It might be objected that this way of presenting the matter merely begs the question of the identification of Brownson with Brown. However, not only does it accord with many people's intuitions, but, more importantly, it is powerfully supported by materialist theories of the mind. If the mind just is the brain, as the mind/brain identity theorists robustly claim, or if, less strongly, the mind is supported by the brain and is supervenient upon it, either as a collection of non-physical properties or as a function or program incarnated in the hardware of the brain, then surely we are bound to conclude that Brownson is Brown, not Robinson. According to these materialist theories, where my brain goes, there go I, either because I just am my brain, or because my existence as a conscious being depends upon my brain. In such a case, the identity of a person's body is neither necessary nor sufficient for the identity of the person. It is not necessary because Brown survives in someone else's body – in this case, Robinson's. We have here a situation in which there is a different body, i.e. Robinson's, but one and the same person, i.e. Brown. It is not sufficient because Robinson, before he dies, briefly survives in Brown's body. The contrasting situation here would be the situation where we have one and the same body, i.e. Brown's, but a numerically different person, i.e. Robinson.

Let us grant that this thought-experiment succeeds in destroying the continuity of the body theory of personal identity. It does not, however, eliminate the possibility that the identity of the person depends upon physical continuity, namely, the physical continuity of some crucial part of the person's body – i.e. the person's brain, or even just possibly some set of physical arrangements which function equivalently as the brain. I shall return to this theme later.

9.7   Fission

Not long after Shoemaker had proposed the thought-experiment of brain-transplantation, other philosophers, including David Wiggins and Derek Parfit, came up with an even more bizarre suggestion. They considered what we should say if a person's brain were divided in two by severing the commissural fibres which hold the hemispheres of the brain together, one hemisphere then being placed in a suitably evacuated skull, and the other being inserted into another empty skull. Now consider the questions posed in Exercise 9.4 in light of this suggestion.

Exercise 9.4

Does the original person survive the split or not? If he does survive, does he survive as the left hemisphere or the right? Or as both? What do you think is the right response to this question? Think about the issue and discuss it with someone else before reading on.

This fantasy was not engaged in purely for amusement; there was a serious point behind it. Up to the point when the thought-experiment of splitting the brain and transplanting each of the halves was envisioned, the central concern of philosophers, as this exposition reflects, was with identity. What does it mean to say that a given person, P1, is numerically identical (or not, as the case may be), with another apparently different person, P2? This question was particularly pressing in relation to the question of life after death. If I die, and do not continue to exist as a ghostly Cartesian soul, but then God resurrects my body by gathering up the bits of which I was made and putting them back together again just as they were when I was alive, do I continue to exist or not? The concern with identity meant that there were only two possible responses to this question. Either I am one and the same as the resurrected person, or I am not. Identity is an all-or-nothing relation: either it obtains or it does not. There is no halfway house or matter of degree such that it would make sense to suppose that something could be more or less numerically identical with some other thing. To repeat: regarding identity, either X is numerically identical with Y, or it isn't.

The problem with the resurrection theory, in which, at death, the body is either slowly dispersed in the grave, or scattered in the vast breath by the crematorium fires, is that, in keeping with the considerations advanced in section 9.5 above, death spells the final end for us. Even if all the molecules of the pre-mortem person constituted the body of the post-mortem resurrectee, even to the extent of occupying the same places and causal roles they had before the person's demise, the resurrected person would not be one and the same as the pre-mortem person, but only a brilliant replica. To say that this would not be very satisfying would be to understate the case. The great appeal of doctrines of life after death is surely that they are supposed to provide for one's own personal survival. To be told that the matter of which you were composed will go back to the void, ultimately to comprise parts of other people, animals and plants, is not at all comforting, precisely because these other things are not me. Similarly, although I might comfort myself now that people will not forget me, that I will 'live' in their memories or hearts, or will continue through my children or the books I write, ultimately I have to recognize that my life will come to an irrevocable and permanent end, precisely because I am not my children, my books or other people's memories of me.

More mystical doctrines, which maintain that the soul, like a drop of water, will merge with a great ocean of spirituality and, in dissolving into it, lose all identity and individuality, are similarly unsatisfactory, because my survival as an individual with a consciousness of himself and his past and present life is lost according to such a doctrine.

However, the split-brain thought-experiment raised for consideration the possibility of something that had not been contemplated before, namely that there could be survival without identity. To appreciate how this is meant to be possible, let us suppose that a present student of mine, Florence, is the person whose brain will be split. The operation is performed, and afterwards the left hemisphere of Florence's brain goes to a body on the left to make up the person Florence(1), whilst the right hemisphere goes to a body on the right to make up a person Florence(2). After the operation has been successfully performed both Florence(1) and Florence(2) wake up. When asked who they are, they both say they are Florence. Moreover, both Florence(1) and Florence(2) make identical memory claims which exactly fit Florence's life. They are, moreover, claims about what Florence did and underwent 'from the inside' – that is to say, they are made not from the point of an external third-person observer of Florence, but, rather, as far as we can determine, from Florence's private, first-person perspective, i.e. as the person who did or underwent the things in question. Florence's situation is illustrated in figure 9.3.

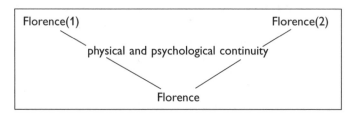

Figure 9.3   Split-brain

Notice that I say Florence(1)'s and Florence(2)'s memory claims fit Florence's life, not that Florence(1) and Florence(2) both remember what Florence did. The reason why I say this can be explained as follows. Let us suppose that what Florence(1) and Florence(2) both claim to remember doing before Florence had her brain divided is being taught by me last week. Florence(1) will most naturally express this memory claim by saying 'I remember being taught by Keith Maslin last week', and Florence(2) will say the same. But this sentence can be expanded to read: 'I remember that I was taught by Keith Maslin last week', and this means that the first occurrence of 'I' in this sentence must refer to one and the same person as the second occurrence of 'I'. To state more simply what I am saying, what the sentence is claiming is that I, Florence(1), am one and the same person as Florence who was taught by Keith Maslin last week. Similarly, the sentence issuing from the mouth of Florence(2) is also claiming is that I, Florence(2), am one and the same person who was taught by Keith Maslin last week. Florence(1) has as much right to make this claim as does Florence(2) (and vice versa), but the problem should now be apparent. If Florence(1) really is one and the same as Florence, and Florence(2) really is one and the same as Florence, then we shall be forced to embrace the contradiction that Florence(1) is one and the same person as Florence(2). Quite clearly, this is manifestly untrue, since Florence(1) and Florence(2) exist in two different places, one on the left and one on the right.

The principle that leads to this conclusion is called the transitivity of identity: if X is numerically identical with Y, and Y is numerically identical with Z, then logically X must be numerically identical with Z. To set this out formally:

Let '=' mean 'is numerically identical with'
Then, if

1   Florence = Florence(1), and
2   Florence = Florence(2), then
3   Florence(1) = Florence(2)

and this is manifestly an absurd result.

The problem comes about because in standard English usage the statement 'I remember being taught by Keith Maslin', implies that the person or persons making the memory claim, in this case Florence(1) and Florence(2), are one and the same person who underwent the thing that is remembered. But Florence(1) and Florence(2) cannot both be remembering in the standard sense in the case in question, because if it is granted that they may both legitimately say that they remember being taught by Keith Maslin before the fission, this will lead, as we have seen, by the transitivity of identity, to the nonsense claim that Florence(1) and Florence(2) are one and the same person.

To get round this difficulty, philosophers had a simple device. Instead of saying that both Florence(1) and Florence(2) remember being taught by Keith Maslin, we should say instead that they quasi-remember or as-if remember. Quasi-memory is just like ordinary memory of events, not made from a third-person perspective but from a first-person viewpoint, 'from the inside', except that the effect of the term 'quasi' is to cancel out the implication that the person doing the quasi-remembering is one and the same as the person who did the action quasi-remembered. Ordinary remembering by a person of something they did can then be viewed as a form of quasi-remembering; it will in effect be quasi-remembering where the person doing the quasi-remembering is one and same as the person who did the action remembered.

However, to return to our original question, what happens to the original Florence when the fission takes place? Some responses appear to be ruled out from the start. Firstly, we have no grounds for saying that Florence is identical with Florence(1) rather than Florence(2), nor that Florence is identical with Florence(2) rather than Florence(1), since both Florence(1) and Florence(2) have an equally good claim to the title. Secondly, we are prohibited, upon pain of contradiction, from saying that Florence is numerically identical with Florence(1), and that Florence is also numerically identical with Florence(2). Thirdly, it seems wrong to say that Florence no longer exists. If both transplants take, and both people wake up with quasi-memories of Florence's life, there seems to be a sense in which Florence is still around. As Parfit once put it, how could a double success amount to a failure?

One way to approach this problem is to imagine that you are Florence and about to undergo the fission operation. Would you regard the prospect as equivalent to death, or do you think that in some sense you, or at least a significant part of you, will survive? Compare what happens when a tulip bulb divides. The tulip in some sense does survive, as both halves. The fission of a tulip bulb is not equivalent to pounding the bulb to pulp. The bulb certainly does not survive the pulping, whereas, in going on to form two new plants, there is a sense in which it does survive.

In the same way, we are invited to think that fission does not spell the end of a person. Florence survives as both Florence(1) and Florence(2), even though, upon pain of contradiction, Florence cannot be said to be numerically identical with both. As Florence(1), Florence survives with a store of quasi-memories of her past life intact.

From Florence(1)'s viewpoint, these quasi-memories are no different from genuine memories of Florence's life since they were produced in essentially the same way that ordinary memories are produced when no fission is involved. Similarly, Florence also survives as Florence(2), who, from her viewpoint, also has a store of quasi memories that fit Florence's life and are as good as the real thing. (In a sense, from the first-person perspectives of Florence(1) and Florence(2), the quasi-memories of Florence's life *are* the real thing, because they are phenomenologically indistinguishable from genuine memories.)

What the fission case would appear to establish is that we can have personal survival without identity. It does not matter that we cannot have identity. What we are really interested in is survival, and the fission example is person-preserving in that it gives us what we want, namely continuity in some form, even though neither of the products of the fission, Florence(1) and Florence(2), can claim to be strictly numerically identical with Florence.

An important feature of the fission case just outlined, is that we have both physical and psychological continuity. Indeed, it would appear in this case, that there is psychological continuity only because we have physical continuity. The physical processes that go on in each half of the brain support the mental life of each of the resulting persons, Florence(1) and Florence(2), just as the processes in the entire unsplit brain supported the mental life of the original person, Florence.

This prompts the question: can we envisage a situation in which we had psychological continuity without the physical continuity of the brain? If so, then perhaps we could survive the death and destruction of our own brains. This leads us, by a natural progression, to psychological continuity as a theory of personal identity, which forms the subject of the next chapter.

Questions to think about

1 Could I remember being someone other than who I now am?
2 What philosophical difficulties are involved in supposing that, after my death, God will resurrect me?
3 Does the possibility of brain-fission establish that what matters for personal survival is physical *continuity* and not *identity*?

Suggestions for further reading

- There do not appear to be many texts on personal identity written primarily as introductions to the topic. In *Introducing Persons: Theories and*

Arguments in the Philosophy of Mind (London and Sydney: Croom Helm, 1986), Peter Carruthers helps to plug this gap, and the relevant parts of his book are recommended for those new to this area of philosophy.

- Sidney Shoemaker's *Self-Knowledge and Self-Identity* (Cornell: Cornell University Press, 1963) is the book that launched a revival of interest in personal identity in recent times. It is highly recommended.
- In *Problems of the Self* (Cambridge: Cambridge University Press, 1973), Bernard Williams has made original and important contributions to the debate, and this book collects together many of his important papers. It is essential reading for anyone interested in personal identity.
- Sidney Shoemaker and Richard Swinburne's *Personal Identity* (Oxford: Blackwell, 1984) is an interesting and lively debate between two influential thinkers favouring different approaches to personal identity. It is highly recommended.

PERSONAL IDENTITY AS PSYCHOLOGICAL CONTINUITY

Objectives

As a result of reading this chapter you should:

- understand Locke's memory account of personal identity and the objections by Reid and Butler which can be raised against it;
- understand Parfit's psychological connectedness and continuity account of personal identity and the objections which can be raised against it;
- be able to evaluate critically Hume's bundle theory of the self;
- understand how survival without identity is supposed to be possible and be able to evaluate critically this claim;
- understand how psychological continuity without physical continuity is supposed to be possible and be able to evaluate critically this claim;
- understand Unger's claim that physical continuity in the shape of the continued existence of the brain is essential for the preservation of personal identity and be able to evaluate critically this claim;
- understand the differences between reductive and non-reductive accounts of personal identity and be able to evaluate critically these options.

10.1 Introduction

John Locke (1632–1704) was the originator of the theory that personal identity consists in psychological continuity. To provide an outline of the theory, we can no better than to quote Locke's own statement of it:

> For, it being the same consciousness that makes a man be himself to himself, personal identity depends on that only, whether it be annexed only to one individual substance, or can be continued in a succession of several substances. For as far as any intelligent being can repeat the idea of any past action with the same consciousness it had of it at first, and with the same consciousness it has of any present action, so far it is the same personal self. For it is by the consciousness it has of its present actions that it is self to itself now, and so will be the same self as far as the same consciousness can extend to actions past or to come, and would be by distance of time no more two persons than a man be two men by wearing other clothes today than he did yesterday, with a long or short sleep in between: *the same consciousness uniting those distant actions into the same person, whatever substances contributed to their production.*[1]

The essence of the Lockean approach is this: personal identity consists neither in the persistence of an organized portion of matter, the human body or an important part of that body, the brain, nor in the continuance of an immaterial Cartesian soul, but, rather, in a certain kind of continuity and connectedness between a series of experiences. The substances in which these experiences are incarnated are irrelevant to the identity of the person. This is reminiscent of functionalism. What makes mental states what they are is not the stuff, whether material or even just possibly immaterial (see chapter 5, section 5.1), which happens to embody them, but the input/output relations that can be specified purely formally. Similarly, what Locke is claiming is that as long as there is a connected series of experiences, we have personal identity, even if this chain of mental states were to be transferred from one physical substance, or even from one immaterial substance, to another.

Put more precisely, Locke is claiming that a present person at time t1 is one and the same as a past person at time t0 if, and only if, the present person can remember what that past person did: 'For as far as any intelligent being can repeat the idea of any past action with the same consciousness it had of it at first, and with the same consciousness it has of any present action, so far it is the same personal self.'[2]

However, this immediately raises the following question: is memory of a past event, say an action that you performed, necessary to make the person doing the remembering one and the same as the person who did the action? Think about this, and look at Exercise 10.1, before reading on.

Is a person X, one and the same as a person Y, only if X can remember, from a first-person perspective, what Y did?

Exercise 10.1

10.2   Reid's objection to Locke's account

The first objection that may occur to you is this: surely you can forget that you did certain things, and yet this does not mean that you were not one and the same person that did them. I may have forgotten that it was me, and not my wife, who put the rubbish out last week, and yet, for all that, I am one and the same person who put the rubbish out. More dramatically, Ivan Demanyuk might genuinely insist that he has no memory of committing horrors in the Nazi death camps, and yet for all that he may have been the person who perpetrated those atrocities.

This objection was developed by Thomas Reid (1710–96), via the following story. Consider a soldier who was once a boy who stole apples from an orchard and was flogged in consequence. Later still, that same boy became a brave ensign who captured a standard in battle.

Afterwards, the ensign gained promotion and ultimately became a famous general. If memory is supposed to be necessary for personal identity we get the following result:

a   The brave ensign can remember stealing the apples, so he is one and the same person as the boy who stole them and was flogged.
b   The general can remember taking the standard, so he is one and the same person as the brave ensign.
c   The general, however, cannot remember stealing the apples as a boy, so he is not one and the same person as the boy.

Now look at Exercise 10.2.

What does Reid's counter-argument show, would you say? Consider your response before reading on.

Exercise 10.2

It would appear that if the general is the brave ensign by (b), and the brave ensign is the boy by (a), then the general is the boy (by the transitivity of identity: if $x = y$, and $y = z$, then $x = z$). But according to (c) the general is not the boy, because he cannot remember what the boy did. Hence the general both is, and is not, one and the same person as the boy. But this is a manifest contradiction, hence we must reject memory as a necessary condition of personal identity.

10.3   Dealing with Reid's objection

Locke was on the right track, according to the contemporary philosopher Derek Parfit,[3] but he overstated his case in insisting that a present person X could not be identical with a past person Y who committed some crime, unless X remembered committing the crime. Parfit suggests that X can be Y just as long as there is enough of what he calls continuity and connectedness – C & C – between memories as well as other psychological features. By connectedness, Parfit means direct memory connections: if X can remember what Y did a number of years ago, from the inside, then X is identical with Y. But even if direct connections are lacking, there may still be continuity. The idea here is that there is an overlapping chain of direct memories. Thus on Sunday I can remember some of what I did on Saturday, but perhaps nothing of what I did on Friday. However, on Saturday I can remember some of what I did on Friday, although nothing of what I did on Thursday. On Friday, though, I can remember some of what I did on Thursday, but none of what I did on Wednesday . . . and so on and so forth. Revising Locke's criterion in this way, we can say that X is identical with Y because there is sufficient continuity and connectedness between them. We can see the proposal represented diagrammatically in figure 10.1.

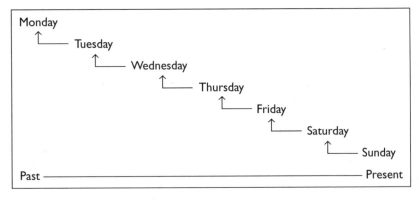

Figure 10.1   Overlapping memory chains

The corollary of this account is that if there is no C & C of psychological features at all, as in the case of total amnesia imagined in chapter 9, section 9.4, then it appears we are entitled to conclude that a present person is not one and the same as a past person, even though there is physical continuity in terms of the persistence of a body and brain.

Parfit's modification of Locke can accommodate other sorts of psychological C & C besides memory, for example the connection between an intention to do a particular action and the later performance of that act. There are also connections between past beliefs and desires and present states of mind, as well as connections between past and present personality traits, habits and abilities.

Parfit points out that, as identity is a transitive relation (if $x = y$ and $y = z$, then $x = z$) and connectedness is not a transitive relation (if on Monday I remember what I did on Tuesday, and on Tuesday I remember what I did on Wednesday, it does not follow that on Monday I remember what I did on Wednesday), then connectedness alone cannot count as the criterion of identity. What is also needed is continuity.

Furthermore, Parfit distinguishes between strong and weak connectedness, because connectedness is a matter of degree. For X to be identical with Y there must be enough psychological connections between X and Y, in other words, there must be strong connectedness. Whilst 'enough' cannot be precisely defined, Parfit maintains that it can be said that X is numerically identical with Y if the number of connections on any day is at least half the number of connections that hold, over every day, in the lives of every actual person.

Parfit is now enabled to use the notion of strong connectedness in defining personal identity. Unlike connectedness, continuity is a transitive relation. If X on Monday is continuous with Y on Tuesday, and Y on Tuesday is continuous with Z on Wednesday, then X is continuous with Z. Parfit suggests the following definition of personal identity, what he calls the psychological criterion:

(1) There is psychological continuity if and only if there are overlapping chains of strong connectedness. X today is one and the same person as Y at some past time if and only if (2) X is psychologically continuous with Y, (3) this continuity has the right kind of cause, and (4) it has not taken a 'branching' form. (5) Personal identity over time just consists in the holding of facts like (2) to (4).[4]

At this stage, however, the meaning of conditions (3) and (4) and the reason for their inclusion may not be very clear. However, I will briefly postpone an explanation of them, as this task is best left until I have dealt with other objections to the Locke/Parfit model of personal identity as psychological continuity.

10.4   Butler's objection to Locke's argument

Certainly, if X can genuinely remember in the usual way from the inside what Y did, then it follows that X is Y. If I now can remember teaching Florence last week, then I must be one and the same as the person who taught Florence last week. The reason, as we saw earlier, is obvious. 'I remember teaching Florence last week' is elliptical for 'I remember that I taught Florence last week'. For this sentence to make sense, the reference of the two occurrences of the pronoun 'I' must be to one and the same person throughout. But this leads to a very telling objection first formulated by Bishop Joseph Butler (1692–1752), namely that Locke's account is circular. Butler wrote: 'One should really think it self-evident, that consciousness of personal identity presupposes, and therefore cannot constitute personal identity, any more than knowledge, in any other case, can constitute truth, which it presupposes.'[5]

In other words, if it really is true that I remember teaching Florence last week, then this presupposes I am one and the same person who taught Florence. If it wasn't me that taught Florence, then I am mistaken, and therefore I can't really be remembering after all. My numerical identity with the person who taught Florence is being used as the criterion of whether or not I have a genuine memory of teaching her. It is precisely in this way that the notion of genuine memory presupposes personal identity and why memory cannot be appealed to in order to constitute personal identity.

10.5   Dealing with the circularity objection

Parfit's elaboration of Locke's theory still leaves it open to the charge of circularity. To avoid this problem, Parfit suggests that the notion of memory is replaced with quasi-memory, as that was defined earlier (chapter 9, section 9.7). I have a quasi-memory of teaching Florence last week, an apparent memory of instructing her, but this leaves it open as to whether it really was me that taught her or someone else. Hence, the identity of the person doing the quasi-remembering is not presupposed, and circularity in the analysis is circumvented.

To make Parfit's modified analysis as clear as possible, consider the following real-life case. I remember that when I was 3, my father and I witnessed a lifeboat being launched at Exmouth in Devon. Any attempted analysis of my identity over the intervening years since I was 3 which uses the notion of memory presupposes personal identity, as we have seen, so let the analysis be put instead in terms of quasi-memory, thus:

1   I seem to remember the lifeboat being launched.
2   Someone did see the lifeboat being launched.
3   My apparent memory is dependent, in the right kind of way, on that past experience.

This formula leaves it open that the someone in (2) might not be myself. I might quasi-remember someone else's experiences. It will probably be objected that this never happens. I never in fact do remember someone else's experiences 'from the inside', that is, from a first-person rather than a third-person perspective. True, but must this necessarily be so?

Suppose memory is somehow encoded in brain cells and surgeons develop a technique of transplanting these cells from one person to another. This could enable the recipient to access the memories of the donor, from the inside, so that it seemed to the recipient that he was remembering what the donor experienced from the inside. The experience of seeming to remember the donor's experiences would be just like remembering one's own experiences, except that it would, in fact, be quasi-remembering someone else's experiences. The fact that they were someone else's experiences would not enter into the mode of presentation of those experiences – the experiences would be presented to me just as if they were my very own original experiences.

In terms of my seeming to remember seeing the lifeboat being launched, what could have happened is this. Over a number of years I totally lost all memory of seeing the boat launched, but my father did not. Subsequently, I had some of his memory cells implanted in me, and as a result it seems to me that I am remembering seeing the launch of the boat. In reality, I am only quasi-remembering the launch, since it is my father's experience of seeing the boat coming out of the lifeboat shed that is causing my apparent memory of the event, and not my experience of seeing the boat launched that is causing my memory of it.

What this slightly fanciful example is designed to bring out is that memory is a causal notion. The same applies to quasi-memory. For a present experience to count as a memory experience, or even a quasi-memory experience, it must have been caused by someone's original experience, either one's own experience in the case of ordinary straightforward memory, or someone else's in the case of quasi-memory. If what seemed to be a memory experience was caused, say, by the injection of a drug or a bang on the head, then it could not count either as ordinary remembering, nor even quasi-remembering. The experience would not be any kind of memory experience at all.

However, to return to the main argument, let us remind ourselves that what we are looking for is a non-circular account of personal identity framed in terms of the causal notion of quasi-remembering, of one past experience causing another present experience, where this relation is couched in such a way that the identity of the person whose experiences are in question is not presupposed. The three statements presented above may appear to have captured what is needed, but unfortunately there is a problem with spelling out what is required by condition (3).

To appreciate the difficulty, let us consider a modification of the lifeboat example. Suppose that having seen the boat launched, my father totally forgets this experience. I, however, do not, and some years later remind him of the event. This has the effect of reviving his memory. However, some time after this I myself totally forget the original experience. Many years pass, until one day my father tells me how we saw the lifeboat launched. At a yet later date, I forget his telling me this. However, as a result of his telling me, it subsequently seems to me that I really do remember seeing the lifeboat launched. In reality, I do not, however. This is because my memory impression has resulted from his words and not directly from either my experience of seeing the boat launched, nor even from his experience of the event. Thus I am not genuinely recalling the experience, nor even quasi-remembering it. It only seems to me that I am. Nevertheless, my original experience of seeing the lifeboat launched has played a role in producing my apparent memory, and hence conditions (1), (2) and (3) are satisfied. The problem is that (3) is not satisfied in the right way. What we needed for (3) was that my experience of seeing the lifeboat launched directly caused quasi-memory of it. On the present account it did not, because the causal chain reaching from that original experience to my apparent quasi-memory of it took a wayward route through an external agent, namely my father.

The difficulty cannot, however, be avoided by specifying that for an apparent quasi-memory to count as a genuine quasi-memory, and therefore to qualify for inclusion in the analysis of personal identity, the causal chain reaching from the original experience to the quasi-memory of it must run internally through one and the same person and not pass externally through other persons. The reason why this stipulation cannot be made should be plain, namely, that it employs the very concept of one and the same person for which we are supposed to be accounting in a non-circular way.

Let us reconsider afresh what Parfit is trying to do. What seems to emerge, at the end of the day, is that Parfit's aim is to provide a theory of personal identity purely in terms of the causal relations that obtain between experiences and other psychological features. Ultimately, that is all that personal identity really amounts to for Parfit, a chain of experiences and other psychological features causally related to each other in the right, that is, in 'direct', non-wayward sorts of ways. However, it seems doubtful that even this modified analysis can avoid the importation of circularity into it.

Yet, be that as it may, it is of some interest to note that Parfit's account has a historical precedent in that it bears more than a passing resemblance to Hume's bundle theory of the self. Hume's theory arose in the following way. He wanted to be clear what the subject of the experiences, the 'I' or self to which they all belong, really was. This subject of experiences, it seems, could not itself merely be another experience, but was to be set over and above them as a different sort of item, the kind of thing capable of possessing experiences, but which is not reducible to any one of them, or, indeed, even to their totality.

Hume believed that all meaningful concepts, or ideas as he called them, ultimately derived from sense experience which supplied what he called 'impressions'. Accordingly, for Hume, the way to get clear about any concept that is obscure is to trace it back to its origins in sense. Lack of clarity about the self, he thought, meant that one must try to find the sense impression from which the concept of the self is supposed to be derived as a faint image. In order to find this sense impression, Hume introspected to find the self who is the owner of experiences. However, as he famously reported, he could not find it. The most he could discover were particular experiences that he was undergoing and which kept rapidly changing. He was thus driven to the conclusion that there is no self, no subject of experiences, no 'I', over and above the experiences themselves. The self, then, he concluded, must ultimately be nothing more than a bundle of experiences related in appropriate ways. But what are these ways? If we consider six experiences, E1, E2, E3, E4, E5 and E6, by what principle do we decide if we have just one self consisting of six experiences, or two selves consisting of three experiences each, or three selves consisting of two experiences each, or three selves consisting of two experiences each, or even six selves consisting of just one experience each?

Hume observed that there were just three ways in which they could be related to each other. Firstly, they could be contiguous, that is, close to each other. Secondly, they could resemble each other. Thirdly, they could be related causally. Which of these relations, if any, can be used to decide which experiences are to constitute which self? Think about this question and then consider the question posed in Exercise 10.3.

Exercise 10.3   What difficulties can you find with Hume's proposal? Discuss this with someone else before reading on.

To begin with, contiguity does not seem to be of much use because it is not clear in what sense experiences can be contiguous to each other as opposed to what the experiences are experiences of. Hume's own example in his *Enquiry concerning Human Understanding* is of apartments that are next to each other. However, whilst rooms can literally be contiguous to each other, it is difficult to attach sense to the claim that people's experiences of seeing rooms are next to each other, unless this is merely an obscure way of saying that two flesh-and-blood people, each of whom is having an experience of seeing one of the rooms, are standing next to each other.

Secondly, similarity of experiences is neither necessary nor sufficient for determining which experiences belong to which people. It is not necessary because it is possible that someone could have a stream of experiences, none of which resemble each other. It is not sufficient because different people's experiences could resemble each other.

That leaves causality. Is it necessary for an experience to be causally linked to other experiences to count as part of the bundle that constitutes the self? The idea of a particular experience, which has no causal relation to any other experience and yet counts as the experience of one and the same person, does not seem unintelligible. But whatever the truth is in deciding this difficult question, a causal relation between one experience and another does not seem sufficient to make them part of one and the same self. This is because it makes sense to suppose that one person's experience could give rise to another person's – my sadness, for example, could make you feel sad – and yet, despite the causal link between the two experiences, my experience of sadness would still be mine, whilst yours would remain yours. Going back to the case where my father's experience of seeing the lifeboat launched is supposed, after some of his brain cells have been placed in my brain, to cause my quasi-memory of the launch, the fact that his original experience causes my later quasi-memory is not sufficient to classify the original experience as mine rather than his. In fact, as I have already pointed out, this talk of quasi-remembering someone else's experiences, but genuinely remembering my own experiences, would appear to be invoking the correlative notions of numerically the same and different people, which is, of course, the very notion that we are supposed to be providing an analysis of purely in terms of the connectedness and continuity of experiences and other psychological features. Hence, it seems that the circularity that Parfit's invocation of quasi-memory is designed to eliminate creeps back in at the end of the day. As Colin McGinn has aptly observed, it seems that causal theories can seldom deliver sufficiency.[6]

Parfit, I think, would be unfazed by these criticisms. What his position amounts to, it seems to me, is this. There are human bodies and brains and there are also experiences. Some of these experiences are causally related to each other. When enough experiences are related to each other by strong connectedness and continuity in the sense explained earlier (see section 10.3), then we have a (one) subject of experiences. As Parfit himself says:

Because we ascribe thoughts to thinkers, it is true that thinkers exist. But thinkers are not separately existing entities. The existence of a thinker just involves the existence of his brain and body, the doing of his deeds, the thinking of his thoughts, and the occurrence of certain other physical and mental events. We could therefore redescribe any person's life in impersonal terms. In explaining the unity of this life, we need not claim it is the life of a particular person. We could describe what, at different times, was thought and felt and observed and done, and how these various events were inter-related. Persons would be mentioned here only in terms of the descriptions of the content of many thoughts, desires, memories, and so on. Persons need not be claimed to be the thinkers of any of these thoughts.[7]

There could be a few experiences that are causally related to those linked by strong continuity and connectedness, but which do not exhibit strong continuity and connectedness themselves. But these less strongly linked experiences would not count as the memories of a single self. They would, perhaps, constitute quasi-memories instead, that is, memories, from the inside, of other people's experiences. Besides my experiences, which are my experiences on Hume's/Parfit's view precisely because they exhibit strong continuity and connectedness and therefore comprise the central core of myself, there will be a few other experiences that are causally linked to this core, but more tenuously. These extra experiences will include quasi-memories such as my quasi-memory of seeing the lifeboat launched, which was given rise to by my father's original experience in the case where his brain cells were implanted into me. There is, unavoidably, a certain indeterminacy about just how strongly linked experiences have to be to count as a tract of a person's history. This means, as Anthony O'Hear has pointed out, that there is, on Parfit's view, 'no clear criterion for deciding when one self ends and another begins.'[8]

This leads Parfit to what he finds a consoling view of death. After he has died, Parfit explains, there will be no one living who will be him. There will, however, be many experiences, none of which will be linked to his present experiences by such direct connections as those presently obtaining in the case of his memories, or which are involved when a present intention is fulfilled by a later act. But some future experiences will be related to his present experiences in less direct ways. Some memories will be of his life, and there will be some thoughts and policies influenced by Parfit's thoughts when he was alive. 'My death', he says, 'will break the more direct relations between my present experiences and future experiences, but it will not break various other relations. . . . Instead of saying, "I shall be dead", I should say, "There will be no future experiences that will be related, in certain ways, to these present experiences." '[9] This way of redescribing death makes it less bad for Parfit, although he observes that for Hume it made it much worse, throwing him into 'the most deplorable condition imaginable, environed with the deepest darkness',[10] from which the only cure was dining and playing backgammon with friends. By contrast, for Parfit it removes the glass wall between him and others and makes him care less about his own death. All his own demise amounts to, he claims, is that after a given time certain experiences will no longer be related to his present experiences, in certain ways. And that, he thinks, cannot really matter very much.

10.6   Identity and survival without physical continuity

Parfit's theory enables him to deal comparatively easily with what happens in the case of split brains. The experiences supported by the two hemispheres after fission will be linked by chains of strong continuity and connectedness to the experiences which occurred before the split. Although, because of the transitivity of identity, neither of the two fission products can be literally identical with the original person, the two sets of experience comprising each of the fission products will be strongly continuous with the original person's experiences. Hence, there is a sense in which the original person is not annihilated but continues to exist as two streams of causally related experiences. A river that divides, similarly, does not disappear, but continues to exist, as two separate but individual flows of water continuous with the original river. In this way there can be survival without identity.

There is, moreover, Parfit claims, another way in which survival without identity is possible, but which does not involve dividing brains or ultimately even any tinkering with a person's physical aspects at all. Interestingly, for reasons that will shortly become clearer, this other possibility is much closer to Locke's original suggestion that personal identity has nothing to do with the identities of material or immaterial substances, but is definable purely formally, as Parfit maintains, in terms of the relations between experiences.

To appreciate the point Parfit is making, we are invited to imagine a device called the brain-state-transfer-device. This consists of a cubicle, which you enter and are then scanned, the relative positions of the molecules in your body being recorded by the machine. Your body and brain are then vaporized, after which the information stored in the machine is transmitted to a distant planet where a molecule-for-molecule replica is created out of the materials on the planet's surface. This person looks exactly like you, and has all your skills, abilities, character traits and habits. Moreover, everything he claims to remember fits your life in every detail. Before reading on, consider the question posed in Exercise 10.4.

Is the replica person identical with you, or merely a brilliant duplicate? What is your reaction to this thought-experiment? Consider reasons for and against the claim that the replica is you.

Exercise 10.4

According to Parfit, the person is you. After all, everything that really matters for your survival is in place, namely, strong continuity and connectedness of mental and psychological life generally. Granted, you do not have the one and the same body that you had on earth, but why should that be important? If you survive in the brain-transplant case with a numerically different body, then why not in this situation? It is merely that the transference of the person in this case is carried out in a more sophisticated, less messy, way. To be sure, in the case of the brain transplant you still ended up with one and the same brain, whereas in this situation you acquire a totally new brain, the old one having been vaporized. But again, why should that matter, as long as your psychology and memories are intact? Further, let us suppose that after you have been on the distant planet some time you become bored and wish to go travelling. Accordingly, you enter the brain-state-transfer-device again many times, each time being transported to a different planet and acquiring a new body and brain at every stop. This fits what Locke said about personal identity precisely: 'For, it being the same consciousness that makes a man be himself to himself, personal identity depends on that only, whether it be annexed only to one individual substance, or *can be continued in a succession of several substances.*'[11]

Parfit can also deal very easily with a second scenario, in which you enter the cubicle as before, but this time the machine malfunctions and does not vaporize your body before transmitting the information to the distant planet. Consequently, we end up in a situation such that the person who entered the transporter is psychologically and physically continuous with the person who stepped out of it on earth, while the person on the distant planet is psychologically, but not physically, continuous with the original person on earth. This situation is represented diagrammatically in figure 10.2.

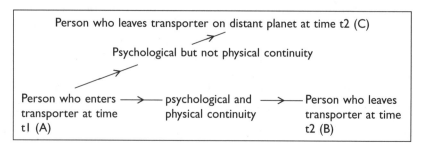

Figure 10.2   Physical and psychological continuity

Which person has the better claim to be you: B or C (see figure 10.2)? By the same logic that we applied in the split-brain example, the claim is that you survive as B and C, though the transitivity of identity prohibits you from being identical with either. The fact that one of the pair, B, is physically continuous with you, whereas C is not, is irrelevant to whether or not you survive on the Locke/Parfit approach. In matters of survival, psychological, not physical, continuity reigns supreme. The Locke/Parfit theory also easily provides for personal identity. In keeping with the sketch that has been given of the theory, we have personal identity in just those cases where no branching occurs. After fission has taken place, if one of the hemispheres dies and the other survives, the survivor will be you. There is no other competition for the title, which you win by default. Similarly, when the brain-state-transfer-device does not misfunction and only creates a single replica, that replica is you, there being no other candidate available for that honour. This should hopefully have now made it clear why condition (4) was included in Parfit's formal statement of personal identity as psychological continuity in section 10.3.

As we saw above, the Locke/Parfit approach is analogous to treating you as a function or program run on the hardware of the brain, the material embodiment being strictly irrelevant to your identity and survival. You could go from body and brain to body and brain, just as information on a floppy disc can be transferred intact to another disc if the original disc becomes damaged.

In the fantasy above, this is all managed by the brain-state-transfer-device, but this possibility can be given a theological twist. God, being all-powerful, can do anything that is logically possible. So whatever the transporter can do, God can do equally well, if not better. This is how life after death is possible, according to this view. At death your body and brain are destroyed, but God preserves the programme, the stream of experiences which exhibit strong connectedness and continuity. He preserves these experiences not in physical hardware, but in his mind. After all, there is no objection, as functionalists agreed, that a program could not be equally well instantiated in non-material as well as material arrangements, since the program possesses an abstractness which means it cannot be strictly identified with the arrangements which realize it (cf. chapter 5, section 5.3). Actually, God, being all-good as well as all-powerful, goes one better than conventional program-storing devices. What he does is to delete some imperfect or damaged parts of the programs, and in this way perfects us for Heaven. He is, thus, essentially a moral physician, cleaning up and purifying the person's soul and ridding them of sin.

The following objection may, however, have occurred to you. Are we really entitled to conclude that the replica on the distant planet is you? Without some kind of physical continuity, do you really survive being scanned in the machine? Is the machine not better described as an execution chamber, which swiftly and painlessly disintegrates you? On this view, the replica of you on the distant planet is just that, a mere replica, a brilliant forgery. The survival of this replica no more provides for your survival than does the fact that your appendix will be preserved eternally in a bottle, as Anthony Flew once memorably remarked.[12]

I suspect that many people's intuitions will accord with the conclusion that the brain-state-transfer device, when it does not malfunction, is not person-preserving. When the machine goes wrong, the person who enters it survives by a lucky accident because his body and, most importantly, his brain are left undisturbed. But the full rationale of this response needs to be articulated, and this leads us back to physical continuity as a criterion of personal identity.

10.7   Physical continuity revisited

Peter Unger has powerfully argued that physical continuity is necessary for the preservation of personal identity.[13] Although it is impossible to do justice here to the full range and subtlety of Unger's discussion, his central thesis can be put directly and simply. He acknowledges that the preservation and continuity of a person's psychological life are crucial to their survival and identity over time. If your brain were scrambled so that all memories and other psychological features were lost, you too would be lost. Moreover, if you are to exist at a future time, there must be, from now until that time, the continuous existence of your basic mental capacities. Unger puts great emphasis on the continuous preservation of psychological capacities. These capacities can continue to exist, even when they are not being exercised, or even during those periods when they could not be exercised, as, for instance, if your brain were frozen.

By comparison with Descartes, who thought that the human mind must be conscious even during periods of dreamless sleep and in the mother's womb, Unger only requires the preservation of the capacities, not their actual exercise during periods of consciousness. The brain, rather than the rest of the body, is vitally important here, because, in common with other materialists, Unger believes that the brain supports mental life. In fact, he is prepared to go further, maintaining that each conscious experience is a physical process in the brain. But this is not a position he argues for, nor, as he points out himself, is he required to, in order to give the account of personal identity which he does. He remarks that he could quite happily be a non-reductive monist as far as his account of personal identity goes.

Unger presents his theory that personal identity is ultimately grounded in physical continuity of the brain, not as a matter of logical or conceptual necessity, but just because that is the theory that the facts as we know them will support.[14] He is willing to allow for the possibility that there are worlds where personal identity is not materially based, but these possible worlds are not our world. In our world, personal identity does, as a matter of fact, depend upon the continuous preservation of a person's psychology by their brain.

Let us now see what Parfit, in contrast, says about the importance of physical continuity to personal identity. Parfit distinguishes between what he calls the strong, intermediate and weak versions of the psychological criterion.

According to the strong version, the physical cause of psychological continuity must be the normal cause, that is, the brain. The weak version, at the opposite extreme, maintains that even if the cause is abnormal, personal identity is preserved. The brain-state-transfer-device is supposedly just such an abnormal cause of psychological continuity. The thought here is that although normally the brain preserves the continuity of mental life, the working of the brain-state-transfer-device, albeit a somewhat unusual way of carrying out the same function, will do just as well. How the preservation of psychological continuity is actually carried out by a set of physical arrangements doesn't really matter, as long as one way or the other it gets done. The intermediate version, as the name implies, wants the best of both worlds. The cause of psychological continuity must either be the brain, or at least something not too different from the brain, for example, an ordinary organic brain that has been gradually transmuted by the replacement of its parts by bionic replacements into an inorganic structure supposedly subserving the mental function carried out by the original brain.

All three versions are agreed on the importance of psychological continuity for survival and personal identity. They differ only with regard to how this may acceptably be achieved. Unger strongly disagrees with the weak version. He thinks that the description of the scanning device as a brain-state-transfer-device begs the question. The trouble with this kind of description and science fiction example – compare the transporters in *Star Trek* – is that it encourages the belief that the person is transported and makes its acceptance appear inevitable. We play along with the idea that the person is transported for the sake of a good story and because it satisfies our imaginations.

But it would be better, Unger proposes, if the scanning machine were called, more neutrally, a taping device, which merely records the information regarding the position of your molecules. The transmission of this information to a distant planet, where it is used to construct a replica of you out of suitably modified local materials, hasn't the slightest tendency, Unger maintains, to show that you actually succeed in making the journey. When you enter the taping device, your body and brain are vaporized, and that is the end of you. The dissolution of your brain spells the end of the preservation of your psychological capacities in a way that some of the other things that might be done to your brain do not, for example, the gradual replacement of all its working organic cells with bionic replacements, as the intermediate criterion envisages. Freezing your brain, quartering it, putting it back together and thawing it out might all be consistent with the preservation of your psychological capacities. But shattering your brain into thousands of nerve cells, even if subsequently these are all reattached to each other in the original structure before the catastrophe occurred, is not. The newly assembled brain may well support a person's mental life, but this person would not be you in any sense, you having disappeared permanently at the moment your brain was scattered to the elements.

If this last statement is correct, then not even God is capable of resurrecting you by reassembling all your molecules. He might well put all the particles of which you were made back together again as they were when you were living, and he might thereby create a new living person. But this would not be you. The new person would merely have been made out of the materials of which you formerly had been constituted, the organizational structure that existed continuously whilst you were alive and which during that time grounded your psychological capacities, having been lost. Compare the following case: a statue made of a lump of gold cannot exist without the gold, but it is not the same as the lump. The lump survives being melted down, but the statue does not. Hence, something is true of the lump that is not true of the statue, and by Leibniz's Law (see chapter 2, section 2.7.1) this rules out their identity, even though, with seeming paradox, there could be no statue without the material that comprises the lump. If the melted-down material was then recast in the form of the original statue, and even if by some freak of chance all the molecules ended up back in their original relations to each other, it seems that it would not be one and the same as the original statue. This is not like the case in which a ship or a bike is disassembled and then reassembled. These are composite objects whose very nature consisted in being assembled and which allow for their parts to be gradually changed and for them to be taken apart and put back together again, whilst still retaining their identity. We may not permit ourselves the same licence with regard to lumps of stuff.

In stressing the importance of the continuity of the brain and its structure in preserving a person's psychological capacities, and hence their identity, it might be wondered whether this leads to the strange-sounding thesis that a person is identical with nothing but, ultimately, his or her brain. Marx called this kind of position Cartesian materialism. The mind/brain identity theorists appear to be committed to this position, and Thomas Nagel has also toyed with the idea. The strangeness of the position may be brought out when we reflect that, according to the Cartesian, we cannot say that Keith Maslin is five feet two inches tall, or weighs so many pounds. Strictly, we have to say that Keith Maslin's body, but not Keith Maslin, has these physical characteristics, the real Keith Maslin being an immaterial soul who lacks all physical features.

Maintaining that the person is the brain leads to a similarly odd result. According to this view, as for traditional Cartesianism, you have never met me because you have never seen my brain. Equally, if I am my brain, we would surely be prohibited from saying that I am weeping, falling in love, getting angry, forgiving someone, watching the television, reading a book or playing the piano, for brains can do none of these things.

To identify me with my brain is surely to identify me with a part of me, albeit a vitally important part without which I doubtless could not do any of the things just mentioned. Fortunately, however, even if the continued existence of my brain determines my continuance and identity over time, it does not follow that I must be identical with my brain. Returning to the example of the statue and the lump of gold, the identity of F things might be fixed by the identity of G things, without Fs being identical with Gs, as Brian Garratt points out. The statue cannot be identified with the lump for the reasons given earlier, but 'the identity conditions for the lump fix the identity conditions of the statue in the following way: necessarily, if the statuesque lump continues to exist with its shape pretty much unaltered, then the statue continues to exist'.[15] And, we may add, if not, not.

In bringing this section to a close, I conclude that physical continuity of the brain, or something very closely equivalent to the brain, which makes possible and supports a person's psychological capacities continuously, even if those capacities are not and cannot temporarily be exercised, is essential to personal identity. Shaun now (whom you will remember from chapter 9) is one and the same person as Shaun then if, and only if:

1　Shaun now has psychological continuity in the sense of the preservation of his psychological capacities.
2　There is also physical continuity which is responsible ultimately for the psychological continuity. The cause of (1) is a normal cause, i.e. Shaun's brain, or perhaps something very like Shaun's brain, such as a gradually evolved bionic replacement. The so-called brain-state-transfer-device does not count as a normal and acceptable cause of psychological continuity.
3　Branching, which would supply another equally good candidate for the status of being Shaun, has not occurred.

10.8　Personal identity and non-reductionism

There are philosophers today, though probably only a small minority, who reject the reductive accounts of personal identity in terms of either physical or psychological continuity, or a combination of the two, outlined above. For such philosophers, personal identity is a conceptually primitive notion, unanalysable into other concepts such as the physical continuity of the brain, or causal relations between various psychological states or conditions, notably memory. The persistence of the subject of consciousness, the ego or self, that to which 'I' is supposed to refer, is represented as a further fact over and above the holding of mental or physical relations between various states. Hence, the persistence of the self or subject of experience cannot be reduced to the holding of such relations. In the past this view was most famously associated with the eighteenth-century philosopher Bishop Joseph Butler, who, in rejecting a reductionist view of the self, was making a move similar to those who have rejected a causal theory of the persistence of physical objects, the theory that the persistence of such objects can be regarded as a temporally extended series of time slices or stages which are causally connected to each other. The persistence of a physical object is something over and above, and therefore not reducible to, the obtaining of causal relations between its physical states at different times, or its continuity in space.

Contrary to what the psychological continuity theory implies, a non-reductionist account of personal identity entails that a person could suffer complete and radical amnesia of the type mentioned earlier and yet still be one and the same person. Moreover, all past experiences and old psychological features could be swept away, and a new set of experiences and characteristics installed, and yet it would be one and the same consciousness, one and the same self, throughout the changes. If it is true that personal identity consists in a further fact over and above mental connectedness, then no contradiction can possibly result from the supposition that a person will survive the very radical changes to their psychological life that we are envisaging. It will be one and the same person after the changes as it was before the drastic alterations were implemented.

In support of such a claim, Richard Swinburne writes:

> Many religions have taken seriously stories of persons passing through the waters of Lethe (a river whose waters make a person forget all of his previous life) and then acquiring a new body. Others who have heard these stories may not have believed them true; but they have usually understood them, and (unless influenced by philosophical dogma), have not suspected them of involving contradiction.[16]

Equally, according to the theory which regards personal identity as primitive and unanalysable, the identity of a person has nothing to do with the identity of their body, or any part of it. At the end of the day, what does or does not happen to the body, including the brain, has no effect upon, or relevance to, the person's identity.

By now, it should be becoming clearer that what, in effect, the non-reductive account of personal identity amounts to is an espousal of substance dualism. The self, the subject of consciousness, cannot be identified with a material object such as the body or the brain, nor as consisting in a succession of physical states causally related to each other. But neither is the self reducible to the series of mental states which it enjoys during the period of its existence. It is that which has the mental states in question but which cannot be identified with the states it has. Since the self is that single thing, that unitary subject of experiences, which persists and stays the same throughout even very radical changes in its psychological life, and since, in addition, its identity has nothing whatsoever to do with the persistence and identity of material things such as the body and the brain, it seems to follow that the self has to be conceived of, *pace* Cartesianism, as a simple, logically indivisible substance.

This theory, if correct, has important consequences for the thought-experiment conducted earlier concerning the splitting of the brain into the two hemispheres, each of which is then transplanted. This was supposed to demonstrate the possibility of survival without identity, personal identity constituting the special case where non-branching occurs, as is effectively the case when one of the transplanted hemispheres does not survive the operation. The surviving hemisphere is, to all intents and purposes, identifiable with the original person, there being no other suitable candidate available.

For the dualist, however, none of this will do. Unlike cases where tulip bulbs, amoeba or rivers divide and thus in some sense survive as the parts of new entities, simple soul substances cannot divide. Such souls are not made up of smaller soul-like parts, hence, although when the brain is divided, part of it goes to the right and part to the left, it is not meaningful to speak of half the soul going to the left and half to the right. Thus, in the case of souls we are prohibited from having survival without identity. If the soul survives the brain split (and there is every reason to suppose it would, since it does not depend for its existence on physical states of affairs), then there are only three possibilities as to what happens to it in relation to the two resulting physical organisms whose skulls contain the left and right hemispheres of the original brain. Firstly, the soul goes where the right hemisphere goes. Secondly, it goes where the left hemisphere goes. Thirdly, it goes to neither hemisphere. If this third possibility were realized, then the result would be the creation of two soulless organisms – zombies, in effect – as no mentality would be associated with either entity. There would be a living functioning body containing a functioning brain, yet because mentality is not supervenient upon, nor identical with, brain processes, these bodies would lack any vestige of a mental life. There would, so to speak, be no one at home in each of these cases.

However, if we discount this third possibility, then the person, as a soul, survives either in connection with the right hemisphere, or with the left, but not with both simultaneously. In a way, this is a satisfying result, because it bears out an intuition about personal identity that it is hard to shake, namely, that is all-or-nothing and does not admit of degrees, contrary to what psychological and physical continuity theories appear to imply. There could be another reason why this result may be thought to be satisfying. Imagine that you yourself are going to have your brain divided because your original body is riddled with inoperable cancer. You are worried about whether you will survive, but are reassured by the surgeon, who has read Parfit, and who tells you that the outcome is better than death, because you will survive partially as two people. The single view that you now have on the world will be split into two, so you will be able to view the world from two different perspectives, both of which in some sense will be yours. After the split, you will no longer be able to know, without observation and inference, what is going on in your other mind, but you will, somehow, still be around as two distinct and independent centres of consciousness and experience.

However, you may well baulk at this description of what will happen to you, complaining that it smacks of incoherence. How could your present single viewpoint on the world become two such viewpoints in the future? How could what appears to be essentially a single viewpoint become two such viewpoints? A variation on this theme is supplied by Bernard Williams's fantasy of a mad surgeon who says that after your hemispheres have been transplanted, one of the resulting people will be horribly tortured, whilst the other will be set free and awarded a million pounds. How should you regard such a prospect? What you want to know is whether you will be unlucky and get the torture, or whether you will be lucky and get the million pounds. But for those who believe in partial survival without identity, this stark choice of alternative outcomes does not apply. Instead, we are forced to say that as one of the people you get the torture, and as the other person you get the million pounds, but there is no single person who gets both the torture and the million pounds. Thus no clear determinate answer emerges as to what will happen to *you*, the single subject of experience as you stand at this moment, in the future after the transplants have taken place.

By contrast, if you are a soul, there must be a determinate answer to the question of what will happen to you after the operation. Either your soul will go where the right hemisphere goes, or it will go where the left hemisphere goes, and one of the resulting individuals will get the torture, and the other the million pounds. Thus, on the dualist thesis, we can be sure that a single individual will either get the torture or the million pounds. There is, in other words, a definite answer as to who ultimately gets tortured and who gets rewarded. Before the operation takes place, the person in question can only hope that, as a soul, he will go with the hemisphere which helps to constitute the person that is rewarded and not tortured. Swinburne claims that neither natural laws nor philosophical reasoning can determine with which transplanted hemisphere the soul will ultimately be associated. The allocation of a particular hemisphere to a particular soul, is, Swinburne maintains, either down to God or to chance.

However, in keeping with the non-reductive monist theory of mind espoused by this book, I agree with J. L. Mackie's remark that 'a materialist view of the thinker is less controversial than a materialist view of thoughts'.[17] Thus, whilst there are very strong reasons for *not* attempting to reduce mental states to brain states, equally strong reasons pull in the opposite direction when it comes to the nature of the subject of consciousness. It is more plausible to view the identities of persons as dependent upon those physical structures that underpin and make possible the continuity of the various sorts of psychological capacity. Besides, as we saw in chapter 2, the problem of how incorporeal souls are to be individuated and identified means that substance dualism is ultimately a deeply unattractive account of the nature of persons, and hence a reductive view of personal identity is much more likely to be true.

Questions to think about

1   How plausible is Parfit's account of personal identity in terms of psychological continuity?
2   When Captain Picard in *Star-Trek* beams down to a planet's surface and back, is it really Picard who steps out of the transporter or a brilliant replica?
3   What philosophical problems are raised when endeavouring to establish our continuing identity through time?
4   Is it possible for you to survive as each of two different people?
5   If you were going to suffer a complete memory wipe, should you be worried about will happen to your body afterwards?

Suggestions for further reading

- A key text in the modern debate is Derek Parfit's *Reasons and Persons* (Oxford: Clarendon Press, 1984). It is lively, original and fun, and highly recommended.
- J. Dancy (ed.), *Reading Parfit* (Oxford: Blackwell, 1997) contains an important collection of papers on Parfit.
- Peter Unger's *Identity, Consciousness, and Value* (Oxford: OUP, 1990) is an important book which makes a highly persuasive case for the physical continuity account of personal identity.
- B. Garrett, *Personal Identity and Consciousness* (London and New York: Routledge, 1998) brings together physical and psychological accounts of personal identity, and is useful for the overview it provides as well as the clarity of its discussions.
- A book that contains intriguing discussions of multiple personality and the effects of commissurotomy is K. V. Wilkes, *Real People: Personal Identity without Thought-Experiments* (Oxford: Clarendon Press, 1988). It is also useful for its discussion of consciousness and Aristotle's picture of the mind.
- See also Wilkes's paper 'Psuche versus the mind', in M. Nussbaum and A. O. Rorty (eds), *Essays on Aristotle's* De Anima (Oxford: Clarendon Press, 1992).

NOTES

Chapter 1   The Mind/Body Problem

1   Hence Dickens's joke, embodied in Mrs Gradgrind's words in *Hard Times*: 'I think there is a pain somewhere in the room, but I couldn't be positively sure that I have got it.' Hume would have disagreed: 'Whatever is distinct, is distinguishable; and whatever is distinguishable, is separable by the thought or imagination. All perceptions are distinct. They are, therefore, distinguishable, and separable, and may be conceiv'd as separately existent, and may exist separately, without any contradiction or absurdity' (Appendix to *A Treatise of Human Nature*, ed. L. A. Selby-Bigge (Oxford: Clarendon Press, 1978), p. 634). What Hume means by a perception is an experience, i.e. a mental item. Thus he is claiming that individual experiences can exist loose and separate without dependence upon anything else.

2   G. W. Leibniz, *Monadology*, first published posthumously in J. E. Erdmann (ed.), *Leibniz, Opera Philosophica*, 2 vols (Berlin, 1840).

3   Admittedly there have been some strange and aberrant cases, as in one reported by Michael Lockwood in his book *Mind, Brain and the Quantum* (Oxford: OUP, 1989) in which a hypnotized subject who was asked to keep his left hand in a bucket of ice-cold water denied with apparent sincerity that he was feeling pain, yet upon being given pencil and paper started writing with his right hand that he was feeling terrible pain. This case resembles occurrences of so-called 'blindsight', a term that was coined by the psychologist Larry Weisskrantz. Oliver Sacks describes a case of blindsight in his fascinating book, *An Anthropologist on Mars* (London: Picador, 1995). A patient called Virgil had suffered brain damage owing to a lack of oxygen and insisted later that he was blind and could not see anything. Yet he would reach for objects and avoid obstacles – in short, he behaved exactly as if he were seeing except that he denied, with sincerity, that he had any consciousness of seeing. It is difficult to know how to account for such cases; it appears

that signals are received from the eyes and responded to, but that nothing filters through to the person's consciousness. I suggest that we can allow for the existence of these highly unusual cases just because they are not the norm and do not upset the normal use of the concepts of feeling a pain, or seeing things. If the situation altered so that blind-sight and unfelt pain became predominant and what we now regard as normal seeing and feeling pain were the exceptions, then our notion of what it is to feel pain and to see would undergo a conceptual revolution to accommodate the change.

4　I leave aside the complications posed by concepts such as repression, unconscious mental states, self-deception and so forth, for reasons of space.

5　Some philosophers, controversially, have tried to interpret the *causes* of sensations as being what the sensations represent, what they are about. See, for example, Michael Tye's *Ten Problems of Consciousness* (Cambridge, MA: MIT Press, 1995), ch. 4.

6　F. Brentano, *Psychology from an Empirical Standpoint*, trans. A.C. Pancurello, D.B. Terrell and L.L. McAlister (New York: Humanities Press, 1973), p. 88. Originally published 1874.

7　J. Heil, *The Nature of True Minds* (Cambridge:'CUP, 1992), p. 152.

8　D. Hume, *A Treatise of Human Nature*, book I, Part IV, p. 234.

9　Compare A. Kenny, *The Metaphysics of Mind* (Oxford: Clarendon Press, 1989), p. 39.

10　M. Proust, *À la recherche du temps perdu*, trans. C.K. Scott Moncrieff (London: Chatto and Windus, 1913–21), pp. 123–4.

11　J. Conrad, *Lord Jim* (New York: Bantam Books, 1957), p. 5.

12　Heil, *The Nature of True Minds*, pp. 154–5.

13　C. McGinn, *The Character of Mind* (Oxford: OUP, 1982), pp. 6–7.

14　G. Strawson, *Mental Reality* (Cambridge, MA: MIT Press, 1994), p. 245.

15　J. Hopkins, 'Wittgenstein and Physicalism', *Proceedings of the Aristotelian Society* 75 (1974–5), pp. 121–46.

16　H. Robinson, *Perception* (London: Routledge, 1994).

17　Ibid., p. 104.

18　Ibid., p. 105.

19　McGinn, *The Character of Mind*, p. 7.

20　Aristotle, *Politics*, 1253a 8–13, in J.A. Smith and W.D. Ross (eds), *The Works of Aristotle* (Oxford: Clarendon Press, 1910–52).

Chapter 2　Dualism

1　T.S. Eliot, *Collected Poems, 1909–62* (London: Faber and Faber, 1963).

2　Aristotle, *Categories*, 2a 12. In J.A. Smith and W.D. Ross (eds) *The Works of Aristotle* (Oxford: Clarendon Press, 1910–52).

3　For a good discussion of property dualism, see Dale Jaquette, *Philosophy of Mind* (Englewood Cliffs: Prentice-Hall, 1994).

4　Plato: *Phaedo*, 80a–b. In E. Hamilton and H. Cairns (eds), *The Collected Dialogues of Plato* (Princeton: Princeton University Press, 1961).

5   The other arguments, which you are encouraged to explore for yourself, can be found principally in the *Phaedo*, the *Meno*, and the *Republic*, and a good exposition and criticism of them is to be found in A.G.N. Flew's *An Introduction to Western Philosophy* (London: Thames and Hudson, 1971), as well as in Stephen Priest's *Theories of the Mind* (Harmondsworth: Penguin, 1991).

6   G. Ryle, *The Concept of Mind* (Harmondsworth: Penguin, 1973 [1949]), pp. 180–1.

7   Lest I should be accused of offering a crude caricature of Cartesianism, I should point out that I am presenting the standard interpretation of his philosophy of mind which is commonly taught in A-level and undergraduate courses. It is also to be found in the reactions to his work by philosophers such as John Locke (1632–1704) and David Hume (1711–76) and, more recently, in Gilbert Ryle's (1900–82) celebrated *The Concept of Mind* (1949), to which we owe Cartesian dualism's deliberately abusive characterization as 'the dogma of the ghost in the machine'. However, just as it is often said that Marx was not himself a Marxist, so nowadays it is increasingly being claimed that Descartes was not a Cartesian dualist! See, for example, G. Baker and K.J. Morris, *Descartes' Dualism* (London and New York: Routledge, 1996).

There is some truth in this radical claim. For example, even by the time he was nearing the end of his most famous work, the *Meditations*, Descartes was already substantially moving away from the view of the nature and relation of mind and body which he had expounded earlier in the *Second Meditation*; and further refinements and differences can be found in his letters and other published and unpublished works. An investigation into these other elements of Descartes' thought belongs in another place, however. In conclusion, Cartesian dualism as traditionally understood certainly represents a possible position – in fact, according to some philosophers it represents the common-sense view of what the mind is – hence my reason for (largely) confining myself to it in this early chapter.

8   R. Descartes, *Meditations* (London: Everyman Classics, 1986), p. 88.

9   R. Descartes, letter to an unknown correspondent, August 1641. In P. Geach and G.E.M. Anscombe (eds), *Descartes: Philosophical Writings* (Nelson University Paperbacks for The Open University, 1970), p. 266.

10 R. Descartes, *The Principles of Philosophy*, Section IX (London: Everyman Classics, 1986), p. 167.

11 Cf. R. Descartes, *The Passions of the Soul*, ed. S.H. Voss (Indianapolis: Hackett, 1989), i, 6, 5.

12 R. Descartes, *The Discourse on the Method*, trans. J. Veitch (London: J.M. Dent and Sons, 1912), p. 44.

13 R. Descartes, *Discourse on the Method*. In Geach and Anscombe (eds), *Descartes: Philosophical Writings*, pp. 41–2.

14 Ibid., p. 41.

15 B. Spinoza, *Ethics*. In E. Curley (ed.), *The Collected Works of Spinoza* (Princeton: Princeton University Press, 1985), Preface to Part III, note to proposition 2.

16 R. Descartes, *Meditations*. In Geach and Anscombe (eds), *Descartes: Philosophical Writings*, p. 117.

17 Ibid.

18 J. Cottingham, *A Descartes' Dictionary* (Oxford: Blackwell, 1993), p. 75.

19 Descartes, *Meditations* (Everyman edn), p. 86.

20 A. J. Ayer, *The Problem of Knowledge* (Harmondsworth: Penguin, 1956), p. 82.

21 Descartes, *Discourse on the Method*. In Geach and Anscombe (eds), *Descartes: Philosophical Writings*, p. 32.

22 T. Hobbes, 'Second Objection of the Third Set of Objections and Replies containing the controversy between Hobbes and Descartes'. In Geach and Anscombe (eds), *Descartes: Philosophical Writings*, p. 128.

23 Ibid., pp. 114–15.

24 A. Kenny, *Descartes* (New York: Random House, 1968), p. 84.

25 M. D. Wilson, *Descartes* (London: Routledge, 1978), p. 193.

26 Quoted in ibid.

27 Quoted in ibid., p. 196.

28 Quoted in ibid., p. 195.

29 J. Cottingham, *Descartes* (London: Phoenix, 1997), p. 35.

30 Quoted in Wilson, *Descartes*, p. 179.

31 I. Kant, *Critique of Pure Reason* (various editions), A.363.

32 Ibid., A.360.

33 Ibid.

Chapter 3   The Mind/Brain Identity Theory

1 J. J. C. Smart, 'Sensations and Brain-Processes', *Philosophical Review* LXVIII (1959). Reprinted in C. V. Borst (ed.), *The Mind/Brain Identity Theory* (London: Macmillan, 1970), pp. 52–66.

2 T. Nagel, 'Physicalism', in C. V. Borst (ed.), *The Mind/Brain Identity Theory* (London: Macmillan, 1970), p. 218.

3 Compare R. Brandt and J. Kim's way of putting it: 'Identity is a symmetric relation; it does not favour one of its terms at the expense of the other.' 'The Logic of the Identity Theory', *Journal of Philosophy* 64 (1967), p. 515.

4 See M. Tye, *Ten Problems of Consciousness* (Cambridge, MA: MIT Press, 1995); F. Dretske, 'The Intentionality of Conscious States', *Midwest Studies in Philosophy* 5 (1980), pp. 281–94; J. Fodor, *The Language of Thought* (T. Y. Crowell: New York, 1975).

5 See J. Searle, *The Rediscovery of the Mind* (Cambridge, MA: MIT Press, 1992), p. 51; G. Strawson, *Mental Reality* (Cambridge, MA: MIT Press, 1994), ch. 7; D. Jaquette, *Philosophy of Mind* (Englewood Cliffs, NJ: Prentice-Hall, 1994), ch. 4.

6 Jaquette, *Philosophy of Mind*, p. 96.

7   D. Davidson, in S. Guttenplan (ed.), *The Blackwell Companion to the Philosophy of Mind* (Oxford: Blackwell, 1994), p. 232.
8   Compare J. Kim, *Philosophy of Mind* (Boulder, CO: Westview Press, 1996), p. 58.
9   I have been very much helped in my understanding of these issues by ibid., ch. 9.
10 Searle, *The Rediscovery of the Mind*, p. 40.
11 S. Kripke, *Naming and Necessity* (Oxford: Blackwell, 1972).
12 Compare what David Chalmers has to say in *The Conscious Mind* (Oxford: OUP, 1996), p. 147:

> Kripke runs the argument in two different ways, one against token-identity theories and once against type-identity theories. Token-identity theories hold that *particular* pains (such as my pain now) are identical to particular brain-states, (such as the C-fibres firing in my head now). Kripke argues ... that a particular pain could occur without the particular associated brain state, and vice versa, so they cannot be identical. Type-identity theories hold that mental states and brain states are identical as *types*: pain, for example, might be identical as a type to the firing of C-fibres. Kripke holds that this is straightforwardly refuted by the fact that one could instantiate the mental-state type without the brain-state type and vice versa. Overall, we can count four separate arguments here, divided according to the target (token or type identity theories) and according to the method of argument (from the possibility of disembodiment or from the possibility of zombies).

13 K. V. Wilkes, *Physicalism* (London: Routledge and Kegan Paul, 1978), p. 102.
14 D. M. Armstrong and N. Malcolm, *Consciousness and Causality* (Oxford: Blackwell, 1984), p. 99; emphasis in original.
15 My position is essentially the same as Karl Popper's. Writing about eliminative materialism – which he refers to as promissory materialism – he says: 'there is rationally, not of more interest to be found in the thesis of promissory materialism than, let us say, in the thesis that one day we shall abolish cats or elephants by ceasing to talk about them; or in the thesis that one day we shall abolish death by ceasing to talk about it. (Indeed, did we not get rid of bed-bugs simply by refusing to talk about them?)' See Popper, *The Self and Its Brain* (London, Heidelberg, New York: Springer International, 1977), p. 97.

Chapter 4   Analytical Behaviourism

1   For a very precise and rigorous formulation of analytical behaviourism see John Foster's *The Immaterial Self: A Defence of the Cartesian Conception of the Mind* (London: Routledge, 1991), pp. 33–46.
2   See Norman Malcolm, *Dreaming* (London: Routledge and Kegan Paul, 1959). Malcolm disputed that he was claiming that dreams are nothing

but waking experiences – for example, he writes: 'Indeed I am not trying to say what dreaming is: I do not understand what it would mean to do that', and 'It is not easy to understand the relation between dreams and waking convictions of having dreamt. The dream and the waking conviction are not one and the same thing, in the sense that the morning star and the evening star are one and the same' (p. 59). Nevertheless, the general philosophical verdict seems to have gone against Malcolm and the position he was espousing was felt by a number of philosophers to amount to the reduction of dreams to waking impressions.

3   Hume's first analysis of causation can be found in his *Enquiry concerning Human Understanding and concerning the Principles of Morals*, ed. L. A. Selby-Bigge and P. H. Nidditch (Oxford: Oxford University Press, 3rd edn, 1995) in section 7 of the first enquiry concerning human understanding. Hume later improved on it, recognizing that although knowledge of cause and effect may be based on experience of regularities, it need not reduce to mere regularities. The causal relation is better captured, Hume recognized, by the formula 'if the first object had not been, the second had never existed'. This statement is what philosophers call a 'contrary-to-fact conditional' and it is not equivalent to the claim that whenever one sort of event occurs, it will be followed by another sort. Rather, it states a dependency of one event upon another, saying that if one sort of event were not to occur, then neither would the other sort.

4   This is reminiscent of a man, reported by Oliver Sacks in *The Man who Mistook his Wife for a Hat* (London: Picador, 1986), who suffered from visual agnosia, and seemed confined to being able to produce such descriptions. He could not see a glove as a glove and describe it in human terms as an article of clothing designed to fit human limbs and fulfil human purposes, but could only characterize it scientifically as 'a continuous surface, infolded upon itself. It appears to have five outpouchings, if this is the word' (p. 13).

5   C. Hempel, 'The Logical Analysis of Psychology', reprinted in Ned Block (ed.), *Readings in the Philosophy of Psychology*, vol. 1 (Cambridge, MA: Harvard University Press, 1980), p. 19.

6   Ibid., p. 17.

7   The utterance of any sentence is not necessarily an affirmation or statement of some fact intended to convey information, in this case how it is with that person experientially. 'I have a toothache' could be produced, as indeed it is now being, not to convey how I feel, but merely to provide a philosophical example. For a different reason, if a person were to produce the words 'I have a toothache' in their sleep, this could not be construed as the report of a toothache, because the person has no awareness that words are coming out of his or her mouth, and no operative intention to utter those words.

8   Foster, *The Immaterial Self*, p. 29.

9   See Geoffrey Madell, *Mind and Materialism* (Edinburgh: Edinburgh University Press, 1988), pp. 37–8.

10   See Foster, *The Immaterial Self*, pp. 42–3:

> And so, in trying to spell out the meaning of 'Smith believes D to be due north', he [the analytical behaviourist] will find himself falling back on sentences of the form:
>
> 3) If Smith were to have, additionally, such and such other mental states, he would be behaviourally disposed to behave in such and such ways and thus he will find himself relying on a further range of psychological concepts whose behavioural analyses still have to be supplied. But now it is clear that, if it is structured in this way, the analytical process will be unending, and indeed, until it starts to turn back on itself, ever-widening. The behaviourist will never be able to reach an ultimate construal of the original want-statement, since each time he turns his attention to a given mental state which he has so far taken for granted, he is forced to take other mental states for granted in specifying its behavioural significance.

11   S. Shoemaker, and R. Swinburne, *Personal Identity* (Oxford: Blackwell, 1984), p. 99.
12   G. Ryle, *The Concept of Mind* (Harmondsworth: Penguin, 1973). See Alan Donagan's observation that *The Concept of Mind* 'is a classic of modern analytic Aristotelianism, dressed in a behaviourism now out of style' in *Choice: The Essential Element in Human Action* (London: Routledge and Kegan Paul, 1987), p. ix.
13   Ryle, *The Concept of Mind*, p. 23.
14   Ibid., p. 17.
15   Ibid., p. 57 (my emphasis).
16   Ryle's disinclination to engage in the kind of analysis Hempel was aiming for is illustrated in his remark that *The Concept of Mind* would be stigmatized, harmlessly, as behaviourist. He is also reported as having said that he was never anything more than 'only one arm and one leg a behaviourist' (see Alex Byrne's 'Behaviourism', in S. Guttenplan (ed.), *A Companion to the Philosophy of Mind* (Oxford: Blackwell, 1994), p. 135).
17   Ryle, *The Concept of Mind*, p. 43.
18   H. Putnam, 'Brains and Behaviour', in Putnam (ed.), *Mind, Language and Reality: Philosophical Papers*, vol. 2 (Cambridge: CUP, 1975), p. 330.
19   Ryle, *The Concept of Mind*, p. 234.
20   Compare Christopher Peacocke's fantasy of a marionette, outwardly just like a minded human being, but actually radio-controlled from Mars, and lacking all internal mental states: *Sense and Content* (Oxford: Oxford University Press, 1983).
21   Putnam, 'Brains and Behaviour', p. 334.

Chapter 5   Functionalism

1   T. Crane, *The Mechanical Mind* (Harmondsworth: Penguin, 1995), pp. 93–9.
2   N. Block, 'Troubles with Functionalism', in N. Block (ed.), *Readings in the Philosophy of Psychology*, vol. 1 (London: Methuen, 1980).
3   K. V. Wilkes, *Physicalism* (London: Routledge and Kegan Paul, 1978).
4   S. Shoemaker, 'Functionalism and Qualia', in N. Block (ed.), *Readings in the Philosophy of Psychology*, vol. 1 (London: Methuen, 1980), p. 261 (my emphasis).
5   In their book *Philosophy of Mind and Cognition* (Oxford: Blackwell, 1996), David Braddon Mitchell and Frank Jackson thus choose to call metaphysical functionalism, common-sense functionalism.
6   Block, 'Troubles with Functionalism', p. 276.
7   This possibility was first mooted by John Locke (1632–1704) in *An Essay Concerning Human Understanding*, Book II, xxxii. 15): it is possible that 'by the different structure of our organs it were so ordered, that the same object should produce in several men's minds different ideas at the same time. v.g. if the idea that a violet produced in one man's mind by his eyes were the same that a marigold produced in another man's, and vice versa'.
8   F. Jackson, 'Epiphenomenal Qualia', in W. Lycan (ed.), *Mind and Cognition* (Oxford: Blackwell, 1990), pp. 469–77; and 'What Mary Didn't Know', in D. Rosenthal (ed.), *The Nature of Mind* (Oxford: OUP, 1991), pp. 392–4.
9   The imaginary case of Mary can be supported by a dramatic real-life incident. In *An Anthropologist on Mars* (London: Picador, 1995), Oliver Sacks describes the case of Mr I who had been a successful artist, but following a car accident suddenly and permanently lost all his colour vision. In a letter to Dr Sacks, Mr I wrote:

> 'My vision was such that everything appeared to me as viewing black and white television. Within days, I could distinguish letters and my vision became that of an eagle – I can see a worm wriggling a block away. The sharpness of focus is incredible. BUT – I AM ABSOLUTELY COLOUR BLIND. I have visited ophthalmologists who know nothing about this colour blind business. I have visited neurologists, to no avail. Under hypnosis, I still can't distinguish colours. I have been involved in all kinds of tests. You name it. My brown dog is dark grey. Tomato juice is black. Colour TV is a hodge-podge.' (p. 1)

The unfortunate Mr I went on to describe the leaden world which he had come to inhabit as not merely one in which colours were missing, but as one in which what he did see had 'a distasteful, "dirty" look, the whites glaring, yet discoloured and off-white, the blacks cavernous – everything wrong, unnatural, stained and impure' (ibid., p. 5).

Mr I's case is the reversal of Mary's. She comes to know what it is like to experience colour, whilst he loses the ability to know. But the philosophical point remains, namely that if the visual experience of the entire human species had been like Mr I's visual world from the very start, could we know, purely on the basis of a knowledge of our neurology, what it is like to see the flaming red of sunsets, the iridescent azure of a Morpho butterfly or the fresh green of horse-chestnut leaves in spring?

10   P. Churchland, 'Reduction, Qualia, and the Direct Introspection of Brain States', *The Journal of Philosophy* LXXXII (January 1985), pp. 8–28.

11   Jackson, 'What Mary Didn't Know', p. 393.

12   The distinction between 'knowledge by description' and 'knowledge by acquaintance' can be found in B. Russell, *The Problems of Philosophy* (Oxford: OUP, 1959), pp. 25–32.

13   D. Lewis, Postscript to 'Mad Pain and Martian Pain', in Lewis, *Philosophical Papers*, vol. 1 (Oxford: OUP, 1983), pp. 130–2, and 'What Experience Teaches', in Lycan, *Mind and Cognition*, pp. 499–519; L. Nemirow, Review of T. Nagel, *Mortal Questions*, *Philosophical Review* (1980), pp. 475–6, and 'Physicalism and the Cognitive Role of Acquaintance', in Lycan, *Mind and Cognition*, pp. 490–9.

14   Jackson, 'What Mary Didn't Know', p. 394.

15   J. Searle, *Minds, Brains and Science* (Harmondsworth: Penguin, 1984).

16   J. Searle, *The Rediscovery of the Mind* (Cambridge, MA: MIT Press, 1992), p. 210.

17   Ibid., p. 213.

18   The phrase 'something it is like to be us' is taken from Thomas Nagel's well-known essay 'What is it like to be a bat?'. Nagel claims that no amount of information gleaned about a person from a third-person, objective perspective can tell us what it is like to be that person. What it is like to be a person is something that can only be known from a first-person, subjective perspective. Similarly, what it is like to be a bat can only be known from the bat's subjective viewpoint. We are so different from bats, and bats are so different from us regarding sensory and intellectual modes and capacities, that we will never fully grasp the nature of a bat's experience as it seems to a bat, and bats, likewise, will never properly know what is like to be us from our perspective. Nagel's article, which is well worth reading, can be found, among other places, in his *Mortal Questions* (Cambridge: CUP, 1979), pp. 165–80.

19   A. Kenny, *The Metaphysics of Mind* (Oxford: Clarendon Press, 1989), p. 152.

20   Ibid., p. 153.

21   D. Dennett, *Brainstorms* (Brighton: Harvester Press, 1978), p. 123.

22   Searle, *The Rediscovery of the Mind*, p. 213.

23   W. James, *The Principles of Psychology*, 3 vols (Cambridge, MA: Harvard University Press, 1976; originally published 1890), p. 179;

quoted in O. Flanagan, *The Science of the Mind* (Cambridge, MA: MIT Press, 1984), p. 42.

24   Ibid.

Chapter 6   Taking Consciousness Seriously

1   D. Davidson, *Mental Events* (1970), reprinted in Davidson, *Essays on Actions and Events* (Oxford: OUP, 1980), p. 214.
2   J. Kim, *Mind in a Physical World* (Cambridge, MA: MIT Press, 1998), pp. 5–6.
3   If the disappearance form of the mind/brain type-type identity theory were true, it would sound odd to say that the mental supervenes on the physical, as this would be tantamount to claiming that a single phenomenon, characterizable as either mental or physical, supervenes upon itself. Perhaps a supervenience theorist could try to get round this, however, by maintaining that there can be no change in the description of a person's mental state, unless there is a change in the description of the person's physical state (brain state). The identity of the mental and the physical could be seen as the limiting case of supervenience. Identity caters for the other features of supervenience outlined above. The mental will vary according to the physical because it is the physical, and the mental will depend for its existence on the physical, because, again, it just is the physical. The one feature the reductionist identity theory cannot cope with is that supervenience is supposed to be asymmetric – the mental cannot change unless the physical changes – but the physical can change without the mental changing because of the possibility of the multiple-realizability of mental states by physical states. If the type-type identity theory were true, then it would be equally the case that the physical could not change unless the mental changes, because the mental *is* the physical.
4   R. M. Hare, *The Language of Morals* (Oxford: OUP, 1952).
5   Ibid., p. 145.
6   S. Burwood, P. Gilbert and K. Lennon, *Philosophy of Mind* (London: UCL Press, 1998), p. 36.
7   J. Searle, *Rediscovery of the Mind* (Cambridge, MA: MIT Press, 1992), p. 1.
8   J. Searle, *Intentionality* (Cambridge: CUP, 1983), p. 267.
9   E. Lepore and R. van Gulick, *Searle and His Critics* (Oxford: Blackwell, 1991).
10   Ibid., p. 182.
11   J. Searle, *The Mystery of Consciousness* (London: Granta Books, 1997), pp. 194–5.
12   Ibid., p. 8.
13   Searle, *The Rediscovery of the Mind*, p. 126.
14   T. Nagel, 'What is it Like to be a Bat?', repr. in Nagel, *Mortal Questions* (Cambridge: CUP, 1979), pp. 165–80.
15   C. McGinn, *The Problem of Consciousness* (Oxford: OUP, 1991), p. 1.

16   G. W. Leibniz, 'Monadology', first published posthumously in J. E. Erdmann (ed.), *Leibniz, Opera Philosophica*, 2 vols (Berlin, 1840).

17   C. McGinn, 'Can We Solve the Mind/Body Problem', in *The Problem of Consciousness*, pp. 11–12.

18   D. Chalmers, *The Conscious Mind* (Oxford: OUP, 1996), p. 121.

19   The charge of mystery-mongering levelled at McGinn has been labelled the 'New Mysterianism' by Owen Flanagan in his book *Consciousness Reconsidered* (Cambridge, MA: MIT Press, 1992), p. 9. The Old Mysterians were substance dualists who thought consciousness was a feature of the non-physical soul, and thus in principle beyond the reach of scientific explanation. The New Mysterians reject substance dualism but still nevertheless believe that the nature of the link between brain processes and consciousness will never be uncovered and the relation will eternally remain a mystery. See also McGinn's book, *Minds and Bodies: Philosophers and their Ideas* (Oxford: OUP, 1997), pp. 106–7, for the intriguing revelation that the New Mysterians borrowed their title from a defunct 1960s rock band called Question Mark and the Mysterians.

20   D. Hume, *A Treatise of Human Nature*, ed. L. A. Selby-Bigge, rev. P. H. Nidditch (Oxford: Clarendon Press, 1978), p. 247.

Chapter 7   Psycho-Physical Causation

1   D. Davidson, 'Mental Events', in Davidson (ed.), *Essays on Actions and Events* (Oxford: Clarendon Press, 1980). This article first appeared in L. Foster and J. W. Swanson (eds), *Experience and Theory* (Cambridge, MA: University of Massachusetts Press and London: Duckworth, 1970).

2   L. Tolstoy, 'The Death of Ivan Ilyitch', in *The Works of Leo Tolstoy*, vol. 15 (Oxford: OUP, 1934).

3   T. Burge, 'Mind-Body Causation and Explanation', in John Heil and Alfred Mele (eds), *Mental Causation* (Oxford: Clarendon Press, 1995), pp. 102–3.

4   D. Davidson, 'Actions, Reasons and Causes', in Davidson (ed.), *Essays on Actions and Events*.

5   D. M. Armstrong and N. Malcolm, *Consciousness and Causality* (Oxford: Blackwell, 1984), p. 71.

6   Ibid., p. 72.

7   D. Davidson, 'Actions, Reasons and Causes', p. 4.

8   Ibid., pp. 16–17.

9   Ibid., p. 17.

10   D. Davidson, 'Thinking Causes', in Heil and Mele (eds), *Mental Causation*, p. 13.

11   Ibid.

12   Ibid., p. 6.

13   J. Kim, *Philosophy of Mind* (Boulder, CO: Westview Press, 1996), p. 232.

14   J. Searle, *The Rediscovery of the Mind* (Cambridge, MA: MIT Press, 1992), p. 126.

15   Compare Samuel Guttenplan's discussion of this point in his article 'An Essay on the Mind', in Guttenplan (ed.), *A Companion to the Philosophy of Mind* (Oxford: Blackwell, 1994), section 3.4, pp. 84–6.

Chapter 8   The Problem of Other Minds

1   Obviously there could be a doubt about the existence of other brains if scepticism about the existence of an external world is invoked. But this doubt would equally embrace the existence of one's own brain and body, and not merely those of other people. I leave this extreme generalized scepticism to one side because it has no relevance or application to the specific problem of the existence of other minds.

2   I exclude the possibility of telepathy on two grounds. Firstly, its existence does not seem to have ever been convincingly established. Secondly, and more importantly, it is far from clear that it is a coherent notion. How, for example, if certain thoughts come into my mind, am I supposed to be able to identify them as yours rather than mine?

3   Strictly speaking, the behaviour in question will have to be characterized in non-intentional terms, that is, in terms that do not already attribute, or imply the existence of, states of mind to the alleged person with whom we are concerned. If we are not careful to characterize the behaviour in neutral, non-mentalistic terms, the question about the existence of other mental states will be begged in their favour. We must avoid assuming from the outset the existence of that whose existence we are supposed to be establishing.

4   H. Putnam, *Brains and Behaviour in Mind, Language, and Reality*, vol. II (Cambridge: CUP, 1975), p. 330 (italics in original).

5   This has led some philosophers to wonder whether inductive inference really is a species of inference at all, and has given rise to the notorious difficulty of how induction is to be justified, a large issue in its own right which cannot be pursued further here. See David Hume's *An Enquiry Concerning Human Understanding*, section IV, parts I and II, and section V, part I, for a famous discussion of the problem of induction.

6   J.S. Mill, *An Examination of Sir William Hamilton's Philosophy*, 6th edition (New York: Longman's Green and Co, Inc., 1889), p. 243.

7   I am grateful to Roger Lindsay for this analogy.

8   I. Kant, *Critique of Pure Reason*, trans. N. Kemp Smith (London: Macmillan, 1963) A52, p. 93.

9   G. Frege, 'On Sense and Meaning', in P. Geach and M. Black (eds), *Translations from the Philosophical Writings of Gottlob Frege*, 3rd edn (Blackwell: Oxford, 1980), p. 59. See also Samuel Guttenplan in *A Companion to the Philosophy of Mind* (Oxford: Blackwell, 1994), p. 55.

10   L. Wittgenstein, *The Blue and Brown Books* (Oxford: Blackwell, 1964), p. 2.

11   L. Wittgenstein, *Philosophical Investigations* (Oxford: Blackwell, 1968), para. 33.

12   Ibid.
13   L. Wittgenstein, *Zettel* (Oxford: Blackwell, 1967), para. 332.
14   Wittgenstein, *Blue and Brown Books*, p. 5.
15   Wittgenstein, *Philosophical Investigations*, para. 198.
16   Ibid., para. 580.
17   O. Hanfling, *Wittgenstein's Later Philosophy* (London: Macmillan, 1989), p. 122. In this connection, see also P. Hacker, *Wittgenstein* (London: Phoenix, 1997), p. 19.
18   Hacker, *Wittgenstein*, p. 38.
19   G. Strawson, *Mental Reality* (Cambridge, MA: MIT Press, 1994), pp. 223–4.
20   Hanfling, *Wittgenstein's Later Philosophy*, p. 126.
21   Wittgenstein, *Philosophical Investigations*, para. 246.
22   Wittgenstein, *Philosophical Investigations*, para. 224^e.
23   L. Wittgenstein, *On Certainty* (Oxford: Blackwell, 1969).
24   L. Wittgenstein, *Philosophical Investigations*, para. 303.
25   P. F. Strawson, *Individuals* (London: Methuen, 1959), p. 99.
26   Ibid., p. 100.
27   G. Graham, *Philosophy of Mind: An Introduction* (Oxford: Blackwell, 1993), pp. 39–40.
28   A. J. Ayer, *The Concept of a Person* (London: Macmillan, 1963), pp. 105–6.
29   Ibid., p. 108 (my emphasis).
30   Ibid.

Chapter 9   Personal Identity as Physical Continuity

1   B. Williams, 'Personal Identity and Individuation', reprinted in Williams (ed.), *Problems of the Self, Philosophical Papers, 1956–72* (Cambridge: CUP, 1973), pp. 1–19.
2   Some philosophers would disagree. For example, Leibniz, writing about this possibility in *New Essays concerning Human Understanding*, trans. and ed. P. Remnant and J. Bennett (Cambridge: CUP, 1992), paras 236–7, wrote:

> Thus if an illness had interrupted the continuity of my bond of consciousness, so that I did not know how I had arrived at my present state even though I could remember things further back, the testimony of others could fill in the gap in my recollection. I could even be punished on this testimony if I had done some deliberate wrong during an interval which this illness had made me forget a short time later. And if I forgot my whole past, and needed to have myself taught all over again, even my name and how to read and write, I could still learn from others about my life during my preceding state; and, similarly, I would have retained my rights without having to be divided into persons and made to inherit from myself.

Compare J.L. Mackie in *Problems from Locke* (Oxford: Clarendon Press, 1976), p. 190:

> Memory and character are not as evidence alternatives to bodily continuity; they serve, in law and in all ordinary cases, as evidence of personal identity only in so far as they are evidence of bodily continuity. Such continuity occupies a similar position as evidence even of my own identity as a person. Whenever and wherever in the past the same man as I am was conscious and active, I presume that it was I who was there and who did whatever this man did. I am quite ready to ascribe to myself innumerable actions and experiences which I do not now remember once I am satisfied of the bodily continuity of that person with me.

3 S. Shoemaker, *Self-Knowledge and Self-Identity* (Cornell: Cornell University Press, 1963), ch. 1, sections 8–10.

Chapter 10   Personal Identity as Psychological Continuity

1 J. Locke, *An Essay concerning Human Understanding* (London: Everyman's Library, 1961), vol. II, chap. XXVIII, sec. 10, my emphasis.
2 Ibid.
3 See D. Parfit, *Reasons and Persons* (Oxford: Clarendon Press, 1994).
4 Ibid., p. 207.
5 J. Butler, 'Of Personal Identity', in J.H. Bernard (ed.), *The Works of Bishop Butler*, vol. II (London, 1900).
6 C. McGinn, *The Character of Mind* (Oxford: OUP, 1992), p. 112:

> Since it is perfectly possible for there to be relations of causal dependence between mental states of distinct persons – as when one person comes to have a belief as a result of what another says – we clearly need some restrictions on which causal relations are such as to link states of the same person. And it is in fact surprisingly difficult to supply any restrictions which do not import circularity and yet have a chance of working.

7 Parfit, *Reasons and Persons*, p. 251.
8 A. O'Hear, *What Philosophy Is* (Atlantic Highlands, NJ: Humanities Press International, Inc., 1985), p. 252.
9 Parfit, *Reasons and Persons*, pp. 281–2.
10 Ibid., p. 282.
11 Locke, *Treatise concerning Human Understanding* (various editions), II, XXVIII, sec. 10, my emphasis.
12 A.G.N. Flew, *Body, Mind and Death* (New York and London: Macmillan, 1964), p. 5.
13 P. Unger, *Identity, Consciousness, and Value* (Oxford: OUP, 1990).
14 Ibid., p. 102. Compare John Mackie:

I would say that it is an empirical question what makes co-consciousness possible [and by implication, personal identity], just as it is an empirical question what inner constitution generates the more readily observed properties of gold. And if it is an empirical question, we now know at least the outline of the answer: what makes co-consciousness possible is the structure of the central nervous system and the persistence of that structure through time ... The concept of personal identity, as we are now interpreting it, is not the concept of bodily continuity, but it is the concept of something that turns out to be the continuity of a certain part of the body [the brain]. It is conceivable that personal identity should have been the persistence of some immaterial substance, since it might have been upon this that the possibility of the co-consciousness of experiences depended. We have no reason to suppose that it does: but it is an empirical, not an analytic truth, that we do not survive bodily death.

This interpretation of the concept of personal identity is, of course, closely analogous to Armstrong's view of the mind as by definition the inner cause of behaviour, and, hence, contingently, the central nervous system. But it is a more satisfactory answer to this question because the awkward issue of property-identity does not arise here. A materialist view of the thinker is less controversial than a materialist view of thoughts. (*Problems from Locke* (Oxford: Clarendon Press, 1976), pp. 200–2.)

15   B. Garratt, *Personal Identity and Self-Consciousness* (London: Routledge, 1999), p. 10.
16   R. Swinburne, *Personal Identity* (Blackwell, Oxford, 1994), p. 25.
17   Mackie, *Problems from Locke*, p. 202.

GLOSSARY

a fortiori

Latin: 'from the stronger'. It is used to mean all the more or even more so. For example, at the heart of the cosmological argument for God's existence is the ontological argument, and since this latter argument is deeply flawed, then a fortiori, the cosmological argument is rotten to the core.

a posteriori

Known on the basis of, or after, experience. For example, causes can only be known through experience and not independently of it. Propositions whose truth or falsity can only be known on the basis of experience are said to be a posteriori propositions.

a priori

Known to be true independently of, and therefore before, experience. For example, the propositions of mathematics and geometry, such as '2 + 2 = 4' and 'All Euclidean (flat-plane) triangles have angles totalling 180 degrees', are known to be true by virtue of the meanings of the words they contain. They cannot be confirmed, or disconfirmed, by observation and experiment.

Aboutness

An informal term for mental states which exhibit **intentionality**, the feature of being directed upon, or being about, other states of affairs, including those that do not exist. In other words, intentional mental states, such as beliefs, dreams, desires and thoughts, represent the world as being in a certain way, and thus possess representational content. For example, my belief that there are fairies at the bottom of my garden represents my garden as having fairies in it. Even though nothing in reality corresponds to this belief, that is what the belief is about. When the world is as the belief represents it as being, the belief is true.

Agential description

An agential description is one that characterizes someone's behaviour using mental terms, including those that describe the behaviour as an action performed by an agent. A non-agential description, by contrast, describes behaviour using only concepts drawn from physics and carries no implication that mentality is present. For example, 'He raised his arm' would be an agential description because it attributes an action, performed intentionally and chosen for a reason. By contrast, the description 'A human limb seen to move through intervening regions of space in such and such a way and over such and such a period of time', carries no implication as to whether an action was performed or not.

Ampliative

A term that is applied to **arguments** whose conclusions contain further information not found in their **premises**, and thus amplify what is to be found in those premises. **Inductive arguments** provide the standard case. For example, the conclusion that the sun will continue to rise because it has always risen in the past goes beyond our present evidence for this belief.

Analytical behaviourism

A form of reductionism that claims that all talk about mental states can be rendered, more perspicuously and without loss of meaning, into talk about actual and possible patterns of behaviour.

Analytical reduction

The basic idea behind analytical reduction is that talk about a certain class of things can be rendered, without loss of meaning, into talk about another class of things in a way that makes it clearer what is being asserted. For example, it has been proposed that talk about physical objects can be translated, without loss of meaning, into talk about actual and possible experiences that someone might have. Similarly, analytical behaviourism maintains that talk about the mind is translatable, without loss of meaning, into talk about actual and potential public behaviour. See also **ontological reduction**.

Argument

In philosophy, an argument is not a row, but an attempt to move rationally or logically from statements called '**premises**' in order to establish the truth of another statement called the 'conclusion'. There are two kinds of argument, deductive and inductive. In a **deductive argument** which is valid, the conclusion logically follows from the premises, so that if the premises are asserted and the conclusion denied, a contradiction results. The conclusions of **inductive arguments** do not logically follow from the premises but go beyond them in the sense explained under the entry '**ampliative**'.

Atomistic

Intentional mental states, such as beliefs and thoughts, are **holistic**. That is to say, they presuppose and entail a whole network of other intentional states and cannot occur in isolation. The belief that the dustman has not collected the rubbish, for example, entails all sorts of other beliefs, such as what day of the week it is, the existence of a rubbish collection service and so forth. By contrast, non-intentional states like sensations are atomistic in the sense that they can occur on their own and carry no implications for the existence of any other state of mind.

Bi-conditional

A bi-conditional is a statement that states logically **necessary and sufficient conditions** and takes the form 'if p then q, and if q then p' where p and q stand for propositions. This is often abbreviated to 'p if, and only if, q' or 'p iff q'. For example, 'if Martin is an only child, then he has no brothers and sisters and if Martin has no brothers and sisters, then he is an only child'. This may not sound very illuminating, but in the philosophy of mind an attempt has been made to find true bi-conditionals of the sort 'x is in mental state m if, and only if, his brain is in physical state p'. If this last statement were true, then mental states would be one and the same class of phenomena as brain states and the mental would effectively have been reduced to the physical.

Biological naturalism

This is a term associated with the philosophy of mind of the American philosopher John Searle. Mental states are a class of natural phenomena, namely biological phenomena. They do not lie outside the order of nature in a supernatural or non-natural world, but are as much a part of our biological history as processes such as digestion and the secretion of bile by the liver. There is an implication that mental states can be associated only with organic life-forms and not inorganic artefacts such as computers and robots.

Cartesianism

Broadly the set of doctrines and beliefs associated with René Descartes (1596–1650), but in the context of the philosophy of mind the **dualistic** doctrine that human beings are composed of two radically different kinds of thing, body and soul, capable of existing independently of each other but joined in life. The soul is non-physical and lacks extension, whereas the body possesses extension but lacks thought.

Causation

Causation operates where one event brings about, or necessitates or makes happen, another event. How the concept is ultimately to be analysed and understood is a major issue in philosophy. Hume proposed a famous analysis of causation that saw it as the constant conjunction of events – one type of event regularly following another – with no discernible connection or 'glue' to bind one to the other. Hume also suggested that 'A causes B' could be understood as saying that if A were not to occur, then B would not happen.

Cognition

Cognition refers to the operations of the intellect and understanding by means of which we arrive at knowledge and beliefs.

Computation/computational

The operations by a computer to carry out a sequence of defined operations in order, for example, to find the solutions to arithmetical or mathematical problems. The computer performs a series of discrete steps, called an algorithm, which require no insight or intelligence to be carried out. The computational theory of mind claims that the mind is best understood as a computer program run on the hardware (wetware?) of the brain. See in this connection **functionalism**.

Conation/conative

That aspect of the mind that is to do with acting, willing and trying.

Counterfactual conditional

A counterfactual conditional is a statement that takes the form 'If x were to occur, then y would occur' or 'if x had not occurred, then y would not have occurred'. All true causal statements, including the laws of nature, entail counterfactuals, and are not mere statements of regularities. 'The striking of the match on the box caused it to burst into flame' entails 'if the match had not been struck on the box, all being equal, it would not have burst into flame' and 'if the match were to be struck on the box, all being equal, then it would burst into flame'. The point of the 'all being equal' clause is to rule out the operation of interfering causes, such as the matches getting wet, which would prevent the normal outcome of striking the match.

De dicto/de re necessity

De dicto necessity is the kind of necessity that attaches to words, for example, that necessarily all bachelors are unmarried, or that necessarily $2 + 3 = 5$. *De re* necessity is the kind of necessity that relates to things. To understand this we need to use the terminology of possible worlds. Thus we can say that there is a possible world in which Clinton was never the President of the United States, but there is no possible world in which Clinton was not Clinton. Similarly, although there is a possible world in which Clinton was bald, there is no possible world in which he was not human. Charles Dodgson might not have written *Alice in Wonderland* in some possible world, but in every possible world he could not have been other than Lewis Carroll.

Deduction/deductive argument

In an **argument** that is deductively valid, the conclusion is logically entailed by the **premises** so that to advance the premises but deny the conclusion leads to a contradiction. This is because the information contained in the conclusion is already present implicitly in the premises.

Disjunction/disjunctive

A disjunctive statement is of the 'either/or' variety and states alternatives. There can be inclusive disjunctive statements – e.g. you can have either beer or cake or both – and exclusive disjunctions – e.g. you can have either beer or cake, but not both.

Disposition/dispositional

A dispositional property of a thing states how that thing would behave were certain conditions to be fulfilled. 'Solubility' is a dispositional property of sugar, that is to say that when immersed in water, for example, it will dissolve. Similarly, a person who has an irritable disposition need not actually be fuming and fussing, but is prone to do so in circumstances that would otherwise lead others of a more serene temperament to remain unruffled. See also **occurrent**.

Dualism/dualistic

Dualism takes two forms: substance dualism and property dualism. According to substance dualism, human beings are composed of two radically different kinds of substance or things: non-physical minds and physical bodies, each capable of existing independently of the other. Property dualism postulates only physical substances but claims that these possess two radically different kinds of property: physical properties and non-physical mental properties such as consciousness. See also **non-reductive monism**.

Eliminativism

Associated particularly with the work of writers such as Richard Rorty and Paul and Patricia Churchland, eliminativism not merely denies there are such things as mental states, but advocates expunging all psychological and mental terms from our vocabulary, recommending that these are replaced by terms drawn from the sciences, especially computational and cognitive science.

Epiphenomenalism

Epi is the Greek for 'on top of', so epiphenomenalism literally means 'one phenomenon occurring on top of another'. The basic idea is that one phenomenon produces another which is dependent upon it, just as a suitably placed light and object cast a shadow on a wall. The behaviour of the shadow is dependent on the behaviour of the light and the object and cannot vary independently of the way they behave. The shadow is powerless to produce any alteration in the light and the object. In a similar fashion, it has been argued that physical processes in the brain produce and sustain mental states, but these states can have no effect on the brain processes upon which they depend, and are causally impotent to bring about any physical changes.

Epistemology/epistemological

Epistemology is the theory of knowledge and concerns itself with issues such as what is knowledge, how do we know, and can we know anything.

Existential and universal quantifiers

There are two quantifiers in logic, the existential quantifier ($\exists x$) that says 'there is at least one thing that is x . . .' and the universal quantifier strictly ($\forall x$) that says 'for all things that are x . . .'. These quantifiers are definable in terms of each other and they occur in the predicate calculus. For example, ($\exists x$)(Fx and Gx) says that there is at least one thing x such that it has the property F and the property G. Let F = 'is a man' and G = 'is bald'. Then this statement says that there is at least one man who is bald, i.e. some men are bald.

Functionalism/psycho-functionalism

Functionalism conceives of the mind as a function, run on the hardware of the brain, whereby sensory inputs are converted into behavioural outputs.

Metaphysical functionalism provides a purely conceptual philosophical analysis of the inputs and outputs which constitute a mental state – say, pain. Psycho-functionalism investigates empirically what actual neural mechanisms are involved in embodying and discharging the function. Functions are abstract in nature and cannot be strictly identified with the arrangements that happen to embody them, whether these comprise physical, or even conceivably non-physical states of affairs.

Holism/holistic

Holism is the feature whereby **intentional** mental states logically presuppose the existence of other intentional states, thus comprising a network or background. Unlike sensations that are non-intentional, intentional states cannot exist in isolation from each other. A possible analogy is with a jigsaw piece, which assumes the existence of the other pieces of the jigsaw. See also **atomistic**.

Homunculus fallacy

Homunculus (plural: *homunculi*) literally means 'little man' or 'manikin', and has come to denote the error in the philosophy of mind of attributing to some internal agent, either the brain or the soul, the very features the agent was invoked to explain in the first place. For example, in the children's section, 'The Funday Times', of *The Sunday Times* there used to be a cartoon called 'The Numbskulls'. The Numbskulls are a group of little men who lived inside the skull of 'Uncle' and explained how he was able to do various things such as seeing and thinking. A little man, for example, looked out of Uncle's eyes and steered him round the world. Another little man in the brain, suggested various thoughts to him. The problem, of course, is how do these little men in turn see and think? Do they have yet smaller men inside them? Clearly, a vicious infinite regress threatens, in which case the explanation comes to nothing. Descartes committed the homunculus fallacy when he explained what it is for us to see by postulating that the person, conceived of as a ghostly soul, views images of the outside world projected onto the pineal gland in the middle of the brain.

Induction/inductive argument

An inductive argument is one in which the **premises** do not logically entail the conclusion, because the conclusion contains information beyond what is to be found in the premises. Such **arguments** are thus said to be **ampliative**. The typical form of an inductive argument is: 'All the Xs observed so far have been Ys, therefore all the Xs there are, are Ys.' We use this kind of reasoning a thousand times a day and it is clear that if we did not, there would be little beyond the data given by present experience which we could claim to know. The problem of whether induction can be rationally justified, to which Hume (1711–76) first alerted us, remains a much-debated issue to this day.

Intentionality/intentional

Intentionality is the feature whereby many mental states possess a representational content. Some intentional states, such as beliefs, purport to represent how the world actually is. If the world is as a belief represents it as being, the belief is true, otherwise it is false. Other intentional states, such as desires and intentions, represent how the agent wants the world to be. Desires and intentions that do not succeed in bringing about the states of affairs at which they aim are frustrated or unfulfilled. See also **aboutness**.

Intrinsic and derivative intentionality

Many philosophers, of whom the American John Searle would be a prime example, have claimed that intentional states are intrinsic to brains and not derived from other intentional systems. Computer programs, by contrast, are not intrinsically about other states of affairs, and do not possess genuine underived intentionality. The contents of such programs exist only because we are there to interpret the programs. In a world devoid of minds, computer programs would lack a content, as would language, books and symbols in general. Two pieces of wood, formed into a cross, mean nothing in themselves. We invest such a structure with meaning, thereby turning it into the Christian symbol for the redemption of mankind by Christ.

LAD (language acquisition device)

The American linguist, Noam Chomsky, claimed that learning theory which is founded upon stimulus/response psychology cannot explain how children acquire language so quickly, nor their ability to understand and to generate an indefinite variety of sentences and constructions they have never encountered before. To explain this, he postulated a LAD, a language acquisition device, incarnated in the neural machinery of the brain, which embodies an innate universal grammar, not learned from experience, that provides the rules the child needs to recognize and classify the different examples of utterances which it encounters. In this way, the child quickly learns what utterances are meaningful, and which are to be discarded.

Leibniz's Law

Leibniz's Law, formulated by the great German philosopher Gottfried Leibniz (1646–1716) is also known as the 'identity of indiscernibles'. It states that if an object, X, is one and the same thing as an object, Y, then all the properties of X must be the same as all the properties of Y. Hence, if X possesses at least one property lacked by Y, and vice versa, then X and Y cannot be numerically identical, i.e. one and the same. Leibniz's Law is a useful tool for evaluating identity claims. For example, if mental states are identical with brain states, then all the properties of mental states must be possessed by brain states, and vice versa. If just one property can be found that is possessed by a mental state but not a brain state, and vice versa, then mental states cannot be brain states. There are exceptions to Leibniz's Law. It will not work, for example, with verbs that denote intentional mental states. It may be true that Lois Lane is imagining she is kissing Superman and not imagining she is kissing Clark Kent (so something is true of Superman but not Clark Kent), but this cannot establish that Superman is not Clark Kent (we know full well that he is).

Logical positivism

Logical positivism was associated with members of the Vienna Circle which flourished between, approximately, 1924 and 1936. The logical positivists were much concerned with the unity of science and scientific method. A central aim was to formulate a criterion that would demarcate meaningful utterances from meaningless ones, and this led to formulation of the **verification principle**, according to which a statement was meaningful if, and only if, it could be verified in principle on the basis of experience. Later, under the pressure of criticism, the verification principle transmuted into the falsification principle, according to which a statement was devoid of literal meaning unless it could in principle be falsified empirically.

Materialism/physicalism

According to materialism, all that really exists are physical objects and physical phenomena. Mental states, ultimately, are nothing over and above physical states of affairs, including properties.

Mental phenomena

Mental phenomena comprise states of mind, including mental happenings and processes. A prime example of a mental state is consciousness, and consciousness, in different sorts of ways, appears to be integral to the existence not only of non-intentional states such as sensations and moods, but also of the vast panoply of intentional states such as beliefs, thoughts, desires and emotions.

Metaphysics

Metaphysics raises questions about the nature of existence which lie beyond the scope of the sciences. Typical questions in metaphysics are: what is the nature of causation? What is the mind, and how does it differ from, and relate to, the body? What constitutes the identity of a person over time? What is the difference between things and their properties?

Monism

Monism is the view that only one type of thing exists. Materialistic monism maintains that the sorts of thing which exist are physical in nature. Immaterialistic monism maintains the opposite: only spiritual substances, i.e. non-physical souls and their properties, exist.

Naturalism

The view that everything that exists is part of the natural world and explicable in terms drawn from the natural sciences, such as physics, chemistry and biology.

Necessary and sufficient conditions

This is best explained by means of an example. A necessary condition of being a bachelor is that the person in question is male. But this is not sufficient, because a newly born male infant is not a bachelor. What more needs to be added is that, firstly, the person in question is of marriageable age and, secondly, that he has not been married before. These two conditions, together with maleness, are logically necessary and sufficient to comprise bachelordom. Consider now the notion of sufficient condition. A sufficient condition of being a British citizen is that one was born of British parents in Britain. But it is not necessary, since citizenship can also be acquired in other ways, such as by marriage. See also **bi-conditional**.

Nomological

From the Greek nomos, i.e., law. Thus, nomological is 'law-like'.

Non-intentional mental states

These are mental states such as sensations and moods, which are not about, or directed upon, a content, so that they do not represent other possible states of affairs, unlike intentional states. Non-intentional states are non-**holistic**.

Non-reductive monism

Non-reductive monism maintains that only physical entities exist, but these possess both physical and non-physical mental properties, the latter resisting reduction to the former. Property-**dualism** is an example of non-reductive monism.

Normative

Governed by rules or standards.

Occasionalism

The doctrine of the mind/body relation associated with the French philosopher Nicholas Malebranche (1638–1715). Malebranche held that the mind, conceived of as a non-physical soul, has no causal commerce with the material body, but that when mental and physical events occur, God is present on every occasion – hence the title of the doctrine – to ensure that the right sorts of correspondence between the mental and physical occur, so that it is as if they affected each other. Malebranche adopted the doctrine to get round the Cartesian problem of how physical and non-physical things could possibly have any effect on each other.

Occurrent

Occurrent mental states are those that are currently present to consciousness – for example, the ache in my shoulders I am experiencing at this moment. Occurrent states contrast with **dispositional** states, which manifest themselves when certain conditions are fulfilled. My beliefs are dispositional in the sense that I am not currently conscious of them, but I can call them to mind if and when the occasion demands, in which case they become occurrent.

Ontology/ontological

The branch of metaphysics which concerns itself with the nature of what exists.

Ontological reduction

An ontological reduction contrasts with an **analytical reduction**. An analytical reduction maintains that talk about one sort of thing can be rendered in different words without loss of meaning. Thus, talk about triangles can be translated, without loss of meaning, into talk about three-angled figures. The two kinds of talk are equivalent in meaning. An ontological reduction never maintains that descriptions of a phenomenon and the analysis of it are equivalent in meaning, but only that the terms which figure in the analysis constitute all the facts about the phenomenon which is being ontologically reduced. Thus, talk about heat is not analytically reducible to talk about the behaviour of molecules – the two kinds of talk have irreducibly different meanings – but nevertheless there are no heat facts at the macro-level over and above behaviour of molecules at the micro-level.

Ostensive definition

An ostensive definition is one that takes place by pointing. Not all words can be defined purely in terms of other words. There must come a point where a term has to be defined by pointing at the non-linguistic state of affairs to which it may be applied.

Personal identity

The central question is: what makes a person X at the present moment one and the same as a person Y in the past? The request is for the **necessary and sufficient conditions** of the numerical identity of the person over time.

Phenomenalism

Phenomenalism is a species of **analytical reduction** and tries to render all talk about physical objects in terms of actual and possible experiences.

Physical phenomena

It is extremely difficult to define physical phenomena, but one would expect them (1) to be publicly available in theory to all subjects of experience; (2) to be spatially located and to occupy a volume or area of space; (3) to exist independently of all observers; (4) frequently to be measurable and quantifiable. Natural objects, human artefacts, phenomena such as light, gravity, magnetism, mass, solidity and so forth are typical examples of physical phenomena.

Physicalism

Physicalism is very close to **materialism**, and maintains that everything that exists is physical. It often makes the additional claim that the only genuine explanations of events are physical explanations, and the only proper concepts are physical concepts.

Plato/Platonic

Plato was born in Athens in c.428 BC and is most famous for his writings on ethics and his theory of Forms. According to this theory, the real world, what might be called Platonic Heaven, is a world of universal characteristics – universals – which are perfect, unchanging and eternal, known only through intellectual acquaintance after training in mathematics, geometry and philosophy. The world we see around us is an imperfect, changing evanescent world of particulars perceived by the senses. Particulars are made to be the kinds of thing they are by sharing in the nature of the Forms, or by being imperfect copies or reflections of them. Knowledge is acquaintance with the non-sensory Forms, belief acquaintance with sensory particulars. Plato also espoused **dualism**, and thought that the nature of the soul was similar to that of the Forms.

Premise

A premise is a statement supporting a conclusion and is supposed to lead to it. In valid **deductive arguments**, the premises of the **argument** logically entail the conclusion.

Psycho-physical causation

Mind-to-body causation. In other words, mental states act as causes to bring about bodily behaviour. There is still a puzzle as regards what mental states must be like to be able to do this. **Materialists** and **physicalists** straightforwardly hold that mental states must ultimately be physical in nature, but there are serious difficulties in reducing the mental to the physical as this leaves out consciousness and **qualia**.

Psycho-physical parallelism

This theory, invented by Leibniz, was designed, like Malebranche's **occasionalism**, to avoid the problem posed by **Cartesian** dualism, namely how it is possible that a non-physical soul (mind) can affect the physical body, and vice versa. Mental events and physical events run parallel to, and are synchronized with, each other. This is because God, who winds up the mind and body clocks, synchronizes the right kinds of mental event with the right kinds of physical event, and then sets the clocks ticking. Unlike Malebranche's God, Leibniz's does not have to be around on each and every occasion to make sure the appropriate mental/physical correspondences obtain.

Qualia

Qualia comprise the felt or phenomenological aspects of experience, such as the itchy feel of a blanket, the dull ache of cramp or the vivid green and golden of a field of young rice. Qualia are supposed to be subjective and private to the individual person, and exist in addition to public, physical events in the brain and central nervous system.

Ramsey sentence

Invented by the Cambridge philosopher Frank Plumpton Ramsey (1903–30), the aim of a Ramsey sentence is to eliminate circularity in analyses of phenomena. For example, to avoid defining an item like 'positive charge' in terms of its opposite 'negative charge', and vice versa, the way out of the circle is to talk about both charges more neutrally and without commitment, by saying there is something that has property F and there is something that has property G; things with F attract those with G and repel things with F, while things with G attract things with F and repel things with G; and G can be induced in a rubber comb by rubbing it with wool.

Reify/reification

To reify an item is to treat is as a thing. This usually occurs because of the mistake of thinking that all nouns acquire their meanings by naming things, but quite often this is a mistake. The word 'pain' is a noun, but is a pain a thing? Rather, we should think of it as some state or condition of a person. Similarly, is the meaning of a word an object, or is it better thought of, as Wittgenstein suggested, as the use of the word? The noun 'body' names a thing, but need this be true of the noun 'mind' contrary to what substance **dualists** maintain.

Res cogitans

A thinking thing, from the Latin *res*, 'a thing', and *cogitans*, 'thinking'. This was how Descartes characterized the mind or soul. It is a thing whose whole essence is to think. By thinking or, in French, *penser*, Descartes meant consciousness in general, and not mere intellection or ratiocination.

Res extensa

An extended thing, i.e. physical, space-occupying bodies. Descartes divided the whole universe into the two mutually exclusive realms of *res cogitans* and *res extensa*.

Semantics and syntax

Semantics is the study of the meaning of statements and how it is possible. Syntax is the study of the language structures by means of which statements get made.

Solipsism

The view that only oneself and one's experiences exist. A weaker version would add 'as far as one can tell'.

Substance/logical substance

A substance is a thing that can exist in its own right, in logical independence from anything else, unlike properties, which have to be the features of some substance or other. However, just as properties must belong to substances, it would equally seem that there cannot be featureless or propertyless substances. Substances and properties were made for each other. It is a marriage made in metaphysical heaven, which no philosopher can put asunder. Some philosophers, e.g. Spinoza (1632–77), have maintained that, strictly speaking, God is the only genuine substance, because God, unlike all else, does not depend for his existence on anything external to him.

Supervenience/subvenience

A supervenient phenomenon arises from, and depends for its existence upon, a subvenient base. Moreover, there can be no changes in the supervenient phenomenon with a corresponding change in the subvenient base, but the converse does not apply, owing to the possibility of the multiple realization of the supervenient phenomenon by a variety of subvenient bases. The exact nature of the supervenience relation is controversial.

Syllogism

A syllogism is a form of deductive inference in which a conclusion is drawn from two premises. For example, 'All fish live in water', 'All things that live in water are cold-blooded', so 'All fish are cold-blooded'. Each premise contains an expression, which occurs in the conclusion, and an expression, called the 'middle term', which doesn't. In this case, the middle term is 'live in water'. There are four basic forms of statement that can figure in syllogisms: These are: 'All A are B', 'No A are B', 'Some A are B', and 'Some A are not B'. There are 256 ways in which these statements may be combined, but only 14 of these combinations represent valid arguments, i.e. arguments where the conclusion logically follows from the premises.

Tautology

A tautology is a kind of necessary truth because it merely repeats itself. For example, the line 'A rose is a rose is a rose' (by the poetess Gertrude Stein) is a tautology.

Verificationism/verification principle

Verificationism is a central doctrine of the **logical positivists** which maintains that unless a statement could be verified empirically, i.e. established as true in principle on the basis of experience, it is devoid of meaning. (This did not apply to necessary truths and falsehoods.) The problem is that there are all kinds of statements that cannot be verified and yet are meaningful – e.g. a city will never be built on this spot (an example given by the American philosopher, Hilary Putnam). In addition, how is one supposed to verify the verification principle itself – by observation or experiment? The cardinal error made by the principle is that whilst it must be possible to specify what state of affairs, if it occurred, would make a statement true if that statement is to be meaningful, it is entirely another matter to be able actually to find out, even in principle, whether that state of affairs obtains. There may be all kinds of statements whose truth we will never be able to discover, even in principle, but that does not make them meaningless.

SELECT BIBLIOGRAPHY

Aristotle, *De Anima*, Books II and III, translated with an introduction and notes by D. W. Hamlyn (Oxford: Oxford University Press, 1968).

Armstrong, D. M., *A Materialist Theory of the Mind* (London: Routledge and Kegan Paul, 1968).

Butler, Joseph, 'Of Personal Identity', in J. H. Bernard (ed.), *The Works of Bishop Butler*, vol. II (London, 1900).

Chalmers, David and Searle, John, 'Consciousness and the Philosophers: An Exchange', *New York Review of Books* (15 May 1997), 61.

Churchland, Patricia, *Neurophilosophy* (Cambridge, MA: MIT Press, 1986).

Churchland, Paul, *Scientific Realism and the Plasticity of Mind* (Cambridge: Cambridge University Press, 1979).

Davidson, Donald, 'Thought and Talk', in Samuel Guttenplan (ed.), *Mind and Language: Wolfson College Lectures 1974* (Oxford: Clarendon Press, 1975).

Dennett, Daniel, *The Intentional Stance* (Cambridge, MA: MIT Press, 1987).

Dennett, Daniel, *Consciousness Explained* (Boston, MA: Little, Brown, 1991).

Dennett, Daniel, *Kinds of Minds: Toward an Understanding of Consciousness* (New York: Basic Books, 1996).

Dennett, Daniel and Hofstadter, Douglas (eds), *The Mind's I* (New York: Basic Books, 1981).

Descartes, René, *Meditations on First Philosophy*, trans. John Cottingham (Cambridge: Cambridge University Press, 1986 [1641]).

Evnine, Simon, *Donald Davidson* (Cambridge: Polity, 1991).

Fodor, Jerry, *The Language of Thought* (New York: T. Y. Crowell, 1975).

Fodor, Jerry, *Psychosemantics* (Cambridge, MA: MIT Press, 1988).

Haugeland, John, *Artificial Intelligence: The Very Idea* (Cambridge, MA: MIT Press, 1985).

Heil, John, *The Nature of True Minds* (Cambridge: Cambridge University Press, 1992).

Hume, David, *A Treatise of Human Nature*, ed. L.A. Selby-Bigge and P.H. Nidditch (Oxford: Clarendon Press, 1978 [1739]).

Jackson, Frank, 'Mental Causation', *Mind* 105 (1996), 377–41.

Kant, Immanuel, *The Critique of Pure Reason*, trans. Norman Kemp Smith (London: Macmillan, 1964 [1787]).

Kim, Jaegwon, *Supervenience and Mind: Selected Philosophical Essays* (Cambridge: Cambridge University Press, 1993).

Kirk, Robert, 'Zombies vs. Materialists', *Proceedings of the Aristotelian Society*, supplementary vol. 48 (1974), 135–52.

Kirk, Robert, *Raw Feeling* (Oxford: Clarendon Press, 1996).

Kripke, Saul, *Naming and Necessity* (Cambridge, MA: Harvard University Press, 1980).

La Mettrie, Julien Offraye de, *Man a Machine*, trans. R. Watson and M. Rybalka (Indianapolis: Hackett Publishing Co, 1994 [1747/8]).

Leibniz, Gottfried Wilhelm, *Monadology* (1787), repr. in Mary Morris and G.H.R. Parkinson (trans.), *Philosophical Writings* (London, 1973), 94.

Locke, John, *An Essay Concerning Human Understanding*, ed. P.H. Nidditch (Oxford: Clarendon Press, 1978 [1690]).

Lockwood, Michael, *Mind, Brain, and Quantum* (Oxford: Basil Blackwell, 1989).

Lockwood, Michael, 'The Grain Problem', in H. Robinson (ed.), *Objections to Physicalism* (Oxford: Clarendon Press, 1993), 271–91.

Lowe, F.J., *Locke on Human Understanding* (London: Routledge, 1995).

Lowe, F.J., *Subjects of Experience* (Cambridge: Cambridge University Press, 1996).

Lycan, W.C., *Consciousness* (Cambridge, MA: MIT Press, 1987).

Mackie, John, *Problems from Locke* (Oxford: Oxford University Press, 1976), esp. ch. 6.

Nagel, Thomas, 'What is it Like to be a Bat?', *Philosophical Review* 83 (1974), 435–50.

Nagel, Thomas, *Mortal Questions* (Cambridge: Cambridge University Press, 1979).

Nozick, Robert, *Philosophical Explanations* (Cambridge, MA: Harvard University Press, 1981), esp. ch. 1.

Parfit, Derek, 'Personal Identity', *The Philosophical Review* 80 (1971), 3–27.

Perner, Josef, *Understanding the Representational Mind* (Cambridge, MA: MIT Press, 1991).

Perry, John, 'Can the Self Divide?', *Journal of Philosophy* 69 (1972), 463–88.

Perry, John (ed.), *Personal Identity* (Berkeley: University of California Press, 1975).

Place, U.T., 'Is Consciousness A Brain Process?', *The British Journal of Psychology* 47 (1956), 44–50.

Poland, Jeffrey, *Physicalism: The Philosophical Foundations* (Oxford: Clarendon Press, 1994).

Putnam, Hilary, *Mind, Language, and Reality: Philosophical Papers*, vol. 2 (Cambridge: Cambridge University Press, 1975).

Putnam, Hilary, *Reason, Truth, and History* (Cambridge: Cambridge University Press, 1981).

Quinton, Anthony, 'The Soul', *Journal of Philosophy* 59 (1962), 393–403.

Rorty, Amélie (ed.), *The Identities of Persons* (Berkeley: University of California Press, 1976).

Rosenthal, David (ed.), *The Nature of Mind* (New York: Oxford University Press, 1991).

Ryle, Gilbert, *The Concept of Mind* (London: Hutchinson, 1949).

Searle, John, *The Rediscovery of the Mind* (Cambridge, MA: MIT Press, 1992).

Searle, John, 'Consciousness and the Philosophers', *New York Review of Books* (6 March 1997), 43–50.

Shoemaker, Sydney, 'Causality and Properties', in Peter van Inwagen (ed.), *Time and Cause* (Dordrecht: Reidel Publishing Co, 1980), 109–35.

Skinner, B. F., *Science and Human Behavior* (New York: Macmillan, 1953).

Sterelny, Kim, *The Representational Theory of Mind: An Introduction* (Oxford: Blackwell Publishers, 1990).

Stich, Stephen, *From Folk Psychology to Cognitive Science: The Case Against Belief* (Cambridge, MA: MIT Press, 1983).

Strawson, P. F., *Individuals: An Essay in Descriptive Metaphysics* (London: Methuen, 1959).

Stroud, Barry, *Hume* (London: Routledge, 1977).

Swinburne, Richard, 'Personal Identity', *Proceedings of the Aristotelian Society* 74 (1973–4), 231–48.

Turing, Alan, 'Computing Machinery and Intelligence', *Mind* 59 (1950), 434–60.

Watson, J. B., 'Psychology as the Behaviorist Views It', *Psychological Review* 20 (1913), 158–77.

Wiggins, David, *Identity and Spatio-temporal Continuity* (Oxford: Oxford University Press, 1967).

Wiggins, David, *Sameness and Substance* (Oxford: Oxford University Press, 1980).

Williams, Bernard, *Problems of the Self* (Cambridge: Cambridge University Press, 1973).

Wittgenstein, Ludwig, *Tractatus Logico-Philosophicus*, trans. D. F. Pears and B. F. McGuinness (London: Routledge and Kegan Paul, 1961 [1922]).

Wittgenstein, Ludwig, *The Blue and Brown Books* (Oxford: Oxford University Press, 1958).

Wittgenstein, Ludwig, *Philosophical Investigations*, trans. G. E. M. Anscombe (Oxford: Basil Blackwell, 1968 [1953]).

Wittgenstein, Ludwig, *On Certainty*, eds G. E. M. Anscombe and C. H. von Wright, trans. Denis Paul and G. E. M. Anscombe (Oxford: Basil Blackwell, 1969).

INDEX